THE NAZIFICAT

Art, Design, Music,
Film in the Third Reich

edited by
Brandon Taylor and Wilfried van der Will

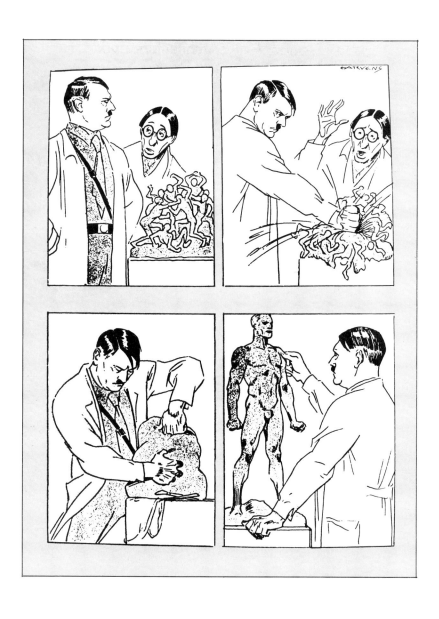

THE NAZIFICATION OF ART

Art, Design, Music, Architecture and
Film in the Third Reich

edited by
Brandon Taylor and Wilfried van der Will

The Winchester Press
Winchester School of Art
Park Avenue, Winchester, Hampshire

Front cover: Arno Breker, *Wounded Soldier* (bronze), 1942

Frontispiece: Cariacature from the German satirical magazine *Kladderadatsch,* 1933.

First edition published in the United Kingdom 1990 by:
The Winchester Press
Park Avenue
Winchester SO23 8DL
Hampshire

Typesetting by Artset Ltd, Southampton
Printed by Billings and Sons Ltd, Worcester

British Library Cataloguing in Publication Data:

The Nazification of Art: art, design, music, architecture and film in the Third Reich.
(Winchester studies in art and criticism)
1. German visual arts, history
I. Taylor, Brandon   II. Will, Wilfried van der
709'.43

ISBN 0 9506783 9 2

CONTENTS

PREFACE AND ACKNOWLEDGEMENTS

Any book about so controversial a subject as the Nazi contribution to artistic culture must make clear at the outset its principal claims and limitations. The editors have put forward a particular line of argument on National Socialist art and design — in particular on the propriety of studying its practices, its aesthetics and its institutions. Collections of essays are necessarily the work of many people, however, and it is important to state that no set of guidelines or principles was — or could be — discussed and agreed upon in advance. There are many differences of emphasis and methodology. Yet despite this necessary diversity, we believe that a substantial consensus has emerged around a number of important propositions. All the contributors to this book are firmly convinced that Nazi culture forms an important, if frequently disturbing, object of investigation within the modern European tradition. More specifically, the contributions show a general agreement that National Socialist culture represented a complex combination of immense mass appeal and highly simplified, even banal aesthetic programming; that art was used by National Socialism as an agent of social cohesion and simultaneously as an instrument of repression and social marginalisation; and that it is the peculiar and highly problematic tension between these two poles that lends Nazi art its grim fascination and its undoubted terror. A further proposition underlying the greater part of this book is that National Socialism as a political movement was founded upon an appeal to yearnings for order and wholeness that could be found in all countries which had suffered the experience of social fragmentation engendered by capitalism at an advanced stage; and that art was moulded by National Socialism both as an expression and as a vehicle for those yearnings. The editors have also proposed that the fact that such sentiments were widespread and intense — and remain historically repeatable today — is part of what lends to Nazi culture its macabre relevance, its status as both paradigm and symptom, virus and cure. Another focal proposition concerns the contradictory posture of Nazism vis-a-vis modernity and artistic Modernism. On the one hand it was obvious to National Socialist leaders that no political culture purporting to be progressive could afford to ignore the modernising impulses contained within technology and technological development. Yet at the same time, as is well known, certain forms of international artistic Modernism came in for extensive and implacable abuse from National Socialist propaganda. And yet what forms of negotiation the Third Reich entered into with artistic Modernism remains — for many — a centrally important subject for debate.

The editors' introductory chapter 'Aesthetics and National Socialism' explains the close, even generic connection between National Socialist political culture and the resources of 'art'. It also discusses and evaluates different explanations for the rise of Fascism in Germany, thus preparing a context for the chapters which follow. Wilfried van der Will in 'The Body and the Body Politic: Symptom and Metaphor in the Transition of German Culture to National Socialism' then goes on to examine the evidence from older as well as modern cultures which suggests that National Socialist corporatism played upon a deeply rooted desire for the organic cohesion and wholeness of society, a desire which both on the Left and the Right also expressed itself in a culture of the naked body and nudism. Nazi culture raises particular problems for the representation of women, however. As Annie Richardson points out in her paper 'The Nazification of Women in Art', the types of discourse capable of explaining how women are represented in a heavily 'masculinist' culture are still very much open to debate and formulation. By investigating how images of women were 'read' by contemporary audiences she delineates Nazi conceptualisations of the body which permeated National Socialist culture at several points.

In the section devoted to art institutions we reproduce an early text by Robert Brady which presents a particularly concise statement of how the cultural politics of the Nazi regime were organised and administered. This is then followed by a specific study, Christine Fischer-Defoy's article 'Artists and Art Institutions in Germany, 1933–1945', which attends to the troubled evolution of Berlin art teaching establishments under the onslaught of the various stages of Nazi art policy. Here is an initial discussion of the problem of Nazism vis-a-vis Modernism. This is elaborated further in John Heskett's contribution 'Modernism and Archaism in Design in the Third Reich', and in Brandon Taylor's chapter 'Post-modernism in the Third Reich'. Both attempt to deal with the paradox — as it must now seem — that Modernism contributed crucially important aesthetic paradigms to National Socialist policy after 1934, and that National Socialist artists and designers deployed these prescriptions in a considerable number of ways. The question whether this double attitude of Modernist anti-Modernism was an early form of Post-Modernism in the contemporary sense is a question that will undoubtedly attract more comment.

In architecture, Nazi stylists such as Troost and Speer have long been regarded with the gravest suspicion — as harbingers of an appalling monumental, ceremonial and imperial manner. That verdict must now be seen in a more complex light, as we begin to appreciate the extent to which Speer's buildings to a very noticeable degree succeeded in assimilating the international Thirties style of public architecture which was then being pursued, as a modernising Classicism, by architects as diverse as Piacentini in Italy and Azema in Paris, not to mention Wallace Harrison and the Rockefeller Centre architects in New York, or Charles Holden in his London University buildings after 1932. Hartmut Frank's study of Paul Bonatz illustrates the case of an architect who rejected both Nazi Classicism and international Modernism, and in doing so opened the possibility of a 'third way' for architecture which explored the use of materials and forms as integral to a relationship between buildings and a given landscape.

There follow two further studies of specific cultural media — music and the graphic arts — in 'The Political Poster in the Third Reich' by Andreas Fleischer and Frank Kämpfer, and Erik Levi's 'Music and Fascism: the Politicisation of Composition, Criticism and Performance'. In the latter, particularly, we encounter not only the transposition of 'blood and soil' ideology into the relatively abstract field of music, but also the policy inconsistencies and reversals that included certain 'Modernist' musicians as 'nationalists' while condemning other rearguard composers purely because of their racial connections. This illustrates how the Nazi culture machine became progressively caught up in policy contradictions, by the imposition of conflicting criteria.

Films above all were employed in National Socialist Germany both as propaganda tools and for demonstrations of state power. Susan Sontag's essay 'Fascinating Fascism' looks at the career of Hitler's favourite film-maker Leni Riefenstahl and draws from it the preoccupations of National Socialist culture not only with power but also with sexuality and death. Eva Warth's 'The Fascist Reconceptualisation of Women's Roles: an Analysis of *Die Frau Meiner Träume*' opens questions about the difficulty for Nazism in maintaining the propagandistic image of femininity in the increasingly crisis-ridden atmosphere of the war.

The book ends with Walter Grasskamp's article 'The De-Nazification of Nazi Art: Arno Breker and Albert Speer Today' in order partly to dispel any impression that the nature of National Socialist culture is a settled historical matter, or that its consequences and ideological reverberations have completely died away. It is clear that German artists, architects and planners are still grappling with the issue of how to frame, use, destroy, rehabilitate, describe or display the culture of the Nazi past.

This book began in a symposium entitled 'The Nazification of Art' which was held under the auspices of the German Art and Politics Study Group at the Goethe Institute, London, in November 1985. Three of the original seven papers were selected for the present volume, though all have been extensively rewritten. Of these, Christine Fischer-Defoy's paper has been published in the *Oxford Art Journal* in 1986 and is reprinted here with her and the Journal's permission. Eva Warth's paper appeared in a more detailed version in *Frauen und Film*, Vol 38, 1985; Erik Levi's paper appears here for the first time. Of the additional eight chapters in the present book, Wilfried van der Will's paper is an extended version of his contribution to the earlier symposium 'The Body: Physical Culture in Weimar Germany', also held by the Art and Politics Study Group. John Heskett's paper appeared in *Block*, no 3, 1980, and is reprinted here unchanged with the author's and *Block*'s permission. Hartmut Frank's essay on architecture appeared in an earlier form in both Italian and English in *Lotus International*, Milan, no 47, 1985. His contribution in this book is substantially reworked and is translated into English by Wilfried van der Will. The essay by Robert Brady appeared as part of his *The Spirit and Structure of German Fascism* (1937) and is reprinted here with minor amendments with the permission of Viking Penguin, New York. Susan Sontag's essay 'Fascinating Fascism' first appeared in 1974 and was reprinted in *Under The Sign of Saturn*, London 1983. It appears here with the permission of the author and of Farrar, Straus and Giroux, New York.

We are grateful for the help afforded by a number of individuals and institutions: particularly Andrew Stephenson of the Art and Politics Study Group; Iain Boyd-White of the Department of Architecture at Edinburgh University; Michael Butler, Leon Pompa (both of Birmingham University) and Steve Hinton (Technical University of Berlin), for having read and commented upon parts of the manuscript; Arnold Fester, Munich, for giving us access to the pictures of the various exhibitions staged in the 'Haus der Deutschen Kunst' in the Third Reich; the staff of the Wiener Library in London, the Deutsches Filmmuseum in Frankfurt, the Fritz-Hüser-Institut für Arbeiterliteratur in Dortmund, and the Archiv für Zeitgeschichte in Munich; and to Frances Childs, who typed one version of the manuscript.

B.T. and W.v.d.W.
Winchester and Birmingham
January 1990

Chapter One

AESTHETICS AND NATIONAL SOCIALISM

Brandon Taylor and Wilfried van der Will

The mass appeal of National Socialism in Germany after 1933 was in a number of ways obviously linked to aesthetic and artistic phenomena. Fascism could even be defined as a form of government which depended on 'aestheticised' politics[1], featuring, for example, the marshalling of masses in geometrical formations, the expression of party-political and governmental functions through uniforms, insignia and ranking symbols and the integration of individuals in secular rituals of acclamation and submission (*Figs 1 and 2*). The aesthetics of political symbolism do, of course, play an essential part in all systems of mass politics. This can be readily observed in the cult of the national flag in the United States, in the ritualisation of royalty in Britain and in the commemorations of revolution in the Soviet Union. The difference in Fascism is the frequency, intensity and omnipresence of such practices. Furthermore, in Germany the public discourse of multi-party politics, which had characterised the Weimar period, was replaced from 1933 until the end of the Nazi era by the rule of one party and the rhetorical exaltations of its dictatorial leader. Hitler's penchant for politics as theatre, his coaching by an actor in how most effectively to strike oratorical poses, and his preference for the stage settings of Wagnerian opera as decorative models for Nazi festivities have often been remarked on. Assisted by the media, Hitler cultivated certain role models in the presentation of his public persona: the lover of serious music, art and architecture, the unsung ordinary soldier of World War I, the heroic fighter for the 'decent' German cause within the treachery of the Weimar party jungle, the deep thinker and instrument of providence as a statesman, and so on. His agitatory theatricality even gained him the nickname 'the drummer', both because his often repetitive speeches were understood to be 'drumming in' a certain message and because the drum as an instrument for summoning crowds and animating them into a rhythmic mass was associated with Nazi techniques of propaganda. Both he and Goebbels, the Minister for People's Enlightenment and Propaganda, explicitly compared themselves to artists. In a letter to Wilhelm Furtwängler, Germany's leading conductor, Goebbels had written: 'Politics too is an art, perhaps the highest and most comprehensive there is, and we who shape modern German policy feel ourselves in this to be artists who have been given the responsible task of forming, out of the raw material of the mass, the firm concrete structure of the people.'[2] Goebbels frequently cultivated this image of the mass of the people as putty in his 'creative' hants. The media was his 'piano' whose tunes he could manipulate at will.

1

1. Commemoration of the dead of the 'movement': bodies of members of the Right-wing putsch of 9 November 1923 are transferred to the memorial temples on the Königlicher Platz, Munich, 9 November 1935

Nazi politics is best understood as a string of captivating scenes in a series of dramas driven from climax to climax and aimed at mobilising the people. In addition to the regular regional and national Party rallies, there were special mass spectacles, parades and Party gatherings which were arranged to coincide with important events such as the opening of public buildings and the celebration of anniversaries. This was but one well-known means by which the Nazis were able to infuse tradition with new meanings, manipulate their followers ideologically and impress upon both them and the rest of the world the extent of their mass support and the splendour of their accumulating power. The *Führer's* birthday, the First of May as a festival of the *Deutsche Arbeitsfront* (German Labour Front), and Christmas redesigned as the Winter Equinox, are some of the more familiar examples of this genre. Carefully calculated forms of symbolic expression and aesthetic presentation stimulated mass-psychological effects. The colouring and design of the Nazi flag is a prime instance of the meticulous attention paid by the Nazi leaders to the presentation of meaning through the precise integration of design, scale, colour and choice of material. Thus Hitler wrote in *Mein Kampf*,

2

2. Party Rally, 1934: the dedication of the Nazi standards

I myself, after countless attempts, had laid down a final form: a flag with a background of red cloth, having a white circle, and, in the centre, a black swastika. . . . As National Socialists we see our programme in our flag. In the *red* we see the social idea of the movement, in the *white* we see the nationalistic idea, and in the *swastika* we see the mission of the struggle for the victory of Aryan man and at the same time for the victory of the idea of creative work, which in itself always was and will be anti-Semitic.[3]

The National Socialist regime itself commissioned, or made possible, works of art in all the traditional media — paintings, sculptures, buildings, musical scores and design work — which would reflect and hold in place National Socialist ideology. Art in this incarnation was to be no mere decoration on the surface of ordinary life, but a moral force permeating the whole of German society. From the building of the *Haus der Deutschen Kunst* (House of German Art) after 1933 to the seven vast exhibitions held in it between 1937 and 1944; from the party decrees on National Socialist tasks in the cultural sphere — including the notorious diatribes against 'Jewish' and 'Bolshevik' art enunciated by Rosenberg, Goebbels and Hitler himself — to the buildings of Speer, Mach and Troost; from the musical score of the Horst-Wessel song or the exploitation of a famous conductor, Wilhelm Furtwängler, to the layout of cultural magazines; art under National Socialism was assigned an indispensable part in the propagation of ideology and of politics as spectacle. It may reasonably be argued that within the Fascist state the role played by art, design, music and architecture was of considerably greater importance than that which is generally bestowed within 'liberal' or 'socialist' cultures.

However, the paintings, sculptures and other artefacts of the Nazi period have been subjected to only partial analysis within the context of contemporary aesthetic and historical criticism. To date, there exist a mere handful of publications on the Nazification of art in English, French and Italian. In Germany, a lively, if highly polemical, debate is in progress on the merits or demerits of placing National Socialist art in museums, but in most standard German books on art history any argument about the aesthetic characteristics of Fascist art in general and Nazi art in particular appears to have been largely avoided.[4] Furthermore, many studies have followed the 'liberal' assumption that all art under National Socialism was repellent and barbaric, even to the point of being too repellent and barbaric to analyse; and that aesthetic interest attaches only to that art which National Socialism set out to crush and destroy.

There are a number of practical and psychological reasons why this simplistic view could be held for so long. In the first place a large number of Nazi drawings, paintings and sculptures was confiscated by the Allied Powers at the end of World War II and consequently have not yet been examined extensively by art historians either in Germany or in the English-speaking countries. Those of the *Propaganda-kompanie* (a unit accompanying the German troops at the front), for example, were impounded in Washington D.C. Only since their return to the *Bayrisches Armeemuseum* in Ingolstadt can the scholarly examination of these works — mostly drawings — now begin. However, access remains severely restricted, just as it is to the paintings of the exhibitions of 'Great German Art' between 1937 and 1944 that are now stored, expertly in some respects and carelessly in others, in a huge customs and excise depot in Munich (*Hauptzollamt München-West*). It has become a matter of heated debate in West Germany to what extent they should be given a place in provincial city museums, exhibited only at special showings, or be kept together more permanently in the new historical museums that are being planned by the Federal German government.

Apart from such difficulties of a substantially logistical nature there are, of course, more important moral and ideological explanations for the tendency to reduce and simplify the output of National Socialist culture and thus to ignore or deny its inherent complexities as ideology and as art. One of the most prominent of these is the understandable reluctance of both museum curators and historians to enter into discussions about National Socialist art for fear of being accused of implying support either for the works under review or for the regime which sponsored them. On the other hand, the tendency to condemn all such works as 'horrific' to an equal degree is a sure sign that the process of historical, social and aesthetic analysis has yet to begin.

Indeed, the contributors to this book are united in believing that the time has come for this position of out-of-hand dismissal and exclusion from debate to be subjected to fundamental re-evaluation. The aim of this book is therefore not to attempt an exhaustive presentation of the fate of all the arts under National Socialism but rather to open up reflections of how that art might be placed within European developments from Modernism to Post-Modernism. Correspondingly, it is the task of this introduction to outline some of the more recent approaches to the historical assessment of National Socialism itself which have informed the re-interpretation of its art and which underly the various chapters of this book. The West German, British and American scholars who have collaborated on this volume have left undecided the leading question of the *Historikerstreit*[5] (the battle of the historians) which has recently preoccupied German academics, namely whether the Nazi crimes stand out by their heinous singularity or reveal in exemplary fashion the nature of modern state-induced, technological crimes. However, the essays in this volume have proceeded on the assumption that the works of National Socialist culture can be subjected to the same spirit of enquiry as that which makes us seek to understand the works of any culture, whatever its ideological foundation. We are not, after all, prevented by moral or political scruples from examining the paintings, sculptures, architecture and music of other imperialist powers, past or present. Knowledge of the most inhumane ruthlessness does not prevent us from examining the art of the Roman Empire either B.C. or A.D., or that of Florence between the 14th and 17th centuries, or that of Napoleonic France at the turn of the 19th century, or that of the United States after 1945. Rather, it makes such analysis more urgent. Nor have other academic disciplines such as economic and social history, sociology or psychology been slow to exhume the body of National Socialism for careful scrutiny. It may be argued, perhaps, that against a background of violence, murder and destruction, the imperialist cultures of the past have nevertheless made genuine contributions to civilisation, while German National Socialism has left us only with a negative heritage. Whether or not this is the case, the immensely troubling events of that period — all the more troubling because of their occurrence within a supposedly civilised country — should not prevent us from subjecting its culture and art to candid and scholarly analysis.

Nor should we feel constrained by any preconceived idea about the most appropriate social function of art. It may be precisely because of the fact that the prevalent role allotted to art in liberal-bourgeois society is becoming primarily that of an adornment to leisure, or a speculative object for investment, that the very idea of art as a social, political and ideological phenomenon connected centrally with the exercise of power seems abhorrent. Equally, the still current modernist attitude that art is an expression of individualism can serve to exclude from serious discussion artefacts that lend themselves to political uses. If it were applied with any rigour, we would have to condemn out of hand the monumental architecture of the Pharaohs as well as the triumphal arches of the Roman Empire and the frescoes of Florentine victories over other Tuscan cities, to name but a few examples.

In the context of today's debates about Post-Modernism, another reason for wishing to understand the aesthetic characteristics and ideological burdens of Fascist art arises from the well-known National Socialist antagonism to the values of international Modernism, which had, after all, been so influential in the Germany of the first three decades of the 20th century. Yet this antagonism is another stereotype that deserves to be re-examined. Is Nazi art in its entirety simply to be regarded as retrogressive in comparison with painters like Kandinsky, Picasso and Klee, sculptors like Barlach, Lipchitz and Lehmbruck, or composers like Schönberg, Hindemith and Stravinsky? Or is National Socialist art better regarded as the exemplification of a radical ambiguity between Modernism and anti-Modernism which, however differently inflected, can be traced in most advanced industrial countries of the West during the 1930s and 1940s? In the context of the overall re-evaluation of Modernist culture which is under way in the English speaking countries, the study of the art-works of Nazi Germany may become a matter of considerable, perhaps even compelling interest. The question here is whether the crude assessments normally associated with an 'antagonism' between Modernism and its reversal can be replaced by a dialectic in which the adversaries might define their positions in relation to each other. On the face of it, their deficiencies seem in many ways complementary. Thus it was the avant-garde of Modernism which purported to capture the harsh realities of life in the big cities, but, arguably, created an art which was inaccessible to most city-dwellers. It was the Modernist architects who addressed themselves to the pressing problems of insufficient housing and office space, but then proceeded to trap thousands of people in functionalist, high-rise layouts and development 'schemes'. Conversely, it was the genre-artists favoured by National Socialism who created a popularly accessible art that was yet sugar-coated with a social harmony quite absent in real life. Equally, there are striking parallels. Modernism showed a marked predilection for the innocence or 'primitivism' of the child, while National Socialist art showed a pronounced liking for the innocence of the simple country folk and the stable values of traditional rural life.

Thus a third reason for wishing to re-open the debate on Nazi culture is the conviction that an examination of the axioms of European Modernism would scarcely be complete without an equal examination of its presumed antithesis or converse. Such a re-examination is by no means as straightforward as might be supposed. Against the liberal doctrine that Nazi culture occupies the unacceptable or 'extreme right' in aesthetics and that Modernist art unequivocally occupies the acceptable 'centre' or 'left', there arise at least two considerations which must serve to complicate the picture. One is that various artists and intellectuals during the period of Nazi culture were attracted to Fascist doctrine while at the same time remaining stylistically Modernist in inclination or expression—Nolde in painting, Yeats, Pound and Gottfried Benn in literature, Carl Orff, Paul von Klenau, Richard Strauss and Werner Egk in music. Moreover, this grouping shades off into a host of other artists who were not at any time sympathetic to Fascism, yet were staunchly antipathetic to Modernism. De Chirico's nationalism, for example, brought him close to Mussolini in 1935; but it remains problematic whether he can be positively associated with the Italian Blackshirts, and, if so, by what precise sympathies and connections. Another consideration is that a third paradigm came to exist *between* National Socialism and European Modernism in the form of Germany's war-time rival, the Soviet Union, which, in the doctrine of Socialist Realism, took a stand that was hostile to both international Modernism *and* to Fascism, and yet shared stylistic features with the latter and a boundless optimism about the possibilities of technological modernity with the former.

The Soviet Union, during the 1930s, provides a particularly significant example of shared similarities with developments in culture and art under National Socialism, despite the ostensibly unbridgeable ideological gulf between the two regimes. In terms of its much vaunted 'revolutionary romanticism', its advocacy of naturalistic technique and its support for a 'positive', 'healthy' and 'heroic' approach to life, Socialist Realism is to be placed inevitably alongside the technical and conceptual axioms of National Socialist art. Official programmatic statements in Germany and the Soviet Union on the social and ideological importance of art show clear resemblances to each other. Just as Hitler and Goebbels insisted on art being accessible to the people and a representation of their concerns, rather than remaining the prerogative of an educated élite, so the doctrine of Socialist Realism stressed the necessity of popularising a 'revolutionary romanticism' (Zhdanov) of the socialist hero. Both regimes extolled the virtues of a collectivist culture, both claimed to speak and act on behalf of the 'masses' or 'the united people', and both castigated the excessive individualism of capitalist culture. In terms of their cult of the charismatic leader and their fervent approach to nationally approved priorities such as industrial modernisation and the central organisation and dissemination of ideology, the two systems obviously invite comparison. Both regimes exerted manipulative control over the media. The timings of their key moments in the cultural field are also uncannily close: the 1936 statement by Goebbels on the state control of art criticism and the 1934 Soviet Writers' Congress which endorsed (but did not initiate) Socialist Realism as the appropriate Communist style; the foundation of the *Reichskulturkammer* (National Chamber of Culture) in 1933 and that of the *Komitet po delam iskusstv* (Committee for the Arts) in the USSR in 1936; the Munich *Ausstellung 'Entartete Kunst'* (exhibition of 'degenerate' art) in 1937 and the purging of those who deviated from 'Socialist Realism', which reached a peak in the same year; the idolatry of the *Führer* and the Stalin-cult, which after the mid-1930s was well established in painting, sculpture and the other arts. Finally, the institutionalisation of an ideology of art meant that in both societies conformist writers could act as public ideological judges of other writers, painters denounced other painters, musicians other musicians, and so on. In Germany the selection and requisitioning of paintings for the Nazi exhibition of 'degenerate' art was the responsibility of the painter Adolf Ziegler, who had been installed as president of the *Reichskammer der bildenden Künste* (National Arts Chamber). In the Soviet Union, where the process of setting up various Party- and state-controlled professional associations in the arts had started earlier, the processes of denunciation and official discrimination began in the late 1920s. One of the first victims was Evgeny Ivanovich Zamyatin who in 1929 was pressured to leave the All-Russian Writers' Association because one of his novels had been published in an émigré magazine in Prague. He resigned his membership for he did not wish to belong to 'a literary organisation which, albeit indirectly, takes part in the persecution of a fellow member.'[6] The criticism contained in his letter of resignation — which was to find echoes in many others that were to follow both in the USSR and Nazi Germany — officially went unheeded, and denunciatory practices became an established part of Stalinist Russia, both inside and outside the realms of culture and art.

However, despite these points of similarity, marked differences remained. Within the socialism of the Soviet Union racism could never be made into a central policy platform, and despite talk of 'international class warfare' in the 1930s, the Soviet Union, while seeking to extend its spheres of influence abroad, cannot be compared with Nazi Germany in terms of military aggression, either in fact or intention. Further, it must be acknowledged that socialism in whatever form cannot be completely assimilated to Fascism. Only through some mystical unity-of-opposites argument can the two be brought together into complete and final coincidence. German Fascism was mendacious even in the name it had adopted: it was nationalistic but certainly not socialist. The differences between the two political orders demonstrate clearly that reactions to international Modernism could arise from significantly divergent ideological precepts, could be dissimilar in form and content, and could be variously motivated aesthetically. This strongly suggests, in turn, that Modernism and Fascism can no longer be understood as 'inevitably' or 'naturally' opposed.

The Soviet example may bring to mind a further complication in the prevailing view of Nazi art as irredeemably inartistic, unworthy of being examined and unfit for exhibition. This arises from the gradual change which has occurred in the last couple of decades regarding our view of the Fascist period in German history. Once standard accounts of German Fascism — essentially of a liberal tendency — viewed the rise of National Socialism in a sophisticated, modern nation as an aberration, a tragic mistake, an absurd interruption in the otherwise comprehensible trajectory of twentieth-century German life. Implicit in this view was the proposition that such a mistake could only be repeated if a similar inexplicable eruption of dark and deathly forces occurred, and that in any case it would require a demon with the charm, the fanaticism, the rhetorical skills and the destructive personality of an Adolf Hitler to provide the fateful spark. Suffice it to say that with the growth of evidence of the mass popularity of the National Socialist movement, of the acceptability of its 'innocent' face in everyday life, of its skilful exploitation of ordinary administrative practices in peacetime and during the emergency situation of war, the credibility of such liberal explanations has declined. The evident appeal of the Nazi propaganda machine and its attendant culture industry to millions of Germans from all classes, but particularly to the lower middle class, is surely incompatible with the idea of a chance emergence within history of a charismatic homicidal maniac.

The reverse of such liberal explanations is no less implausible. According to this version Hitler merely represented the culmination of a process within German history stretching back to the times of Luther and the *Obrigkeitsstaat* (a state demanding unquestioning obedience from its subjects) which made possible the fashioning of subservient religious minds and apolitical citizens. This is a German syndrome which Hitler was certainly able to exploit for the establishment of his dictatorship. Yet it must not be overstated, lest it serve a linear, excessively deterministic explanation reducing the complex constellation of rival, oppositional and contradictory social, cultural and political forces to the assertion of a monocausal set of agents that continuously produce more of the same: conformist personality structures and passive obedience to state authority. Such explanations effectively isolate Germany from the rest of European history. Yet they can explain neither the considerable potential for disobedience to authority that is evident in numerous periods of German history—for example in the Reformation itself, in the uprisings of 1848 and in the struggles of the democratic, republican and revolutionary constituency of Weimar Germany — nor the specific features of Nazi ideology and the way these were designed to play up to revanchist desires for economic, political and racial superiority kindled by the outcome of World War I.

But if liberal versions of fascist history have proved unsatisfactory, then so have certain traditional Marxist accounts (many of them generated in the late 1920s and early 1930s), albeit in a different respect. The 'vulgar' Marxist theory that Fascism was an off-spring of capitalism — final proof, perhaps, that advanced capitalism would deteriorate into dictatorship when the profit rate threatened to collapse[7]—relied heavily upon the proximity of the acute financial crises that swept the whole of the Western World between 1929 and 1932. By this account, Germany was the falling keystone signalling the collapse of the whole dome of the capitalist order. Several attempts have been made to prove that the connection between Fascism and capitalism in crisis was revealed beyond doubt by the funding of National Socialism from the coffers of private industry.[8] Capitalism in these accounts is seen as an inherently unbalanced system and the bourgeois democratic state that went with it as a highly corruptible order. German capitalists were believed to be behind-the-scenes manipulators financing the Nazis as their puppets, in order then to seduce the mass of the population by demagogy. The basic motive for the capitalist support of Hitler's Party was supposed to stem from the idea that the promised policies of the NSDAP would provide guarantees against both the bankrupting fluctuations of market demand and the politically incalculable disaffection of the low-wage workforce and the unemployed. Once the NSDAP had gained power it would use the machinery of the state, and in particular the armaments industries, to regulate the former and to deal with the latter by disciplining the mass of the proletariat. Such expectations did indeed exist, notably in the circle of industrialists, bankers and large-scale landowners (junkers) around Wilhelm Keppler.[9] Nor were these expectations entirely unrealistic. However, there is little hard evidence to suggest that the vast majority of capitalists were prepared to pay for Hitler's ascendancy, although they saluted him readily enough once he came to power. Substantial funding of the Party derived from individual rather than from banking or industrial sources. Nor is there evidence of any large-scale connivance by the business bosses with National Socialism before 1933. Majority opinion in the *Reichsverband der Industrie* (Reich-Federation of Industry) appears to have favoured not Hitler but Kurt von Schleicher who envisaged a certain balance of interests between employers and employees, bourgeoisie and working class, industrialists and trade unionists.[10] Such donations from industry to the National Socialists as there were before 1933 tended to come from individual capitalists in particular industries, like Thyssen, who represented the hard-pressed steel producers. The chemicals and electrical industries, however, kept their political options open[11], as did Mercedes-Benz whose political donations were spread over a number of parties. Understandably, the moment Hitler took power, the scene changed and most industrialists and financiers assured him and his movement of their co-operation.[12]

A further difficulty with the thesis that National Socialism was nothing more than the executive arm of capitalism is its inevitable conclusion that the *Führer* was merely the stooge of the capitalist bosses. Nothing could be further from the

9

truth, since Hitler introduced a planned economy that ultimately had to dance to the tune of the military, and hence to Hitler's own martial stratagems.[13] The introduction of a four-year plan in 1936 effectively geared the whole of industry to the requirements of a military machine that was preparing for an aggressive war against the Soviet Union. There was a clear supremacy of politics and ideology over economics within the National Socialist state. The Nazi leaders constantly sermonised against big business as an alienating force in society, largely run by Jewish financiers who were out to rob the people. It was important for National Socialism to exploit the anti-capitalist sympathies of the majority of white-collar workers, small traders and businessmen, with all the romantic and racist overtones that their attitudes demanded. At the same time, German capitalism was to be made into a subservient tool of Hitler's political designs.

Thus a cardinal explanatory fact is that the National Socialist dictatorship, whatever its connections with capitalist economic interests, was founded substantially on mass acclamation, and there can be little doubt that at least during its initial years in power it could be sure of eliciting precisely such a response from the majority of the population. Such was his mass acclaim that, according to his own testimony, Hitler did not have to squander the powers of the executive on keeping down an internal opposition. Indeed, he could plan for his war against the Soviet Union with concentrated rapidity.[14]

The vulgar Marxist argument of conceiving German Fascism as merely the executive arm of capitalism presents the further difficulty of being unable to explain why it took so long for National Socialism to take power. After all, the collapse of share prices at the New York stock exchange on 24 October 1929 (Black Friday) did not initiate, but rather significantly exacerbated, a fundamental economic crisis that had already set in a year earlier. It is difficult to see why the Nazis were left to struggle for a sizeable share of the vote for four years (without ever attaining an absolute majority), if they were indeed the spokesmen for the combined agrarian and industrial lobby. Had the latter really commanded such a decisive influence, the National Socialists would surely have been manipulated into power at the beginning of the crisis rather than left to seize it for themselves at its end.

Signs of a more thoroughly dialectical and historically more precise explanation have been emerging in recent scholarship, which has been able to absorb elements of both the liberal and the Marxist theories while at the same time pointing beyond them in ways that promise, amongst other things, to make the art of National Socialism a rewarding object of study. Such explanations have aimed to link certain traditions dating back to the nineteenth century, which fed yearnings for national grandeur, with specific features of the rise of Fascism in Germany and elsewhere in Europe during the 1920s. The Wagnerian myths of tragic Germanic greatness, infused with a hefty dose of anti-semitism, the xenophobia, the militarism and chauvinism, the envious zeal of vying with the British 'John Bull', had all fostered an amalgam of nationalistic perceptions and prejudices before World War I which lent themselves to further modulation in the 1920s when it became clear that dreams of world dominion had failed to produce German hegemony even in Europe. Internally, Germany was weakened by divisions. The Weimar Republic, which began with one of the most remarkably democratic constitutions anywhere in the world, suddenly released such a diversity of political parties and ideological platforms that a sharply divided society emerged. The notion of 'Weimar Germany' became inseparable from the very idea of an internally riven society. It became a battleground which proved incapable of coming to terms with its own inherent contradictions other than by allowing them to be smothered with lulling illusions of the 'one nation', the indivisible *Volk*. A sense of national solidarity proved capable of being built only against the plural nature of Weimar culture and on the basis of mass resentment against the divisions of class, ideology and race. The imagined enemy was now neither Britain nor France[15], but the international Jewish community which supposedly ruled both the 'plutocracy' of the United States and, nearer home, the 'compact authoritarian ideology' (Hitler)[16] of Bolshevism.

The virulence of these resentments provided Fascism with the chance of agitating not only for radical political solutions but also for a fundamental transformation of politics itself. Art, too, was transformed, both in terms of style and in terms of its importance within German society. Inspired by Walter Benjamin's observation as early as 1936 that Fascism introduced the aestheticisation of politics and the politicisation of aesthetics, and following Bertolt Brecht's and Ernst Bloch's propositions on similar lines[17], a number of post-war critics and historians have furnished detailed analyses which give powerful support to Benjamin's original thesis. Independently, Gerhard Szczesny in a German pamphlet of 1946 entitled *Europa und die Anarchie der Seele* (Europe and the Anarchy of the Soul) had talked of the tribal patterns of identification that the Nazis in their various organisational formations (Hitler Youth, Storm Troopers, SS, Party organisation, administrative divisions etc.) attempted to attain through hierarchy and symbolism. The argument here is that the collectivism of the horde was intended to give the individual a feeling of unquestioned togetherness and provide an affirmation of shared values against enemies both within and without. This argument certainly applies to the German petty bourgeoisie (the *Kleinbürgertum*) and the white collar workers (*Stehkragenproletariat*) who, given their dread of proletarianisation, their traditional feelings of inferiority to the higher class and their fear of the organised might of the lower one, fell back into a state of political puerilism. This petty bourgeoisie began to long for authority and stability in the wake of the acute ideological insecurities and the disorientating Modernism of the Weimar Republic. It was this large and internally varied lower middle class which became uniquely vulnerable to the temptations of the *Führer*-cult, the anticapitalist rhetoric, the anti-communism, the anti-Bolshevism, the anti-semitism and the heavily popularised dreams of the supremacy of the Germanic *Volk*. It was here that National Socialism gained its biggest majorities, while making distinct but only limited inroads into other social classes.[18] How the Fascists were able to consolidate their power so rapidly and exert so powerful a fascination over the mass of the population by the aesthetic production of politics and ideology has gradually come to light through detailed historical investigation. This research has rightly laid a particular stress on the 'theatrical direction of public life'[19], the 'pseudo-religion of the brown cult'[20], the 'liturgy and symbolism'[21] of mass-democracy movements and the use of 'magic and manipulation'[22] under National Socialism. Such analyses, while sometimes in danger of overestimating the irrationalist side of mass politics, are either explicitly or implicitly anchored in concrete manifestations of complex class interests and in the psychology of individual responses to the fragmentary and fragmenting experience of cultural Modernism.

Within such an approach, the parades and public spectacles of the years between 1933 and 1939 must be seen as more than mere 'expressions' of a stage-managed rank-and-file movement or a dictatorial philosophy of mass organisation and propaganda. Above all, they displayed the essentially designed nature of National Socialist existence, the opening up, in spectacular fashion, of ritualised ideological arenas which the lower middle class and also sections of the middle and the working classes could enter *(Fig 3)*. Within these arenas, which were kept free from the open show of violence and the blatant criminality of the ruling powers, the Party and state apparatuses could play to and excite the prejudices of the mob, while at the same time giving the dictatorship a façade of respectability and legitimacy. To describe this set of scenarios as the liturgy of National Socialism does much to demonstrate the religious and mythological borrowings which are to be found within the aesthetic phenomenology of Fascism. At the same time, the realisation of mass politics as an aesthetic design served to hide the contradictory nature of its contents and the ambiguity of the concepts, ideologies and emotions it could draw on and absorb with such virtuoso eclecticism. Hence the German Fascist could conceive of himself as an anti-socialist, but with the proviso that he was a 'better' socialist than those internationalist Social Democrats and 'Bolshevik' Communists whom he was proud to have defeated. Likewise, he may have lost his allegiance to the Christian churches, but could persuade himself that he possessed a deeper faith in Christian values than mere churchgoers. Finally, he could be motivated to fight for 'culture' against the 'Bolshevik hordes', but, as Goering had said — borrowing a phrase from a play by Hanns Johst[23] — he would stand ready to release the safety catch of his Browning as soon as he heard the word 'culture'.

This is sufficient by itself to suggest that art played a complex and contradictory role in the practices of National Socialism. For all the indubitable power of the *Führer* standing aloof from the intense inter-departmental rivalry in the machinery of Fascist government, that power still had to reproduce its legitimacy by constantly rallying the masses to ever renewed acts of faith in the leader and by establishing in the minds of the many that his fate was identical with that of Germany. He had to be projected as a tool of divine providence. All the arts, from the theatrical rhetoric of the political orator to painting, music, architecture and film, would be used to this end.

This does not and should not be taken to imply that all art under National Socialism was directly engaged in extolling the virtues of Nazi power. On the contrary, many of the paintings — to name but one category — that appeared in the extensive Munich art exhibitions were pieces of idyllic painterly 'beauty', executed to a considerable standard of technical accomplishment. Typically, painters supported the racial ideology not by overt identification with Nazi propaganda but by their preference, sometimes unquestioned and unconscious, for blond and blue-eyed 'Aryan types' as the subjects of their canvasses. Art did not have to battle for attention but, on the contrary, quickly achieved a privileged position within German society. By 1937, the regime, far from being popularly regarded as hostile to culture, appeared to be inaugurating a veritable renaissance of art. Thus in 1938, there were 170 competitions for painters, sculptors, architects and graphic artists with 1.5 million marks in prize money involved. In 1941 there were over 1,000 special art exhibitions all over the Reich.[24] However, pointing to the importance and wide-spread nature of aesthetic activity within the Fascist state is never to relegate National Socialist art to the role of adornment or superficial decoration of an otherwise implacable and nihilistic military machine. It is rather to suggest that, perhaps more in tragedy than in grace, art and aesthetic practice could be entered into at a variety of social and political sites and made to captivate the

3. *Lichtdom* (cathedral of light): Party Rally, Nürnberg, 1937

awareness of very substantial numbers of people in answer to their perception of national crisis; that it could mould the context of public and private communication; that it could structure the psychology of interpersonal relationships; and that it could draw on various styles and formal predilections which, ironically, it tacitly shared both with its 'plutocratic' enemies in Wall Street and its 'Bolshevik' adversaries in the Kremlin. It is in this respect, too, as much as for its protest against and connivance with Modernism, that an understanding of the sculpture, painting, musical composition, architecture, film and interior design of National Socialism must remain an essential part of the educated memory of an era that wishes to be called 'Post-Modern'.

Chapter Two

THE BODY AND THE BODY POLITIC AS SYMPTOM AND METAPHOR IN THE TRANSITION OF GERMAN CULTURE TO NATIONAL SOCIALISM

Wilfried van der Will

Responses to Modernity and the Rise of National Socialism

National Socialism may in some respects be the result of peculiarly German developments, of Germany having travelled down a *Sonderweg* (idiosyncratic route), as some historians have argued. The chief concern of this chapter, however, is to trace within National Socialist society the symptoms of a break-away from Modernity to Post-Modernity. In other words, it is proposed to 'read' in National Socialism the relatively early manifestations not of a purely national, but of a European cultural transition. It is set within a new political grammar which maginalised the 'modern' one of class struggle. The Germany of the 1930s signalled a departure from traditional class politics, for it is impossible to explain the power of National Socialism in Germany in terms of conflicting economic and class interests. The nature of Fascist politics, while ready to accommodate and exploit such interests, was essentially anchored in an organic concept of society, expressed in symbolic representation and cultural hierarchy. It could therefore build its support on a wide sociological stratum of voters and, once in power, was obliged to no particular class fraction. The victory of National Socialism in the Germany of the 1930s meant the replacement of a political grammar based on economic precepts and class struggle by one based on the symbolism of hier-archical integration. The latter implied ideological and racial exclusion and pre-supposed a re-feudalisation of social perception. This is clearly illustrated in the painting and drawing of the time, for example in the nostalgic portrayal of pre-industrial village life as an allegorically visualised source of instant rejuvenation (*Fig 1*), and in the heraldic design for a *Luftwaffe* officers' mess signifying the defence of community (*Fig 2*). National Socialism gained mass acceptance because it promised to overcome the alienations wrought on individuals by modern capital-ism and instead transform society to become a large integrated community. In reality, of course, National Socialism intensified the secular fate of alienation to the point of leading society into destruction. Yet we must ask whether the yearning for a socially more integrated community, on which the propaganda of National

1. Paul Beuttner: *Old Wives Mill* (in Tripstrill near Heilbronn), 1939 Exhibition in Haus der Deutschen Kunst, Munich

Socialism had played, does not survive today in many, typically non-Fascist, forms of Post-Modernist protest.

Such propositions call for a reconsideration of the context of cultural history out of which National Socialism arose. In trying to understand the degeneration of a sophisticated Central European state into barbarity, a number of diverse factors may spring to mind. For example, many Germans wanted a fundamental revision of, if not revenge for, the Treaty of Versailles, which had concluded the hostilities of World War I without laying any foundations for a possible reconciliation between the adversaries. Furthermore, a large percentage of the German electorate at the end of the Weimar Republic was ready to follow a leader who promised work at a time when there were over six million unemployed and when many more had only a subsistence income from part-time or temporary employment. Such voters came

15

2. Karl Heinz Dallinger: *Tapestry for an Officers'
Mess of the Luftwaffe*; Legend: 'Florian Geyer be
our captain and let none of our enemies escape';
from *Die Kunst im Dritten Reich*, 1938

less from the ranks of the unemployed themselves than from the lower middle
classes who felt the threat of proletarianisation and a collapse of law and order.
Many people, traditionally accustomed to the ideological and psychological
securities afforded by the clear stratifications of an authoritarian state, became
disorientated. They were unsettled first by a period of revolutionary upsurge
(1919 – 21) which followed the defeat in war and later by the extreme pluralism of
political parties, each fighting a hopeless battle for dominance in an increasingly
confused and chaotic political discourse. Others abhorred not only the ideological
disunity of the nation, but also its social division into haves and have-nots, into the
leisured chic and the workers, into privileged and underprivileged classes.

Although Hitler never attained more than 43.9% of the vote in a free general
election, he appeared to many to be the answer to all these problems, for we have to
assume that the plebiscites he held *after* he had attained power did in fact produce
large acclamatory majorities, even if the final results were manipulated by the
Nazi propaganda machine.[1] As long as there was peace Hitler was not a dictator
who had to live behind an impenetrable shield of security men. Nor was National
Socialism a political and ideological creed which fed merely on its sectarian
delusions. Hitler denied these occult roots of his ideological education in Vienna[2]
precisely because his political instinct told him that only the exploitation of
'respectable' cultural traditions would confer political legitimation in the eyes of
the 'broad masses' both on him and on his movement. After all, National Socialism
had to provide what to many were plausible responses to the confusing reality of
lived experience at that time. It could not do so without incorporating in its culture

16

a perception of society that had a long European heritage. I shall attempt to show that the attractiveness of one of its central propaganda motifs, the vision of a united *Volk* (nation) (also used in compound nouns like *Nationalvolk, Staatsvolk, Volksstaat, Volkskörper*), derived from older, distinctively anti-modernist arguments that were European in origin though German in inflection. They were nourished by venerable ideological traditions which could also be traced in other countries, notably Britain. Furthermore, I shall demonstrate that these traditions hold utopian attractions which have by no means lost their force even in the 'Post-Modernist' culture of present-day Western societies. For the utopian anti-Modernism, on which National Socialist propaganda and art were founded, can be seen to suffuse modern culture and is re-emerging, whether ironically or accompanied by ideological ardour, in the iconographic and architectural imagination of the present.

In order to explain the events of the Nazi era in Germany historians have increasingly felt compelled to look beyond pure political analysis. They have sought to unravel the dominant life styles, the hegemonic ideological currents, the shifts in the social composition and the social psychology of the German people since the beginning of the twentieth century and have tried to follow a number of threads going back hundreds of years into German history. There can be little doubt that long-standing traditions of authoritarianism, nationalistic myth-making and anti-semitic prejudice were indeed absorbed into Nazi propaganda. The danger of such social and cultural history is that deterministic developments are perceived where there are none and that special characteristics are highlighted which were by no means typical of Germany alone. There is, for example, no convincing evidence that certain stock features which are supposed to constitute the 'German character' are in fact specific to Germany. For example, anti-semitic intolerance was far more militant and widespread in Poland, the Ukraine and the Austro-Hungarian Empire than in the German *Reich*. As for nationalist, chauvinist and imperialist sentiments, they were extremely strong in all the major nation states of nineteenth and early twentieth-century Europe. It is difficult to prove that attitudes of passive obedience were noticeably more marked in Germany than they were in other European societies. If Hitler is nevertheless to be regarded as the culmination of such traditions, then we must search for manifestations in twentieth-century German culture, themselves pointing back into European history, which indicated such pronounced reactions against modern developments that they were capable of pulling Germany in crisis in a significantly different direction from that taken by other Western societies. Accordingly, within the limits of this chapter, a set of intense and inimical responses to modernity will be traced which give evidence of extensive nostalgia for a vividly imagined traditional, 'organic' society, free from the alienation of capitalist industrialism. This will help us to understand how Nazism could appropriate the best parts of an illustrious German cultural tradition. At the same time it will explain how attitudes that were by no means exclusive to Germany could, there, form a distinctive and seductive ideological mixture which in turn prepared the ground for a policy of murderous extremes.

Clearly, we cannot attempt here a comprehensive study of the cultural dynamics within which incipient changes of attitude, the political radicalisation of the 1920s, and the refabrication of tradition by National Socialism led in the 1930s to mass allegiance to a ruthless dictator. We shall instead have to content ourselves with the study of one aspect within the sketch of a larger picture. By concentrating on some powerfully suggestive images and symptomatic movements since the turn of the twentieth century, which were either completely absent from other European societies or relegated to marginality there, it is possible to reveal deep-seated yearnings that in Germany demanded political attention and that called for a rhetoric targeted at the dissatisfied mass. The images both of nudity and the organic cohesion of society which we have in mind were neither necessarily of National Socialist provenance nor could they be considered suitable material for the programmatic pronouncements of a mass party. Yet they carried messages and dreams of social organisation with the broadest appeal. They represented a storehouse of utopian promises that in the 1920s and before World War I was being raided by groupings from the far Left to the extreme Right. The latter was able to use such images within the manipulatory network of Fascist ideology and skilfully popularise them in a period of economic, social and cultural crisis; through them was suggested a necessary return to heroic values and a communally integrated life. In other words, distinctive elements within German tradition served to negate the present and were used to create a myth of the past that could feed the convictions of majorities and influence their attitudes and decisions regarding contemporary politics.

The Crisis of Modernity

The long-term factors which were operative within the crisis of the 1920s could be found everywhere in Europe, rooted as they were in the secular transformation from a traditional authoritarian society to one of democratic pluralism. During the inter-war years the evolutionary character of this transformation faltered in Germany. Until then Germany had, with considerable lag behind Britain, embarked on the European transition to modernity. This process, which at times showed distinctly revolutionary features, can be traced over three centuries. It includes the post-Renaissance victories of modern science over superstition and medieval scholasticism, the disintegration of feudal-absolutist authority and universal religious faith, the development of global commerce, the emergence of machinofacture and the evolution of an industrial capitalist society, large-scale urbanisation and the replacement of communalist attitudes by bourgeois individualism. These developments necessitated changes in the existing political structures which would make them more responsive to the plural interests of growing mass populations. The foundation of modern political parties and the splitting of society into party-political groupings, the growth of the print mdia and their use by different ideological factions in the *Kaiserreich* and, finally, the crescendo of intensely nationalistic state propaganda were typical historical features that found their parallels elsewhere in Europe. World War I was the outcome of a situation where competing nationalisms had patently grown too big for their boots. In Germany, which had been pushed into hurried industrialisation over a single generation after the Franco-Prussian War (1870 – 71), the transition to modernity was then significantly accelerated again, perhaps overaccelerated, by the abolition of the monarchy and the introduction of a republican, liberal-democratic constitution in 1919. The momentum of social change, still not fast enough for sections of the urban proletariat who had little to lose, proved too fast for the majority of the conservative middle and lower-middle classes, who felt the loss of social prestige and material income and clung to ideas of a more traditional social order. The process of transition first produced frenzied party-political, ideological and social contradictions in the Weimar state and was then halted — though not in all respects — by the emergence of National Socialism and the establishment of the Hitler dictatorship, only to be completed in the Federal Republic of the post-Adenauer period and in the post-Honecker period of the German Democratic Republic. The demagogy of the Nazi movement and of Hitler in particular, however unconvincing it may have been to large sections of the electorate — the majority of workers, of Catholics and of the educated/liberal middle classes — was assured of ever greater public approval the more it could project the vision of an undivided nation. The abolition of all party-political and ideological divisions within a volatile multi-party state and the promise of forging the German people into one united body energised by the same 'blood' was a counsel of despair, but it held considerable attractions. Notions of the 'body' — both in its specific sense as the material shape of human beings and in its wider meaning as a metaphorical designation for the nation in the sense of the 'body politic' — had been gaining steadily in importance since the dawn of the twentieth century.

It was at this time in Germany that a society with an increasingly modern class structure appeared, together with its attendant social tensions and internal contradictions. These were clearly articulated in the political, economic and cultural spheres. The German parliament, the *Reichstag*, may have been overshadowed by the power of the *Kaiser*, his chancellor and a traditionally authoritarian government bureaucracy, but it steadily increased in political weight and, with the spread at least of male universal suffrage, gave expression to a plurality of political interests and representation to different social classes and class factions. A scenario of conflict emerged which became even more dominant in the Weimar Republic. No superior authority, such as that which before 1918 had staked its claims in terms of 'divine right' (*Gottesgnadentum*), could now override political divisions. Germany exhibited the typical fissures of a secular society, in which religious creeds were on the decline and numerous *Weltanschauungen* (ideologies) and divergent political programmes competed with each other. Even the university sciences were no longer considered to be free of ideology. Significantly, a scholar as eminent as Max Weber felt compelled to devote several treatises to the distinctions between social science, which was concerned primarily with facts and their location in an historical context, and ideology, which involved beliefs about ultimate values and their relatedness to political action.[3] University chairs in *Weltanschauungslehre* (theory of ideology) began to appear — notably based on the work by Karl Jaspers, Max Scheler and Romano Guardini, with memories of the book entitled *Weltanschauungslehre* (1908) by the much earlier Heinrich Gomperz — because it was hoped that this would promote 'mutual acquaintance and understanding among the races, classes and parties within the political life of this country'.[4] Philosophers as well as writers expressed their disquiet over 'value pluralism', 'value relativism', 'the decay of values' and 'nihilism'. Theories about the 'sociology of knowledge' which challenged all illusions of objectivity became fashionable. In other words, dissonances, not just in musical composition — where they were revolutionary — but in ordinary cognition became a basic experience. Josef Goebbels was right to stress in an article of 1935 that the reaction against the confusing democratic pluralism and the internal dissensions of the Weimar Republic was a major element in the acceptance of National Socialism by a majority of the German people: 'Never before had particularism of every kind revelled in such orgies at a time when we badly needed internal unity.'[5]

Whether in the intellectually challenging cosmopolitan environment of the universities or in the rural backwoods, whose idyllic retardation was daily disturbed by the metropolitan media, all sections of society in the 1920s were drawn into a politicised contemporaneity which manifested itself in ever greater participation rates at elections. These shot up from an already respectable 75.6% in February 1928 to 88.7% in March 1933. Feelings of alienation, of being let down by society, were in the late 1920s not confined to the modern wage-dependent labourer, nor to the sensitive literary avantgarde of the educated bourgeoisie from Rainer Maria Rilke to Gottfried Benn. Instead, they became the central psychological, intellectual and social experience of members of all classes. Similarly, the economic crisis broadened. Earlier, it had mainly been the small savers of the lower and professional middle classes who had lost their money as a result of the hyperinflation of 1923. Now, the Black Friday crash of 1929 affected shareholders, sharedealers and financiers as well, at the same time worsening further the position of white and blue-collar labour. Dissaffection with the existing political system became so widespread that, from the elections in September 1930 through three further general elections up until March 1933, a steadily increasing majority in the *Reichstag* joined in a shrill chorus of extremist propaganda in favour of abolishing parliamentary democracy.

The Utopian Content of Nudism and Fascist Corporatism

It was in this situation that a rhetoric gained ground which celebrated the return to rural simplicity and close-knit community pre-dating industrial civilisation. The appeal was to the harmony of the body as a metaphor of social balance, natural inequality and co-operation in a complex organism. At the very time when the designs of the Bauhaus and the New Objectivity in art and literature were achieving creative triumphs of Modernist culture, the most violent moment of an anti-modernist backlash was being prepared in politics, supported by the extensive spread of an anti-modernist mentality in large sections of the population. This is neither to say that Modernism actually breathed its last the instant that National Socialism came to power, nor that Hitler's policies stopped the forward march of industrialisation. Yet the utopian visions of organic wholeness which were played on by Nazi propaganda campaigns drew on anti-modernist protests such as those organised since before World War I by adherents of the nudity cult, the many branches of the neo-romantic *Bündische Jugend* (the German Youth Movement), and right-wing publishing houses with influential journals such as *Die Tat* (The Deed — Eugen Diederichs Verlag, Jena), *Deutschlands Erneuerung* (Germany's Renewal — J. F. Lehmanns Verlag, Munich) and *Deutsches Volkstum* (German Folk — Hanseatische Verlagsanstalt, Hamburg).[6] All these groupings, which gained their clearest articulation in writers associated with the 'Conservative Revolution', were more or less fiercely elitist, hoping for a *Diktatur der Geistigen* (dictatorship of the intellectual/spiritual élite) and believing in a special cultural mission of Germany. They sought to promote *Ganzheit* (wholeness), *Einheit* (unity) and *Bindung* (social and ideological incorporation) against *Individualismus* (individualism), *Weltanschuungsvielfalt* (ideological pluralism) and *Fortschrittsdenken* (idea of steady progress). While these were typical rightwing, proto-fascist responses to modernity, they were attractive to all segments of German society, whose respective sense of social distinction and ideological division became intensified at the same time. Thus, on the left too there was an ardent search for incorporation and collective commitment amongst the members of the socialist worker culture organisations, despite the internationalism of their outlook. The novels and theories of the communist 'cultural bolshevists' invoked the all-encompassing capacity and wisdom of the *Volk* (the nation, the ordinary people). Communist and socialist youth organisations were founded which emulated the bourgeois youth movement, the symbolism of its banners and styles of clothing and the practices of exploring the countryside and living together in tent colonies. Nudism too burst out of its bourgeois enclaves. By the late 1920s the lure of the nudist arcadia had extended its influence across the best part of the ideological spectrum and thereby furnished clear proof that the naked body could become the focus of reformist, educational and aesthetic ideas in quite divergent ideological camps. It was a telling symptom of the degree of material uncertainty and mental anxiety then prevailing that human beings felt compelled to return to the most basic point of orientation, the body, in order to redefine their perception of society and their relation to it. Far from providing any guidance towards 'pure', 'natural' or 'original' values, however, the body turned out to be a chameleon, reflecting the different colours of quite diverse ideological environments.

The cult of the naked body had its origins in Germany around the turn of the twentieth century. The German FKK clubs—the literal translation of *Freikörperkultur* is 'bare (or open-air) body culture'—from which naturism took its cue, retain even now some of the high-minded ideals associated with nudism in the first third of the century. These ideals appear to have successfully defied the suspicions of debauchery which the congregation of naked men and women initially kindled everywhere in petit-bourgeois police forces. The nudists' erstwhile campaigning zeal has today lost its provocative edge, having been smothered in reluctant acceptance or active tolerance of nudity on beaches, near lakes, in naturist resorts and, in Germany, even in public city parks. Nudity in the sun has become one of the regular enticements of the package holiday industry. Idyllic corners of sun-belt Europe, governed until recently by carefully circumscribed moralities of provincial decency, have in the 1970s and 1980s imperiously been invaded by the pale-skinned, money-bearing sun-seekers from the North. Yet even in this thoroughly commercialised environment nudity still seems to radiate to some extent the utopian equality of human beings and the dream of a re-union with nature, both of which are played on by the advertising industries. Nudity could and can also suggest the purity of life before it became depraved by the sophistication, cultural corruption, social disunity and decadence of overcrowded urbanised civilisations.

Nudism was an attempt to regain, in the face of the ravages of industrialisation, physical and ideological spaces for the restoration of life in harmony with nature. At its inception it was embedded in a rarified cult of beauty which, it was assumed, had reached its unsurpassed cultural climax in the polis of classical Greek antiquity. Because of this overt connection of nudism with political thought any study of the naked body in the 1920s and 1930s must inevitably be set against the larger background of utopian hopes and aspirations which suffuse the entire period of Modernism and which receive the most articulate expression in the Germany of the inter-war years. Here, the body and the body politic revealed themselves as part of a joint ideological history. The many branches of the German Youth Movement had, since the turn of the century, expressed their longings for both charismatic leadership and a fresh reconciliation with nature. The right-wing nudity cult and the organicist thinking that went with it appeared to hold some of the answers. To conceive the state neither as a collectivity (as in the USSR) nor as a contractual association of individuals (as in liberal capitalism), but as a wholesome organism, stimulated the recovery of supposedly traditional values which modern civilisation had destroyed: the ties of kith and kin, the purity of racial blood relationship, the unity of racially identical folk, the ennoblement of rich and poor alike into members of the finest race, the comradeship of the tribal, regional or military group in the service of their leader and their nation, and the conception of life as a struggle between different races competing against each other for expansion and domination. The state was thus regarded as a combative athlete, continually testing its strength against others and regenerating itself like an organic body. Oswald Mosley, the English Fascist leader, put the basic idea most succinctly: 'Our policy is the establishment of the Corporate State. As the name implies, this means a state organised like the human body.'[7] It was this kind of anti-modernist thinking which shaped Hitler's ideas, without there being much evidence that he took any special notice of nudism as such, although we can assume that he would have come across references to it in the occult journal *Ostara. Briefbücherei der Blonden und Mannesrechtler*[8] (Ostara. Library of the Blond and Masculinists) which he collected in Vienna. Some of its issues were devoted to the nudity cult. However tenuous Hitler's connections with it may be, he was steeped in organicist notions. In *Mein Kampf* he rejected the modern form of the state as a cold 'monstrosity of human mechanism' (*ein Monstrum von menschlichem Mechanismus*[9]), preferring instead the idea of the individual serving as a sacrificial member of the community (the horde):

> The Aryan is not greatest in his mental qualities as such, but in the extent of his willingness to put all his abilities in the service of the community. In him the instinct of self-preservation has reached the noblest form, since he willingly subordinates his own ego to the life of the community and, if the hour demands, even sacrifices it.[10]

Even in the nineteenth century we find a dichotomy in conceptions of the state and society as between images of dead mechanism on the one hand and vibrant organicism on the other. That dichotomy had its roots in the opposing conceptions of the Left and the Right, with the latter accusing the former of imagining that society could be 'shaped thus and thus at will', with 'aggregated men, twisted into this or that arrangement' by Acts of Parliament. Society had become the product of a mere 'manufacture'. This sort of thinking, in the eyes of conservatives as far back as Edmund Burke, had led to the 'erroneous conception of a society as a plastic mass instead of as an organised body', as Herbert Spencer put it in *The Man versus the State* (1881).[11] Hitler's notion of the state was deeply corporeal and corporatist. He had clearly been influenced by a stream of neo-conservative thought that had many tributaries, from Wagner and H. S. Chamberlain to Rosenberg and Lanz von Liebenfels. Individuals could only be conceived of by him as the constituent parts of a greater body, sentient in its own right, delegating the fight for its survival to all its individual members. This animal remained awsomely anonymous. Only the image of a vast *Volkskörper* (body of the nation) suited it in National Socialist rhetoric. Hobbes's *Leviathan* was contractual and hence repudiated as a model by National Socialist lawyers and political thinkers, and 'Behemoth', the Old Testament beast, had far too strong Jewish connotations to be appropriate. The only creature which within the iconography of the Third Reich projected the fearless unity of nation was the specially stylised *Reichsadler* (imperial eagle) under whose protective wings the peaceful trades of a pre-industrial community of artisans could flourish. This, at least, was the vision which

3. Karl Heinz Dallinger: Tapestry for an Officers' Mess of the Luftwaffe; Legend: 'We are one people and no-one can break us; we remain a united people and the world cannot ever conquer us'; from *Die Kunst im Dritten Reich*, 1938

fired Karl Heinz Dallinger in his tapestry design for a casino of the *Luftwaffe* (*Fig 3*).

Shortly before the attempt on Hitler's life on 20 July 1944 he gave a rambling, philosophising speech to leading personalities in industry and commerce. Here he returned to the subordination of the individual to the social organism as a whole. He reiterated his belief that the foremost objective of the state was the optimal preservation of the nation, *Volkserhaltung*. Against the collectivism of the Bolshevist state, and the individualism of the liberal bourgeois one, he sought to project the idea of the National Socialist state where 'the creative activity of the individual must work for the benefit of the whole of society'[12]— fine words, indeed, which were in tune with his belief that no nation could be victorious by dint of military power alone and that it therefore had to develop an ideology superior to that of its enemies. Hitler failed to understand, however, that such an ideology must carry conviction not only within the nation but also outside it and that, in order to be of material assistance in victory, it must have attractions for the conquered, transforming them into convinced allies. This was impossible for National Socialism because it blinkeredly saw different nations built on the foundation of unequally rated 'racial elements'. Racial exclusiveness meant that mass assent by the conquered could never be forthcoming and that costly and brutal mechanisms of repression had to be deployed. These were, of course, also in evidence within the *Reich* itself. The huge bureaucracy of the *Reichssicherheitshauptamt* (Central Reich-Security Office), however, would not have been sufficient to control the ninety million people with their distinct regional traditions in Hitler's Greater

Germany. A continuous ideological war, sensitively attuned to majority feelings, had to be waged in order to reproduce if not a mass consensus then at least broad assent for the public actions of the regime.

Significantly, the policies of the holocaust were kept secret. The regime obviously felt the need for such secrecy because it could not be sure of public opinion at home, despite the fact that it had the media under its manipulative control. While the chief target of that policy was European Jewry, it embraced mass executions on general racial and ideological grounds, so that large numbers of Poles and Russians perished in the concentration camps, as well as German anti-fascists. This murderous side of the regime was but the violent reverse of its theatre of public rhetoric with its constant celebrations of the *Volksgemeinschaft.* There was, of course, always the threat of coercion, of physical sanction against anyone who actively resisted persuasion through propaganda. The permanent objective of this propaganda, even when not explicitly stated, was to conjure up a society that fervently believed in *Ein Volk, ein Reich, ein Führer,* the Nazis' most effective slogan by far. In other words, this propaganda assumed that, above all, it had to establish in the German populace both a sense of togetherness in nationhood and an acceptance of fascist leadership. Nationhood was conceived as a racially identical bloc of people united in a single political will. In it, the individual was expendable, whether or not he or she happened to be endowed with the awareness which, according to Nazism, befitted humans in a mass, namely of being only 'a dust particle of that order which shapes and forms the whole universe' (A. Hitler) or, as a well-known slogan of the Third Reich had it: *Du bist nichts, dein Volk ist alles* (You are nothing, your nation is everything).[13]

Modernity as the Loss of Organic Community

As has often been observed, Germany was a relative late-comer in the historical process which led to the formation of modern nation states in Europe. It had also lagged behind Britain and parts of France in achieving general industrialisation, although it was clearly not so backward as to have no hope of catching up. The transformation from an agrarian society to one based predominantly on machine technology was very sudden when it came in the latter part of the nineteenth century. Germany's backwardness and, at the same time, the presence within it of a sharply critical literary and philosophical intelligentsia, meant that the society of that country could become a prime, though by no means exclusive, reservoir of anti-modernist attitudes and of anti-modernist criticism. In the past, German society, chiefly made up of rural and small-town communities, had been marked by a strong sense of cohesion. It was now plainly reluctant to cut the umbilical cord with the land, to expropriate its small-holding peasantry and to abandon its regional allegiances. Because of this local cohesiveness, rooted in medieval tradition, some German writers (notably Kant, Schiller and Goethe) acutely perceived the very earliest threats that the advent of modernity posed. Precisely because Germany, especially when compared to Britain, was at that time an extremely antiquated society, it could provide a stark backdrop for the harbingers of anything that was at all modern. Strongly influenced by the remarkable school of Enlightenment philosophers, historians and political economists in eighteenth-century Scotland, German writers around the turn of the eighteenth to the nineteenth century voiced concern and protest at the specialisation and fragmentation of human faculties through the division of labour and the elaboration of bureaucracy in modern society. They perceived a contradiction between the modern mode of production and the attainment of a rounded personality. Yet it had long been recognised that technical, intellectual and social advances were possible only through the progressive division of labour. The creation of wealth depended on it. Adam Smith was aware that such specialisation brought about inevitable problems, namely the division of individuals into occupational particularity and the separation of society into social estates with special functions, such as the military, the agrarian and the industrial classes. Even before Smith we find in John Millar's *The Origin of the Distinction of Ranks* (1771) and in Adam Ferguson's *An Essay on the History of Civil Society* (1766) remarkably clear-sighted though brief descriptions of the divorce of man from the roundedness and integration of his own individuality and from the social totality of the Common Weal. The state, Ferguson held, had become a machine, people 'part of an engine' and human beings were but 'stones in a wall' to modern government. Manufacturers prospered most, Ferguson observed, 'when the mind is least consulted', referring here to the stupefying subdivision of the labour process into separated specialisms. This led men to become indifferent to the polity as a whole and the citizen ceased to be a statesman, so that both in an individual and in a collective respect Ferguson was moved to speak of the 'fatal dismemberment of the human character'.[14]

All this is repeated and amplified with great rhetorical skill in Friedrich Schiller's extraordinary treatise *On the Aesthetic Education of Man*. It was written in response to the French Revolution, in sympathy with its fundamental ideals of liberation, yet in opposition to the violence, terror and brutishness it unleashed. With all his sharpness of observation, his philosophical skill and his poetic genius Schiller proposed a programmatic counter-model to the emergent panorama of bourgeois-capitalist society. Within the context of our argument it is important to note firstly that in defence of a classical ideal of human individuality Schiller, in conjunction with other German writers, particularly Kant, posited the harmonising powers of an autonomous aesthetic sphere as a bulwark against the fragmentation of modern society. Secondly, by constructing a radical opposition between antiquity and modernity, he presented the latter in a series of barren metaphors and could thus engage in a scathing critique of the alienating tendencies which had become most distinctively discernible in France and in Britain and from which he wanted to save his blessedly backward Germany:

> The polypoid character of the Greek states in which every individual enjoyed an independent existence but could, when need arose, grow into the whole organism, now made way for an ingenious clockwork, in which, out of the piecing together of innumerable lifeless parts a mechanical kind of collective life ensued. State and Church, laws and customs were now torn asunder; enjoyment was divorced from labour, the means from the end, the effort from the reward. Everlastingly chained to a single fragment of the Whole man himself develops into nothing but a fragment; everlastingly in his ear the monotonous sound of the wheel that he turns, he never develops the harmony of his being and instead of putting the stamp of humanity upon his own nature he becomes nothing more than the imprint of his occupation or of his specialised knowledge. But even that meagre, fragmentary participation by which individual members of the State are still linked to the Whole, does not depend upon forms which they spontaneously prescribe for themselves . . . it is dictated to them with meticulous exactitude by means of a formulary which inhibits all freedom of thought. The dead letter takes the place of organic understanding . . .[15]

Against tendencies of mechanistic, universal rationalism in the French Enlightenment Johann Gottfried Herder, an older contemporary of Schiller, had in his *Ideas for a Philosophy of the History of Mankind* (1784–91) stressed the meaning of the historical process as one in which the many-sidedness and national plurality of human nature would in time unfold. History was seen by him as the organic growth process that would reveal the totality of the human potential, just as nations were seen by him as distinct personalities, held together in organic cultural community. Goethe's novel *Wilhelm Meisters Lehrjahre* (Wilhelm Meister's Apprenticeship, 1796) traced the steady, organic formation of an individual towards the full elaboration of his talents. The novel inaugurated the German tradition of the *Bildungsroman* (novel of individual development). At the same time Goethe opposed those aspects of modern science which tore objects out of their natural context and isolated them for experimental observation (cf. his opposition to Newton in *Zur Farbenlehre*, On the Theory of Colours, 1810). Modern technology was criticised by him for its inherently self-destructive megalomania in Faust II (1833) and in his visionary poem *Der Zauberlehrling* (The Sorcerer's Apprentice, 1798).

The point here is this: despite the relative backwardness of Germany in becoming an industrialised, bourgeois society on the basis of a modern capitalist economy — and perhaps because of this backwardness — there was operative in German thought at the threshold to modernity an almost obsessive fear of the mechanistic reduction of the organic community to a cold, anonymous, alienated association and of the individual to a fragment of his/her human potential. In a country which had experienced the influence of medieval thought and medieval social structures for so long, the collapse of the medieval ideology of anthropomorphic organicism which had held together the social entity caused the greatest sense of crisis. The erosion of the medieval vision of the organic interdependence of individuals and estates within the homely environment of the extended social family induced an anti-modern protest in Germany even before modernity had properly been established. It raised the spectre of uprootedness, dislocation, alienation and disorientation which in Germany was particularly intense and which fed ultimately into the ideological currents of the 1920s and 1930s.

History of the Body Metaphor

In order to understand the strength of the organicist myth in twentieth-century anti-modernism we must rediscover the tradition of the metaphor which lay behind the idea of the body politic. This is especially necessary in view of the fact that this metaphor has apparently lost all its fascination within the affluent, pluralistic societies of the West. Yet well into the twentieth century there was, within the tradition of European political thought, an ever renewed analogy between the human body and state-ruled society (*Staatsgesellschaft*). In Britain and the United States fictions of society as a great family or organism are sometimes invoked by politicians, but in truth the ideological persuasiveness of such images began to be eroded with the onset of modern bourgeois society, i.e. in the seventeenth and eighteenth centuries. The incipient anonymity of competitive capitalism in which all social interdependence threatened to be regulated by money was lamented most vociferously in a country where, similar to Italy, medieval regionalism, medieval social structures and medieval ideology had been firmly entrenched for so long. Germany had not been ruptured by any successful revolution, glorious or bloody. It was here that the leaders of the Romantic Movement invented the image of an organically integrated society in the Middle Ages in an attempt to stem the tide of modernity. What then was the precise form of the body analogy in the Middle Ages and what was its purpose?

It is in John of Salisbury's *Policraticus* in the middle of the twelfth century that we find an excellent example of the elaborate metaphor of the state as a body in which all internal social bonds were forged in strict hierarchical order to make up an indivisible living organism:

> In the commonwealth the prince takes the place of the head, subject to God alone and to those who act as His representatives on earth, even as in the human body the head is animated and ruled by the soul. The senate corresponds to the heart, from which proceed the beginnings of good and evil deeds. The offices of eyes, ears and tongue are claimed by the judges and governors of the provinces. Officials and soldiers correspond to the hands . . . Treasurers are like the belly and intestines, which, if they become congested with excessive greed and too tenaciously keep what they collect, generate innumerable incurable diseases, so that ruin threatens the whole body when they are defective. Tillers of the soil correspond to the feet, which particularly need the providence of the head because they stumble against many obstacles when they walk upon the ground doing bodily service; and they have a special right to the protection of clothing, since they must raise, sustain, and carry forward the weight of the whole body . . .[16]

The organic corporatism of this medieval analogy between the human body and the body politic served an ideologically legitimatory purpose, namely to keep the entire hierarchical structure firmly in place, ruled ultimately by the Church and based on the exploitation of the peasants. John of Salisbury, who incidentally was an ally of Thomas a Becket, was an erudite man. Having been educated at Chartres and at the University of Paris (under Abelard) he could draw on a rich fund of knowledge. His was but one version, remarkably secular, of a body metaphor which had been used by many medieval writers to refer, in the first place, to society as the ecclesiastical body of Christ. Religious or secular, the metaphor fitted in with and expanded on another crucial depiction of medieval society, the ternary image[17], which suggested a division into those who pray (*oratores*), those who fight (*pugnatores*) and those who work (*laboratores*). The image of the three orders and that of the body were both used very widely throughout medieval Christendom. One of the earliest cases was that of Wallafried Strabo in Germany.[18]

Whatever Salisbury's medieval precursors, the reference to the 'senate' reveals that his sources reached back to Roman antiquity, and it is indeed very likely that the Roman origins of the body metaphor were known to him. According to Camden's *Remains of a Greater Worke, Concerning Britaine* (1605) John of Salisbury had the story from Pope Adrian, an Englishman from Middlesex. In Hadrian's version the analogy appears more or less as it did originally in Livy, where it is attributed to Menenius Agrippa, a Roman Senator:

> All the members of the body conspired against the stomacke, as against the swallowing gulfe of all their labors; for whereas the eies beheld, the eares heard, the handes labored, the feet traveled, the tongue spake, and all partes performed their functions, only the stomacke lay ydle and consumed all. Hereupon they ioyantly agreed all to forbeare their labors, and to pine away

their lasie and publike enemy. One day passed over, the second followed very tedious, but the third day was so grivous to them all that they called a common Counsel; The eyes waxed dimmer, the feete could not support the body, the armes waxed lasie, the tongue faltered, and could not lay open the matter; Therefore they all with one accord desired the advise of the Heart. There Reason layd open before them that hee against whome they had proclaimed warres, was the cause of all this their misery: For he as their common steward, when his allowances were withdrawne, of necessitie withdrew theirs from them, as not receiving that he might allow. Therefore it were a farre better course to supply him than that the limbs should faint with hunger. So by the perswasion of Reason, the stomacke was served, the limbes comforted, and peace re-established. Even so it fareth with the bodies of Common-weales; for albeit the Princes gather much, yet not so much for themselves, as for others: So that if they want, they cannot supply the want of others; therefore do not repine at Princes heerein, but respect the common good of the whole publike estate.[19]

This sermon in political science was clearly addressed to those who might be tempted to doubt that the existing social classes were God-given, natural and immutable. The organic metaphor of the state as a huge, finely balanced metabolism functioned as a perfect legitimation for the division of labour, the unequal distribution of wealth and the separation of human beings into social estates. It could serve superbly well as a compelling illustration of the necessity for a ruler and a ruling class, while at the same time the metaphor could help spread the warm glow of community, of cradled security enfolding all individuals from the highest to the lowliest in one harmoniously co-ordinated body.

It was the nostalgia for such a totally 'natural', totally integrated community in a society blatantly exploited by a magisterial feudal-absolutist aristocracy which prompted Rousseau's cry, 'Back to Nature'. A similar nostalgia, prompted by a social reality pregnant with the incubus of capitalism, inspired the relentless criticism by the German Romantics of society as a soulless machine, a dis-membered body whose lifeblood had flowed away:

> You see artisans but no human beings; priests but no human beings; masters and servants, young and old, but no human beings; is it [i.e. society] not like a battlefield where hands and arms and all other limbs lie in a fragmented heap, while the lifeblood is spilt in the sand?[20]

This quotation shows that Schiller was not alone in his warnings about certain tendencies inherent in modern society. It is taken from a novel entitled *Hyperion* which in the late 1790s spelt out the misery of life in Germany compared to that of classical Greece. Modern society was largely seen as the dismemberment of an old, organic body politic. Less pessimistically, another important Romantic poet, Novalis, likened society to a human body and turned the metaphor round, 'Every human being is a small society',[21] only then to give it a new twist: 'Law courts, theatres, courts, the church, the government, open assemblies, academies, colleges etc. are only the special, internal organs of the mystical individual of the state.'[22] The state, Rousseau had taught three and a half decades earlier, was not just an indifferent machine, but the executor of a will. The Romantics built on this idea and saw the state as a superindividual. Hegel demystified this notion in two ways, firstly by insisting that the state as the guarantor of law and order protects the property and liberty of the individuals associated under its authority. To this extent it has a purely contractual nature, allowing any arbitrary collection of individuals to make up a state. Secondly, however, the state in general is recognised as 'objective spirit', i.e. the result of dialectical interaction between the general will and the will of individuals. Any particular state is the externalisation of a particular people, its particular ethos, which finds expression both in the morality underlying its constitution and in the consciousness of its citizens. (*Philosophy of Right*, § 274). The state therefore retains the special properties which make up the organism (§ 259) of a people. It is the conscious form of collectivity, its reason, developed by the nation over centuries. Despite the stress on 'objective spirit', on the state as externalisation of human reason — in contrast to nature which is seen as an externalisation of divine reason — Hegel retained the organicist anchorage of any given state in the mentality of a people or nation.

The dual character of the state as a legal persona regulating the relations of private citizens on the one hand and as an incarnation of social reason itself on the other is rehearsed in later theory. It can be found, for example, towards the end of the nineteenth century, in the writings of Ferdinand Tönnies. He was a seminal figure in the rise of modern sociology, author of the thesis that modern societies were the result of a historical shift from *Gemeinschaft* (organic, rural community) to *Gesellschaft* (urbanised, industrial association), from the personableness of neighbourly ties to the anonymity of bureaucratic control and mass existence.[23] While he had no illusions that this process was in fact irreversible, his analysis was nevertheless used by representatives of the 'conservative revolution'[24] in the 1920s and by National Socialist sociologists to indulge retrogressive cravings. The organic body as a metaphor for the integratedness of community grew in ideological importance just as individuals were increasingly subjected to the cold anonymity of state bureaucracy and the industrial labour process. A bifurcation of ideology and reality was developing in which the two were not simply separate but fed on each other. The more German society was becoming a modern association the more it appeared to need the comforts of an ideology of organic community.

Aspects of German Nudism: Bourgeois, Proletarian and Fascist

It was in order to rediscover the lost organic ideal that the nudity cult arose within elite, upper-middle class circles in Germany after the turn of the twentieth century. The aim was to re-live an assumed ideal of ancient Greek beauty, to adhere to an elevated notion of sexual purity, and to keep aloof from what was regarded as the primitive sexuality of the proletarian masses. In their zest for maintaining sharp distinctions between sexuality and nudity the early bourgeois nudist clubs came close to a projection of gender as sterile, arcane frigidity. The organisational structure of these clubs was pervaded by, and indeed modelled on, the secrecy and hierarchy of masonic lodges. Membership could only be gained after an apprenticeship and required the sponsorship of several senior members. This period of nudism has sometimes been referred to ironically as its 'Bronze Age', since the stress was on the exposure of the body to the sun in the open air and on the display of its beautiful proportions. The main journal documenting this spirit of the early nudity cult was significantly called *Die Schönheit* (Beauty). It ran from 1902 until 1931, first published in Berlin and then, from about 1910 onwards, in Dresden. Some of its special numbers appeared simultaneously in German and in English. The working classes were entirely excluded from the aesthetic concerns of

Die Schönheit, not least because their bodies tended to show evidence of occupational misshapenness.

In their aesthetic seclusion the early nudist clubs did not particularly care about rebuilding organic communities; they were at best a sectarian, perhaps a titillating side-show in the ideological panorama pre-1914. But this situation was to change very rapidly. For these clubs, even before 1914, began to take on board other ideological freight. A member of a proletarian nudist organisation in the 1920s sarcastically summed up this development of the bourgeois nudist clubs before the Great War:

> They soon fell for ideas of eugenics and racial hygiene: the blue-eyed, blond young lady with her soul full of longing was searched out by that equally blue-eyed, blond, boneheaded Germanic youth. Accordingly the majority of these lodges and clubs were swimming in the anti-semitic *völkisch* tide from which they have not emerged until the present day.[25]

Die Schönheit, while upholding general ideals of human progress, was certainly by the early 1920s illustrating 'Greek spirit in a new German manner'. It betrayed its racialist leanings and, as it stated in one advert, hoped for a new cultural efflorescence through the body cult. One only needs to look at the prolific and unbearably self-laudatory writings of an author like Richard Ungewitter to appreciate the accuracy of the quotation's appraisal. In 1905 Ungewitter had published a book advocating the ideals of nudity from an anthropological, moral and health-care point of view. It was titled *Die Nacktheit* (Nudity). Three years later he published *Nackt* (Nude), which was impounded. It showed a sharp development towards ultra-Right ideas. In 1913 he brought out another book on the same subject, entitled *Nacktheit und Kultur* (Nudity and Culture). The subtitle announced 'New Demands by Richard Ungewitter'. In 1920 he published *Nacktheit und Aufstieg* (Nudity and Ascendancy). In the preface he explained why its completion had been delayed by a special contribution which he felt he had to make towards the war effort. That explanation included his ideological self-portrait:

> My pen too was put in the service of this sacred issue and, together with thirty collaborators, I wrote *Germany's Rebirth Through Blood and Iron*, which aimed at the renewal of the German people on a national-political, Germanic-racial, *völkisch*-social, moral and cultural basis.[26]

The main guideline for his collaborators had been to point out the unbridgeable gulf between the idealistic, Germanic *Weltanschauung* and that of the Jewish, democratic, petty-shopkeeper mentality. He saw Germany threatened by three powerful international conspiracies: 'the red, the gold and the black conspiracy', colours which symbolically stood for socialism, 'Jewish' finance capitalism and popish catholicism. Black, red and gold were, of course, the colours of the German flag of the Weimar Republic and of democratic Germans in the nineteenth century. This flag was therefore intensely hated by those who thought like Ungewitter. Evidently, a powerful brew of Fascist propaganda material was being fermented at the beginning of the 1920s. It had mixed into it a poisonous paranoia of a Germany haunted by superior, inimical forces both without and within. Ungewitter's ideas were obviously not a mere absorption of those held by the early bourgeois nudist clubs. He was not elitist in the sense of striving to uphold class privilege. He was elitist on a much more dangerously comprehensive scale, namely on a racial basis, fashioning an image of the German people as the master race of the world. It is worth noting that even as early as 1920 his writings had achieved total sales of 220,000 copies. Racial consciousness, he held, was to be coupled with the *völkisch*-social idea. The cultivation of nudity was for him a vital element in the preparation of an uprising of the Right against all the decadence of Western civilisation that this author believed impaired true Germanic uprightness and undermined the integrity of Germany's political mission. The basic assumptions behind his view of the present blended in with those of the cultural pessimists (like Oswald Spengler, Ludwig Klages and others) but differed from their fatalism by the persistent tone of aggressive racism. This ideological mix was more or less identical with what later came to be called National Socialism.

For a while, however, it appeared that it was not the Right but the Left which was going to make the running in the Weimar Republic. Interestingly, a nudity cult, stimulated by yearnings for health and a return to nature, also developed on the Left. Here, it was not racist. But it did have an important ideological function, for it was intended to create attitudes favourable to radically reformist or revolutionary change. Socialist advocates of nudism implied that people should not only discard their clothes but with them the whole armour-plating of authority-fixated conditioning which held proletarians in deference to their masters: parental authority, the paternalism of school and church, the mass media, and the organs of law and order. Nudity was understood as a strengthening of the individual's potential for opposition: 'It helps to form strong characters, hardened for battle, which is what is wanted by the proletariat.'[27] Proletarian nudity was intended as a purgative of deep-seated anti-sensual prejudice and a radical method of discarding the chains of bourgeois ideas around proletarian minds. Gymnastics in the nude was designed to give individuals the feeling of being in tune with common rhythm and an integral part of a larger, harmonious pattern (*Figs 4 and 5*). New dance schools sprang up in Hamburg, Berlin, Leipzig and Cologne which, inspired by Rudolf von Laban's ideas about *Bewegungstanz* (rhythmic movement dance) and themselves developing *Ausdruckstanz* (expressive dance), strove to show naked bodies in gracefully configured motion (*Figs 6 and 7*). Gymnastics in the nude also inspired sculpture, which accentuated the streamlined strength of the human body (*Fig 8*).

The *Proletarische Freikörperkulturbewegung* (proletarian naturist movement) became a subsection of the huge Worker Sports Organisation, which in turn was part of a large Worker Culture Movement in the Weimar Republic. That movement thought of itself as an indispensable 'third column' in a three-pronged attack on capitalism which, it was believed, could not be defeated solely by being politically outmanoeuvred (by proletarian parliamentary parties) or economically transformed (by strategic trade unionism).[28] Hundreds of thousands of workers came together in the richly diversified sections of the culture movement, which provided an all-encompassing counter-cultural environment for the organised working class, covering young and old, male and female, sports, singing, photography, theatre, tourism and many other activities. Together with similar endeavours in Czechoslovakia, Austria, Switzerland, Belgium and Holland it represented the most comprehensive attempt of any working class in a capitalist society to build an organisational and creative cultural framework of its own. Those involved in it had few illusions about the difficulties of the task they faced. In particular, the proletarian nudists shared with many activists in the worker culture movement an acute awareness of the philistinism and petit-bourgeois attitudes that suffused the everyday life even of many party and trade union functionaries.

31

4. Adolf Koch School, Open-Air
'Body Culture', 1920s

5. 'The Naked Body Gives a Harmonious and Natural
Expression'; from *Köperbildung — Nacktkultur*, 1920s

6. 'Joy of the Body'; from *Körperbildung —
Nacktkultur*, 1920s

7. Hagemann School, Hamburg, Seminar of Gymnastics and Breathing Technique, late 1920s

8. Seidenstücker: Female Swimmer Jumping off the Starter Block, late 1920s

In other words, the morality of the petit-bourgeois life style was challenged, so that an altogether more egalitarian, anti-authoritarian and democratic lifestyle might take its place.

The man who like no other developed the idea of proletarian nudism was Adolf Koch, a primary school teacher and educational innovator. For him nudity was above all the symbol of a new start, of the building of a new society freed from the distorting and crippling influences which predominantly affected the proletarian classes. He sought to counteract these influences and the malformations and listlessness of the body by using so-called 'organic-rhythmical exercises' in his pedagogic practice. His work began in Berlin in the early 1920s. When he introduced his methods into two Berlin schools Koch ran into an outcry from the conservative press. But, with the support of the Social-Democratic government in Prussia, he was eventually able to build up a school which was dedicated to his methods and which towards the end of the 1920s had some 3,000 pupils. Throughout the worker culture movement the nudist sections numbered 60,000 members. They were therefore significantly more numerous than the bourgeois nudists, who were organised in the *Reichsverband für Freikörperkultur* (Reich-Association of Naturists), in the *Reichsbund für Freikörperkultur* (Reich-Corporation of Naturists) and the *Liga für freie Lebensgestaltung* (Libertarian League), numbering merely 12,000 in all. The main publication of the proletarian nudists was *Körperbildung—Nacktkultur, Blätter freier Menschen* (*Fig 9*). It is clear from this publication that proletarian nudism, while ideologically at one with the reformist and revolutionary ideals of socialism, was also fulfilling important compensatory tasks by strengthening exhausted and neglected proletarian bodies through providing facilities for gymnastics, showers, swimming pools and sun lamps. The stress on such compensatory functions at times blunted the oppositional mentality and blurred the differences from the bourgeois clubs. It is therefore not surprising that in the late 1920s, probably under the influence of Magnus Hirschfeld, an eminent liberal-humanist sexologist, proletarian nudists who were opposed to racialism did nevertheless advocate eugenics and the physical ennoblement of the nation.

Nudism, then, meant renewal, a fresh beginning and the reconciliation of man and nature. The photographers, no matter whether they were operating in a left-liberal (*Fig 10*) or in a right-wing environment (*Fig 11*), attempted to capture this spirit by concentrating on moments which showed exuberant movement and the enjoyment of the open air. The naked round dance of women became a stock-in-trade image of utopian bliss, both on the left (*Fig 12*) and on the right (*Fig 13*), and probably goes considerably further back in history than Lucas Cranach's late medieval 'Golden Age' (*Fig 14*). Technological objects were banished from these pictures. It is clear from such examples that the crisis of modernity produced similar reactions in both the Left and the Right, despite their different party-political preferences. Their aesthetic tastes, though distinct, show striking similarities, the former perhaps being less demonstrative and stylistically more informal (*Fig 15*). The nudists of the extreme Right, of course, stood out by their racist aestheticism, intent on the cultivation and photographic reproduction of bodies whose beauty was supposed to demonstrate superiority over human beings from other races. Once the ideological trends that supported such ideas had triumphed, proletarian nudism, along with the entire worker culture movement, was declared illegal. The not inconsiderable property assets of the various socialist cultural organisations were confiscated on the basis of a law of 26 May 1933 concerning the arrogation to the state of communist and socialist property, in conjunction with a law of 14 July 1933 decreeing the confiscation of all property 'inimical to the people' (*volksfeindliches Vermögen*). Adolf Koch's schools of physical culture in both Berlin and Hamburg were closed down. The *Verband für Volksgesundheit* (Association for People's Health), to which these schools belonged, was declared illegal, together with all the other subsections of the *Zentralkommission für Arbeitersport und Körperpflege* (Central Commission for Workers' Sport and Hygiene). According to police informers its membership in 1932 had stood at

9. Title pages of Adolf Koch's Journal of the Worker Nudist Culture, late 1920s, early 1930s

10. Dance School Hertha Feist, Berlin

11. Illustration Taken from Hans Surén's *Der Mensch und die Sonne*, 1924ff

12. Working Women, Dancing, 1920s, Fritz-Hüser-Institut, Dortmund

13. Illustration Taken from *Der Mensch und die Sonne*, 1924ff

14. Detail from Lucas Cranach (1472–1553):
'Golden Age', Munich, Alte Pinakothek

15. Socialist Youth Group at the Tonsee near Motzen, late 1920s

1,456,162.[29] Although its Central Committee had disbanded, many of its subsections attempted a so-called 'Trojan-Horse policy', i.e. they sought to invade and secretly control equivalent National Socialist organisations. These tactics failed against the police forces of a modern state which was supported by thousands of sympathisers acting as ideological scouts. Any hopes of overcoming the alienations of modern man via the socialist road to a new society, in which people might live in peace with each other and reconciled with nature, appeared to be scotched. With such agencies as a Ministry for People's Enlightenment and Propaganda, a daily press brought in line with the wishes of National Socialism, a film industry, architecture and sport purposefully put to use for the new state, with Mediterranean cruises for the masses (*Kraft durch Freude*— Strength through Joy), cheap radio sets (*Volksempfänger*) and controlled broadcasting, the most massive apparatus of ideology, public communication and culture in modern times began to operate. It was supported by coercive institutions of the Nazi party and a reorganised police. Never before had a state tried so drastically and so systematically to intervene in the circulation of ideas. Their production and dissemination was now highly selective and manipulatory. Never before had an ideologically intolerant government had such organisational and technological means at its disposal for shaping ideas, tastes and prejudices and for determining the level of information.

It was, of course, neither a philosophy of the body nor a particular branch of the 'bare body culture' which won through in 1933. But, as I have demonstrated, it is within the environment of the body culture movements that the ideas of the Left as well as those of the Right assumed a remarkably unorthodox, clearly utopian character. If the former might well be said to encapsulate some of the most peaceful features of a vision of freely associated human beings, then it must also be recognised that it was within the context of nudism that the Right developed the typical, innately aggressive expression of its most extreme ideology even before World War I. On the eve of World War II a certain Hermann Wilke published a book entitled *Dein 'Ja' zum Leibe. Sinn und Gestaltung deutscher Leibeszucht* (1939— Your 'Yes' to the Body. The Meaning and Organisation of German Body Discipline) in which he argued that German breeding stock ought to be selected with a view to racial improvement. The terms used in this connection are those of an interventionist racialism as a positive means of social engineering: *Aufartung* (upgrading of the species) and *Aufnordung* (nordification). The activist political logic of National Socialism did not shy away from drawing analogies with the breeding of cattle or chicken. The invocation of the *Führer* in this context provided the necessary legitimation:

> If the German people were told by the *Führer* that the most well developed bodies had to come together in order to achieve a new beauty in the people, then he meant the whole body . . . The healthy, well-formed naked body— since clothes cover up and deceive— becomes the most important means of improving the race.[30]

Racial upgrading, without the term *Aufartung* being available at the time, had already been propagated by Richard Ungewitter, who wished to see German nudists as protagonists in the struggle to strengthen the 'racial basis' of the nation. 'The improvement of the human race', but within a distinctly Germanic context, had been the avowed aim of a well-known (and government subsidised) film of the (bourgeois) nudity cult, entitled *Wege zu Kraft und Schönheit* (Ways to Strength and Beauty), which was released in 1925 (*Fig 16*). The same aim was evident— and

38

calculatedly expressed by the accompanying photographs—in one of the most successful books of *völkisch* nudism, *Der Mensch und die Sonne* (1924—Men, Women and the Sun) by Hans Surén. Sales reached 61,000 in one year, increased to 145,000 in 1936 and to over 200,000 by 1940. In his preface of 1924 Surén had stated:

> I did not include any pictures of communal life, because I wanted to show exemplary, well-built bodies and these unfortunately are exceptional.[31]

It was probably because this argument made the case for a racial elitism which was all too exclusive and showed up unfavourably the average quality of the supposed master race that this section of his book fell prey to elision in later editions. However, it is clear from this and other right-wing nudist publications that, in contrast to the photographs to be found in socialist publications, they were not snapshots but carefully staged events for the camera (*Fig 17*), even if this involved uncomfortable nude poses on skis in the alpine snow (*Fig 18*)! Not only are the bodies selected with a view to showing ideal racial types, they are also given especially shiny skins with the help of cosmetic oils. Surén, who had developed his nudist practices as head of the German Army Gymnasts' School in the early 1920s, kept the sexes strictly separate during training sessions. It was, of course, this overt racism and sexism (*Fig 19*) which most sharply marked off fascist from socialist nudism.

16. Still from *Wege zu Kraft und Schönheit* (The Judgement of Paris), 1925, directed by Wilhelm Prager

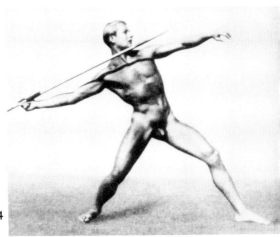

17. Javelin Thrower, Illustration from *Der Mensch und die Sonne*, by Hans Surén 1924

18. Man on skies in the Alps, from *Der Mensch und die Sonne*, 1936

40

19. A group of men from *Der Mensch und die Sonne*, 1936

However, in the 1920s the Right and the Left occasionally joined forces against a hostile conservative press which asserted that any public display of nudity, far from being appreciated as a protest against the decadence of modern society, could only be understood as a symptomatic confirmation of it. In 1924 a certain Dr. Altrock, who apparently belonged to right-wing circles, significantly lent the full authority of the learned institution to which he belonged to Koch's cause when he defended the latter's use of rhythmical gymnastics in the nude. In a lecture he drew on the strongly anti-Manichean sentiments shared by all nudists. Such counter-attacks on the common enemy of religious and petit-bourgeois philistinism brought about a precarious togetherness between Right and Left as they sought to defend their ideals against vilifying press campaigns. The proletarian nudists, being by far the bigger organisation in the Weimar Republic, had to bear the brunt of the displeasure voiced by the conservative press, as illustrated by the following example:

> Ecstatic dances greeting Spring in front of 4,000 people . . . 250 men, women and children, old and fat, young and slim. This public filth of the 29th March 1932 in the Grand Theatre (*Grosses Schauspielhaus*) in Berlin, organised by this red nudist teacher, Adolf Koch, and a state authority which did not forbid this filth, are the reasons why Germans are ashamed of their fatherland . . .[32]

The pompous defence of public decency was almost invariably linked with hints that the moral health of the nation was at stake. Representatives of the more affluent classes seem to have met with gentler treatment by the press. In *Licht—Lust—Leben. Monatsschrift für Schönheit, Gesundheit, Geist, Körperbildung* (Light—Pleasure—Life. Monthly Periodical for Beauty, Health, Spirit and Body Culture) we find reports on a court case in Tegernsee (south of Munich) against the nudists of the *Bund der Lichtfreunde* (Corporation of the Friends of Light) who in 1925 had held their national congress in a remote valley near Bad Kreuth. Their members were mostly from the professional classes and the aristocracy. They had had the good fortune that, when apprehended by the police, no objections were raised and they were allowed to continue. The public prosecutor nevertheless brought a law suit on account of causing a public nuisance and congregating without official permission. The judge, concurring, imposed a small fine. The press desisted from raising a public outcry, but then the *Lichtfreunde* had met in perfect seclusion and would never have been found by the police had it not been for a tip-off by a jealous wife.[33]

Female nudity was meanwhile fairly common in the review theatres of the big cities. In this context the significations of the naked body became complex and contradictory. For example, a well publicised drawing of the black French singer and dancer, Josephine Baker (*Fig 20*), who in 1926 was giving performances in the Berlin *Theater des Westens* would have been an image of degeneration and decadence to some, while to others the figure represented the multi-cultural and multi-racial modernity of life in a European capital.

20. Drawing of Josephine Baker in a Review Scene of the Theater des Westens, Berlin, 1926

The first reaction to the nudity cult when the Nazis came to power was to impose a general ban, at least in Prussia where Hermann Goering issued a decree on the 'repression of the nudity cult'. It was said to lead women to lose their natural feelings of shame and men to lose their respect for women. However, the *Reichsverband für Freikörperkultur* had many National Socialist sympathisers and was an easy target for ideological and organisational incorporation (*Gleichschaltung*). The journal of the Nazi naturists, *Die Deutsche Freikörperkultur,* openly opposed Goering's decree.[34] The nudists became part of the *NS-Verband für Leibesübung.* The old principles of 'ideal beauty' and 'healthy living' could easily be re-accentuated as demonstrations of racially ideal types and para-military fitness training. The re-issue of Hans Surén's book of 1924 was given a modified title to take account both of the arrival of National Socialism and the Olympic Games in Berlin and to signal the full acceptance of the former: *Mensch und Sonne. Arisch-olympischer Geist* (Men, Women and Sun. Aryan-Olympic Spirit). Leni Riefenstahl's famous film of the 1936 Olympics showed the beauty of youthful, naked bodies. When *Das Schwarze Korps*, the weekly periodical of Hitler's SS (*Schutzstaffel*—Protective Guard) addressed itself to the question of 'nudity or indecent exposure' a year later it castigated both Christian 'renunciation' of the sensual body and the exploitation of the 'racial beauty cult' for sensationalist ends by 'numerous revues and magazines which previously served concealed and unconcealed vice'. Rather loftily, the (anonymous) author held that 'nakedness in the North can only be convincing when it makes transparent the revelation of something divine'.[35] The author's attitude to the photographic display of naked, if perfectly shaped, bodies in the press was ambiguous, since he believed that the 'illustration of Nordic racial types' was but a pretext for the titillation of the baser senses. This ambiguity was indicative of the uncertainty in matters of public morality which prevailed within the SS. Its leader, Heinrich Himmler, when formulating directives about the procreation of children by SS personnel, either within marriage or with unmarried women in *Lebensborn* (SS procreation centres and maternity hospitals), had to resort to more cautious formulations than he would have liked. He might otherwise have alienated large numbers of SS-men whose moral ideas, when not serving the 'emergency needs' of the state, were ordinarily petit-bourgeois. Nudism had meanwhile become integrated into Nazi ideology. By 1938 the *Bund für Leibeszucht* (Federation for Body Discipline) was allowed to hold an open-air summer camp again. A nudist film, *Natürliche Leibeszucht* (Natural Body Discipline), was given official approval by being designated as 'educative for the people'. Finally, naked bathing was allowed in a police decree of 1942. The initially ambiguous attitude of National Socialism towards nudism should not detract from the symptomatic importance of the bare body culture within the ideological developments of the time.

Eugenics was a further point of contact between left and right-wing body culturists. But caution is necessary at this juncture: eugenics did not mean the same thing in both camps. On the Left it merely meant a change of attitude. Education and better information could achieve improved bodies through healthy (and hence selective) breeding. On the Right the stress was on race. Hence the immediate closure in 1933 of institutions like the *Reichsverband für Geburtenregelung und Sexualhygiene* (National Association for Birth Control and Sexual Hygiene), the *Verband für Sexualreform* (Association for Sexual Reform), the *Gesellschaft für Sexualreform* (Society for Sexual Reform) and the *Einheitsverband für proletarische Sexualreform und Mutterschutz* (United Association for Proletarian Sexual Reform and the Protection of Mothers). All these bodies were deemed to be typically 'cultural-Bolshevist', i.e. internationalist, anti-racist and socialist in outlook. According to a law passed in December 1933 the minimum age of voluntary sterilisation was set at ten and that of compulsory sterilisation at fourteen in the case of persons considered to be racially or biologically 'impure'. In Prussia there were some 31,000 compulsory sterilisations — enforced by special courts called *Erbgesundheitsgerichte* (Hereditary Health Courts) — in 1934, and 50,000 in the following year. The figures for the whole of Germany were 45,000 and 65,000 respectively. Additionally there were thousands of individuals who were never dealt with by these courts, being referred instead to special institutions where they were kept for a time and then murdered.

With the hindsight of historical knowledge the sheen on the bodies of Fascist nudes was that of the pretension to master-race status which carried a death warrant for those who could not satisfy the legally and bureaucratically enshrined criteria of racial conformity. Himmler had calculated that, with the strict application of the laws and directives on 'racial hygiene' the German people could be gene-coded into a pureblooded 'Nordic' race within a period of 120 years. The special role of the Germans as leaders between the nations of the East and the West was underpinned by a philosophy of irrational and anti-rational organicism which must briefly be traced here. It involved the ultimate perversion of the old organicist metaphor of the state and society and served as legitimation for the imperialist claims of National Socialism in Europe.

Organicism Versus Individualism and Collectivism

There are three books to which reference must be made in this context: Roderich von Engelhardt's, *Organische Kultur. Deutsche Lebensfragen im Lichte der Biologie* (Munich, 1925 — Organic Culture. Vital German Problems in the Light of Biology), Paul Krannhals's, *Das organische Weltbild. Grundlagen einer neuentstehenden deutschen Kultur* (Munich, 1928 — The Organic World View. Foundations of a New German Culture) and Edgar J. Jung's, *Die Herrschaft der Minderwertigen. Ihr Zerfall und ihre Ablösung durch ein neues Reich* (The Government of the Racially Inferior. Its Disintegration and Replacement by the New Realm). All these books heralded the cultural ascendancy and eventual rise to power of the ultra-Right, prophesied by Ungewitter, and terminologically captured in a booktitle of 1931, *Deutsche Kulturrevolution* (German Cultural Revolution). It is not necessary within this context to give a faithful summary of these works. They should perhaps be entirely forgotten. But it remains of some importance for our understanding of the development of Germany in the twentieth century to see how the desirability of a German road to Fascism was argued and advocated in them. They are, of course, only some examples in a flood of similar publications. Within the terminology employed by these authors a number of recurring ideological disjunctures can be discerned, for example (Western) 'civilisation' and (German) 'culture'. These are easily recognizable as transpositions of the unquenched desires of German imperialism. According to the paranoid and aggressive logic behind these mutually exclusive ideas Germany held a prime geopolitical location. The authors bolstered their case further by hypostases and presumptions about national distinctions which purported to be based on ultimate, irreducible metaphysical principles.

In these publications Germany appeared as the land whose people yearned for and upheld the dream of the organic wholeness of their society. They were lauded as the historical protagonists of the organic principle. Hence they stood alone in the glory of heroic resistance, defending the values of rank, biological differentiation and racially (or nationally) rooted culture against the egalitarian and cosmopolitan mêlée of mechanical, unnatural and rootless civilisation. They were therefore ranged as much against the social and cultural dislocation, democratisation and social fragmentation of the West as against the totalitarianism and deadening collectivism of the East. They invoked the contrasts which, according to a German tradition of thought, were spelled out by the terminological pair, *Kultur* and *Zivilisation*. Thomas Mann at his most conservative had given it a new respectability at the beginning of the 1920s by using it to explain the conflict in World War I between Germany, as a representative of *Kultur*, of the cultivation of the spirit, and the West, as a representative of *Zivilisation*, of modern conveniences and flat-headed conversation. Towards the end of the 1920s the neo-conservatives held that in the West the principles of an unnatural, rationally constructed society reigned supreme. They were based on the French Revolution's slogans of liberty, equality and fraternity, which they believed inaugurated the process of internal social dissolution. Allowing for a further egalitarian-collectivist perversion of these principles, the same was considered to be true of Russia since the Bolshevik revolution. Against this degeneration and the suffusion of society with Western influences it was claimed that Germany must defend itself and re-instate the organic principles of coercion (*Zwang*), distinction of rank (*Ungleichartigkeit*) and subordination (*Unterordnung*). It was argued that these principles held the various parts of the body together. An overt analogy was therefore being made between political and social culture and the biology of organisms as perceived by a politicised science. The books referred to above characterised the position of Germany between its Western and Eastern neighbours in terms of inimical tensions, which, it was thought, could only be resolved by a military cataclysm. Initially, however, the *innere Feind* (enemy within) had to be conquered and defeated.

Recurring terminological oppositions, some of which went back further than Thomas Mann's *Betrachtungen eines Unpolitischen* (Reflections of a Non-Political Man) to Nietzsche, Goethe, Herder, et al., spelt out the internal tensions of society as the neo-conservatives saw them. The concepts cited first within the following pairs of terms were advocated by liberals and socialists — not always in the same negative formulation and without any disparaging connotations. Those cited second gave the neo-conservatives' and National Socialists' position: civilisation — culture (*Zivilisation — Kultur*); intellect — intuition (*Intellekt — Intuition*); superficiality — depth (*Oberflächlichkeit — Tiefe*); aesthetic and ethical pluralism — hierarchical order (*Wertverflachung — hierarchische Ordnung*); democracy — leadership principle (*Demokratie — Führerprinzip*); mechanical — organic (*mechanisch — organisch*); dead (static) form — living growth (*tote [statische] Form — lebendiges Werden*); French Revolution — Prussian duty and obedience (*Französische Revolution — Preußische Pflicht, preußischer Gehorsam*); mixed races, multiple racial stock — racial purity (*Völkermischmasch — Rassenreinheit*); contractual society — national community (*Vernunftstaat — Volksstaat*). In other words, there was before 1933 in Germany a highly articulate right-wing intelligentsia able to furnish explosive ideological ammunition by claiming for Germany a unique historical mission which had to be safeguarded against powerful enemies both internally and externally. This situation called for a heroic ethic which was indeed propagated by many journalists, philosophers and lawyers sympathetic to National Socialism both before 1933 and after 1933, when the conceptual oppositions cited above recurred, for example, in a number of pamphlets on National Socialist 'cultural politics'.[36] The terminology evolved in this struggle was not new. It exploited the long, and by no means entirely disreputable German tradition of anti-modernist criticism. In doing so it was able to draw on sedimentations of real historical experience, usurping them for the rhetorical arsenals of the Right and thus denying the Left access to the same sources. At the same time, the Left was identified with all the unsettling Western invasions which had led to the long-term decay of values and the dismemberment of the organic order. National Socialists appeared to embrace in all seriousness and with great ardour the ideals of *Gemeinschaft*: the spontaneous will of individuals to form community, to identify not only with their kith and kin but also with their artisanal or other occupational skills, which were hallowed by tradition, to structure their social being by norms sanctioned by religious beliefs, acts of faith and the ritualisation of creeds. National Socialists could thus project themselves as protagonists of an overdue revision of the social, cultural and ethical dissections modernity had wrought. It seemed to many that the modern had to be subjected to the correctives of the old which had too lightly been disposed of in the name of progress. Exploiting popular perceptions of the crisis, German Fascism was able in the most cynical fashion to make the whole of society into a function of dictatorial will and hence become used for the reverse of what had been promised. By means of a colossal manipulative machine for the dissemination of their ideas they enlisted the support of majority opinion for a brutal administrative exercise. Far from reinstating the values of

Gemeinschaft it reduced groups and individuals to mere *Menschenmaterial* (human beings as functional counters). By exacting an oath of allegiance from the German army, the party membership and the civil service, individuals, political and state institutions were made into executioners of the destructive designs of the Nazi leadership.

In conjuring up the idea, by constant propagandistic repetition, that the German people were a united body bonded by the same 'blood', that the German nation had a right to a united terrain and that both were symbolically and actually incorporated in the political will of the one leader, National Socialism appeared not only to feed the hopes of German minorities outside the *Reich*, it also seemed to be offering solutions to the crisis of Modernism. All Germans would be re-united in the one splendid organism of an extended state which would bind all its members into an integrated demonstration of power and racial harmony. Social classes, estates and the rankings of individuals, far from being denied, were actually affirmed as meaningful components of the whole body politic. The ideological appeal of National Socialism was its promise to restore a clear organic social order, in which those who were included could feel privileged, not least by looking at the wretched condition of those who were denied that privilege and condemned at best to slave existence or at worst to annihilation.

As an ideology of the organic utopia, National Socialism needed not only a rich symbolism expressing the adherence of individuals to certain orders, group-ings and ranks, but also an art that would basically provide images of power (*Fig 21*), social inclusion, the rootedness of the individual in the group (*Fig 22*) and in nature, and of racially acceptable femininity and masculinity (*Figs 23 and 24*). Racial exclusion was implied in these images and hence — with few exceptions — did not need to be explicitly executed. Art under National Socialism was given a privileged place because it could create visions and symbolic demonstrations — in stone and paint, in static and moving pictures, in recited and printed words — of the new racial harmony of the body and the reintegration of the individual in a pacified society. At the same time, the actually existing discrepancy between the Fascist utopia and social reality meant that artists had to be subjected to ideologi-cal control in order not to 'fall back' into the contradictory pluralistic panorama of the Weimar Republic. This ensured the reduction of social reality to ideologically acceptable forms of representation. Artists who did not accept these standards had to face the grim fate of exclusion. Those who did were used as celebrated exponents of the 'new spirit' and served as important consolidators of the National Socialist regime. Its ostentatious political glories and its racial verities called for artistic real-isations in dimensions of the demonstratively colossal or the quietly intimate. It is therefore not fortuitous that the practice of the various art forms assumed two basic aspects under National Socialism: the idyllic and the monumental, with the latter bifurcated into mythical and industrial images. Thus, on the one hand, there were pictures which showed idylls of family life and of naked, open-air beauty; on the other there were those of Germanicised classical myth (*Fig 25*), of monu-mentalised Nordic peasant (*Fig 26*) and warrior, or those showing the achieve-ments of 'workers of the fist and those of the forehead' (*Arbeiter der Faust und Arbeiter der Stirn*) such as motorway bridges (*Fig 27*) or the giant strength of steel-works foregrounded by a wheatfield with harvesting peasants (*Fig 28*). Similarly, in architecture, we find on the one hand monumental constructions, particularly those planned for the new Berlin, and on the other a predilection for half-timbered houses with neatly pitched roofs (*Fig 29*). Monumental neo-classicism and idyll

21. German Poster, 1939; Legend: 'Victory is with Our Flags'

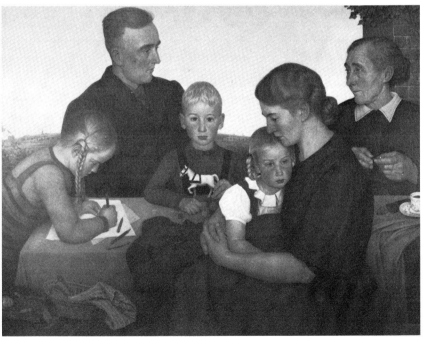

22. Adolf Wissel: *Kahlenberg Peasant Family*, Oil, 1939 Exhibition in Haus der Deutschen Kunst, Munich

23. Julius Engelhard: *Dip in the Mountain Lake*, Oil, 1944
Exhibition in Haus der Deutschen Kunst, Munich

24. Professor Richard Klein (Munich): 1937,
Etching, from *Kunst im Dritten Reich*, 1937

25. Ivo Saliger, The
Judgement of Paris, Oil,
1939 Exhibition in Haus
der Deutschen Kunst,
Munich

26. Oskar Martin-Amorbach: *Sower*, Oil, 1937
Exhibition in Haus der Deutschen Kunst (it
usually hung in Hitler's Headquarters in
Munich), Munich

27. Carl Theodor Protzen, *The Führer's Roads*, Oil, 1940 Exhibition in Haus der Deutschen Kunst, Munich

were the artistic expressions of genuine organicist longings which served simultaneously as a triumphal façade for a mercilessly repressive regime.

The Weimar Republic was a discordant battleground, lacerated by competing ideas, ideologies, groups and classes. In referring to the above list of black and white ideological counters used by the Right and in tracing the peculiarities of anti-modernist protest, I in no way wish to suggest that a relentless historical determinism was at work which catapulted Germany into Fascism. There were powerful political and social forces that worked creatively for a democratic culture. They were defeated and for a time forgotten, but they were not destroyed. Nor do the pairs of oppositional terms quoted above do complete justice to the real historical picture. Germany, after all, was an industrially advanced country which, as much as any other, had a need for sophisticated technology and in which the basic social stratifications of capitalist society and the expression of its plural interests could not easily be wiped out. German culture in the Weimar Republic had evolved clearly Modernist forms and, to this extent, had revealed the tensions and alienations of such a society in an exemplary fashion. The organicist longings to which it gave rise and which were exploited by Fascism were peculiar to Germany only in their intensity and in their racialist inflection. But the same basic longings were operative elsewhere in Europe, and have resurfaced in many strands of Post-Modernist culture. The utopian anti-Modernism, the yearning for an organically integrated, mythically heroic and idyllically rural society, so clearly in evidence in the art and architecture of the Third Reich, evidently did not die with it. Similar romantic desires make themselves felt with renewed vigour today, and

28. Bernd Templin: *Furnesses in Huckingen*, Oil, 1939 Exhibition in Haus der Deutschen Kunst, Munich

29. H. Dustmann, R. Braun (Architects): Hitler-Youth Building, Hanover, from Die Kunst im Dritten Reich, 1937

they are sometimes expressed with some militancy when, for example, the bland functionalist architecture of public and private corporations is rejected.

There is now sufficient visual evidence in the art and architecture of Post-Modernism to propose that the kind of imagination which Fascism in Germany (and Italy) drew upon cannot be restricted either to these countries or to their erstwhile political systems. These in their time had appropriated European traditions of culture and thought, which they redefined and used for their own purposes, and certain aspects of these traditions may have become universally discredited after the defeat of Fascism. The tendencies in contemporary (European) societies which might lead to a revival of such politics have not been entirely overcome. Some will identify elements in much of contemporary art as ominous symptoms of the belief that the best way forward is the way back. Yet it is difficult to dismiss as illegitimate the kind of human longings evinced in many 'Post-Modern' pictorial and architectural realisations simply because they appear to have National Socialist ancestors. National Socialism had, after all, for its own part been heir to distinguished artistic traditions and could, successfully for a time, project itself as their true guarantor. In architecture, for example, Greek classical styles provided the model for the Nazi demonstration of power through government buldings; traditional half-timbered and pitched-roof construction was used for private and communal dwellings, while flat roofs and rectangular functionalist blocks were reserved for industrial buildings. The actual relation of Fascism to the past and the present was, however, not conservationist but clearly expedient and manipulative. This is a trait it shares with Post-Modernism. Both seek to gain advantage by the use of tradition. For all its playful pastiche and its ironic self-consciousness, the Post-Modernist recovery of classical canons in architecture and its regressively utopian world of civic and bucolic reconciliation in painting appears like a latter-day democratic version of earlier, National Socialist attempts in the same formal direction. This could be demonstrated by a comparison of the pictures inspired by the pre-industrial utopia of the classical idyll in the exhibitions of the *Haus der deutschen Kunst* with those of the US painters Paul Resika, Milet Andrejevic, Lennart Anderson, Thomas Cornell and Edward Schmidt in the late 1970s and early 1980s. The monumental, natural-stone neo-Classicism demonstrating Nazi might can be found refracted in the architecture of Ricardo Bofill and his Taller de Arquitectura in post-1970 France[37], just as the morphology of the less elaborate, traditional pitched-roof, half-timbered houses can be seen everywhere in contemporary European Architecture. Such comparisons lay themselves open to horrible misunderstandings. They are nevertheless suggested here because of the compelling nature of the formal similarities. This is not because the Post-Modernists are Fascists of any sort but because both draw on a very similar utopian inspiration as a protest against the alienating dismemberment of life under the continuing onslaught of modernisation.

Chapter Three

THE NAZIFICATION OF WOMEN IN ART

Annie Richardson

Introduction

My aim here is to reconstruct the field of associations that images of women in the art of the Third Reich might have evoked. 'Might have evoked', because art history has sought in vain for a method equivalent to oral history to uncover subjective meanings for a range of viewers. It has tended rather to view meaning in terms of intended meaning (most commonly the artist's or patron's) or meaning-within-a-context, where meaning is sought in a more open-ended inquiry that seeks to reconstruct the relevant factors determining the production and reception of the work. Art historians might reasonably argue that the responses of a wide public are not available to them and can only be deduced from such evidence as critic's writings or the interests of purchasers, and that in any case it is appropriate to prioritize intended over received meanings. Why does this standpoint become especially problematic in the case of Nazi art?

Nazism has always presented a methodological as well as an interpretative problem for the cultural and political historian. How can 'criminal' actions be 'understood' without being rendered normal or acceptable in the process? Is it not morally safer as well as philosophically more reliable to view Nazism as a pheno-menon determined by economic, political and social structures, as Fascism in other words, rather than as the product of individual actions? Recently, however, the study of the Third Reich has shifted its emphasis from structural theories of Nazism to lived experience, via regional studies and oral history. An attempt is being made to 'get behind the propaganda façade' of the unrepresentative stated intentions of a few politicians and encompass the paradoxical feelings and deci-sions of everyday life.[1] However, attempting to gauge the individual intentions of the artist in Nazi art is not generally attempted. The monographic literature on artists favoured by the regime, such as Josef Thorak, is almost exclusively from the Third Reich itself and the later art historian is therefore faced with the construc-tion of particular ideological artist-types ('the man of the woods'[2]), while rare quotations by the artists themselves do not really read like personal insights. The artist's Nazism, opportunism or naïvety, his status as 'Nazi artist' (read non-artist) are presumed to place his personal intentions outside the area of enquiry. More-over, in the case of images of women in the Fine Arts generally, artists' stated inten-tions have proved of limited explanatory value when questions on the feminist agenda are raised, such as how images of women in high art circulate alongside more popular forms of imagery and a variety of discourses to produce meanings in a particular historical context.

However, these are not reasons which compel us to fall back on theories of structural determination; to ask only how and why this is Nazi art, rather than what it would have meant. There are of course no predetermined limits to art history which prevent it from prioritising received over intended meanings, merely considerable difficulties. The art historian can certainly utilize oral accounts and can attempt to estimate associative values by other means.

However, to date, the more analytical studies of Nazi art have been directed principally at showing how the images 'functioned for Fascism' and thus at demonstrating the 'Fascist' qualities of the work.[3] For this reason they do not give much separate consideration to images of women, for they consider that images of women functioned both to compensate and to reward the male viewer in the Fascist state. In this view images of women are only particular instances of the more general trend, exemplified in Nazi genre painting and sculptures and paintings of the female nude, to compensate and reward, enabling subjective contemplation for the bourgeoisie by disguising the real workings of capitalism. It is as the object of male fantasy that an image of woman is considered for it is male rather than female fantasy that is thought to be put to work to secure the Fascist, capitalist state.

The following sections give separate consideration to the questions and difficulties arising from the examination of Nazi images of women within the disguise-and-reward scheme outlined above. Firstly, the question of ideology: viewing Nazi images of women in terms of disguise-and-reward has entailed viewing their function as ideological. How useful is this? Secondly, the question of which images in art are most representative of Nazi ideology and a developed Nazi aesthetic: the disguise-and-reward scheme grants representative status to images of men, but should it? What happens when the focus is shifted to images of women? Thirdly, to return to the key question on the feminist agenda mentioned above, what happens when images of women in art are considered alongside non-art images and other discourses? What issues are brought together, what meanings are suggested by the relationships set up between them? Given that the disguise-and-reward scheme has considered the gender of the viewer to be unproblematic, what associations can be reconstructed for the female viewer alone? This final question will be considered in each of the three following sections.

Images of Women and Ideology

Within the disguise-and-reward scheme of Berthold Hinz's *Art in the Third Reich* (1974), the female nude and peasant mother in Nazi art are said to perform a number of valuable ideological functions for the Fascist state. Firstly, they shift attention away from the present, away from the actual roles of male and female workers and from the role of the mother as reproducer of these, by being made to convey essential and absolute truths. Thus an allegory of the nation at war, which depicts a peasant mother as a madonna enthroned amongst soldiers, farmers and workers, is analysed by Hinz in terms of the way it works to naturalise and sacralise war and work. Secondly, the female nude and peasant mother are said to suggest that an imminent natural order is being re-established and that this will stabilize the present and guarantee the future. Thirdly, Hinz argues that, in their address to the male viewer, female nudes harness and encourage sexual aggression, compensating the exploited male in capitalism by offering him the position, as viewer, of the (sexual) exploiter. This analysis hypothesises the success of Nazi images of women in being able to invoke singular preformed ideologies to the extent that they will effectively suppress reference to reality or to alternative perceptions.

What happens if this analysis is tested against a text by a Nazi ideologue that attempts to argue for the existence of a preformed ideology in relation to images of women in art? *Deutsche Kunst der Gegenwart*, 1943, (German Art of the Present) by Werner Rittich[4], frequent contributor to the Nazi art magazine *Die Kunst im Dritten Reich* (Art in the Third Reich) and author of several survey books on art, certainly attempts to provide a coherent rationale for a wide variety of contemporary paintings. Rittich's choice of images featuring women confirms Hinz's argument that allegorical nudes, scenes of peasant life, native types, and the peasant madonna predominated in Nazi art. The two peasant madonnas from Rittich's survey are reproduced as *Figure 1*: Erich Erler's *Ripeness* and Ferdinand Andri's *Mother and Child* (no dates are given). Furthermore Hinz's argument for the intended 'naturalisation' of reality is confirmed by the employment in Rittich's text of various concepts of 'the natural'. According to Rittich, Nazi art has a distinct character which he terms 'Naturalism', to which he applies the important qualifiers 'intensified' and 'religious'. The definition is weakened however by a string of negative caveats: the 'natural' in question is less natural than the Naturalism of the past; not so natural as to include effects of nature for their own sake, not so unnatural as to be idealisations. Rittich employs the typical strategy in Nazi definitions of its own position, concentrating first and foremost on what the Nazi position was not and what it was opposed to, indeed what it was rescuing the nation from. Positions described as 'socialism' or 'liberalism' would first be constructed, then the Nazi position would be presented as precisely not these things. It tended to be harder to say positively what the Nazi position was.

Thus Rittich's definition of Nazi art suffers not only from over-emphasis on what it was not, but it suffers too from contradictions: on the one hand everything, even animals, are said to be elevated to essences and symbols; on the other hand Erler's and Andri's mother-and-children are said to stay within the range from 'comprehensive symbolism' (presumably the Erler) to 'the instantaneous' (presumably the Andri). But would the 'instantaneous' then not be Naturalism pure and simple?

The 'natural' is given a second meaning in Rittich's text: it is said to signify a natural or instinctive response, for Rittich asserts that the new naturalism presupposes 'an uncomplicated receptive capacity for experience'. According to him this demonstrates the relation between this art and the 'ideology of our time'. Nazi ideology was not of course 'natural' but frequently relied on the assertion that it did no more than develop people's innate, biologically and racially determined capacities and would therefore necessarily evoke 'natural' responses. Rittich himself employs this ideological construct of an art that will evoke 'natural' responses, but at the same time ensures that any response will be followed by reflections along the lines he directs. The images he singles out for special attention to show how the new Naturalism is linked to 'the ideology of our time' are scenes of peasant life and life-cycle allegories featuring the female nude. But he directs no particular attention to the presence of women in these images and attempts to capture their relationship to ideology with the brief warning that they are not merely costumed people set in a landscape, but are images of a people's attachment to blood and soil and to destiny. Apparently of greater use (especially given the war-time context) is the allegorical nude, whose basis he suggests is the 'confirmation of life, the fulfillment of life on *this* earth' ('*Diesseitigkeit der Lebenserfüllung*', presumably as opposed to life beyond the grave).

It seems to me then that the art writing of one Nazi ideologue confirms Hinz's argument that the female nude and the peasant madonna were intended to 'naturalise' reality. More precisely we should say that such images, accompanied by Nazi discourses, were used to construct notions of 'the natural' and then to apply them to the ideological tenets of Nazism. In effect Rittich claims that if you respond to these simple images, balanced somewhere between the symbolic and instantaneous or physical, it is because you share 'our' ideology, with its 'generally valid' truths.

Are we justified in assuming though that such writings targeted male rather than female viewers? Should we assume that male rather than female viewers would have received these 'truths' unprompted or rather prompted by the use of images of women? Reception of Rittich's book would surely have depended on a number of factors. One would be the extent to which the images he brought together appeared consistent with one another. Would luscious nude and peasant madonna seem 'natural' juxtapositions? Another would be the political standpoint of the viewer. A third would be the viewer's gender; and a further factor would be the extent to which these paintings would refer to and invoke propaganda and specific events or circumstances. These factors are interdependent. For example, while Nazi propaganda in the Third Reich did rely heavily on images and texts which constructed women as 'life-source of the people', in terms of a biological and racial essence expressed in motherhood, such a construction would have seemed positive, natural and shared to the committed Nazi woman. As one woman leader reported of her time in a Nazi women's group: 'Womanhood gives us a community, a source of strength for the entire *Volk* [with which we] forge a powerful unified movement among all women and girls for moral renewal.'[6] If we unpack this statement, and uncover some of the constituents of the ideology of committed Nazi women, we will be in a position to ask how Rittich's choice of mother images (*Fig 1*) might have answered to and confirmed the views of this particular group.

The ideological position of Nazi women puzzled non-Nazis and foreign reporters who commented that women seemed to be emerging as the most zealous of the Nazis' supporters and yet, paradoxically, were offering their support to a party which defined womanhood as non-participation in male spheres of action such as politics. Claudia Koonz's study *Mothers in the Fatherland* (1987) suggests some reasons for this paradoxical attachment with the help of a 1936 survey of Nazi supporters. Some of the reasons for support stated in the survey were of course given by both male and female supporters. Both for example celebrated in quasi-religious terms the idea that they had been called upon to be ready for total self-sacrifice.

But in what ways did women's responses differ from men's? On the one hand women were actively seeking their equivalent to the male form of self-sacrifice in battle. During the 1920s when Nazi ideology was a conglomeration of views held by a number of groups, both ideologically and geographically diffuse, its vision of the future drew on images of a past based on natural hierarchies and of marital bliss based on 'natural' gender roles (as in Goebbels' novel *Michael*: 'the female bird pretties herself for her mate and hatches the eggs for him'[7]) which seemed to hold an emotional appeal for men and women alike. The more calculating women supporters (and those women who joined the National Socialists in the twenties

1. (Left) Erich Erler, *Ripeness* and (right) Ferdinand Andri, *Mother and Child*, reproduced from Werner Rittich, *Deutsche Kunst der Gegenwart*, 1943

tended to be activists) found the ideology of the separate spheres realistic as well as emotionally appealing. Outside the male political framework it was possible to find self-affirmation: to work for the party in women's groups and to expand this all-woman sphere.

There was also an element of editing out in the conscious rationalisation of support. Koonz suggests that just as racism was played down when supporters told themselves they personally did not hold racist views and that in any case the party would drop its most extreme policies once in power, so too the misogyny of sections of the party leadership was rationalised: 'Hitler would never turn women into brood mares.'[8] However, even the most committed Nazi women did not form a homogeneous group. Some of them were not prepared to rationalise misogyny, and in the late 1920s and early 1930s articulated demands for recognition of women's talents and achievements, which were then perceived by opponents within the Party as 'feminist'.

Thus while the criticism mounted by the Nazi feminists was suppressed by the Party, the images of woman they projected — the talented career woman or the combative Nordic warrior woman of prehistory — were not; rather these strong, positive images, conveyed by military vocabulary (their magazine for example was called *Die Deutsche Kämpferin*, The German Woman Fighter) were incorporated into an essentially flexible image which proved capable of carrying a variety of other connotations and, most importantly, responding to successive changes in policy on women. For example, the 'mother' image did not prove an irrelevance or embarrassment as the economy developed an ever greater need for female labour: women were channelled into what was termed 'womanly work', and if they were unmarried this was described as their 'spiritual maternity' for the nation; and when, on rare occasions, it was suggested that some women had a vocational calling, this was still termed a 'maternal force', one to which they would respond, like the mother, in a spirit of self-sacrifice.[9] Thus illustrated books on and for women, for example those used as propaganda for the Labour Service, set photographs of women caring for children or cooking next to photographs showing them working in the fields or doing physical exercises. One such book commented that the new type of German woman, muscular and weathered, made laughable the reproach that National Socialism made women into 'baby machines'.[10]

It is doubtful whether women who were Nazis would have had a 'singular preformed ideology' which mother and child images such as those reproduced by Rittich could invoke; rather, they inherited a set of reassuring notions associating the past, the family and the nation, and for some women these would draw on religious faith, any number of which they then transferred to the Party. For many Nazi supporters, the mother image as one of 'genuine' womanhood, one associated with pre- and post-Weimar days, would have been a gratifying affirmation of themselves and of the Party in which they had been given semi-independent status, and a moral and practical role which recognised the qualities they possessed as mothers. Speaking of the time after the Munich putsch, when Hitler was in prison, a Nazi woman later recalled: 'We women had to pick up the thread of life from the floor and keep on spinning for the sake of our children'.[11]

Mothers in a timeless, or rather a pre-industrial, setting could accommodate a range of Nazi views on women from the mainstream conservative desire to value women within their own sphere, to the more extreme views such as the advocacy of matriarchal socialism by neo-conservative and *völkisch* wings of the Party.[12] The latter conjured up an 'original matriarchy' in which earth spirits ruled their enchanted broods with magic and feeling. For those feminists whose version of matriarchy involved fantasies of warrior women, the mother image would perhaps not have been palatable but, as I shall argue in the next section, the mother image is not necessarily a representative image in either art or propaganda. The point to be made here is that Nazism was eclectic, its ideology drew on traditional bourgeois concepts but also on mystical, *völkisch* beliefs. Any image produced by such an eclectic mix of potentially contradictory sources as matriarchalism and bourgeois anti-feminism will potentially address a wide range of viewers for whom it will have a variety of associations.

From the Party's point of view, images which were aimed at self-recognition by women specifically coincided with their recognition in the early Thirties of the extent of women's support and their 'inspired' behaviour at meetings. Women's ability to keep faith with the Party's long-term aims and their value as targets for the chain-reaction effect of propaganda were noted and well understood by Hitler and by his followers.[13] Images of men were understood to have a role in this targeting too. Comments by Hitler and Nazi leaders on the persona Hitler presented to women included a Christ figure, a Saviour inspiring faith and religious ecstasy, and a matinée idol producing similar adulatory reactions. In one comment Hitler noted that in meetings women were in fact the main target of the Party: 'The crowd is not only like a woman, but women constitute the most important element in an audience.'[14]

For the less committed Nazi supporter, or the Nazi opponent, the mother-and-child paintings Rittich reproduced might have passed unnoticed, were it not for the specific circumstances in which propaganda aimed at women then occurred. In 1943, when Rittich's survey was published, the debate about the desirability of conscripting women had dragged on for years due to Hitler's personal prejudices.[15] It was finally resolved in January 1943 when conscription for women's war work was introduced. It proved unpopular. Propaganda therefore aimed to reassure women about protective labour legislation. Would images like Andri's work to reinforce the idea of the government's protective attitude, or would it not rather have pointed up the contradiction between circumstances and ideology?

For most of their time in power, the Nazi women's organisations, administered by Gertrud Scholtz-Klink, projected to women a self-image of homely warmth and pragmatism. *Deutsches Frauenschaffen*, the annual of the *Reichsfrauenführung*, took care to describe its new offices in Berlin in a way that stressed its differences from a male bureaucracy. It was warm, clean, and comfortable. Even its waiting rooms were carpeted. It was a place where cares could be unloaded in the aura of a welcoming motherly presence.[16] Indeed, Scholtz-Klink's later claims to have cared mainly about pragmatic concerns, such as home economics and child care, nutrition and physical fitness, have been substantiated. Although in 1933 women activists were calling either for fighting images of women's spiritual powers on the one hand, or religious images of self-sacrifice on the other,[17] the Party found an appeal to the practical concerns of the housewife far more successful. The mother-images by Andri and Erler might well have been more to the taste of the old-time idealists than the new style administrators, though even the latter relied frequently on purple passages about the deep, mysterious capacities of the mother in its propaganda. It was certainly of great importance to the Party that its women's administration should mediate its ultimate concern for fertility at the expense *of* the family via an image of motherly concern *for* the family.[18]

A further circumstance that Andri's and Erler's images might have referred to was the notorious 'breeding programme'. From 1938, Himmler, exercised by the birth and marriage figures, had been advocating various measures, including urging his 3 million SS men to sire as many babies as possible at state expense and not necessarily via marriage.[19] The outcry resulted in a retraction. However, by 1943, the combination of women's conscription, the drop-off in funding for women's programmes, and the introduction of the SS breeding scheme, meant that opposition and supporters alike perceived the gap between the earlier pro-family propaganda and the harsher war-time measures. Understandably, Himmler's scheme was made much of by opponents who ridiculed the *Bund deutscher Mädel* (League of German Girls) as the *Bund deutscher Milch Kühe* (League of German Milk Cows).[20]

It is also worth noticing that Andri's *Mother and Child*, emblematic and stylised, not attempting to refer directly to peasant life as do the genre paintings in Rittich's survey and without a husband in sight, might well have been disquieting to women at this time. Regardless of official policy which said the unmarried mother merited special praise, the *Bund deutscher Mädel* dismissed members who became pregnant without getting married. Many sections of the Nazi women's organisation were vocal in their opposition to the policy of targeting breeding at the expense of family life. The blatant immorality of the suggestion horrified them. Likewise Rittich's juxtaposition of Andri's 'instantaneous' mother and child with Erler's was meant to place *Ripeness* in the category of the 'comprehensively symbolic', the madonna and child. Rittich could have supported this categorisation by referring to the flattened space and restrained symmetry suggestive of a Renaissance altarpiece. However the presence of male harvesters in contemporary dress prevents the image's removal from the category of peasant genre painting. The image would undoubtedly have been understood as a reference to the madonna, but whether the added connotation of fertility in the title and the contemporary setting would have seemed unproblematic is less clear.[21]

Clearly we cannot assume the smooth ideological functioning of Nazi images of women in art. Even though the mother images discussed so far worked to address that broad spectrum of women who had shown that emotional investment in some aspects of motherhood was a powerful source of government support, it is unlikely that one visual image could hold together all the contemporary connotations of motherhood. Motherhood as an abstract eternal feminine (which in propaganda publications for women could be tacked on to articles about practical concerns), motherhood as prehistorical or utopian matriarchy, motherhood as the source of positive character qualities, especially its staying power for the Party's long-term goals: these are potentially compatible. Indeed the appeal of the traditional bourgeois ideology of woman's 'mission', from the 19th century onwards, has always been its apparent breadth of scope to include a moral alongside a social role, and an apparent equality-in-difference. However, these aspects of motherhood were not compatible while exclusive emphasis was being given to women's biological role, nor were they compatible at a historical moment when it had become apparent that the Party was concerned only with woman's biological or economic functions. Thus while *Ripeness* attempts to combine biological destiny with positive character qualities (Germanic resoluteness of character and clarity of vision was typically signified by the look into the distance in propaganda photographs), the large jug at her side connotes the milk-cow, while her identity as madonna or farm worker is unclear. Rittich no doubt hoped that her halo of hay would pull her into 'the symbolic' and away from 'the instantaneous'. The artist, however, finds it difficult to follow the tactic of the propaganda writer who can foreground the practical work of motherhood, give it social and political importance (woman as consumer), and suppress biological reproduction by references to woman as 'spiritual' guardianess of the race.[22] The propaganda writer can spell out the kind of reassurance the visual image attempts to engender without guarantee of success, namely that the Party does not want to impose a new role on women but only to build on the strengths they already possess *as* women. This is the constant refrain in propaganda for women. For example motherhood schools were said to teach a unified National Socialist attitude, but only by bringing to life those strengths which were already possessed but unknown.[23]

A further significant block to the ideological functioning of images like Andri's and Erler's would have been the class-specific tastes of the viewer. Even the activist, if she were from an educated middle-class family like Melita Maschmann, would find genre painting an embarrassment. Maschmann, a *Bund deutscher Mädel* leader at one time responsible for propaganda at a local level, mentions her tastes in art in her autobiography. This takes the form of letters of confession to a former Jewish school-friend of the errors of her own Nazification. Her parents were wealthy in the 1920's and belonged to the right-wing German Nationalist Party. Her mother filled her with love for the sculpture of Ernst Barlach and Wilhelm Lehmbruck, both denounced as degenerate by the Party. Given her mother's right-wing nationalism, anti-semitism, and constant lamentations about Germany's decline, which the child experienced as both mysterious and pleasurable, Barlach's art seemed to have corresponded to her mother's melancholy prognostications. She seems not to have associated Barlach himself with her mother's view that Germany's culture was sick because it was 'dominated by foreigners'.[24]

Maschmann contrasts the passive melancholy of her mother with her own immediate attraction to the Party and active involvement in the *Bund deutscher Mädel*, and yet her tastes in art apparently remained those of her mother. She was 'bored thoroughly' by Sepp Hilz's *Peasant Venus* (one of several nudes by him in Germanically furnished interiors) or Storm Trooper paintings, and 'never felt comfortable' in the Munich House of German Art.[25]

Maschmann could rationalise the Party's anti-semitism to the extent of spying on her schoolfriend's family, yet not the Party's attitude to art. Is she just trying to assuage her guilt and reach out to her friend (presumably dead) by claiming a retrospective cultural kinship? Upper-middle class taste, if Maschmann is representative, may have regarded genre painting as fit only for inferior tastes (and classes), as unspiritual. Maschmann emphasises elsewhere in the book that youth movement leaders were a cultural élite who deplored 'the scandalous lack of taste' in anti-Jewish propaganda.[26]

Art also had the function for this élite of tapping the sources of religious experience. Maschmann insists that as young women they were not irreligious, even though they scorned the hypocritical muddle of their Christian schoolteachers who attempted to ignore the conflict between their own ideology with the *Bund deutscher Mädel* spirit of the pupils. It would seem that youth too was not free from muddle: 'I can perhaps say that we believed in a Creator God who was revealed to us in the order and beauty of nature and whose mysterious being also touched us when we were confronted with great works of art'.[27] Clearly the eroticised nudes of Sepp Hilz, and genre painting whose tastelessness reduced art to the level of racialist propaganda, could not effect this sublimation of religious feeling. Nor presumably could art which aimed unsubtly to evoke religious associations by means of peasant madonnas.

If one looks in Maschmann's account for what played the biggest part in attracting her to Nazism, it was the sight of marching boys and girls in the torchlight procession celebrating Nazi victory in January 1933, when she was fifteen. It reinforced her sense of having grown away from her parent's anti-socialism; here was the *Volksgemeinschaft* (national community) with its 'magical glow' made visible. It was addressing her group specifically, giving it a sense of purpose: 'You are needed for something important; come!'[28]

These complexities suggest that if the ideological function of images is to mean anything, it must include an account of how specific groups found themselves addressed by images, indeed found their identity in their response to this address. For Maschmann, it was the sight of marching adolescents which seemed to address her. It was not with aggression that she identified, but, seeing a man struck to the ground by one of the marchers, blood streaming down his face, her horror, 'almost imperceptibly spiced with an intoxicating joy', inspired her to feelings of readiness to die. Oral history accounts of girls' experiences in the *Bund deutscher Mädel* confirm that readiness to die as the ultimate test of faith in Germany, and the sacrifice of ego for the cause of gaining honour for Germany, were successfully engendered for many by the group's rituals.[29] Maschmann's account indicates something of the mixture of feelings involved in her attraction to the Party: the simultaneous inclusion of herself and exclusion of others, a sadism directed outwards at others and then increasingly inwards against herself. These are complex feelings, but even if only partly understood they provide better guidelines for enquiry than a mechanistically envisaged process of 'ideological function'. They also of course warn us not to assume that the images of art would necessarily be capable of addressing viewers as powerfully or directly as a march or a rally.

The disparateness of the ideologies which supported Nazism, the flexibility of the mother-image, and the class-specific tastes of viewers all suggest that it is inappropriate to analyse the ideological impact of Nazi art with mechanistic theories of ideological function for a homogeneous viewing public. Is there then a representative image of women in Nazi art?

The Architectural Body: The Form of the Female Body in Nazi Art

On the issue of a representative image in Nazi art, the predominant view has been that the muscular male nude can be taken as the representative image because it best projects the political and ideological intentions of the Party leadership. The formal vocabulary of the muscular male nudes sculpted by Arno Breker for the Reich Chancellery in 1938, *Die Partei* (The Party) and *Die Wehrmacht* (The Armed Forces), is generally thought to express the intentions of a Fascist state: to spur men to identify with an image of masculinity which is so perverted, so de-humanised and desensualised into ultra-masculinity, that it in fact intimidates and terrorises rather than effects identification.[30] 'Olympian distance from the people' is said to be the common denominator of 'the naked form in the representative state sculpture of German fascism.'[31] (*Fig 2*). Yet many of the writers who hold this view also argue that in spite of the block to identification, arousal of men to readiness for battle through such images was both intended and effected. The point here is not only to criticise the blurring of intention and effect, but to put forward arguments for a representative image of *woman* in Nazi art.

Firstly, there are the sheer numbers of female figures in surveys of Nazi sculpture at the time. Secondly, a muscular body-type can be found amongst sculptures of the female as well as the male nude. Thirdly, allegories whose meaning depends on the female nude are as representative of Party and state as Breker's male nudes. For the moment these arguments are considered in reaction to an *intended* representative image. The final section will return to the issue of the reception of art by women. Fourthly, those images of women with some claim to typicality are not primarily images of mothers. For example, paintings of or including women in the Federal government's art collection in Munich, based on the Reich Chancellery's purchases from the Munich House of German Art, mostly contain nudes eroticised by body-type or by poses, noticeably of languorous horizontality. The overwhelming impression is official preference for the pin-up. State commissions from favoured sculptors such as Arno Breker, Joseph Thorak, Fritz Klimsch, Georg Kolbe, and Joseph Wackerle, were for female as well as for male nudes.

But what was the form assigned to the image of women in Nazi art? Art reproduced in contemporary surveys, including *Grosse deutsche Kunstausstellung* reviews and survey articles, in *Die Kunst im Dritten Reich*, suggests a growing preference for sculpture over painting, a valorisation of the nude in sculpture and, within this trend, consistent attention given to the female nude. For example, a small paperback survey of art by Werner Rittich, published by the German Railway Office as part of a series entitled *Deutschlands Werden seit 1933* (Germany's Development since 1933), demonstrates a clear preference for sculpture.[32] While both painting and sculpture are shown to depict German types, Rittich's captions make it clear that it is sculpted figures who are best able to 'embody', in ideal or symbolic form, 'a feeling which points to the future, of strength, courage, energy, joy in life and the will to beauty'. His caption for example to Fritz Klimsch's female nude *Die Schauende*, (The Beholder, *Fig 3*) states: 'This bronze statue is one of the most beautiful representations of the ideal female body. It embodies the striving of

2. Josef Thorak
Kameradschaft
(Comradeship)

German youth for a classical ideal of the body. The statue was exhibited at the Munich House of German Art and made for the staff swimming pool of the IG dye works in Leverkusen'. Furthermore, here and elsewhere Rittich stresses the importance and typicality of sculptures destined for buildings. He argues for a new architectural aesthetic, which had developed since 1933, and which was visible not only in buildings but in the sculpture which complemented them. The new aesthetic was one of monumentality, clear articulation, and the expression of the architecture's ordering principles.

How typical in fact was this aesthetic? Commentators have often noted that in their desire to use art to manipulate the alienation of large sections of the public from avant-garde culture, the Nazis gave less consideration to articulating a National Socialist aesthetic than to castigating modernism.[33] However, a clear and pronounced aesthetic does seem to emerge in the texts of *Die Kunst im Dritten Reich*, that is, from 1937. This takes its cue from the belief that the spirit of the 'movement' 'speaks' through its architecture and finds that sculpture alone can come close to this spirit by being 'like a piece of architecture', its athletic bodies displaying clearly articulated divisions.[34] The terms most frequently applied for this

3. Fritz Klimsch *The Beholder*, 1932, from Werner Rittich, *Deutschlands Werden seit 1933*

architectural aesthetic in sculpture are *Geschlossenheit* (completeness and also connotations of closure) and *Klarheit* (clarity). As it is 'clarity' which is the key term in this aesthetic, its extensive range of meanings must be examined.

'Clarity' is found in Hitler's opening speech for the first *Grosse deutsche Kunstausstellung* in the House of German Art in 1937: 'Deutsch sein heisst klar sein' (To be German is to be clear).[35] In this context it means that clarity of vision is a racial characteristic of the Germans, especially since they have become 'hardened' by recent political events which have 'opened their eyes' to their own decline. Now clear-eyed, they can see who was responsible. Their clarity of vision can find expression in art once again, now that the unnatural and confused sloganising of the Jewish reign of culture is over. Now art requires only normal, 'instinctive' reactions. Art must also therefore be 'clear' in the sense of easy to understand. This meaning — comprehensibility — is linked to the contrast between the transitoriness of Weimar art, reacting to the whims of fashion, and the new art to which only one and the same standard is applied because it is eternal, based on the *Volk* who are a 'still point in the flux of appearances' (*in der Flucht der Escheinungen, der ruhende Pol*). Comprehensibility is linked to political stability.

In the catalogue to the first *Grosse deutsche Kunstausstellung* exhibition, a photograph of Klimsch's *The Beholder* is sandwiched between an upright male nude statue by Kolbe, face frowning and fists clenched, and a semi-reclining male nude in Richard Klein's painting *Das Erwachen* (The Awakening) (*Fig 3*). Klimsch's *The Beholder* is placed directly above a painted portrait of Hitler. In my view Klimsch's sculpture as reproduced here demonstrates the architectural

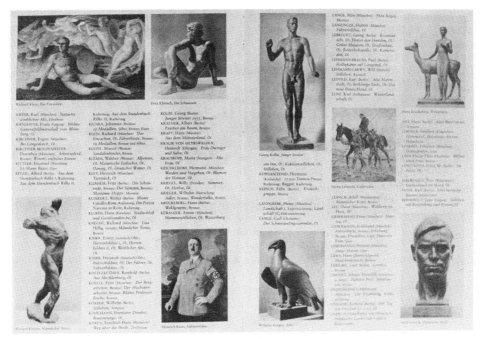

4. Double page spread from the 1937 Grosse Deutsche Kunstaustellung catalogue, Munich, showing from top left Richard Klein, *The Awakening*, Fritz Klimsch *The Beholder* and George Kolbe *Young Strider*

aesthetic precisely as Rittich defined it. The awkward position of the legs, and the deep shadows cast on the body, break down the body into a multitude of surface planes and jointed volumes. In spite of the muscularity of thighs and shoulders, the narrow waist with its deeply incised 'fold' and the small, upright breasts give the nude the appearance of a jointed shop dummy.

Hitler's *Grosse deutsche Kunstausstellung* speech indicates the reassuring resonances that this aesthetic of architectural clarity was supposed to have when applied to the bodies of both sexes: accessibility, timelessness, racial purity, and national stability (the 'still point'). The male and female bodies of the *Grosse deutsche Kunstausstellung* exhibitions were supposed to be ideal racial types, representing the invulnerable and durable body of the *Volk* itself.

There are two phenomena here which require further elucidation: the transference of feelings about the body to the state, expressed through architectural metaphors, and, entailed by this transfer, a reduction in the outward signs of gender difference. The editors of the *Grosse deutsche Kunstausstellung* catalogue, intentionally or not, by reproducing them together make partners of Klein's and Klimsch's male and female nudes. Their poses are mirror opposites, and their bodies are both slim but athletic.[36]

A book which expounded the theory of different racial body-types and standards of ideal beauty, Paul Schultze-Naumburg's *Nordische Schönheit* (Nordic Beauty), published in 1937, casts further light on these two linked phenomena.[37] Schultze-Naumburg's basic argument rests on a racist version of the discredited pseudo-science of physiognomy: the idea that racially determined 'characteristics of the soul' are made visible externally on the body and can be 'read' from it ('*ablesen*').[38] He claims that male and female Nordic bodies, exhibiting the Nordic virtues of contemplativeness and clarity (whose meanings he specifies as both logic and truthfulness), are tall, slim, fine-limbed, and have narrow hips and narrow faces. Schultze-Naumburg discusses different body parts in turn, each assigned their Nordic (or Asian) form. He finds the idea of bodies whose parts are clearly separated, marked off from one another by borderlines provided by the underlying skeleton, highly gratifying. Flabby bodies, whose parts merge together, he finds repulsive, and intends his readers to do so too. Clarity then is a characteristic of the Nordic race because exclusive to Nordic bodies is their 'legibility' in terms of separate parts and borderlines. The Nordic female breast for example has 'chiselled' contours and is small and upright unlike the fast-ageing, fat and overripe breasts of 'orientals', or the huge, formless, spongy breasts of 'mongoloids'.[39]

The text displays a small degree of difficulty over the readability of the female as compared with the male body, however. On the one hand the clear display of Nordic features in women's bodies is essential for the 'right' choice of a (racially pure) spouse, on which the fitness of future generations depends. On the other hand, even the most athletic of Nordic female bodies has softer curves than the male's and is perceived as graceful rather than powerful. Schultze-Naumburg responds to this difficulty by insisting that race has a much stronger influence than gender on physique as it 'imprints' the race's ideal image on the Nordic female as much as the male.[40] Other races are apparently less fortunate, less 'imprinted'. Oriental and Mongoloid women are soft and flabby in art as in life. The Nordic woman is therefore more like the Nordic man than like the women of other races; she has small breasts without prominent nipples, a flat stomach and long legs. She does not have broad hips or narrow shoulders in an absolute sense; there is no feminine or masculine 'form of humanity' according to Schultze-Naumburg. Rather, her hips are only broad in relation to the hips of other races. She therefore reproduces 'the image of the heroic man in its feminine form'.[41] Klimsch's female is just such a 'heroic' equivalent to the Klein and Kolbe males.

Schultze-Naumburg entreats the reader to dwell on the contours of the female torsos in his illustrations (*Fig 5*) and to note in the one bottom-left the gradual broadening of the hips from waistline to thighs. This pleasurable, calm sensation is contrasted with the disturbing sensation the author assumes the reader will have when the eyes jerk down and across the fleshy hips of the nude bottom-right. The author comments, with seeming irrelevance at this point, that in accidents the legs can become separated from the torso without the victim dying. The text and images therefore seem to be attempting to instill the desire for the ideal Nordic body form by associating it with wholeness and at the same time providing verbal and visual images of dismemberment: legless (and in the illustrations headless) bodies. In a text which not only describes but displays Nordic body parts, and enjoins readers to put the Nordic aesthetic into practice by recognising the Nordic imprint or its lack in real bodies, the architectural metaphor is again essential. Nordic bodies, male and female alike, are recognisable immediately in terms of three 'points', nipples and navel, which Schulze-Naumburg likens to building-piles displayed on the corners of buildings. The architectural solidity of the Nordic body is profoundly reassuring for him. It is reassuring not only in its contrast with the softness and illegibility of the bodies of 'others', but also in contrast with the 'dismembered' Nordic body which appears in the text — where body-

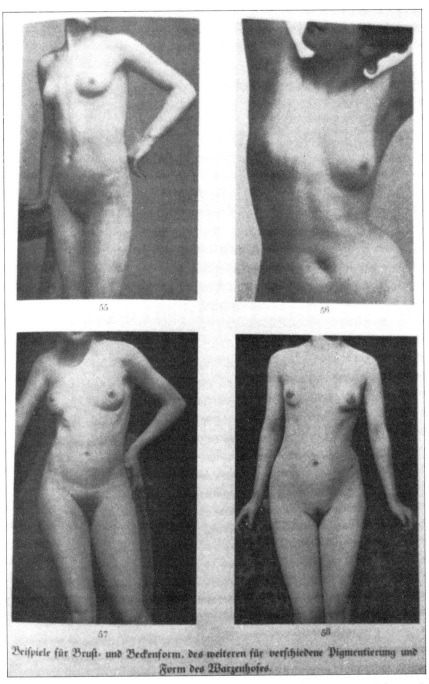

Beispiele für Brust- und Beckenform, des weiteren für verschiedene Pigmentierung und Form des Warzenhofes.

5. 'Examples of breast and pelvis forms also indicating varied pigmentation and forms of the nipple area' from Paul Schultze-Naumburg, *Nordic Beauty*, Munich, 1937

parts are analysed separately in order to build a catalogue of independently identifiable features.

In fact, however psychologically reassuring the architectural body-aesthetic may have been, it did not appear consistently in representations of women in art, partly due to the suppression of the *völkisch* ideology.[43] Nevertheless it did emerge. It was articulated by Rittich and other writers for *Die Kunst im Dritten Reich*. It had a rationale: that monumentality and clear articulation in sculpture rendered it a fitting ornament for architecture. Moreover its standards — clarity and completeness — were entirely consistent with Hitler's expectation that the gratifying comprehensibility of the new art, its 'clarity' the sign and proof of its Germanness, would help to consolidate his power by giving viewers the sense of being newly empowered to make judgements on art by his party's elimination of Weimar culture. They would also be empowered by their new found health and strength, reflected in the bodies of the new art.

If the architectural aesthetic was applied more consistently to the male figure than to the female, there are indications of its applicability to female figures too. It was important here not only in providing an architectural aesthetic for sculpture, but also for constructing an alleged continuity with a lost classical tradition. It was important in its appearance in allegorical sculpture intended for buildings; and it was important in its address to women.

In its attempt to construct a tradition which could be claimed as an artistic heritage that had been lost or perverted, Nazi art discourse relied increasingly, from 1936 onwards, on the notion of a classical heritage. For example, in its 1936 anniversary exhibition, the Prussian Academy of Fine Arts mounted an exhibition of Berlin sculptors, from the late 18th century to the present, in order to show successive phases of Classicism and Baroque. In contrast to early 19th century monumental figures, exemplified in the catalogue by female allegories with heavy bodies, accented drapery and impersonal features, are female figures from the Imperial era with much more naturalistic, softly contoured bodies, unclothed, and shown in coy artificial studio poses. Female figures reproduced in the catalogue to represent the Third Reich, which was said in the text to be witnessing a renewal of classicising and gothicising form, are an ethereal, clothed *Seraphita* by Gerhard Marcks, and a nude *Caryatid* by Ludwig Kasper (*Fig 6*): slim, stiff, primitivised, architectural and impersonal. The Academy's representative female figures, in their 'classicised' or 'gothicised' forms, both accord with the Nordic ideal. Their youthfulness and de-eroticisation are also consistent with the anti-modernist polemic, which singled out the 'distorted' female bodies of Expressionism and Dada for particular execration in 1937. Modernist fragmented bodies, their 'organic form' disguised by broken body boundaries, were attributed to artists' overheated sexual desires and are associated with the 'sickness' of socialism.[45] The relatively unerotic female nude could therefore also be used to construct an apparent continuity with an earlier 19th century 'classical' tradition, where the representative female figures were dignified allegories, disavowing the embarrassments of the Imperial era, as well as advertising the suppression of modernism.

Taking a Werner Rittich text once again as an indication of the development of a consistent National Socialist aesthetic, the valorisation of the sculpted nude was taken as an opportunity to suggest that the nature of allegorical sculpture was changing in the Third Reich. In a 1938 article whose theme is the superiority of architectural over free-standing sculpture,[46] Rittich argued that allegory was being surpassed by 'symbolic' sculpture. Allegorical attributes 'which have no

6. Ludwig Kaspar, *Caryatid*, 1936, reproduced from
Berliner Bildhauer von Schlüter bis zur Gegenwart
(German Sculptors from Schlüter to the Present),
Berlin, 1936

intrinsic relation to the whole' (and perhaps he was thinking here of Imperial female nudes whose sexuality was impossible to ignore) were becoming less important, now that the figure itself, in its structure and relation to site, could express the 'required meaning'. The examples Rittich discussed in his text were female nudes all expressing the same 'required meaning': a racial essence inflected, but only slightly, by a female essence. One example was Joseph Thorak's allegorical *Victory Goddess* (exhibited at the *Grosse deutsche Kunstausstellung* in 1938), which was intended as the central figure in a group of male warriors for the Nuremberg rally ground (*Fig 7*). Thorak's *Victory Goddess* was said to monument-alise the charm of his earlier nudes and to convey through her whole structure 'Sublimity, Dignity, Seriousness and the Supernatural'.[47] Other examples given were female nudes by Thorak and Klimsch, and the adjectives Rittich applied to them also suggested Schultze-Naumburg's racial idea of a basically masculine heroic ideal in female form, a female equivalent: 'powerful but feminine', 'power-ful, natural but proud, bringing the mighty Hellenic spirit into our times'.[48]

Curiously, Rittich's article did not illustrate these architectural-symbolic sculptures, even though he was arguing that they were typical. Instead, the article was illustrated by a double-page spread with four nudes, three female and one male (a format typical in *Die Kunst im Dritten Reich* surveys) (*Fig 8*). The text did not say whether any of these were intended for architectural sites; indeed did not mention them at all. The female nude at one end of the line up was Georg Kolbe's *Young Woman* (far left). She has an athletic body and her arms hang down at her sides so that she is closer in pose and body-type to the male nude at the opposite end of this line-up. In effect the double-page spread which accompanied Rittich's piece is a symmetrical tableau, for the two central female nudes are also 'paired' by their softer contours and exaggerated contrapostos which push out the hips on opposite sides, and by the raised pieces of flimsy drapery. Rittich's claim for the representa-tive status of the 'architectural' female allegory, whose allegorical (as opposed to

69

7. Josef Thorak, *Victory Goddess*, Monument for Nuremberg Rally ground, exhibited in the Grosse Deutsche Kunstausstellung, Munich, 1938

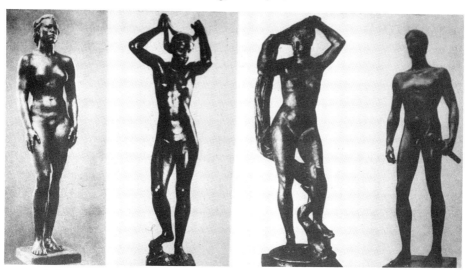

8. Double page spread from Werner Rittich, *Architekturgebundene oder freie Plastik?* (Architectural or freestanding sculpture?) *Die Kunst im Dritten Reich*, August 1938, showing from left to right sculptures by Georg Kolbe, Eugen Henke, Josef Wackerle and Ernst Andreas Rauch

purely erotic) meaning is expressed through body-type, must surely be viewed as wish-fulfilment, for it is clear from the text of the article that Rittich encountered a lack of architectural sculpture in the 1938 *Grosse deutsche Kunstausstellung* show. The 'feminised' female figure was rationalised in Rittich's article and in other articles in the magazine, as evidence that artists were continuing to develop their motifs and techniques in their 'private' interests. This argument for the expression of artists' private interests became particularly useful in later war-time articles in *Die Kunst im Dritten Reich*, where the female body was frequently stated to be evidence that in spite of war there was still freedom of fantasy and continuity of life in the private sphere.[49]

The slim 'architectural' female body was, as Rittich indicates, a suitable choice as a representative *public* form of art, whose athletic body and pose of readiness-for-action could easily be viewed as the female equivalent to male heroism, and could dilute and give contemporary form to the female figure 'called' as if by God, suggested by such titles as *The Chosen One* or *Looking Up (Fig 9)*. Figure 10 shows a divinely inspired female nude (*The Call*) reproduced in the 1937 *Grosse deutsche Kunstausstellung* Catalogue, swooning back, hands raised to shoulder level, palms upward.[50] The Kolbe and Scheibe nudes (*Fig 9*) are modified and de-eroticised versions of this, that take on the connotations of readiness-for-action, especially when reproduced in women's magazines, as I shall show in the final section.

9. Left Richard Scheibe, *Looking Up*, 1938 from *Die Kunst im Dritten Reich*, 1944 and right Georg Kolbe, *The Chosen One* from *Die Kunst im Dritten Reich*, 1942

Woman as the 'Bearer of Culture': Images of Woman in Nazi Discourse

I have argued that while not typical in the sense of statistically predominant, the slim 'architectural' female nude was part of the development of an architectural body-aesthetic in racialist and art discourse. Its terms — clarity and completeness — found expression in metaphors which were intended to encourage the transfer of feelings about the body to the state.

I want now to examine discourses around women in propaganda publications. Firstly, to ask whether an architectural body-aesthetic had any importance outside art discourse and what associations it may have had for women; secondly, to recover some of the wider associations that the female nude in art was intended to have. There can be no doubt that the female, like the male nude, was loaded with associations. As one writer in *Die Kunst im Dritten Reich* expressed it: the nude was far more than merely 'artistic', it had become 'a documentary expression of ideology and cultural history . . . of moral, social and religious attitudes.'[51]

A useful starting point is the widespread notion that woman is the 'bearer of

71

CAUER, Hanna (Berlin) *Nischenfigur*,
Gips
CHRISTLIEB, Hermann (Kleinmach-
now) *Pavianfamilie*, Gips
CLARENBACH, Max (Düsseldorf)
Mondnacht in Friesland, Öl
COESTER, Otto (Wuppertal-Barmen)
Niederrheinische Landschaft,
Radierung; *Mulde*, Radierung
COMPTON, Edward Harrison
(Feldafing) *Aus dem Riesengebirge*,
Öl; *Bernina*, Öl
CRASS, Otto (Hanau a. M.)
*Bildnisbüste Generalintendant
Wilhelm Rode*, englischer Zement

DALLINGER, Karl Heinz (München)
*Dekoratives Bild für Offiziers-
kasino der Luftwaffe*, Malerei auf
Goldgrund
DAMBERGER, Josef (Obermenzing b.
München) *Im Kartoffelacker*, Öl
DARSOW, Johannes (Klasdorf) *Tiger*,
Bronze
DIER, Amadeus Erhard (Berlin) *Turm-
bau zu Babel*, Öltempera; *Legenden
der Liebe*, Öltempera; *Bildnis eines
holländisch-javanischen Maler-
freundes*, Öltempera; *Aktstudie*,
Zeichnung

Elf Eber, *Appell am 23. Februar 1933*

DORRENBACH, Franz (Berlin)
Junges Mädchen, Marmor
DOTZLER, Hans (Landshut)
Schlesische Landschaft, Zeichnung
DRESCHER-ITTER, Hans (Thal-Itter)
Am Frischen Haff, Federzeichnung
DROBIL, Michael (Wien) *Knaben-
kopf*, Marmor; *Mädchenkopf*,

Max Brumme, *Berufung*

BRÜCKNER, Oswald (Nürnberg)
Der Pimpf, Bronze
BRUMME, Max Alfred (Leipzig)
Berufung, Bronze
BRUSENBAUCH, Arthur (Wien)

10. Section of a page from the *Grosse Deutsche Kunstausstellung* catalogue, 1937, showing
left Max Brumme *The Call*, and right Elf Eber *Roll-call on 23rd February 1933*

culture' (*Kulturträgerin*).[52] At one level of course this was a euphemism for bearer
of children, bearer of the German race of the future. However, as I have argued, in
order to address women as mothers, propaganda tended to address women as
housewives, and to link their practical tasks with their role as Guardianess of
Spiritual Values. Female nudes, for example by Kolbe, can be called simply
Guardianess (*Hüterin, Fig 11*) and there is no need to specify whether this is
guardianess of hearth, spiritual values or race. The Party also discovered, indeed
was told in no uncertain terms by its *Bund deutscher Mädel* leaders, that its address
to girls would fail completely if it addressed them only as future mothers and took
no account of their interests as adolescents.[53] 'Bearer of Culture' therefore had a
different meaning in the ideological indoctrination of girls. It is within this system
of indoctrination that the importance of the body, and a body-aesthetic, can be
seen.

Until the outbreak of war, it was not clear exactly how adolescent girls were
meant to be addressed to make them ready for insertion (*Einsatz*) into and sacrifice (*Opfer*) and service (*Dienst*) for the state (to make them *einsatzbereit, opfer-
bereit, dienstleistungsvoll*).[54] In formulating the tasks of the *Bund deutscher Mädel*,
the main focus was therefore on creating a mainly 'educational' organisation, with
the task of inculcating the right attitudes for *Einsaztbereitschaft* (readiness-for-
service). It was considered most effective to do this by working on the 'whole
person'[55]: on the body by sport, on the mind and character, and as I shall show, on
the body too, by political indoctrination and the encouraging of the right 'cultural
attitudes', by which was meant taste in clothes, furniture, household objects, etc.
This would attempt to create practical women with no claims to 'rights as separate
individuals'.[56]

Through the physical and cultural education they received in the *Bund*

11. Georg Kolbe, *The Guardianess* from
Die Kunst im Dritten Reich, August, 1939

deutscher Mädel, the absolute values held up to the girls as objectives were: 'the genuine, the racially pure, the beautiful, the solid, the natural',[57] and the absolute values they were to demand of themselves were: 'loyalty, uprightness, purity, cleanliness and honour'.[58] These ethical and aesthetic values were to be applied to the girls themselves, their bodies, their clothes, and the things they made or might buy.

The role of images as a means of indoctrination of both mind and body was understood and frequently discussed, a common term for a simultaneous effect on body and mind being 'imprint'. Boys might be taught by force, girls, however, could not be taught by 'commando-methods';[59] they had to be taught by means of images. The images involved were mostly of two kinds. Firstly, images of agricultural life, people, their homes, etc., secondly, the face and body of a female leader. So powerful was the effect of looking at an inspiring leader thought to be, that lecturers were instructed not to allow women or girl pupils to take notes. The pupils should look at the lecturer's face and body to 'absorb its expression alongside its content'.[60]

The body of a *Bund deutscher Mädel* leader was therefore of great importance. The autobiography of Ilsa Koehn, daughter of socialist parents forced to live apart because one parent was 'aryan' and one Jewish, recounts how, in common with most other girls of her age, she longed to join the *Bund deutscher Mädel*. Later, conscripted to a flea-infested Labour camp for girls in Czechoslovakia, she delighted in puncturing the *Bund deutscher Mädel* rhetoric of female purity, of

73

bodies 'tough as leather, hard as Krupp steel, swift as greyhounds'[61], while noting that the *Bund* leaders were themselves fat and ate puddings. Even so, one detects in Koehn's reminiscences a longing to be recognised and befriended by these imperfect figures, standing, as they did, *in loco parentis.*

There is, of course, nothing intrinsically 'clean', 'pure', or 'natural' in a slim, athletic body as opposed to a fat one. With the help of competitive sporting activities and the fashionable, narrow-hipped, tailored look of the thirties, it was possible to make it seem as if there were. It was above all the idea and image of 'the natural' that appealed to adolescent girls as a positive ideal. Hiking and camping for example helped to set them apart from the consumer world of their parents.[62]

If the athletic body was given these meanings, and the girl possessed such a body, then she herself 'embodied' the ideal values, as Nazi art discourse was fond of expressing it. She would feel positive about her own body and, as part of the body of the *Volk*, it was expected that she would offer herself as an image of the *Volk* for others. The result of her own indoctrination would be that she in her turn would become the vehicle of ideological rectitude, responsible for 'the first ideological attitudes of the future race'.[63]

Being the 'Bearer of Culture', then, meant being looked at. It also involved looking at others, to judge them, which women were told they were particularly skilled at as mothers, who could tell much about their children just by looking at them. Scholtz-Klink told the readers of *Deutsches Frauenschaffen*, that they could regard looking at others to judge them good or evil as part of their 'mission', their equivalent to man's mission to fight.[64] Melita Maschmann in the autobiography cited earlier reveals her pride in her own decoding look and her ability to withstand the looks of others: she can tell the difference between the newly conquered Poles and the German settlers, and she can withstand the hostile looks of the Poles. Rationalising in retrospect her 'cultural mission' in Poland as an editor for a Youth Movement publication, she explains the power of images of political indoctrination, which had made the Poles seem to her squalid over-breeders, unfit to rule themselves. She also comments on the importance to her of being able to shut herself away from the enemy, of being able to sustain the illusion that she is being constantly watched and yet able to withstand constant looks of antipathy from the Poles. It may have been a relief to get back over the border into Germany and drop the mask, but it seems also to have been a pleasure to preserve this mask, to exist for others, to 'give' herself 'entirely', to experience 'release from the ego' and achieve 'inner stillness'.

By 'inner stillness' Maschmann presumably meant both a certainty of purpose and a lack of individual motivation, a draining of individual identity. Werner Rittich uses the terms inwardness and stillness to describe the difference between Georg Kolbe's female nudes of the Third Reich and those he had done before.[65] He contrasts the 'stillness' of his female nudes of the thirties, some of which were intended to alternate with pillars in a special courtyard Kolbe had designed, with two earlier nudes who are depicted in movement; a dancer with outstretched arms and a kneeling *Pietà*. The later nudes, he explained, seem deprived of physical movement, and yet they are all the more full of an inward movement of the emotions. Like Mary in the Pietà, they too are 'vessels' to be filled, and know their own fate. Both Rittich's and Maschmann's references to the stillness of the inner life seem to me, on the contrary, to indicate its emptiness and lack of real content in the period of the Third Reich.[66]

One might comment here that while there is nothing inherently Fascist about women being looked at, Nazi methods of indoctrination of girls required them to transform the 'normal' experience of being looked at into a draining of individual identity, and to transform their 'normal' ability to accept the looks of men, into a positive feeling of superiority over a racial 'other'.[67]

After all, women in the Third Reich were given considerable practice in 'reading' the female body: women's magazines had competitions to guess the origins of native types, and in one article in *Frauen-Kultur*, crisp, outline drawings of the faces of successful professional women (*Fig 12*) accompanied a reassuring text containing the message that these faces bore the imprint of a natural femininity which had blossomed in whatever career path their owners had chosen. 'Life offers clear answers to those who know how to look.'[68] To read 'femininity' into this series of mostly angular, masculinised faces, is to end any sense of conflict about women's roles. Whatever one does as a woman will be 'natural'. Again, the legibility of externals is made to stand for a gratifying certainty without the problem of individual choice.

12. 'Life offers clear answers to those who know how to look'. Drawing of Gertrud Scholtz-Klink, *Frauen-Kultur*, November, 1936

Given this level of familiarity with images designed to address girls and women, it is hardly surprising that images of women in art featured in women's magazines and were able to draw on meanings established in art discourse, just as art was able to draw on meanings established by rituals of indoctrination. In several issues of the magazine *Frauen-Kultur*, images of women in art were set alongside images of sporting activity or items about clothing or crafts. For example, a slim, adolescent female nude by Kolbe accompanied a 1940 article about Goethe, in which a woman explained that Goethe's books had taught her to be dutiful and to derive strength from this.[69] Thus the idea which women's sports teachers were supposed to inculcate — that sport was undertaken because of 'the duty woman owes to her body, and with it to her descendants'[70] — was mapped onto the idea of loyalty to a German classical literary tradition, equally fit to ensure standards in the future. The other key idea linked to physical training was of pleasure in one's body, in recovery from the strains of life. Thorak, 'interviewed' for *Frauen-Kultur* in an article which reproduced a gigantic pair of male and female athletes by him, was made to say: 'we see with great pleasure how the new age has transformed the bodies of girls, and how sporty women have taken the place of the often coy, worldly, sick female forms [he has no need to add 'of the Weimar Republic']. Now women are full of joy in their physicality'.[71]

Women in sport were depicted in two main ways: either doing callisthenics, which was thought appropriate to the female nature, or at rest in line, hands by sides (as are the Kolbe and Thorak nudes in *Frauen-Kultur*), or holding javelins, standing to attention and ready for action. Perhaps the two types express the two ideas, duty and joy. It is useful to compare the meanings given to a photograph of girls standing in line with javelins (*Fig 13*) in a Party calendar for 1939,[72] with the athletic nudes of Thorak, Kolbe and Scheibe (*Figs 7, 8 and 9*).

13. 'Future Mothers', NSDAP Calendar, 1939

The calendar photograph is captioned: 'Future mothers' and 'earth which lies fallow is not joyful, nor is the woman who has grown beautiful but remains childless for a long time.' The caption and image associated the girls' javelins with spears of corn, in a sense demilitarising a military formation, invoking the ideology of women's separate but equivalent spheres. Sport is emptied here of its Socialist meaning of emancipation. The calendar refers to woman's healthy body as her 'dowry' for her husband and her nation. The military connotations were taken up again later in this calendar by the image of a female athlete with a swastika emblazoned on her T-shirt and with the caption: 'For us the blood is holy and inviolable'.[73] For women, images of female athletes may have been images of themselves as other people were supposed to see them, able to deflect the 'hate-filled eyes of the enemy'.[74] They may also have provided a gratifying reflection of the intense group identity, the feeling of belonging, which many women later remembered as the most important aspect of their *Bund deutscher Mädel* experience. Remember also Maschmann's account of being 'called' by the marching youths.

The female nude in art was also used to support the idea that Germany was a 'culture', a complete whole in which everyone participated, instead of a merely political state, a fragmentary parliamentary democracy. How this could be done is seen in a Strength Through Joy publication *Unter dem Sonnenrad* (Under the Swastika).[75]

This book attempted to demonstrate Hitler's great concern for leisure as a means to recovery, a concern said not to be shown by Marxists who had wanted to fill workers' leisure time with arid political lectures. Workers now, argued the book, do not need lectures because National Socialism is easy to understand. Now that material needs have been provided for, the state is building a culture 'from below'. Images of women were used to illustrate this paradoxical super-imposition of a culture 'from below'.

For example, a photograph of women dancing with their factory in the background was used to suggest a number of different ideas. Firstly, it was used to illustrate the newly found valuation of *Volkskunst* (folk art) which was said to be the special preserve of women (*Fig 14*). They were 'bearers of culture' in this sense too. Secondly, the image was used to sustain the argument that work was no longer a separate activity, no longer the basis of life, as in Marxist ideology. Thirdly, it was useful in casting a positive light on the fact that increasing numbers of women were having to enter the labour force. Rather than allow this to be viewed negatively in terms of their own earlier propaganda, as the unnatural incorporation of women into the male sphere of employment, women dancing, or, as in another photograph, basking in the sun-lit decorated courtyard of a newly built 'recovery area', could suggest a healthy feminine influence on working conditions.

The female nude appears four times in *Unter dem Sonnenrad*: firstly as a sculpture on a plinth outside a factory with workers walking past; secondly, as an antique female nude statue on a plinth in Pompei, whose gesture and position give the impression that she is beckoning to the two Strength Through Joy tourists who look up at her respectfully; thirdly, as a sculpture on a plinth in a factory art exhibition; and fourthly, as a naked model on a platform, arms raised, being sketched by men in an adult education art class. These nudes too helped give the impression of an art of the people that was also brought to the people.

The drawing of the female nude outside the factory, placed next to a sunshade (*Fig 15*), is used to contrast past with present. The description of the past invokes tired battalions of workers streaming to work in a grey morning light, divided from

14. Women and Folk Art, Women Dancing Outside a Factory, from *Unter dem Sonnenrad* (Under the Swastika), Strength Through Joy publication 1938

15. 'Schönheit der Arbeit', Beauty of Work, from *Unter dem Sonnenrad*, 1938

one another into different political parties and envying the capitalist in his luxury villa. Now, the image suggests, such a dim Socialist view of things is no longer appropriate. Now all workers belong to a shared culture where art is available and accessible. Accessibility without 'kitsch' was signalled by the female nude, and perhaps the fact that it was a female rather than a male nude suggested that this new culture was the product of concern rather than imposition. Woman as culture was being used to mediate the male Nazi state, with the ideological impetus again being to reverse the Marxist analysis of the economy and labour relations as the real determinants of culture. Workers were described as having longings for a culture they could participate in, irrespective of wealth, rather than for power or money; and these longings were said to have been 'stilled'.

Thus it would be extremely naïve to analyse the use of the female as 'Bearer of Culture' in terms of sexual gratification or compensation alone. The very terms used in Nazi discourse for the source of gratification that images of women in art were intended to provide, such as 'stilling longings' or 'nourishing the *Volk*',[76] indicate how very much more extensive were its intended meanings and emotional effects than the merely sexual. While in reality Nazification was a process of invading the private sphere and making it public, so the feminised self-image of the state as culture attempted to shore up the illusion that the public sphere was being privatised and returned to a 'natural' state.

Chapter Four

THE NATIONAL CHAMBER OF CULTURE (*REICHSKULTURKAMMER*) (1937)

Robert Brady

The law which established the National Chamber of Culture (September 22, 1933) was the first of three giving 'expression to the world view of the National Socialist leader-state.' The other two were the 'Law for Author Leaders' (October 4, 1933) and the 'Theatre Law' (May 15, 1934). Of these three laws, Dr. Karl-Friedrich Schreiber, Counsel for the National Chamber of Culture, says: 'The law for the National Chamber of Culture, including its enabling clauses, is a law without formal content; an organisation law without material standards. The Law for Leaders of Authors and the Theatre Law, on the other hand, go far beyond form and, with definite rules, reach immediately into the activities of the affected groups.

'The basic idea underlying the three laws can be brought into a simple formula: within the unity of creative function, primacy of the spiritual, suppression of the economic, subjection to the law of the people's community through filling the cultural professions with a definite sense of responsibility to the nation, assembly of a class of spiritual leaders dedicated to the task of overcoming a falsely understood freedom in the exercise of their professions, and thereby of eliminating the police principle of negative control.'[1] This means, that 'it is necessary to merge together the creative elements from all fields for carrying out, under the leadership of the state, a single will. . . .'

The National Chamber of Culture is given a large commission. 'Its main task is, and will be for a long time, to operate within the cultural professions *separating the tares from the wheat*, and to decide *between the fit and the unfit*. But fitness will not be determined by affiliation with this or that artistic trend, over whose ultimate value perhaps only coming generations can decide; but through *inner conformity with the will and being of the people*. To decide between the sound and the transitory, and *to divide by blood and spirit German from alien*, that is the 'direction' of National Socialist cultural leadership, since that is also only the direction of National Socialist will. [Italics by Schreiber.] What within the new forms will be created is a tremendous leader corps, made up out of all who participate in any wise in the process of forming the national will, from the greatest spiritual creations to the most insignificant helper, from the man who does the creative work to the last retailer who hawks literature and journals on the streets and at the railway stations.'[2]

The Chamber is, in short, to include everybody who practises in any of the arts and in any capacity for the sake of making a living. Membership in the chamber is compulsory upon all persons and all associations, whether citizen or foreign, engaged in the production, reproduction, promotion, management, direction, or participation in any other capacity whatsoever in the transmission of written, visual, or audible instruction or entertainment to the German people. Control over membership, associations, and activities is complete in every respect with exception of wages and certain specified price scales — these latter functions coming, respectively, under the control of Labour Trustees and various Price Commissioners.

The organisation of the National Chamber of Culture is extremely interesting, since it illustrates once again the full meaning of the combination of the Nazi 'total' and 'authority' principles. The application of these principles to the arts means that the Ministry of Propaganda and People's Enlightenment, operating through the Chamber, assumes complete 'authority' over the 'totality' of all phases of cultural life.

The skeleton of its structure is comparatively simple, as can readily be seen from *Figure 1*. It is made up of seven constituent member chambers:

The National Music Chamber.
The National Arts Chamber.
The National Theatre Chamber.
The National Literature Chamber.
The National Press Chamber.
The National Radio Chamber.
The National Film (Cinema) Chamber.

Each national chamber includes all activities falling under its control for the entire Reich. The first four and the Film Chamber are regionally divided, having each 31 regional and local representative bodies. A similar arrangement is planned for the Press and Radio Chambers. The local offices of the Radio and Film Chambers are at present under the direct control of representatives of the National Socialist Party.

As usual, the 'Leader' principle obtains throughout. The President, Vice-President, and Secretary of the National Chamber of Culture, and, through him, the officers of each of the member chambers, are appointed by and directly responsible to Dr. Goebbels, Minister of Propaganda and People's Enlightenment. They are personally responsible to him for the conduct of their offices, all the business and professional affairs over which each office has charge, and can be removed or overruled by him for any cause and at any time as he may see fit. The same powers are conferred on each officer under him, so far as the authority of this delegated 'Leader' may extend as defined by decree. . . .

Throughout all organisations the 'leader principle' obtains, and 'leaders', in addition to being always appointed from above, are typically drawn from business ranks. All the separate chambers and their member bodies are known as 'self-managing' groups, and function on the basis of 'private initiative' and competition, all conduct their activities so as to exclude new competition as far as possible and so to regulate prices and output as to be able to make satisfactory returns on capital invested for member enterprises. All are 'co-ordinated' to the 'will' of the National Socialist state that they may promote the goals which their inspired

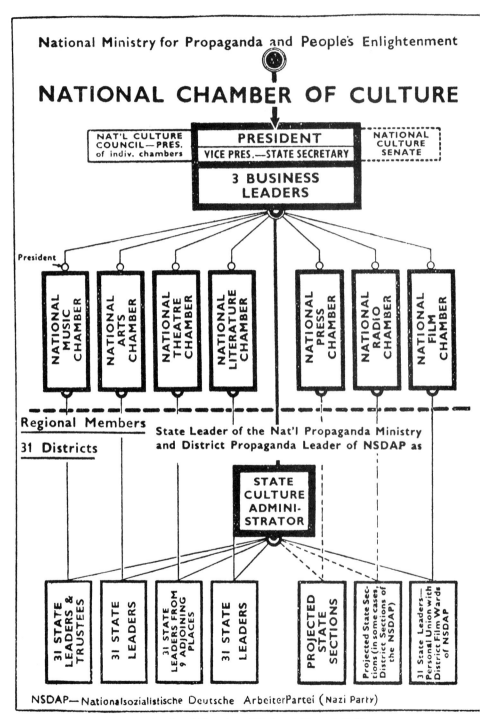

1. The *Reichskulturkammer* (National Chamber of Culture) [from A. B. Krause, *Organisation von Arbeit und Wistschaft*, Otto Eisner Verlag, Berlin]

leader, Adolf Hitler — and those subordinates to whom he may delegate the duty of being inspired — discover for them.

The goals, here as always, appear on the surface to present a serious paradox. If the purpose is to promote the joint economic advantage of the business community and their strong right arm, the army, how account for the rule cited above — that all member bodies of the National Chamber of Culture shall promote 'primacy of the spiritual' and 'suppression of the economic'? The Nazi literature allows no equivocation in reply; the answer lies readily at hand: All employees in all capacities should have their 'eyes diverted from the material to the spiritual values of the nation', and no business man should make money out of any of the arts and sciences by promotion of any point of view which militates against the ingeniously cultivated fancies of the disinherited. It is not that the people should not buy goods — far from it — but that they should not want to buy more goods than they can pay for out of the wages and salaries allowed them by their 'leaders' — 'leaders' perpetually engaged in plumbing the 'longing of the people' and so fulfilling their 'spiritual duties to the National Socialist people's community'!

Special plumber for people's 'longing', and sole mentor for instruction in the proper use of the arts is the National Socialist Community of Culture. Alfred Rosenberg, given charge by the 'Leader' of the 'entire programme for the education of the Party in spiritual and *Weltanschauung* matters', organised the National Socialist Community of Culture immediately upon accession of the Party to power. According to Dr. Ramlow, an official spokesman, the Community of Culture immediately took over the membership of the theatre-goers' union, some 300,000 in number, and from that nucleus expanded rapidly until it came to include, by the end of 1935, better than a million and a half members. According to another version, the bulk of the members now claimed came not from expansion but from absorption in 1934 of two other organisations, the 'Fighting League for German Culture', and the 'National Association of German Theatres', the latter of which counted over 500,000 members on its roster nearly a year before joining the National Socialist Community of Culture.[3]

The Community of Culture, as spiritual mentor of the National Chamber of Culture, concentrates on the organisation of clubs or circles through which the stimulation of the approved art is fostered. Thus the Community of Culture has organised an art ring, a theatre ring, a book ring, and a lecture ring. To these rings any true German may belong, whether or not a member of the Nazi Party. The membership fee is one mark per annum per ring.

By buying in blocks, thereby ensuring a reliable market, the Community of Culture can obviously secure greatly reduced rates on many things for its membership. Whatever it is that the members are interested in buying, they can, according to Dr. Ramlow, generally obtain at one-half the market price or less.

As possessor of the sole legal authority 'to set up an organisation of audiences, the National Socialist Community of Culture considered a strong structure of organisation its foremost problem. Being at the same time a *community of ideals* purporting to make vital contributions to the cultural reconstruction of the people, it *rigorously sees to it that admission to membership means a declaration of allegiance.*' Thus 'strong' and 'centralised . . . it feels united with its millions of adherents in the idea that a genuine reformation of Germany's cultural life can be achieved only through *unconditional devotion and perfect consistency.*'[4] To this end it has not only sponsored, but undertaken active management of, theatrical productions, exhibits, prize competitions, etc., but it has also organised its membership into some 2,000 local groups, each of which is in the care of a 'culture guardian'.

How it functions can be seen from brief examination of two of its main lines of functions: (1) those dealing directly with the theatre, and (2) those involved in agreements for co-operation worked out with other Nazi 'corporate formations'. These latter 'agreements' have been made with a considerable number of organisations; notably, with the Army, the Police, the National Association of Jurists, the National Socialist Students' League, the Labour Service, the General Inspector of the National Highways, the National Socialist Strength through Joy, and the Hitler Youth.

Up to the present the Community of Culture has concentrated upon co-ordination of the theatres to the National Socialist *Weltanschauung.* In performance of this function it sponsors plays, gives advice to Party officials who wish to take their 'followers' to the theatre *en masse,* sponsors the plays of 'unknown' writers who advocate Nazi viewpoints, arranges block sales of tickets, etc. More recently it has gone directly into the field of theatrical production.

The latter are of two sorts — those given in large metropolitan theatres, and those given in rural areas by small travelling theatres. Productions which prove successful in Berlin, Munich, and other large cities are sent out to travel through all the large cities of Germany. For this purpose the Berlin Theater am Nollendorf-platz has been used as a sort of 'culture laboratory' for the development of model plays, model theatrical leadership, model players, and model audiences. Here the Community of Culture has worked out a 'Play Plan' including historic drama, folk plays, and other types of productions which comply with the 'new German style'.

A number of *News in Brief* propaganda leaflets, for the 'information' of foreign journalists, gives examples of the types of plays reproduced. A cantata called *A Man Builds a Cathedral* represented 'the first attempt on a large scale to cast into a mould of art the great experience of the last twenty years and the sentiment and faith of the new "myths"' and 'demonstrated the possibility ... of giving ... a religious meaning to our national resurrection.' An opera, *The Return of Joerg Tilman,* by 'leaning on Greek drama' and employing 'interlocking music' gave 'heroic' effects 'both as to talent and intention' to battle scenes. Of this opera a commentator writes: 'The battlefield an opera! The trench a scene! Does this not imply a danger?' If the excited Nazi can survive the thrills of such 'great music drama expressing the soul of our age' he can then go to a moving picture called *Culture and Everyday* which demonstrates that 'in the last analysis every film ought to be a cultural film.'[5]

Whether this same mixture of pomposity and the *opera bouffe* obtains in the travelling theatres is difficult to say. Apparently, somewhat the same type of production is shown, though there appears to be greater stress on folk plays and subject matter than is the case with the metropolitan theatres. Some 24 of these 'wandering theatres' were active in Germany by the middle of 1935, carrying the gospel of National Socialism into villages and outlying hamlets all over the Reich.

The influence of the Community of Culture does not stop with mere sponsoring and management of theatrical productions. According to Künkler, its 'theatre division has taken over the sifting of the entire dramatic production of the present time'. How extensive its labours have been can be seen from the fact that 'in a single year the censor of the Theatre Division tested over 3,000 manuscripts.'[6]

The criteria by which manuscripts are judged is indicated clearly by Goebbels. Speaking at a meeting of the heads of the various member chambers of the National Chamber of Culture he said: 'The National Socialist state must, on principle, uphold the point of view that *art is free* and that attempts should never be made toward replacing intuition with organisation. *Art as such can only flourish when given the greatest possible freedom of development.* Those who think that they can confine art or civilisation in general within fixed limits are sinning against art and civilisation. When I say 'art is free', I wish to steer clear of the opinion, on the other hand, as though absolutely anarchical tendencies in art should be given free vent. However free art must and can be within its own laws of evolution, *it must feel itself closely connected with the elemental laws of national life. Art and civilisation are implanted in the mother soil of the nation. They are, consequently, for ever dependent upon the moral, social, and national principles of the state.*'[7]

Art and artists have, in other words, 'the spiritual duty' to place themselves 'into a *correct angle* with regard to themselves and the people', and to receive 'inspiration only from the national character in its totality'. That is to say, it must be controlled, root and branch, by the National Socialist *Weltanschauung,* which, as Alfred Rosenberg is very careful to state, expresses 'a definite view of the world'. Preliminary to adoption of this point of view, he says, it is necessary to '*break the philosophy of democratic levelling . . .*' Only then will it be possible to 'attach once more a direct value to our unbiased eye and therewith to our unspoiled instincts as against the speculative theorems of hollow fancies.'[8]

With this same idea of co-ordinating 'free art' to obey such National Socialist doctrinal pronouncements, the Community of Culture has established a special youth division known as the 'Culture Community of the Youth'. Its duty is '. . . to unify all efforts directed towards the cultural education of the youth. Accordingly it endeavours to harmonise all efforts of school officials, the National Socialist Teachers' Federation, the Labour Service, the Hitler Youth, and other service bureaux in order to achieve the cultural objectives of the youth.'[9]

The objective is that 'culture shall become an iron strength in the personal life' of the youth, who, with 'hearts beating in unison' will be 'welded into a voluntary service community which will cut across all formations, occupational groups, and layers of the population.' Culture, in short, will become a weapon for co-ordinating the youth to National Socialism through creating 'receptivity of the ear, the eye, and the heart for the great master of works of German art.' With this receptivity will go, they expect, a willingness to give 'voluntary service because of an inner personal sense of duty. . . .' The youth will thereby be 'assembled and bound into a cultural works community.'

To this end they select those cultural activities for special stress which play most effectively upon youthful love of play, delight in novelty, and sense of humour. Activities promoted include youth theatres and films, puppet theatres, lay and folk plays, holiday celebrations, folk music, and writing competitions. The number of puppet theatres included in this programme is especially extensive, and apparently pretty well attended.

The prize competitions for works written by children indicate somewhat less success. This may be because the competitions are restricted to those with an 'unconditionally reliable *Weltanschauung*', must promote National Socialist doctrines in all respects, and are judged solely by officials from the Nazi Party. At any rate, an announcement of such a prize competition in the *Völkischer Beobachter,* official party medium, gave as the reason for the competition being opened that, 'despite the large number of new publications there is scarcely an inexpensive manuscript in which *Weltanschauung* questions and the necessities of National Socialist instruction in the schools and in the educational work of the youth associations is handled.'[10]

In one other respect the work of the Community of Culture is particularly significant, and that is in connection with the National Socialist Community Strength through Joy. This organisation has control of all recreational activities of the central control body over labour, the Labour Front. Inasmuch as the purpose of the Labour Front is to 'neutralise' anti-employer and pro-trade union sentiment on the one hand, and to 'abolish' the class war on the other through 'diverting the gaze of the masses from material things and towards the spiritual values of the nation', collaboration here with the central Nazi Party organisation to which is delegated responsibility for all 'point-of-view' affairs is of great importance.

A good deal of this work, however, seems to be shrouded in mystery. The Strength through Joy organisation works openly with the Community of Culture in the theatrical field, the latter making a general rule of sponsoring plays being put on in theatres owned by the former. There are a number of such theatres scattered around throughout the larger cities of the Reich. Outside of the theatrical field, little can be told about the exact nature of the co-operation, though it seems clear that the Community of Culture is in close and active contact with the Strength through Joy organisation in all phases of the latter's work with the exception of its excursion and travel programme.

As a final step in explanation of the Nazi programme for the co-ordination of the arts and sciences, mention should be made of the nature of formal governmental control through the Ministries in charge of religious affairs, education, and propaganda.

Three Ministries divide the work of regimenting the mental, emotional, and cultural life of all good Germans. Reichsminister Kerrl has charge in the Ministry for Ecclesiastical Affairs of all religious matters. Rust rules all-powerful over the Ministry for Science, Education, and National Culture. And Goebbels has supreme command of the third and central propaganda co-ordinating body, the Ministry for Propaganda and People's Enlightenment. . . .

Speaking on the subject 'Art and Propaganda', Dr. Goebbels said: 'We have been criticised frequently for degrading German art to the level of mere propaganda. 'Degrade' — how so? Is propaganda a matter to which anything else can be degraded? Is not propaganda as we understand it a kind of art? . . . Would it mean degradation for art, if it were placed side by side with that noble art of mass psychology which was instrumental in saving the Reich from destruction?'

And it is in the hands of Goebbels that all propaganda activity — through newspapers, periodicals, publishing, the radio, the church, the school, the public forum, and all other media for influencing the mass of the people — is centralised. He is at once National Propaganda Leader for the Nazi Party, Minister of Propaganda and People's Enlightenment on behalf of the Government, and President of the National Chamber of Culture in the name of the arts themselves. In each capacity he wields, subject only to check from Hitler himself, all-inclusive, absolute, and final authority. He has the right to suspend any publication, forbid the performance of any play, deny the privilege of utterance over the radio or through any medium to any person, close down any school, institute, or museum, and punish any person for any real or imaginary offence if and when he pleases. He

86

appoints all officials under him, and delegates to them the type of authority he wields over all.

He can issue decrees at will, and rescind those previously issued at his pleasure. He need not in any wise or at any time observe any 'due process of law' except as he may please. And nothing in Germany has any chance of escaping his drag-net. The Ministry is divided into nine main departments — Administration and Law, Propaganda, Radio, Press, Film, Theatre, Defence, Writing, Music and the Plastic Arts. Each department has complete and final control over all activities falling into its bailiwick. And each of them is represented in the 31 regional offices of the Ministry.

Likewise under his immediate direction comes publication of the official Nazi newspaper, the *Völkischer Beobachter* (Alfred Rosenberg as editor), and 310 other newspapers scattered throughout all sections of the country and reaching into every nook and cranny of the Reich. Through the Advertising Council of German Economy he has control over all advertising and public relations activities. Through the German University for Politics he controls the present central 'leader' training school. And finally, as indicated above, through the National Chamber of Culture, and its allied associations, leagues, and guilds, he has complete authority over all the audible, vocal, and visual arts.

As supreme co-ordinator of all attitude-shaping and opinion-forming activities, this immense, complicated, and meticulously organised machinery serves Goebbels in two capacities. In the first place, it is an elaborate and apparently very effective intelligence service, whereby he is enabled to keep in close and constant touch with all expressions of opinion and all changes in popular moods, whether these centre around large national problems, or whether they are focused on minutiæ of administrative routine in the most out-of-way corner of the Reich. 'We wish', he said on one occasion, 'to put our ears to the soul of the people'. And now he has at his beck and call means for catching every modulation of tone, every murmur of dissent.

But scanning the popular mood is only preliminary to constant readjustment of the propaganda for conquest. The second function of the machinery at the call of the Ministry for Propaganda and People's Enlightenment is to put over the Nazi ideology — to put it over with every class, every group, every interest. As the group varies, and the class interests change, so must the propaganda be modulated, fitted, and adjusted. If possible, it must be made palatable to all. But — and on this point Goebbels, as with all other Nazi leaders, is perfectly candid — it must be accepted by each and every man, woman, and child, whether the means be force or guile.

Just what is Goebbels, chief propaganda and public relations director of a capitalist-militarist state, attempting to put across with the German people? What is his principal concern? Wherein lies the heart of his doctrine and the core of his attack? Who most needs to be convinced, and for what purposes? What does his 'ear', as he places it to hear the responses emanating from 'the soul of the people', tell him it is important to do?

A veritable mountain of Nazi literature on ideology prevents all possible equivocation in reply. The new state stresses 'the folk', the 'community', 'comradeship', 'communal labour', 'unity'. As pointed out above . . . these are slogans designed to give a pleasant front to the drive against 'class war', 'Marxists', 'trade unions', 'internationalism'. As Ley, Leader of the Labour Front, expressed it on one occasion, the chief concern of the National Socialist Party was 'the struggle for the worker's soul'. Organised labour, and all groups or interests antagonistic to business capital, are to be crushed completely, finally, ruthlessly, and at all costs.

Goebbels' activities constitute the German answer to the current drive of business men all over the world — to prevent the drift towards the left by neutralising or crushing all organised dissident opinion and all organised opposition activity. The labour programme of the National Association of Manufacturers (U.S.A.) and the 'spirit' of such as the New Deal, of the Oxford Movement, of the Nazi *Weltanschauung*, the novel *Eyeless in Gaza* (Aldous Huxley) and the *A New Nobility out of Blood and Soil* (Darré — in German), spring from the same basic set of drives, and are actuated by the same common goals. To deny division of interest; to circumvent or crush those who believe or act upon such assumptions; to argue, wheedle, entice, and cajole if these methods are effective, but if necessary to use unrestrained force — these are the defensive manœuvres set in motion throughout the capitalistic world today by the ever-widening forces of social unrest.

The crux of the Nazi programme for the sciences and the arts — as, indeed, of all Nazi programmes, civil and military, domestic and foreign — is to be found in their 'struggle for the worker's soul'.

Chapter Five

ARTISTS AND ART INSTITUTIONS IN GERMANY 1933–1945

Christine Fischer-Defoy

Background history and conditions

Before examining the relationship between artists and art institutes under German fascism, I should like first to give some background information to the two institutions which I shall be discussing: the Academy, and the College of Art in Berlin (*Fig 1*). Founded in 1696, their task was to train both artists and craftsmen. Although they shared a common administration until 1931, the College fulfilled a teaching function and the Academy played a purely representative role. In the nineteenth century, influenced by the Romantic concept of art as autonomous, they concentrated upon 'free' art. In 1868 a second college, the Teaching Institute of the *Kunstgewerbemuseum*, was founded, initially as a private school. This was officially recognised in 1885 and equipped craftsmen with skills and techniques.

In 1907 Bruno Paul, one of the founders of the *Deutsche Werkbund*, became director of the Teaching Institute of the *Kunstgewerbemuseum*. At the Academy, however, the appointment of Arthur Kampf as director in 1915 saw no change to the Wilhelminian régime which had characterised the forty-year tenure of his predecessor, the art historian Anton von Werner. After the First World War, Paul sought the reunification and synthesis of autonomous and 'applied' art and founded the *Vereinigte Staatschulen für freie und angewandte Kunst* (Union of National Colleges for Free and Applied Art). In these all the workshops were available for common use, so that the students had the opportunity to move freely between the different departments. Paul explained the concept thus in 1932: 'So, for example, sculptors engage in calligraphy, pattern designers draw nudes, architects do painting exercises and painters from the independent departments take part in architectural exercises. The foundation of the teaching is thus much broader, its outlook directed in a variety of ways to what is practical.'[1]

The *Vereinigte Staatsschulen*'s framework was characterised by a concept of art and teaching embodied in its director, Bruno Paul, a founder member of the German *Werkbund*. This was a concept which integrated the arts and craft skills from their previously separate areas (architecture, painting, sculpture, graphics) and addressed them to the changing and changeable tasks broadly set by the community as a whole. In one of his last talks before his enforced resignation in 1932, Paul redefined the task of the artist: 'Once again the artist's work is today intervening in almost every aspect of economic life. Our trade and industry depends, to a

89

1. The Akademische Hochschule für die bildenden Künste, Berlin, *c* 1920

great extent, on artistic creativity: house building, furniture design, glass, cera-mics, furniture and clothes fabrics, linoleum, tool-making — all this needs guid-ance from the artist. So does the design of houses, office blocks, tramcars, railway carriage compartments and car bodywork.'[2]

At the beginning of 1933 the faculty of the *Vereinigte Staatsschulen* included Karl Hofer, Oskar Schlemmer, Cesar Klein and Emil Rudolf Weiss as well as the sculptors Gies, Gerstel and Scharff. The position of Director was occupied by the painter Max Kutschmann ('already seven years a party member' as he proudly wrote in 1934), who was responsible for co-ordinating the *Künstlervereine* (Asso-ciation of Artists), whose administration and courses were to suffer many changes of personnel and content during the next few years. On an appointed day, 1 April 1933, the German National Socialist Union of Students proclaimed themselves as the embodiment of the 'rage of the people', as they had done during the notorious burning of library books. They erected a banner in the entrance hall of the Hardenbergstrasse building, publicly denouncing Hofer, Gies, Weiss, Klein and the others as being Jewish-Marxist elements and calling for them to be boycotted. The changes in the balance of political power affected the students and their teachers in different ways as they became involved in the interplay of artistic, poli-tical and racist motives which can be inferred from the slogan 'Jewish cultural bolshevism'. The inconsistency of the measures taken during the following few months reflects the general lack of clarity in National Socialist art policies before 1937 (see below) and is characteristic of the arbitrary political repression and intimidation which occurred during the first phase of the 'conquest of power'. Several professors of art lost their jobs (including Richard Scheibe in Frankfurt) but were re-instated under the law governing Civil Service conditions which, until 1937, determined the political and racial boundaries of acceptability. During that year the requisite National Socialist artistic standpoint was legally clarified and enacted and their employment terminated.

A law prohibiting the 'overfilling of German schools and colleges' led to the exmatriculation of nearly ten percent of the enrolled students. This affected student representatives, those involved in leftist student organisations and the few Jewish students. Further radical artistic change and the appointment of a second wave of new personnel took place in 1937–1938. This coincided with the preparation and display of the Munich exhibition of *Entartete Kunst* (Degenerate Art) and with the outlawing of German Expressionism which was replaced by pseudo-classical, heroic, official German art. During the World War II the College finally abandoned all independence and submitted itself to the direction of the German propaganda ministry to fulfil propaganda tasks important to the war effort.

In 1920, Max Liebermann, one of the founders of the Secession, became president of the *Akademie der Künste*. Nevertheless, the Academy preserved its conservative tradition and modern artists never gained leading positions, although they were represented by Käthe Kollwitz, Karl Hofer and Otto Dix, for example. A painting — *Der Tolle Platz* (1931) — by Felix Nussbaum illustrates this: students of the *Hochschule* demonstrate with their paintings in front of the Academy building, which houses the old guard, while Max Liebermann stands on the roof of his collapsing establishment.

In May 1932, Liebermann resigned on grounds of age to be succeeded by the nationalist Max von Schillings. His first vice-president was Hans Poelzig. The National Socialist press denounced him as *Kommunistenförderer und Judenfreund* (Communist supporter and friend of the Jews) and forced his resignation in January 1933. Max von Schillings was an eager advocate of NS cultural policy and forced Käthe Kollwitz and Heinrich Mann to resign their membership because they had signed a political appeal for anti-fascist unity.

The *Berufsbeamtentumsgesetz* (Amendment to the Civil Service Tenure Law) was used to force Jewish Academy members to quit. In spring 1933 they were excluded from taking part in the Academy exhibition, a move followed by a radical 'cleaning up' similar to that in the *Hochschule* during the *Entartete Kunst* exhibition of 1937. Among those who resigned were Hofer, Pechstein, Nolde, Barlach, Mies van der Rohe, Kirchner, Dix and Kokoschka. Until this point members of the AdK had been able to employ one of their few executive prerogatives — the award of the scholarship to the Villa Romana and the *Staatspreis* to be held in Rome — for the benefit of endangered artists. Following the *Grosse deutsche Kunstausstellung* (Great German Art Exhibition) of 1937 in Munich the country's cultural centre became increasingly located in that city. In 1936 the last exhibition of the *Akademie der Künste* took place in Berlin. The war postponed a reorganisation of the *Akademie der Künste* and the replacement of excluded members by new ones was put off. So, for example, Arno Breker never became a member of the *Akademie der Künste*. In 1949 the Akademie was refounded in East Berlin under the presidency of the writer Arnold Zweig. Then in 1954 a second *Akademie der Künste* was founded as a 'counter measure' in West Berlin. The destiny of the *Akademie der Künste* thus became an element in the Cold War and the division of Germany.

Kulturbolschewismus

If individual conformity with the political and racial qualifications imposed on the Civil Service was widely used to enforce the new system in 1933, the decisive criteria after the *Entartete Kunst* exhibition was that of *Kulturbolschewismus* (Cultural Bolshevism). This vaguely defined, and therefore all-embracing, slogan was used as a cultural equivalent to the term 'Marxism' in the field of politics to denote everything that could be identified with the *Systemzeit* or the Weimar Republic. In other words, by disregarding the fatal differences in the workers' movement it could cover the whole range of social democratic, socialist and communist tendencies. *Kulturbolschewismus* gave way to *System-Kunst*, an expression used to cover the whole trail of changes in the arts which had been left in the wake of the November Revolution in 1918. It was distinguished by its openness towards technology and the media; sparseness of means; rejection of decoration and its functionally determined role in the community, i.e. the integration of art in everyday life. To what extent this final aim was achieved is unfortunately questionable. Between 1933 and 1945 the fascist state appropriated and mobilised the concept of a 'healthy popular consciousness' which was antipathetical to these ideas.

A further criterion of Nazi art politics was the rejection of all 'isms' that could be regarded as French or un-German. Any breakdown of form, be it through Impressionism, Expressionism or Cubism, was considered as a manifestation of irrationalism and, in the final analysis, as in the *Entartete Kunst* exhibition, the product of a mentally sick person. This combination of populist awareness and the rejection of 'degenerate art' began to be mobilised long before 1933.

An example illustrating this is the fate of the sculptor Ludwig Gies and his work. Born in 1887, he was a teacher at the Teaching Institute of the *Kunstgewerbemuseum* (Museum of Arts and Crafts) in Berlin after 1917. His *Crucifixion(Fig 2)* for Lübeck Cathedral was put up there on a trial basis. However, opposition to it gathered around the poet Julius Havemann, who wrote: 'When I look at this Crucifixion I am wounded at the deepest level of my religious experience. It is the body of a degenerate, of a withered proletarian, long resigned in its feebleness, poverty and lowness to pedantic selfishness and capitulation in the face of life.'[3] Here, in 1921, art is already being assessed according to criteria that were generally used to determine political art only after 1933. At this early stage, the attack was only directed against this one particular work. Unidentified individuals knocked the head off the Crucifix in 1922 and it was sunk in a mill pond in Lübeck. The figure was reconstructed and displayed once again in 1937, this time at the exhibition of Degenerate Art. As a result Gies lost his job in 1938 and in the same year his sculpture was finally destroyed. After the War, he worked as a teacher from 1950 to 1964 at the Technical School of Art in Cologne and died in 1966.

By isolating its work under the heading of 'degenerate' or 'Bolshevist', the whole of the modern school was effectively banished by 1937–1938. This process reached a climax in 1939 when, in a delayed parallel to the burning of the books carried out in 1933, 1004 oil paintings and 3824 water colours, sketches and graphics were officially burned in the Köpenick fire station in Berlin.

One further example of the campaign waged against 'decadent' art which began before 1933 can be seen in the destruction of Oskar Schlemmer's murals in the Weimar *Bauhaus*; on the orders of Wilhelm Frick, the National Socialist Home Secretary in Thuringia, these were painted over in 1930.

2. Ludwig Gies, *Crucifixion,*
1922

Antisemitism

The expulsion of Jewish artists from cultural life can only be briefly mentioned
here. This fundamental racist violation of human rights was directed against a
part of the population which had made a cultural contribution of enormous qualitative and quantitative significance during the twenties that is too great to discuss
in the context of the arts and Fascism. However, the names of some of those who
lost their jobs or were murdered for racist reasons should be mentioned: the
graphic artist Ernst Böhm; the art historian Oskar Fischel; the painter Curt Lahs;
the student Felix Nussbaum; the student Charlotte Salomon; the architect Franz
von Seeck and the painter Emil Rudolf Weiss.

  While all Jewish College teachers lost their jobs under the law regulating civil
service employment, another ruling allowed for 1.5% of students to be of Jewish
descent as long as their fathers had served in the First World War. The painter
Charlotte Salomon, who studied from 1936–1938, was among these exceptions.
In 1938 she emigrated to the South of France and from there she was deported to
Auschwitz, where she was murdered in 1943. In the years preceding her deporta-

tion she painted her life story in a series of 1000 gouache drawings under the title of 'Life or Theatre'. Through a depiction of the fate of her family in Berlin during the twenties and thirties, these pictures reflect a view which is at once both very subjective and yet captures the universal nature of racial affliction. Visual art, music, theatre and film are displayed as a realm of events occurring against a background drawn from the experience of daily fascist persecution. These two elements are united in a work of cultural history seen from the viewpoint of a Jewish artist who was not yet 25 years old.

The *Bauhaus*

The *Bauhaus* concept and its disintegration under National Socialism can best be indicated here through the example of Oskar Schlemmer. Born in 1888, Schlemmer studied under Hölzel in Stuttgart and game to teach at the *Bauhaus* in Weimar during 1920. In 1923 he designed the murals for the entrance to the workshop building there, where Schlemmer already realised an artistic perspective which conflicted emotionally with the National Socialist view of mankind. He sought to depict forms in their essential simplicity, without emotion and without dramatic movement: 'Because the abstraction of the human figure, if that is what concerns us, creates an image in a higher sense, it creates not the essentially natural man, but a likeness, a symbol of the human figure.'[4] The murals were destroyed as early as 1930 on the orders of the racial theorist and Director of the Weimar College of Art, Schultze-Naumburg.

In 1925 Schlemmer himself moved with the *Bauhaus* to settle in Dessau. When this was closed in 1932, he made some effort to be appointed to the *Vereinigte Staatsschulen*, taking over the perspective section in the Faculty of Fine Arts. This teaching commission came as a result of correspondence and discussion with the College director Bruno Paul and with Paul Hindemith, which in turn led Schlemmer to write to the Prussian Minister for Science, Art and Popular Education setting his ideas out for a teaching post in Berlin. The physical proximity of the *Vereinigte Staatsschulen* in Hardenbergstrasse to the *Hochschule für Musik* in Fasanenstrasse, combined with the hopes for the integration of the two which the *Vereinigte Staatsschulen* had nursed from its inception, seemed to Schlemmer to offer optimal conditions for the realisation of his concept for teaching 'stage-studios'. He had already published several outlines of this in Breslau and it seemed to him to have a realistic chance of success in the German capital: 'What was possible in Dessau, in a small space and with modest means, we can put into practice better and more easily in Berlin, where all the threads of intellectual and artistic life run together.'[5] During ministerial discussions he mentioned such people as Hindemith, Mary Wigman, Gret Palucca, Gropius, Klee, Feininger and Kandinsky as referees.

By the beginning of June 1932 Schlemmer had received a contract of employment to work at the *Vereinigte Staatsschulen* in the Hardenbergstrasse, a fortunate appointment, which he hoped would be unaffected by the Nazi seizure of power. On 8 November 1932 he gave his inaugural lecture. Out of the 300 students at the school, 62 enrolled for his lectures on 'Perspective for Painters and Sculptors'. His plans for the *Bühnenstudios* (stage studios) failed however, both because of the *Vereinigte Staatsschulen*'s internal politics as well as its relationship with the *Hochschule für Musik* which was also in the throes of a political takeover.

Within the *Vereinigte Staatsschule* the arguments over the relationship between free and applied arts had reached a high point, culminating in major attacks on Bruno Paul who, as Director, embodied the idea of unifying the Academy and the School of Technical Crafts. Running in parallel with this was a second political view which complained about the 'Jewish director of the Academy' and which gave some indication of the threatening measures which were employed in the next few years. The two attacks together led Paul to leave his post on 31 December 1932 and to head a disciplinary inquiry against himself.

Oskar Schlemmer's enthusiasm for the teaching possibilities in Berlin at first remained unblemished by the political developments around him. In February 1933 he wrote: 'So far the Academy has escaped the attention of Nazi politics . . . perhaps, if the situation becomes critical, I'll be rescued by "perspective"!' It sounds so unpolitical.[6] On 1 April 1933, however, a banner hanging in the entrance hall to the *Vereinigte Staatsschulen* denounced him together with Hofer, Weiss, Gies, Reger and Wolfsfeld as 'destructive Jewish-Marxist elements'; it called for the boycott of his classes and made confrontation inevitable. A student of the time described the scene retrospectively: 'On both sides of this banner stood students in Nazi uniform, brown shirts. I can still see today Professor Schlemmer coming into the hall, a book in his hand, playfully swinging it to and fro. Hesitating, he stopped in front of the banner. "What lies" he shouted, and hit the banner with his book. But not one of the students in uniform laid a finger on him!'[7] However, his contract of employment was terminated on 30 September 1933.

The letter of departure which Kutschmann wrote to Schlemmer in the college's name was almost cynically pleasant: 'You were one of us for only a short time. You had hoped to work here in the long term, and to pursue your way in peace. It has turned out otherwise.'[8] Schlemmer's reply expressed his hope that a revival of German idealism would overcome the injustices being suffered at present: 'I would like those forces which led German idealism in art to victory, to come alive in the National Union of Colleges. Hope and belief in that may then help appease the injustices which have now befallen me and so many others.'[9] Having lost his job, Schlemmer travelled first to Switzerland. In 1934 he returned to Germany, initially working in a painting firm. His application for acceptance to the *Reichskulturkammer* (Reich Chamber of Culture) was refused on the grounds that his past political leanings together with his form of artistic expression made him a typical exponent of 'cultural bolshevism': 'In 1921 Schlemmer entered the *Bauhaus* in Weimar and was in overall charge of these communist movements. From Dessau he moved to the Union of National Colleges for Applied Art, Charlottenburg. Hardenbergstrasse 33. He was a professor there, but was expelled as a typical representative of degenerate art on 30th September 1933.' He was a member of the 'Sturm- und Aktion' circle . . .[10] In 1940 Schlemmer was taken on in a paint factory and made responsible for camouflage painting in the armaments industry. He died in 1943 in Baden-Baden.

In 1929, Hannes Meyer had been dismissed as director of the *Bauhaus*, accused of being a Marxist. In 1930 he was succeeded by Mies van der Rohe who proclaimed a 'neutral' attitude in the school. Nevertheless, the *Bauhaus* in Dessau was closed in October 1932 and all its staff dismissed. Mies van der Rohe rented an old factory building in Berlin at his own expense and the school's teaching programme resumed in January 1933. In April, the building was searched by the police and afterwards closed. After several months of discussion between van der Rohe and Alfred Rosenberg, the *Bauhaus* received a letter stating his conditions for its re-opening, starting with the dismissal of Wassily Kandinsky in line with the

Berufsbeamtentumsgesetz. These were unacceptable and so the assembly of teachers decided to close the school on 20 July 1933. Most of them emigrated to the U.S.A.

Neue Sachlichkeit (New Objectivity)

The relationship of *Neue Sachlichkeit* to Fascism will be illustrated here by the example of the painter Georg Schrimpf, who was born in Munich in 1889. Trained as a baker, he worked in Leipzig and Berlin as well as travelling around Europe before arriving in Munich in 1913. A legacy enabled him to devote himself to drawing and painting. Apart from eight days spent in a private painting school, he remained self-taught throughout his life. A meeting with Maria Graf (*Fig 3*) and some of the Expressionists decided the line his work was to follow and his first graphics were printed in the magazine *DieAktion* in 1913. He spent the first year of the war working in a chocolate factory and painting posters in the KaDeWe in Berlin. There he met Herzfelde, Grosz and the Dadaists. Having married Marie Uhden, he returned to Munich. Her sudden death on the birth of their first child made a lasting impression on his future artistic endeavours in which he repeatedly returned to the mother and child theme. In 1918 he took part in the revolution in Munich and participated in the *Räterepublik* (Munich Soviet Republic) in 1919. During the same year he joined the KPD and remained with them until 1926. He was also a supporter of the *Rote Hilfe* and its work.

3. Georg Schrimpf,
Portrait of Oskar Maria Graf, 1918

If his early output, particularly his graphics, still carried the traits of expressionism, he became an exponent of *Neue Sachlichkeit* in the mid twenties. The Mannheim *Neue Sachlichkeit* exhibition of 1925 developed the concept into a style which the exhibition organiser, G. F. Hartlaub, referred to as 'post-expressionist' and in the catalogue he praised its search for truth and certainty in a period of resigned pessimism: 'That the artist — betrayed, disillusioned, often resigned to the point of cynicism, nearly himself giving up, after a moment of boundless, almost apocalyptic trust — ponders, in the midst of catastrophe, on what is most immediate, most certain and most durable: truth and craft.'[11]

Two tendencies can be distinguished within the general concept of *Neue Sachlichkeit*: first, the so-called 'left', those who were social critics and who chose objects which referred to the social realities around them (Dix, Grosz, Hubbuch etc.) and second the 'Timeless' or 'Italian' tendency, which orientated itself around the classical eternal laws of Being or necessity in human beings and nature. Connections with the Italian *pittura metafisica* were both formal and personal. Their close relationship with Italian Fascism is widely recognised.

Schrimpf belonged to this latter group. Their ideology, which was held without hesitation in fascist Germany, was defined by Richard Bie in an article published in 1930 in which he describes *Neue Sachlichkeit* expressing a truly German visual approach as opposed to the imported Impressionism of France, Germany's 'hereditary enemy'. In it he finds the values of 'true breeding', 'commitment to discipline and loyalty', 'masculine clarity' realised without any deception but according to the laws of absolute truth: 'The artist must prove himself before nature. He confronts it with deep respect and his craft consists in nothing else than following the harmonious order and purposive simplicity of the world.' The artist's social and political position are expressed through his satisfaction with imposing order on social chaos: 'Everything which in the town tends towards anarchy, here finds its way back to the ordering of men and the world.'[12] If Bie saw parallels with Dürer, who in his eyes was the greatest craftsman in German art, Schrimpf saw himself as inheriting the tradition of Caspar David Friedrich and Rembrandt. In 1933 he described his art as being motivated by the desire to be clear, simple and unambiguous (*Fig 4*).

In 1933 Alexander Kanoldt, who with Schrimpf was one of the earliest followers of the 'Idealist' tendency in the *Neue Sachlichkeit* movement, was appointed to the newly-vacated position of director of the *Staatliche Kunstchule* (National College of Art) in Berlin. Kanoldt, a member of the NSDAP, appointed Schrimpf to the position of professor in the College during the same year, after an SS attack in February had effected a 'clean up' there which resulted in the dismissal of many Expressionist teachers such as Georg Tappert (*Fig 5*). The appointment of Karl Rössing brought another representative of the new movement onto the faculty. He had been directly associated with the 'Leftish' side of *Neue Sachlichkeit* before 1933 (e.g. the series of wood engravings *Mein Vorurteil gegen diese Zeit* (*Fig 6*) but in 1933 joined the NDSAP and committed his future artistic services to the 'glorification' of power (*Fig 7*). These changes guaranteed Rössing's prominence, as numerous state commissions, from Rudolf Hess among others, testify.

In 1937 Kanoldt was promoted, however, and his successor, a party member called Zimbal, exposed Schrimpf's political past and denounced him as a former KPD member. In doing so he made reference to his important contribution to the most recent developments in art as well as to his loyalty to National Socialism: 'I

4. Georg Schrimpf, *View of the Black Forest*, 1936

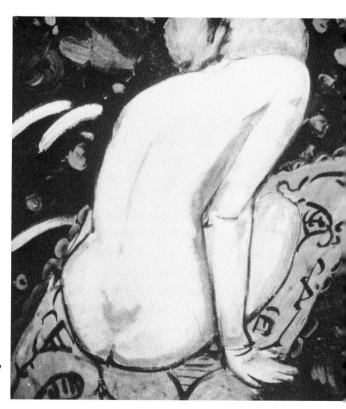

5. Georg Tappert,
Green Nude, 1910

98

6. Karl Rössing, *From the German Märchenwald* (the series My Prejudice Against These Times), 1928

7. Karl Rössing, *Götz von Berlichingen* (undated mural)

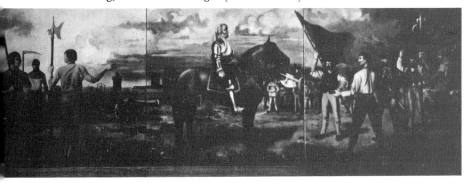

can confirm after the most thorough examination, that Professor Schrimpf is wholly and fully loyal to Adolf Hitler and his Empire.'[13] Schrimpf's situation was further aggravated when his earlier pictures were shown at the exhibition of 'degenerate art'. Under the Civil Service Employment Law, he was now given notice on 23 September 1937. The NS student leader pleaded on his behalf, claiming that he represented the modern German style of landscape painting,[14] but this had no more effect in hindering the dismissal than the fact that Schrimpf was working on a commission for Hess at the time. In spite of his formal dismissal, he nevertheless retained his studio at the Academy and received a further commission at the beginning of 1938. His application for membership of the *Reichskultur-kammer*, which was a prerequisite of any freelance activities, was turned down in February 1938: 'His art developed in the years after the war under the category of "Degenerate Art". Later he changed his outlook and turned to so-called New Objectivity . . . Bearing in mind his earlier and strongly hostile attitude . . . no guarantees of his political reliability can be accepted.'[15] Schrimpf died a few months later on 19 April 1938.

In all of this, Schrimpf is typical of a series of artists (such as Dix and Rössing) whose political positions changed in line with the power relations that developed in the twenties and who found artistic expression which corresponded to that change. While Dix escaped, both physically and artistically, into the German countryside (which like Schrimpf he idealised with the finest brush strokes), Rössing saved himself by means of Party membership and his ability to adapt to the situation in Berlin. The drama around Schrimpf arose only because his political past caught up with him and his extreme conformity to the views of the new holders of power proved to be of no avail. His physical death was the continuation of his artistic self-extermination. In the period after the war, Rössing tried to resume his artistic approach from the twenties and thirties in both theme and style (e.g. *Tiergarten*, woodcutting). Later he tried to find room for himself in the so-called 'modern' school of art, while at the same time persevering in the area of decorative craftwork illustration. Dix, on the other hand, adapted himself first of all in 1945 to the modernistic *Ruinen-Einheitsstil* (unified ruins style) of the post-war period, and then turned to big format oil paintings on the theme of Christ. Here, however, he again failed, after so many years of changes and adjustments, to equal the artistic strength of his early paintings.

The Discussion around the New German Expressionism

Professor Maillard, another teacher at the *Kunstschule*, expressed the opinion to the Ministry of Culture that German art had to be purged of the destructive effects of the chaos and 'isms' that characterised the period before 1933: 'In recent years developments in art have led to chaos . . . The "isms" that have been foisted on German art must be taken care of, everything that encourages subversion must be thrown out, just as the new government has already done in political and economic life.'[16] References to 'isms' here mean particularly 'Impressionism' and 'Expressionism'. However, in the early years of National Socialism, this view did not go unchallenged. Indeed, an open debate arose around the subject of what a specifically German art under National Socialism should be. In June 1933 this led to a clash between the requirements of a 'populist' art and those who saw in the German Expressionism of artists like Emil Nolde or Ernst Barlach an art form which would be an appropriate accompaniment to an aspiring NS movement. The 'political art opposition' gathered together under the leadership of Otto Andreas Schreiber, a student at the College in Berlin and head of the NS Student Union. At a series of organised meetings, he attacked the defamation of the modern school and the persecution of artists like Nolde, Barlach, Schmidt-Rotluff and Kirchner. He openly criticized the crimes against German culture being committed by the *Organisation übellauniger Pinselschwinger* (organisation of heavy-handed daubers), by which he meant the most populist *Kampfbund für deutsche Kultur* (Combat League for German Culture), whose aims he compared with those of amateurs who justified simplistic notions of art by recourse to catchwords like 'nature' and 'populism': 'The painter of garden summer houses and the literary artist are enjoying great popularity because the first mimics nature and declares that the people understand him, the other paints German subject matter and declares his art to be "of the people".'[17]

This conflict came to a head at a student meeting in 1933 billed as 'Youth fights for German Culture'. Schreiber turned against his opponents' dogmatic construction of art history and called for artistic freedom. With this he announced an exhibition of German Expressionist works under the auspices of the NS Student Union. The same debate was also being conducted in parallel in the German press and Karl Hofer was still able to participate. The openness of the discussion in the summer of 1933 seemed at first to indicate an easing in the persecution of 'cultural bolshevism' in favour of a more liberal differentiation, which was perhaps why a painter like Emil Nolde found it possible to reconcile his artistic and political standpoints enough to become an enthusiastic member of the NDSAP.

However, when the 'National Revolution' was declared to be at an end in July 1933, the concessions made in the 'period of struggle' in order to gain youth support were also withdrawn. Otto Andreas Schreiber was charged with being a 'cultural Otto Strasser' (the spokesman of the 'left-socialist' current in the NDSAP). Following this the exhibition of '30 German artists' staged by the Students Union and opened on 22 July 1933, was closed after two days on the orders of the Reich Home Secretary, Frick. It had featured works by Pechstein, Macke, Nolde, Schmidt-Rottluff and other representatives of German Expressionism.

Not until the dual exhibition — *Grosse Kunstaustellung* and *Entartete Kunst* — was held in 1937, was the debate between populist and Expressionist art settled in favour of a third school which accurately reflected the power relationships now established in the country. This school, typified by the gigantic classical canvases of Breker (*Fig 8*) and Thorak continued the populist landscape idyll and the representation of German myth. After this, Expressionism was excluded from all cultural life.

Karl Hofer and Georg Tappert were among the victims of political manoeuvring at the *Vereinigte Staatsschule* in Berlin. Karl Hofer, born in 1878, became a professor in Berlin in 1920. In 1918 he had belonged to one of the *Arbeitsrat für Kunst* (Art Work Councils) and to the *Novembergruppe* which was a group of Expressionist artists. In 1933 he was pensioned off early as a 'cultural bolshevist' and then expelled from both the Academy of Art (in 1937) and the *Reichskulturkammer* in 1938, although he was re-admitted to the latter once he had separated from his Jewish wife. Most of his pictures were destroyed by Allied bombing in 1943, but in 1945 he began to re-construct them with the help of photographs. In 1945 he was taken on as director of the newly-founded Berlin *Kunsthochschule* by the allies.

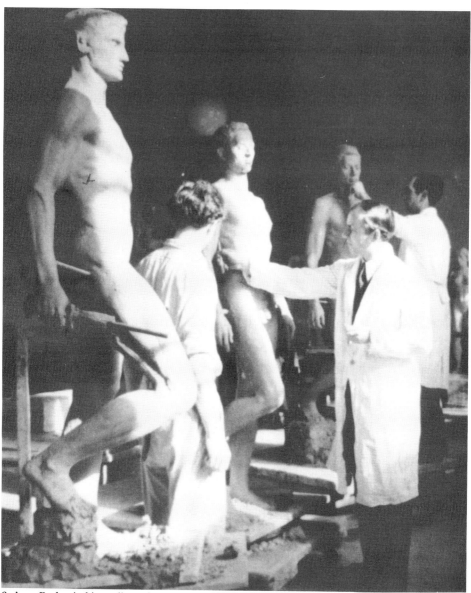

8. Arno Breker in his studio at the Berlin Kunsthochschule

Georg Tappert, born in 1880, spent three years as principal of the Art School in Worpswede after completing his studies. In 1913 he moved to Berlin as a teacher and in 1921 became a professor. Like Hofer, he belonged to the *Arbeitsrat für Kunst* and was a founder member of the *Novembergruppe*. Following the SA attack on the College of Art in 1933, he was first dismissed and then, due to the unresolved status of Expressionism, re-employed. In 1937, however, his dismissal was made final, but in spite of being prohibited from painting, he worked on. He changed, however, from socially critical themes to landscape subjects. In 1944 he took part in

102

the political resistance and was re-appointed to the College in 1945 by Hofer. But he found he could no longer paint. The external pressure to abandon social themes destroyed him as an artist. He never painted another picture after 1945 and instead dedicated himself to teaching. Tappert died in 1957.

Resistance through artistic work

This category includes all those who evaded NS doctrines in their work and whose refusal to adapt became a form of resistance. The price of this refusal was for the most part a mode of existence on the edge of German cultural life, without state commissions or advancement through generous financial support. This, however, should be qualified by noting that there was hardly any artist who did not try at some time to elicit support from the state, although often unsuccessfully. In respect of this, the clear contours of falsely idealised concepts of resistance became blurred by the necessity of everday survival. Thus it was that — to name a particularly unexpected example — even Kurt Schumacher contributed to the decoration of the Karin Hall commissioned by Göring. In so doing he was able, like many others, to accept a commission, grant or prize which served not only to support him materially but also to camouflage political resistance.

Exponents of the position referred to here include the artists from the *Ateliergemeinschaft Klosterstrasse* such as Hermann Blumenthal, Ludwig Kasper and Käthe Kollwitz. Their attitude can be exemplified by the works of Fritz Cremer dating from this time, such as the relief *Trauernde Frauen* (Mourning Women, 1936, *Fig 9*) or the *Selbstbildnis als sterbender Soldat* (Self Portrait as a Dying Soldier, 1937) or his *Soldatenmutter* (Soldier's Mother, 1943). Instead of a resolute soldier's head, representing a removal from all concrete reality, determination to fight and dedication to the task, Cremer's soldier has the reflective expression of the artist himself — a year before the outbreak of war — anticipating his own death. Both the *Trauernde Frauen* and the *Soldatenmutter* assume the style of Kollwitz and Barlach, contradicting through their content the heroic readiness for self-sacrifice demanded by National Socialism.

Taking part in the political resistance

During the fascist period, Elisabeth and Kurt Schumacher (born 1904 and 1905) were students at the *Vereinigte Staatsschule*. Elisabeth studied graphics and photography while Kurt studied sculpture under Ludwig Gies, becoming a senior student after 1932. He shared his studio with Fritz Cremer, who studied under Wilhelm Gerstel after 1929. Student political discussion led all three to join the anti-fascist resistance movement. Elisabeth and Kurt Schumacher made contact with the Schulze-Boysen/Harnack organisation. Their studio served as a postbox for this resistance group for many years. Many persecuted resistance fighters, such as Walter Husemann, or members of the organisation itself, such as Oda Schottmüller, came to the studio under the guise of being models. At night Cremer would print anti-fascist slogans on small leaflets which would be handed over during the modelling sessions for distribution.

Schottmüller, the Schumachers, the writer Adam Kuckhoff, the ceramicist Cato Bont jes van Beck, the photographer John Graudenz and other artists joined the *Rote Kapelle*. This resistance group formed itself around Harro Schulze-Boysen, the government adviser to the Ministry for Economic Planning, and their

9. Fritz Cremer, *Mourning Women*, 1936

activities were concerned with disseminating information and materials concerning the preparation and implementation of fascist war plans. The artists were just as active in producing and spreading pamphlets like *Die innere Front*, as they were in making illegal radio contact with the Soviet Union at the beginning of the war.

Cremer and Schumacher solved the problem of being artist-participants in the resistance in different ways. This had less to do with divergences in their political convictions than with the conditions dictated by their respective forms of artistic expression. Neither of them had belonged to the artistic avant-garde as students in the thirties because the teachers who had represented such a trend had already been dismissed by 1933. Cremer had studied under Wilhelm Gerstel and adopted his rather classical, academic approach to figure work which he could adapt to his own humanistic anti-fascist view (*Fig 10*). So his work remained, for the most part, untainted and even won a state prize at the Academy of Arts in 1936 when there was still uncertainty in the balance of power. This was for his relief *Trauernde Frauen* (Mourning Women (*Fig 9*)) which privately was being called 'Gestapo' and which he dedicated to Käthe Kollwitz. The bursary which accompanied the award enabled him to travel to London where he met such exiles as Bertolt Brecht. Their discussions about the task given to an artist in fascist Germany, led Brecht to write to one of the Me-Ti stories: 'At the time of the severest oppression by the Hijeh, a sculptor asked the Me-ti what subjects he could choose so as to remain consistent with truth but still not fall into the hands of the police. Make a pregnant working woman, Me-ti advised him, and have her gaze sorrowfully at her body. Then you have said much.'[18]

Kurt Schumacher (*Fig 11*) had been influenced by the style of his teacher Ludwig Gies who expressively reformulated Christian motifs with elements from Gothic sculpture. This expressiveness had, to a certain extent, already been ostracised as 'degenerate' in the twenties and led to his being banned from all work and teaching in 1938. Consequently, Schumacher came to do very little independent art work during the war, not least because he wished to mask his political activities. Instead as a form of camouflage, he even accepted state commissions, for example the decoration of the *Arbeitschutzmuseum*.

Whereas Cremer could unite his political and artistic work, Schumacher had to abandon the latter and in his final year concentrated soley on the task of political resistance. The core of the Schulze-Boysen/Harnack organisation was arrested in late 1942. The Schumachers and Oda Schottmüller were (along with Adam Kuckhoff, Harro Schulze-Boysen and Arvid Harnack) condemned to death and executed in Plötzensee on 22 December 1942. In a farewell letter before his execution, Kurt Schumacher, summarising his artistic and political creed, made reference to his artistic heritage: 'By trade I am a sculptor, a wood carver. Riemenschneider, Veit Stoss, Jörg Ratgeb were my great colleagues before whom I bow in humility. They died on the side of the former revolutionaries (. . .). Artists' works only have universal value, are immortal, if they stood and grew at the centre of social events and conflicts (. . .). Why didn't I lead a retiring life, removed from politics? Because then my art would have had only a small value and would not have been living or immortal. So I am dying earlier than if I had lived the trivial life of many — all too many!'[19]

10. Fritz Cremer working on a statue of Oda Schottmüller in his Hochschule studio, 1936

11. Kurt Schumacher, *Worker-Figure*, 1930's

The New Beginning

The period between the cessation of fighting and the beginning of the Cold War can be illustrated by the cases of Ehmsen, Nerlinger and Grzimek.

On 18 June 1945 the *Hochschule der Künste* at the Steinplatz was opened by Karl Hofer, who had been appointed director by the Allies. Together with his deputy Heinrich Ehmsen and George Tappert, who had been employed at the art school in Grunewaldstrasse, he at first succeeded in having all the teaching and administrative posts filled by anti-fascists. This resulted in the integration of all those involved in the teaching of art, and the faculty was overwhelmingly comprised of those like Hofer, Tappert, Ehmsen, Schmitt-Rottluff, Nerlinger and Taut who had been persecuted as anti-fascists. The College co-operated closely with its counterpart in East Berlin. In its early years many professors commuted to and fro between the two parts of the city. This changed abruptly with the development of Berlin as a 'frontier city' in which the Western Allies were allocated three zones. This political division was confirmed by the currency reforms of 1948 and in turn gave rise to the Berlin Blockade, which involved the sealing off of all land routes to West Berlin. The ensuing crisis had a major role to play in whipping up an anti-communist hysteria which had an impact on all areas of social and cultural life in

West Berlin. Only against this background can the fate of some of the teachers in the *Hochschule der Künste* be understood.

Heinrich Ehmsen was born in Kiel during 1886 and studied in Düsseldorf from 1906–1910. He lived in Munich between 1912 and 1929 and was involved with the Munich *Räterepublic*. This activity, and several study trips to the USSR, led to his being arrested several times after 1933. In 1940 he accepted the task of looking after French artists in occupied Paris. In 1942 he was dismissed as politically unreliable, took part in the *Malerstaffel* in the USSR (where he was also dismissed as a 'cultural bolshevist') and then returned to Berlin to take part in the resistance to National Socialism. In 1949, like many of his colleagues, he signed the call for a Congress of World Peace. This 'Congrès mondial des partisans pour la paix' took place in Paris in April 1949. Among the organisers and promoters were Louis Aragon and Pablo Picasso — who also designed the banner with one of his famous doves. As a result of the gathering, delegates from 72 countries founded the Council of World Peace, which still exists today, and proclaimed: 'Art and science for the benefit of mankind can only grow and develop in freedom. We welcome the Congress for World Peace, the progressive intellectuals from all countries who oppose the war-agitators and the war-psychotics in order to prevent the world from sinking, once again, into bloody barbarism. We wish the Congress the greatest success in its aim to unite all those who love peace.'

After this, public opinion was whipped up against the signatories — and Ehmsen in particular found himself the object of castigation. Karl Hofer wrote a letter to the students justifying his signature on the appeal: 'I will recall the text of the letter which removed me from my teaching post: "You are not worthy or suitable to be a teacher of the young." You can read the same thing in the *Tagesspiegel* today (. . .). What's going on? I, without asking permission beforehand from the students, as a private person and with a few colleagues, signed a peace resolution (. . .). We sign any peace initiative, from wherever it may come. I am neither a Russian nor an American, I am a German and want peace for our people.'[20]

On 30 September 1949 the magistrate of Berlin pronounced Ehmsen's dismissal. The Works Council at first withheld its consent and an examining commission was set up which found that Ehmsen had been disruptive at work. This made the dismissal legally effective. Ehmsen left for the GDR (German Democratic Republic), became a member of the East German *Akademie der Künste* and died there in 1964. In the West he remained an unknown figure.

This was the first post-war instance of dismissal on political grounds and it was to be followed by others in the next few years as three further college professors were outlawed. Gustav Seitz was charged with having GDR contacts and both Waldemar Grzimek (*Fig 12*) and Oskar Nerlinger were accused of supporting peace activities against the war in Korea. All three left for the GDR. As a result of the tension around the 'Formalist' debate in the GDR, Grzimek and Seitz later returned to West Germany.

Arno Breker's student Bernhard Heiliger, who in turn had first worked in the GDR, was appointed to one of the newly vacated professorships in sculpture. His work showed an increasing tendency towards abstraction, a trend that was encouraged during these years in the West as a third alternative to the socio-critical art of the twenties and the pseudo-realistic art of the Nazi period which had generally discredited realism. At the same time, a new artistic direction was sought which

12. Waldemar Grzimek, *Concetta,* 1942

13. Bernard Heiliger, *The Flame,* 1969

would be both German and cosmopolitan enough to appeal to the international art market.

In the post-war period this new 'escape into abstraction' failed critically to confront the nature and history of National Socialist art as well as the more general causes and character of Fascism. Rather, after 1945, art effectively assumed the substance and functional character it had under National Socialist — in spite of the apparent differences between the two periods at first glance. So, for example, the *Weibliche Torso* by Bernhard Heiliger (1953) portrays an image of woman which, in its sacrificial pose, can hardly be distinguished from such sculptures as Breker's *Anmut* (Grace, 1940) or Thorak's *Stehende* (1940). His *Flame* (*Fig 13*) on the Ernst-Reuter Platz, although placed at the side away from the central axis, refers — like National Socialist sculptures — to political values, symbolising freedom through the image of the flame. The key to this reference is not in the sculpture itself but rather in its positioning (*Strasse des 17. Juni*). Is it coincidental that works by Breker's students were mounted on the East-West axis of the square which, according to Speer's plans, was meant to be decorated with 23 reliefs (including *Die Kamaraden*, *Der Wächter*, *Der Rächer*, *Die Vergeltung* by Arno Breker)?

All in all it seems to be at least no coincidence that precisely this style of abstract, and hence timeless, value-free, international art in which I believe elements of pre-conquest (or 'collapse' as it is referred to in speeches for the 8th May Memorial Day) German art and culture are still operative, should lead to the production of symbolic objects for official buildings in the period of reconstruction. I would suggest that precisely these artists and their artistic statements could, under the prevailing political climate, become what Bussmann, in reference to Kolbe and Scheibe at the end of the twenties, called the 'Classicists of Transition'.

(*The author would like to thank Paul Crossley for his help in preparing translations.*)

Chapter Six

MODERNISM AND ARCHAISM IN DESIGN IN THE THIRD REICH

John Heskett

Design history encompasses the study of everyday objects of use in the past, such as interior furnishings and fittings, commercial and domestic appliances, and transport vehicles. As an academic discipline in its own right it is still undeveloped and there are naturally problems in defining the content and concerns of the subject, and in developing appropriate methodologies. In this article I will argue that design in the period of the Third Reich in Germany is of interest, not only as a neglected aspect of modern design history, but also because of its potential contribution to an understanding of the emerging role of designers in modern society and to an interpretation of the meaning and significance of their work.

In the majority of publications on design in the inter-war period there is a conspicuous gap. It would appear that modern design in Germany ended with the dissolution of the *Bauhaus* by the Nazi government shortly after its assumption of power in 1933. This interpretation is based essentially upon a limited definition of what constituted modern design in Germany before 1933, which concentrates heavily on the *Bauhaus* and the International Movement, and which has only been seriously questioned in the last two decades. A major defect of this interpretation is its depiction of a particular range of aesthetic concepts and forms as 'modern design'. It thereby excludes a broad range of other work and ideas that in the 1920s was of great importance and widespread concern, much of which was considered to be 'modern' — a term of approbation or opprobrium in those years according to one's standpoint. A consequence of this failure to consider the full breadth of design in Weimar Germany has been the depiction of the Third Reich simply in terms of a negation of the avant-garde tendencies epitomized by the *Bauhaus*. This lack of consideration of what was one of the most crucial periods of German history by design historians is a marked contrast to the wide-ranging and often excellent work that has emanated from other historical disciplines.

One of the first published attempts to discuss design in the Third Reich was a three-part article by Hans Scheerer that appeared in the German design magazine *Form* in 1975.[1] It sought to document 'the usefulness of aesthetics as an instrument of authoritarian state power', and clearly demonstrated the importance of design in the policies of many party organizations. His depiction of the political and economic structure of the regime was somewhat too simplified, however, to clarify the complexities of the period. In particular, the political control of organizations such as the *Reichskammer für bildende Künste* (National Arts Chamber), and the influence of ideologues such as Alfred Rosenberg, were depicted as too deterministic on detailed design work. Despite such differences of opinion, however, Scheerer's article stimulated a serious discussion of design in the Third Reich in its social and political context, a marked contrast to its frequent dismissal by means of undefined phrases or labels such as 'Nazi kitsch'.

Another approach that was disturbing in its implications was revealed in a major exhibition that opened in Munich in 1977, under the title *Schauplatz Deutschland: die Dreissiger Jahre* (The German Scene in the Thirties), in which a limited view of material from the period was presented to justify a specific contemporary view of design. Objects of use were displayed in isolation as pure aesthetic forms under the caption of *Sachlichkeit trotz Diktatur* (Practicality despite Dictatorship). It was a historical irony that the exhibition took place in the former *Haus der deutschen Kunst*, the exhibition complex designed by Paul Ludwig Troost on Hitler's orders as a cultural showplace for the regime. In the relevant chapter of the extensive catalogue, Erika Gysling-Billeter stated that the regime 'determined from now on what art in the Third Reich was to be and what taste the public had to follow'. Despite this, she argued, 'the heritage of the *Bauhaus* and the artists who sympathised with it revealed itself. Functionalism survived! The *Neue Sachlichkeit* outwitted the dictatorship.'[2] The Nazi party was thus depicted as having totalitarian control over the aesthetic taste of the nation with designers playing the role of cultural Schweiks undermining the regime by means of aesthetic form, and thereby constituting a cultural resistance movement. Frau Gysling-Billeter posed the question: 'Were there in fact works of meaning in the Germany of the regime that artistically survived this period?'[3] and came to the conclusion that, 'Thanks to the work of artists such as Wolfgang Tumpel, Wilhelm Wagenfeld, Marguerita Friedländer, Hermann Gretsch etc., 'Good Form' survived in the Third Reich, and after the war could be absorbed into the art of the present without a break.'[4] How it was possible, and why it was important for 'Good Form' to survive was not brought into question. The official positions of the artists named and the relationship between their work and their attitudes to the regime were not discussed. Neither was the attitude of the regime towards those artists and their work. 'Good Form' and its assumed beneficial value were regarded as independent of such relationships by virtue of their aesthetic quality.

Basically, this particular approach was an apologia for the concept of 'Good Form', directed only towards a stylistic or formalistic understanding of the objects displayed, which included a prototype *Volkswagen*, *Volksempfänger* radios and Siemens telephones, as well as a wide range of ceramic and glass wares. Despite the fact that many of these objects were the products of government-sponsored projects, the approach adopted towards them could not offer any answers about the social role of design in this period, since such questions were simply not posed. This is not to suggest that form in design is irrelevant or should be omitted from consideration; the tangible form of designed objects should indeed be the focus of any study of design. Form, however, should be a starting-point, and not an end in itself.

In presenting an alternative view of the period to that described above, it is not possible in a brief account to fully discuss even a representative selection of design or designers in the Third Reich. There are few problems, however, in obtaining material on the designs of the period, since information was widely published and illustrated in journals, books and catalogues, that were often produced on a lavish scale, itself an indication of their importance. The many sources available indicate that there was in fact no single, stylistic tendency or direction, but instead a broad variety of manifestations, encompassing an extensive range of forms, techniques and manufacturing procedures.

Although no simple pattern can be perceived, and although more research is necessary before all the elements of the fuller picture can be identified, two apparently contradictory tendencies are discernible in the objects of the period: one, an emphasis on technical, industrial modernity, the other, an emphasis on traditional craft forms and techniques. A similar polarity has been noted in work on other aspects of the history of the Third Reich, and has been referred to as the 'Janus-headed' nature of the regime. In a discussion of the labour history of the period Tim Mason has identified these two tendencies as 'modernism' and 'archaism', a designation that is highly appropriate to their manifestations in design.[5]

The origins and roots of these tendencies, as with many other aspects of the Third Reich, lie deep in German history. The First World War was an important turning point, however, acting as a catalyst and accelerator of social and economic trends that, together with the trauma of military defeat and the political collapse of the imperial monarchy, heavily conditioned developments and attitudes in the 1920s. In that decade a clear polarization between modern and archaic tendencies became apparent. On one hand, there was an ever-increasing flow of mass-produced articles for an extending range of purposes, whose designers were often anonymous and which were usually identified with the name of the manufacturing company or its trade-mark. Such products were generally manufactured by means of standardized and rationalized mass-production processes after the American model, and exemplified the growth and consolidation of large industrial combines in Germany. On the other hand, there was a continuity of traditional craft organizations and methods, the products of which were made individually, or at most, in limited series, in small workshops. This dichotomy was noted by an American report on German industry published in 1931: 'From the point of view of production, the characteristic feature of German industry is the existence of numerous small establishments side by side with a small number of large enterprises employing a high proportion of industrial workers.'[6]

Another feature of this polarization in the 1920s was that, in addition to traditional industrial and professional bodies, a number of new groups and institutions were founded by both large industry and small craft organizations to promote and publicize their work, methods and interests. Two such institutions that represented new approaches in industry were the *Deutsche Normenausschuss* (German Standards Commission) and the *Reichskuratorium für Wirtschaftlichkeit* (State Efficiency Board).

The *Deutsche Normenausschuss* (DNA) was founded in 1916 as a result of military concern at the disparities and lack of technical compatibility between the products of different firms. Many large companies had established standard specifications for internal use, covering measurements, parts and procedures in the years before the war, but the DNA set out to prepare such specifications on a national basis. Its discussions involved both government and private industry through a network of committees covering all sectors of production. Standards were generally defined by agreement between all the parties concerned on the basis of the best of existing practice and the use of standards was voluntary. Although specific forms were rarely recommended as standards, the publication of a rapidly growing number of *Deutsche Industrie Normen* (DIN or German Industrial Standards) had considerable implications for designers. A major example was the DIN series of paper sizes based on the A-format, since adopted as the basis of an international standard. Published in 1927, it proposed a series of dimensions for sheet-paper that were multiplications or divisions of a basic unit of area, so that any size, from a postage-stamp to large sheets of drawing-paper were exactly proportional. It meant that storage and filing units could also be designed to these basic dimensions, and the result was an extension of the concept of standardisation into three-dimensions with the production of extendable modular storage units.

The *Reichkuratorium für Wirtschaftlichkeit* (RKW) concentrated on the problems of rationalization in industry, commerce, transport and the home. The concept of rationalisation stemmed from the theories of F. W. Taylor on 'scientific management', but the recommendations and publications of the RKW were not only concerned with the rational organization of production, but also promoted the adoption of technically efficient, functional forms. A good example of their approach was in the realm of light-fittings. It is possible to discuss the range produced by the AEG company (*Fig 1*) in formal aesthetic terms as typical of the trend towards functional forms of geometric simplicity that was indeed characteristic of the period. (Attention has frequently been focused in such terms on similar models by several *Bauhaus* designers for the 'Kandem' range of the Leipzig firm of Korting and Mathiesen.) It is clear from the publications of the RKW, however, that there was another important level of meaning to the production of such forms.

INNENRAUM-BELEUCHTUNG

1. AEG Lighting advertisement, 1929

In an article in the *RKW-Nachrichten* under the title of 'Functional Lighting and Rational Economy', published in 1930, it was stated: 'Without a doubt the question of a functional form of light-fitting is also of the greatest significance in economic relationships, in view of the great influence, in psychical and physiological terms, which the light exercises on people.'[7] In other words, and this was strongly stressed, a modern form of light-fitting was an important instrument in attaining higher levels of efficiency in production. The article also reported that efforts were being made by the RKW to evolve general recommendations for the most favourable forms of natural and artificial lighting: 'Endeavours are generally in hand which extend from regulations on single questions of function to the whole economy of lighting, to bring in a more unified, rational approach.'[8] Functional form in lighting was thus part of a wider pattern of developments in industrial efficiency.

That the 'general directions' and 'more unified rational approach' meant a reduction of types in production and an increase in compatibility between types produced was evident in the work of the *Reichsausschuss für Lieferbedingungen* (RAL or State Commission for Specifications), a constituent body of the RKW. The RAL introduced amongst other things, a series of material specifications 'in which, for example, quality requirements, composition, properties, commercial quantities, packaging, sampling, quality control and simple test procedures were laid down.'[9] Quality marks were devised to be affixed to goods satisfying RAL recommendations and procedures, which emphasized a limited range of forms to satisfy specific needs.

The significance of such work, and that of the DNA, was that a considerable quantity of materials and parts produced by and for industry became standardized or subject to standards of performance specification, resulting in a convergence of form and concept between the products of different firms.

It was against this background that the role of designers in German industry evolved in the 1920s. Parallel to the process of standardisation and convergence that accompanied the growth of mass-production and rationalisation, and a direct consequence of it, the work of designers became predominantly oriented towards the creation of artificial and superficial differences between products. An example

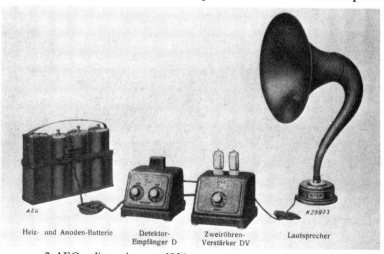

Heiz- und Anoden-Batterie   Detektor-   Zweiröhren-   Lautsprecher
Empfänger D   Verstärker DV

2. AEG radio equipment, 1924

is a series of radio housings produced by AEG between 1924 and 1933. The set of 1924 (*Fig 2*) comprised several units which still have an elementary technical appearance without any attempt to refine or adorn the external form. The models of 1929–30 (*Fig 3*) were still simple and undecorated, but the housings were more consciously formed with an eye to appearance. A major change is evident, however, in the housings for the 1933 models (*Fig 4*). Of pressed plastic, they were a stylistic exercise in the stepped Art Deco fashion of the period, completely eschewing any reference to technical function. The rationale of this trend was summed up in the

3. AEG radios for 1929–30

4. AEG radio housings in pressed Tenacit, 1933

house journal of one of AEG's major competitors, Siemens and Halske: 'The whole attitude of modern people, who see in a radio receiver not a technical apparatus but an object of use, demands ... good-looking radio appliances, whose operation does not require practice or technical knowledge.'[10] Similar trends are apparent across the whole range of consumer goods design, particularly the expanding area of domestic appliances stimulated by the growth of electricity networks.

An unadorned, standardized functionality was therefore considered appropriate to the technical, productive side of industry in pursuit of higher levels of efficiency. With the design of consumer goods, however, there was, in contrast, an emphasis on artifice and fantasy as an instrument of marketing and sales strategies. The attitudes towards purchasers also shows considerable change. As in the example of radio design, the user was no longer considered as an active participant in a technical operation, but as a passive consumer of a packaged article. The role of designers in industry, as it evolved in the context of this transformation, with its emphasis on styling, on aestheticizing the benefits and significance of products for consumers, must therefore also be considered as an aspect of modernity in design.

In discussing contemporary developments in the crafts, it is first necessary to clarify an important difference between the German word *Handwerk* and its usual English translation of 'craft'. The earlier and more extensive process of industrialization of Britain resulted in many traditional crafts becoming obsolete or, if they survived, becoming adapted to or absorbed into industrial structures. The connotations of 'craft' have therefore come to be associated to a considerable extent with the ideas of craft revival associated with the Arts and Crafts Movement. The later industrialization of Germany, however, and its early concentration into a relatively few, highly capitalized units, meant that there was a greater unbroken continuity of traditional craft concepts and business organization. In both numbers employed and range of work encompassed, the concept of *Handwerk*, even though I will use the English translation, is much more extensive than its usage in British design history.

Despite its greater numerical size and economic significance when compared with Britain, the German craftsmen were under considerable pressure as a result of the growth of industry, a process all the more alarming for the speed with which it had taken place. To defend their interests new organizations were also formed in the 1920s. In 1922, for example, a major initiative was the foundation of an umbrella organization, the *Arbeitsgemeinschaft für Handwerkskultur* (The Council for Craft Culture), formed to co-ordinate the efforts of a diverse number of extant bodies. The driving force behind it and a leading figure in its activities was Dr. Edwin Redslob, who held the post of *Reichkunstwart* (State Art Officer) in the Ministry of the Interior, with responsibility for advising on all aspects of government activity that had artistic consequences, ranging from the design of postage stamps, emblems of state and currency, to buildings and public festivities. Redslob's purposes in founding the *Arbeitsgemeinschaft* was 'to systematically maintain the still existing heritage of German achievement in the German crafts, and simultaneously to prepare German work in time for new tasks.'[11] Later, in 1927, he expanded this theme: 'Our age needs a counterbalance to the tasks it has set itself: to dispute the spiritual penetration of machine work with a new appreciation of creative powers as they are evident in the eternally living sources of artistic creativity in the crafts and traditional art.'[12]

116

In pursuit of these ends, the *Arbeitsgemeinschaft* published books, pamphlets, a journal, organized exhibitions and publicized its views wherever possible. Despite these efforts, and Redslob's continuous attempts to evolve a state policy for the applied arts and design in which craftsmen would have an important role, their activities were insufficient to effect a fundamental change in public opinion or state policies.

The political links and influence of bodies such as the *Arbeitsgemeinschaft* and the RKW still require further research. It is clear, however, that in the Weimar Republic a considerable number of *Reichstag* members and government officials, of a broad spectrum of political convictions, consistently represented the different standpoints and policies of such organizations, and attempted to gain and use political influence for the promotion of their views.

The polarization of attitudes and organizations that influenced design at all levels, and political activity and involvement on their behalf, therefore provided a ready field of activity for the growing Nazi party when it began, in the late 1920s, to seek a broader basis of support. In particular, the grievances of the craft class made them very receptive to Nazi propaganda. During the decade, their economic position had continually deteriorated, and there was a similarity between the archaic elements of Nazi ideology, its anti-industrialism and reaction against modernity, and the attitudes of many craftsmen. The vituperative polemics of the debate on art and design that had raged throughout the Weimar Republic's existence were also put to use. From the early 1920's traditionalists had accused modern artists and designers of subverting the roots of German art and life with the rootless cosmopolitanism and 'cultural bolshevism' of their work and ideas. The Nazi front organization for the arts, the *Kampfbund für deutsche Kultur* (Combat League for German Culture) and leading ideologues in the party, above all Gottfried Feder, the party's economic spokesman, continually and carefully exploited the fears and grievances of the craft class. Their support, together with that of similarly aggrieved groups who had become continually more disadvantaged in the Weimar period, became an important factor in the rise to political significance of the Nazi Party.

Indeed it seemed for a short time after Hitler was appointed Chancellor in January 1933, that the plans and ambitions of the craft class to use the power of the new government as a means of re-establishing its former strength in the economic and social life of the country were going to be realized. Although Redslob himself was dismissed when the Nazis came to power for his open disavowal of the regime, the general outlook seemed promising. Craft guilds were reinstated, and at least in their constitutions and legal status, were accorded a new power and recognition. There were also a series of measures to protect craft interests, such as large department stores being forbidden to sell craft products.

Such measures, however, and in a wider sense, the danger of a 'conservative revolution', a return to middle-class oriented production and economic concepts, alarmed the large industrial concerns, who saw their position in the German economy, and their hopes of using the Nazi party for their own ends, endangered by this threat.

The purposes of Hitler's government were clearly revealed by its intervention in this conflict during 1934. Their policies demonstrated that the regime did not intend to simply be a puppet of the disparate forces that had supported its rise to power, neither was its approach necessarily conditioned by its own proclaimed ideology. Even at that early stage, the dominant policy was rearmament and the rebuilding of Germany's military strength, as a precondition and preparation for the territorial expansion that Hitler believed would eventually be necessary. The great industrial concerns were an essential element of that policy, which the so-called 'second revolution' threatened to undermine. Instead of craft workshops, a highly developed technical-industrial base was an absolute necessity. The removal of Feder from power in the party and the elimination of the influence of the SA 'Brownshirt' private army were both steps in denying the 'second revolution' and reassuring the military hierarchy and large industry.

In terms of the effects of these events on design, it appeared that industrial modernity was victorious. The policy of military rearmament and national independence from the restrictions of the Treaty of Versailles meant the full application of the capacities of German industry. There was an increase in design and production in all areas that served the needs of the defence programme, which had considerable secondary influence in the civil sector. The policy of motorisation, which primarily had a military rationale, led also to an acceleration of the autobahn construction programme and a stimulus to the design and construction of road transport vehicles of all kinds.

The economic consequences of these policies, however, created many problems. Resources were diverted from export industries to rearmament, imports were increasing to satisfy the burgeoning goods and materials, and the government's unwillingness to court political unpopularity by imposing restrictions on domestic consumption, led by 1935 to a serious foreign exchange problem.

The government's solution was the Four Year Plan of 1936, which specifically planned to place Germany on a war-footing by 1940. Economic planning was systematized and subordinated to military purposes, though at no time did it become all-embracing, but rather directed towards a limited number of strategic areas and objectives. Many measures were in themselves not new, such as the strengthening of the drive for standardisation and rationalisation begun in the 1920s, and indeed with the same institutions, the DNA and RKW, though now headed by party nominees. The development of new materials, such as plastics and light metals, was encouraged and stimulated, as part of a co-ordinated attempt to reduce the level of imports and make Germany, as far as possible, self-sufficient. There were also some new measures, such as a programme of rationing and allocating essential materials. Collectively, these measures introduced a new dimension into German economic policies that had a strong influence on designers and their work in many sectors of industry. The use of steel-tubing for furniture production, for example, was not restricted on grounds of taste, or because of the avant-garde association of tubular steel furniture in Germany, but because steel was a vital constituent of defence requirements. Thonet steel tube furniture, including designs by *Bauhaus* members that were regarded as classics of modern design, were in fact included in the government-organized exhibition *Schaffendes Volk* (A Working Nation), that was intended to publicize the aim of the Four Year Plan, and which took place in Düsseldorf in 1937. Many aircraft fuselages, however, were also constructed from welded tubular steel frames, and their production, and other similar defence needs, had priority. Where furniture firms, such as Thonet, had an established export trade, though, they could obtain an allocation of materials in pursuit of the vital foreign exchange that was still desperately needed.

The effects of changes in economic policy were also evident, however, in goods produced for the domestic market. The electric-iron produced by AEG in 1937, for example (*Fig 5*), had an enamelled body instead of the nickel-plate finish used on earlier models. Many other domestic implements and fittings were produced from plastics or other substitute materials in the drive for self-sufficiency. Their use was in some cases disguised by conventional forms, as with the upholstered furniture shown at an Arts Chamber exhibition in 1937. A cut-away cross-section of an armchair was shown revealing the extent to which synthetics and substitute materials had been used in its construction. The form of the chair, however, was unremarkable, a high-backed chair with enclosed arms of a type that was wholly characteristic of a broad range of contemporary designs. In other areas, however, new and innovatory forms were necessary to exploit the characteristics of new materials. Articles and speeches in official journals and on numerous public occasions emphasized the need for the process of substituting new materials to be the occasion for a rethink of form and process, in order to at least maintain, and if possible to improve, levels of quality. As a result of this drive, German designers and technicians became very experienced and skilled in the use of many modern materials. By 1939, for example, Germany was producing and using more aluminium than the rest of the world put together (*Fig 6*).

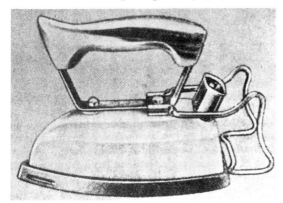

5. AEG electric iron finished in white enamel

6. Junkers 88 transport aircraft fuselage of light metal alloy under construction, *c* 1938

The crafts were not left untouched by these developments either. In 1937, the number of people employed in craft occupations still totalled over 4½ million.[13] Despite their loss of influence at the highest levels of government in 1934, they were simply too numerous to be ignored, and it became necessary to integrate their role and work into the economic plans of the regime. That role was explained in a major speech by Paul Walter, Leader of the German Crafts, at a crafts conference held in Frankfurt in 1937. He began by emphasizing the need for change: 'The way the crafts must go in order to solve the tasks [required of them by the nation] . . . requires a complete change on the part of individual people belonging to particular trades. Many accustomed habits must be thrown overboard. Much that appears self-evident, must make way for these new attitudes.'[14] The major tasks referred to resulted, stated Walter, 'from co-operation on the Four Year Plan'[15], and can be briefly stated as: 1. The manufacture of new finished and semi-finished products from existing and new German raw materials; 2. Reduction of dependence of imported raw materials; 3. Adaptation of material requirements from foreign exchange-linked to existing and new German materials.

The trend of government policy was therefore clearly in the direction of subordinating the crafts to the principle of autarchy that was the foundation-stone of the Four Year Plan. There were further implications of this policy for the crafts, however, which were spelt out in a report of a speech in 1939 at the 'Greater German Crafts Rally' in Berlin: '*Reichshandwerksmeister* Schramm initially outlined the position of the crafts in the present-day economy, which is an instrument of power of the *Führer*. In such an economy, rationalisation has a totally different face to what existed earlier.'[16] He went on to state: 'Of greater further importance is the question of rationalization, that means the higher development of the economic structure in both large and small elements, on the basis of creating room for further improvement in performance.'[17]

Rationalisation, as an instrument of large industry, had earlier been one of the main targets for bitter criticism by the craft organizations, and had been depicted as the soulless subordination of human values to mechanical processes. Now, in pursuit of higher efficiency, they were themselves being asked to conform to the very values they had earlier so vehemently rejected. The realisation of the government's aim required, as a palliative, some acknowledgement of the identity and aims of craftsmen, but this rarely went beyond superficial features. For example, craft forms were often used by government and party organizations for furnishings and fittings in public and official buildings, as a kind of ideological housing or cosmetic (*Fig 7*). In a 'Furniture Book'[18] published by the *Schönheit der Arbeit* (Beauty of Labour) office of the *Deutsche Arbeitsfront* (German Labour Front), the body that replaced trade unions, designs were published for use in factories and offices. These were all of forms derived from traditional furniture, using German timber. Although in formal terms a clear example of archaism, the designs were nevertheless specified in the format of a RAL *Lieferbedingungen*, that is, as a technical specification that was strictly standardised and appropriate to mass-production. In other words, styling, the second aspect of industrial modernity in design, was here used to give an aesthetic, ideological veneer to the underlying aims of the regime.

The subordination of both technology and the crafts to the purposes of the party was consistently justified in Nazi propaganda by stressing the over-riding importance of purpose rather than means. Industry had been the tool, it was argued, and the crafts the victim in the Weimar Republic of the self-seeking ends of

7. Earthenware service for factory canteens, mass-produced but of traditional form and appearance, produced under the auspices of the *Schönheit der Arbeit* organization, 1938

capitalist exploitation, international cosmopolitanism and individual greed. The same means, it was stressed, could be beneficial if placed in the service of the regeneration of the German nation.

The policies of Hitler's government therefore established a framework that had a profound effect upon design in an indirect sense. It is necessary to ask, however, what specific influence these events and innovations had upon form in design and upon the role of designers in the Third Reich. Here, it is necessary to distinguish between propaganda and practice. Continuous efforts were made by party organizations and publicists to identify both technical modernity and traditional craft forms as integral cultural manifestations of the regime and the national resurgence it claimed to have stimulated. Yet an examination of the range of forms produced in this period shows that there was no particular set of design concepts and forms that can be regarded as specific to the regime, apart, that is, from the range of signs and symbols that had the function of a corporate identity programme for the nation. Even when products were manufactured as a direct result of government-sponsored programmes, as with the *Volkswagen* car and *Volksempfänger* radios (*Figs 8, 9*), the forms and design concepts employed in fact predated the regime and were simply appropriated for or adapted to its purposes. Moreover, although the power of the government was extensive, it did not extend to total control over all areas of production in the pre-war period. Individual companies therefore retained a considerable degree of autonomy. Some did indeed attempt to identify themselves with the regime, as in the Adler advertisement of 1938 (*Fig 10*), but again, neither the streamlined car, nor the Berlin exhibition hall in the stripped neo-classical style adopted for official buildings in the Nazi period, were specific to the regime. It could be argued that such attempts to identify with the regime, or what was believed to be the prevailing mood of the time, were as much concerned with commercial opportunism as anything else (see also *Fig 11*). Many firms in fact pursued a policy of self-interest, continuing to exploit sections of the market with goods that had commercial appeal but were frequently castigated as being detrimental to government aims, such as the furniture illustrated in a book entitled *Moderne Gebrauchsmöbel* (Modern Useful Furniture).[19] It con-

8. Foundation stone-laying ceremony of the Wolfsburg plant for the production of Volkswagen cars, 28 May 1938. A prototype model B in the foreground

9. Volksempfänger radio, 1933. Based on a design by Walter Maria Kersting dating from 1928, they were manufactured by several companies to standard specifications and sold cheaply as a means of bringing radio as a propaganda instrument into the homes of the masses

10. Advertisement for Adler cars, 1938, under the slogan 'Forms of the Age'

11. Büssing-Nag 'Trambus'; Kässbohrer streamlined body

tained 120 pages of furniture in an extensive variety of decorative styles for all parts of the house, even the simpler forms based on rural styles having a large, pretentious scale, with heavy proportions set on large ponderous feet being the only overall theme. There was, in fact, a continuity of the diversity found in the 1920s, and, moreover, a continuity of the debates and polemics on the elements of that diversity during the Third Reich. Although furniture such as that illustrated in *Moderne Gebrauchsmöbel* could not be forbidden, such products were the constant target for criticism by official bodies and critics sympathetic to the regime. The basis of the criticism was two-fold: firstly, an advocacy of 'good design' and the beneficial role it could play in improving life; and secondly, the association of that concept with the ideology and policies of the regime. Typical of a large number of similar publications was the book *Unsere Wohnmöbel* (Our Domestic Furniture) by Fritz Spannagel, published in 1937. Spannagel associated the form of domestic furniture with one of the favourite themes of Nazi ideology, that of the family, the womb of the nation: '. . . the great task therefore falls to our domestic furniture to work for the reconstruction of the family and thereby of our state.'[20] In order to do this, furniture should embody the three characteristics of irreproachable quality, functionality, and also 'be so beautiful that through its formal language it delights and brings happiness.'[21] This, he argued, could only be achieved by craftsmanship, though it was stressed that this did not mean hand production. 'No, craft work should know how to use machines and all available technical achievements. But the progress of technology that enables a rational form of work, should above all be placed in the service of an honourable and craftsmanly achievement . . . Machines should not henceforward be used to produce qualitatively inferior mass-products that serve only commercially profit-minded sponsors.'[22] One can see a reflection in Spannagel's argument of the frequently recurring theme of the association and reconciliation of both technology and the crafts in the service of higher national ideals.

The role of design in the policies of the Nazi government, and the clearest and most extensive image of the specific forms it took, were to appear from 1939 onwards in a series of loose-leaved volumes under the collective title of the *Deutsche Warenkunde* (German Index of Goods).[23] Published at the instigation of Adolf Ziegler, head of the National Arts Chamber, it contained an impressive array

124

of designs selected and approved by official bodies for a wide variety of domestic and commercial purposes (*Figs 12, 13*). The standard, in a formalist sense, was generally very good and frequently outstanding, and it included a number of outstanding designs from the 1920s, many by avant-garde designers, that were still in production.

The official view of the function of the *Deutsche Warenkunde* was discussed in an article in the journal of the RKW, which praised the *Warenkunde* as 'visual and educative material for shaping artistic taste and education in the new German way of life. The *Deutsche Warenkunde* should be a guide to a racially pure material environment, free of foreign influences, of stupidities and deformations, that corresponds to our whole German renewal, and in addition stimulates designers and manufacturers of our objects of use to produce beautifully formed, well made and functional creations.' The place of the *Warenkunde* in the government's economic strategy was also stressed: 'The effect of the *Deutsche Warenkunde* in an economic sense relates to two main tasks: the carrying out of the Four Year Plan, and the external trade question. The Four Year Plan requires clarification and direction for producers and users, and it is therefore important to have a means of education by example, of current, characteristic craftsmanship and the increased application of domestic raw materials, which serve simultaneously the principles of efficiency and raw materials freedom. It can also serve foreign trade by providing a comprehensive catalogue of the best German quality manufactures.'[21] The concept of 'good design', subordinated to such ends, can hardly be described as a subversion of the regime, but rather its precise opposite: it was seen as an appropriate expression of government policies and given extensive publicity and heavily-funded support.

Does this mean, however, that the work illustrated in the *Warenkunde* and other official publications was, as claimed, an expression of the regime? Here, one enters a discussion of the nature of the design process and the extent to which creative activity can be regarded as an instrument of social and political relationships. In this respect a quote from an article by Henryk Katz is highly appropriate: 'Every creator is a complicated, autonomous nature with individual relationships and a personal history that can be determined partly by social conditions, but also by biology, from the strength of intellect or by capacity for feeling.'[25] The emphasis in that passage on the need to consider a balance between uniquely individual characteristics and general social forces is important when considering design, since although designers depend upon their individual creative capacity, their work also requires an ability to reconcile the frequently competing demands placed upon them from a variety of external sources and resolve them into a formal unity. The need to cope with these external demands makes a discussion of design untenable without a consideration of these factors, which severely restrict a designer's autonomy. The work of designers became even more restricted in the 1920s as their work evolved as one element in a complex division of labour in large industrial combines. In the Third Reich, their freedom of action was further contained by the government policies described above. Yet although the preconditions for designers' work became more strongly defined, the individual creative power that worked on the basis of those preconditions remained unaltered, enabling many formal solutions of high quality to be created. In this sense, it is possible to construct an argument that designers' work is independent of political and social influences.

To sustain such an argument, however, consideration would have to be

12. W. Wagenfeld, Punch bowl and glasses

13. Door-fittings of pressed plywood by Bruno Paul for the Deutsche Werkstätten, Hellerau, *c* 1939. Illustrated in the *Warenkunde*, it was one of a large number of items that used native or substitute materials

126

limited to the relationship between designer and object, ignoring the social pre-conditions mentioned above, and equally importantly, ignoring the fact that the end product of the creative process of design is an object of use. Use is not an abstraction, but a tangible act that may be identified and responsibility for it established. In this sense, the whole context of design had indeed changed in the Third Reich.

The changes were twofold: firstly, the economic policies of the Third Reich were intended to encourage and tolerate only what was useful for its ends, and it is clear that modernity, on several levels of meaning, was regarded as vitally impor-tant for the realization of those ends; secondly, although the creative work of designers cannot be considered solely as an expression of political conditions, the application of a great many of the products of that creative act were used for the realisation of the aims of the regime, and must therefore be considered as an instrument of those political purposes.

The general conclusions which emerge from a study of this period are that the emphasis on the strand of work and thought represented by the *Bauhaus* in the Weimar Republic and its subsequent closure by the Nazis has obscured the extent of the continuity that existed between Weimar and the Third Reich; further, the depiction of one avant-garde strand of 1920s design as being uniquely 'modern' has obscured the extent to which the Nazi regime not only used modernity, but depended upon it; finally, it places in question the widely asserted equation between concepts of 'good form' and desirable or beneficial political or ethical values. The history of German design between the wars shows clearly that identi-cal design forms and concepts can be used for very dissimilar purposes, and it is therefore necessary in any study of design to include a consideration of the social conditions of production and use as an integral element.

In the 1920s and 1930s in Germany, there was an essential continuity in design in that it became progressively more closely linked to technological innova-tion and industrial organisation and production. But, in the Third Reich, the para-dox existed that modernity was placed in the service of an archaic political ideology and the military preparations for a war of aggression. The ironies and complexities of this situation have their origins not only in the policies of the National Socialist regime, but also in the nature of the modernisation process itself and in the social and economic role played by large industry and craft organisations in Germany in these years, and it is necessary to range far beyond aesthetic factors alone in order to begin to probe this pattern and its meaning.

Chapter Seven

POST-MODERNISM IN THE THIRD REICH

Brandon Taylor

I am concerned in this chapter with the relations between Fascism and Modernism within the cultural context of the Third Reich. My argument is that the generally accepted assumption that Fascism was completely antithetical to the spirit of artistic Modernism itself depends upon taking National Socialist cultural propaganda at face value. Yet this propaganda sought to limit, reduce and simplify cultural Modernism to the point where it could be easily reviled. It did not, necessarily, seek to acknowledge the very various forms which artistic Modernism had taken up to that point, nor to examine its historical, theoretical or social foundations. Against that simplified Modernism, the Third Reich then sought to erect a classical, timeless art that would endure, like the Reich itself, for a thousand years.

The paradox is that any full account of Modernism shows it to consist of many forms which the Reich itself, at various points, employed — the Classic as well as the Romantic, the figurative as well as the abstract, rounded and polished forms as well as the sketchily or loosely conceived. This was true in 1937. It is even truer today, when retro-classicist artists like Carlo Maria Mariani and Stone Roberts — to mention only two who are mentioned in a recent book on Post-Modernism[1] — are recreating a naturalistic, allegedly timeless style. The converse also appears to be true — that the art of the Third Reich in its 'mature' form of 1936 or 1937 came to employ a host of formal and aesthetic devices which Modernism itself had invented.

Yet the rhetoric of National Socialism is apt to confuse us here. Although ostensibly vehemently anti-Modern in each and every way, it takes only a slight shift of perception to see this new aesthetic programme as precisely a novel and heavily militarised form of Modernism itself. Not only must we face the possibility that Fascist 'anti-Modernism' was designed to be a successor style to international Modernism, but that the 'Post-Modernists' of the Third Reich may have shared more than we care to think with the 'Modernists' they so mercilessly antagonised.

The evolution of a National Socialist aesthetic

Strictly speaking, there is no such thing as a National Socialist aesthetic. Too many phases were passed through on the tortuous road to 1937 — the final outburst against 'Modern' art — for us to identify any particular phase as normative for this particular authoritarian regime. We prefer to regard the events of 1937 as defini-

128

tive because only there was the contrast between Modernism and 'true German art' drawn with extreme simplicity. But, I repeat once more, not only was this antithesis drawn by National Socialist ideologists, whose judgements we do not accept elsewhere, but the very simplicity of the antithesis inevitably disguises a far more complex pattern of relationships between the two aesthetic camps.

We need first to notice that in the period before 1933, the *Nationalsozialistische Deutsche Arbeiter Partei* (NSDAP) did not have a precisely worked out artistic and cultural policy, and was unable, at that stage, to make definitive pronouncements either about the style or the content of artistic work. Its interventions were, rather, limited to general and vaguely-worked formulations on artistic direction, and to changes in the administrative structure of the arts, which did, of course, have far-reaching implications.

A sign of the complexity of National Socialist attitudes to the Modern is discernible in 1923. When Hitler dictated *Mein Kampf* to Rudolf Hess in that year, something was beginning to reveal itself about the tone of National Socialist aesthetics, even if its specific measures were as yet unformulated. German culture as a whole was to be based in a mass movement, one in which emotions were simple and deeply felt. The mass was unsophisticated yet hungry, suggested Hitler, hungry for national identification and a sense of purpose. It wished to possess a culture of which it could be proud, and feel, for all that, that it was firmly rooted in old Germany, conceived as a spiritual and at the same time as a national realm. Intellectuals — here personified by the Jew, and particularly by the cosmopolitan Jew — were considered decadent and ultimately subversive. What was needed was not knowledge, but instinct. 'Today we suffer from over-education', Hitler declaimed in a speech in 1923; '. . . the know-alls are the enemies of action. What is needed is instinct and will.'[2] The *völkisch* view of life, Hitler proposed in *Mein Kampf*, stood against 'hybridised and negrified' culture, in which 'all conceptions of the humanly beautiful and sublime, as well as an idealised future for our mankind, would be lost forever'. The Aryan race was central to the future, for 'in this world, human culture and civilisation are inseparably bound up with its existence . . .'[3]

I believe that even in these purple passages we begin to see the origins of a complex and ambivalent attitude to both past and present culture. The suggestion of a return to some long-lost mythologised past is heavily qualified by attitudes which do not belong within a strictly archaic culture — a concern for the future, a reaching for the sublime, mass popularity, the rule of instinct, and so forth.

Such sentiments were far commoner in the Weimar years than is often imagined. At any rate we cannot rely on any simplistic stereotype of Weimar culture as a 'golden' period in which such figures as Brecht, Piscator, Grosz, Dix, Hindemith, Weill and Mendelsohn experimented heedlessly and unopposed. There were far greater ideological problems seeking attention in Weimar Germany, and the Modernists were by no means unique in offering solutions.

With substantial portions of the nationalist press and monarchist judiciary having survived the abdication of the Kaiser more or less intact, with the military machine still active, and with its generals bent on revenge, one might be forgiven for doubting whether liberal 'Weimar Culture' achieved more than the briefest ripple on the surface of a society that was attempting to grapple with deep ideological, social and economic conflicts. Excessively rapid industrialisation in the closing years of the nineteenth century and the first decade of the twentieth, a prolonged and costly World War, an aborted revolution, and then (in 1923) financial collapse, followed by a failed putsch by Göring, Ludendorff and Hitler, had instilled in the German people an acute sense of the deep and unhealed ideological divisions by which their society was characterised. The years between 1923 and the end of the decade were not 'golden' years; only a brief respite from more or less constant upheaval and conflict. Even at this time, 'modern' culture and the culture of traditionists, nationalists and military restorationists were by no means clearly and simply distinguishable. They were already intertwined; already proposing different solutions to the problems of Germany's present.[4]

The collapse of the Wall Street stock market in October 1929 and the Great Depression which ensued had immediate effects which spread throughout the capitalist world. In an already unstable Germany unemployment soared and the economic system nose-dived once again. Incomes plummeted and bankruptcies multiplied. Regional elections in Thuringia resulted in a coalition between conservative parties and the NSDAP, whose Reichstag representative Dr Wilhelm Frick was appointed head of the *Innen- und Volksbildungsministerium* (Ministry of the Interior and Education). Even before the national elections which followed in September 1930, Frick took immediate action to close the Weimar *Bauhaus* and transform it into the *Vereinigte Kunstlehranstalten* (United Institutes for Art Instruction) under the leadership of the highly conservative NSDAP ideologist Paul Schultze-Naumburg. All twenty-nine of the *Bauhaus* faculty were illegally dismissed. Decrees on such racially inflammatory themes as 'Against Negro Culture' & 'For Our German Heritage', issued in May 1930, were typical. Paintings and sculptures by 'Modernists' such as Barlach, Dix, Feininger, Heckel, Kandinsky, Klee, Kokoschka, Marc, Nolde and Schmidt-Rottluff were removed from museums. Here was the beginning of a punitive and exclusive attitude to the Modern that stemmed partly from fear of internationalism, partly from competitive envy, partly from untrammelled ignorance and authoritarianism.

But these repressions scarcely amounted to the assertion of an aesthetic style. Indeed the very absence of a stylistic doctrine within National Socialist ideology — at least at this early stage — may help to explain the need to physically expunge all styles that might have interfered with the creation of a national German art. But what form was such an art to take? The attitudes of an artist such as Nolde may be instructive here. He had supported the NSDAP's attempts to revive and define a specifically national culture since he joined the Party in 1920. Despite the purge of Jewish intellectuals and Jewish artists, it was widely understood as a distinct possibility in 1930 that National Socialist art policy would look to the German Expressionists as the embodiment of the German soul — which, indeed, many of them had attempted to be.

Nolde, for his part — and he may not have been a typical German Modernist — was partly impressed and partly uncomprehending. 'Much was said and the time was full of speeches and assemblies,' he wrote in retrospect. 'At first, I didn't concern myself about anything. Later, I quietly observed events from a distance, while a new order was spoken of in my own area of art, and great promises were made. An unknown, great future for art was prophetically announced. We artists [he speaks here in the plural], often trusting and somewhat unworldly, really didn't know what was happening. All, almost all, lived in tension, full of expectation. Therewith, I heard that my name had been mentioned. Whether in a good or a bad context I didn't know. But a great artistic architecture was being projected . . .'[5]

Nolde's uncertainty was understandable, for in the summer of 1933 and the spring of 1934 a debate raged both in political circles and in the national press about the suitability of 'Expressionism' for conveying the spirit and ideology of the new German nationalism. The context here was the clash between Rosenberg, who disliked Expressionism, and Goebbels, who admired it. Ever since the early 1920's Rosenberg had opposed modernistic—by which he meant abstract, intellectual, individualistic—art.[6] In his best selling book *Der Mythus des 20. Tahrhunderts* of 1930, Rosenberg embellished the thesis that true art should be *völkisch*, now claiming explicitly and repeatedly that *völkisch* art evolved according to its own irreducible laws and denied the influence of sterile formalism or foreign art. *Völkisch* art was in essence unreflective, even naive, and represented the unconscious striving of the *Volksgeist* for self-expression in artistic form. It was the art of the peasant and the artisan, wholesome and warm-hearted, devoted not to the urban individual but to the rural and peasant collectivity.[7]

It needs no argument to show that 'Expressionism' itself could at least be viewed as being premised upon the unreflective nature-feeling of the peasant, and upon a supposedly 'primitive' consciousness; upon 'instinct' and 'will' rather than intellect; upon 'spontaneity' rather than training; and yet these fairly obvious parallels were bypassed in Rosenberg's vitriolic attack on the ills of Modernist culture. In any event, in 1933 a rival organisation was set up under Josef Goebbels, the *Reichsministerium für Volksaufklärung und Propaganda* (RMVAP). Goebbels did not subscribe to the Rosenberg doctrine on *völkisch* art, though he agreed that art should be supported and enjoyed by the *Volk*; and it was here that Expressionist artists believed they saw an escape from the threatened hegemony of the Rosenberg line. Thus, in the debate that ensued, one camp sided with Rosenberg in looking backwards to traditional German themes and folksy stylistic devices; while another camp, supported by Goebbels, saw in Expressionism an adequate foundation for a national style that came near to expressing true German feelings towards the land, nature, and the body, and which joined the fight against the big-city and the machine-minded Modernism of the abstract schools, particularly Constructivist-inspired art that had originated, after all, in the USSR. One such group, the *National-Sozialistischer Deutscher Studentenbund* (League of National Socialist Students), led by the artist and writer Otto Schreiber, published a periodical *Kunst der Nation* from 1932 which supported 'freedom' for the artist precisely as National Socialist cultural workers. This group, and a small number of individuals, were especially concerned about the line taken by Rosenberg's Combat League in its defence of the crafts and in its support of an old culture based on national folk-lore. The Students' League proclaimed that they 'wished to forestall the rejection of the generation of German artists which preceded the present one and whose powers will flow into the art of the future'.[8] The critic Bruno E. Werner was also sympathetic to this view. 'It cannot be denied', he wrote, 'that it was the New Art itself which prepared the way for the national revolution . . . The promoters of the national revolution in Germany were the artists of *Die Brücke* such as Nolde, Otto Müller, Heckel, Schmidt-Rottluff and Pechstein, the artists of *Der Blaue Reiter* such as Franz Marc, Macke, Klee and Feininger [note how Werner lists only the Germans], the sculptors Kolbe and Barlach and the architects Pölzig, Tessenow and Mies van der Rohe, to name but a few'.[9]

It must have seemed for a time as if the debate between Rosenberg and his opponents might have continued for many months, even for years. Such license was contingent however upon the relatively fluid power situation in Germany that still existed in the remaining months of 1933. In 1934 this changed. Schreiber's group, which had already come under attack from Rosenberg in July 1933 when their exhibition '30 German Artists' (with works by Nolde, Pechstein, Macke, Schmidt-Rottluff and other Expressionists) was closed by Rosenberg's agent Frick[10], came under further pressure after January 1934 when Rosenberg was elevated to the directorship of a new organisation for the control of (amongst other things) artistic policy, the *Amt für die Überwachung der gesamten geistigen und weltanschaulichen Schulung und Erziehung der NSDAP* (Department for the Supervision of the Intellectual and Ideological Training and Indoctrination of the NSDAP). Following Hitler's consolidation of power in the summer of 1934, however, speeches began to be made by the *Führer* which did much to resolve the question of *völkisch* art versus Modernism — though he neither followed Rosenberg's doctrinaire policy *nor* supported the Expressionists as the true heirs to German art.

It is from this point onwards that the widely understood 'polarity' between National Socialist and Modernist art began to be constructed. At the Party Congress of the NSDAP in November 1934, Hitler first sided with Rosenberg in warning his audience of 'the saboteurs of art' such as 'the Cubists, Futurists, Dadaists and others' — the Expressionists were not yet identified as a group. The creation of the new Reich would 'not be intimidated by their twaddle', he said. 'They will see that the commissioning of what may be the greatest cultural and artistic projects of all time will pass them by as if they had never existed'. It may be assumed, perhaps, that Goebbels and his Expressionist sympathies was also a target of the *Führer's* invective. But Hitler gave vent to another danger, that presented by those who wished to make 'an old-fashioned German art' based on thoroughly *alt-völkisch* principles without any attempt to take account of modern demands. These people, he said, who would even advocate fashion designs 'based on Gretchen and Faust', were never National Socialists and did not belong to their ranks. Even the Jews thought they were ridiculous.

However, in spite of the condemnation of both Expressionist and völkisch art in the new policy, it remains true that what was still lacking in 1934 was a firm 'theory' developed within the Reich which would positively associate National Socialism with a particular style. Yet the events of the Röhm putsch in the middle of 1934 had shown, if proof were needed, that Hitler was prepared to engage in deliberate and calculating murder to resolve any difficulties which remained in the consolidation of National Socialist power. The task of consolidating a 'total' culture around the activities of the SS, and centred even more explicitly upon the deeds and personality of the *Führer*, was now paramount.

But something else was needed as well. The incorruptible presence of the NSDAP embodied in the person of the *Führer* required not only the silencing of other opinions and of all dissenting voices. It also required the construction of a channel for the expression of hate. The likelihood of venting grievances against the *Führer* would be decreased if it was made possible to hurl redicule at something else, an impure 'other' within the body of the Nazi state. The Jew was one such impurity. But the other could be 'Modern' art. The process had been begun, perhaps, in 1933. Then, in the latter part of 1936 and the whole of 1937 there was launched a further exceptionally fierce assault in which relations between National Socialism and Modernism were finally fixed for all to see.

Exhibitions are by their nature performative and can be easily treated in a propagandistic, theatrical way. Already in the frantic art debate of 1933 – 4 exhibitions had been staged which were openly designed to discredit and ridicule.

132

'Government Art from 1918 to 1933', organised by the painter Hans Bühler, was the first of several such occasions, designed to heap scorn and derision on older Modernists associated with the culture of the Weimar Republic—Liebermann, Corinth, Slevogt, von Marées, and Munch. 'The Spirit of November: Art in the Service of Social Decay', was intended to associate various individuals with the November 1918 revolution, although several of them had no actual connection: Dix, Grosz, Beckmann and Chagall were all included.

Then, late in 1936, Adolf Ziegler was 'empowered' by Goebbels 'to select and secure for an exhibition works of German degenerate art since 1910, both painting and sculpture, which are now in collections owned by the German Reich, by provinces and municipalities'.[11] Ziegler's commissioners in fact exceeded their brief by far: many artists from other European countries were included, Gauguin, Picasso, Kandinsky, Braque, Léger, Lissitsky, Matisse and Roault among them. The *Entartete Kunst* (Degenerate Art) exhibition which opened on 19th July 1937 in the Munich Hofgarten contained 730 works by 112 artists and was displayed, as is well known, in a manner calculated to give the worst of bad impressions (*Fig 1*). Hung in a jumbled, crooked and crowded manner, several of the paintings without frames, the exhibition nevertheless attracted 20,000 visitors a day and proved to be the most popular modern art exhibition ever staged. Carefully constructed captions and messages scrawled over the walls sought to associate Modernism with imbecility, illness and trickery. Comparisons with mental defectives, degenerates, sexual misfits and drunks were legion (*Fig 2*).

One day before, on 18th July 1937, Hitler had opened the first of seven Great German Art exhibitions in the newly built House of German Art. Still lacking a clear conception of the style of National Socialist art, a decision had been taken to begin the series, not with a historical show, but with a competition designed to

1. *Entartete Kunst*, 1937, guidebook cover

2. *Entartete Kunst*, opening, 19 July 1937, Munich

3. P. Troost, *Haus der Deutschen Kunst*, Munich, 1937

attract 'a comprehensive and high quality display of contemporary art'.[12] About 900 works were accepted from the 15,000 submitted, the criteria for selection however being nothing more explicit than the provision that the artists be of German nationality or race. The building was designed by Troost (*Fig 3*). 'When we celebrated the laying of the cornerstone for this building four years ago', Hitler said in his opening speech, 'we were all aware that we had to lay not only the cornerstone for a new home but also the foundation for a new and genuine German Art. We had to bring about a turning-point in the evolution of all our German cultural activities.' His speech also gave vent to a particularly cruel attack on the Modernism of the Hofgarten exhibition: 'What do these artists fabricate? Deformed cripples and cretins, women who inspire nothing but disgust, human beings who are more animal than human, children who, if they looked like this, could be nothing but God's curse on us! And these cruellest of dilettantes dare to present this to today's world as the art of our time . . .'[13]

The Dilemma of Classicism

In self-consciously distancing himself from certain carefully selected Modernist norms, while at the same time claiming to present a very different art precisely as 'the art of our time', Hitler may be described as having heralded a neo-Modernist, or more properly a Post-Modernist, point of view. Two aspects simultaneously characterise this early Post-Modernist posture: the trumped-up appearance of an absolute distinction between the National Socialist and the 'International Modern' styles and, at the same time, an implied claim that National Socialist art represents contemporary civilization in its highest, most progressive, form. A third, dialectical consideration which becomes fully apparent only by hindsight is that the heavily vaunted contemporaneity of Post-Modernist culture (in whatever incarnation) could then and can still be today taken as part of the spirit and essence of Modernity in a wider and more all-embracing sense.

The appearance of an absolute division between the two styles is indeed compelling. On the one hand, and overall, one has the rhetoric of 'incompleteness' levelled consistently against the Modernists by the culture managers of the NSDAP. Hitler's most frequent accusation was that modernist work was 'unfinished', 'merely sketched', 'inept', etc. This is primarily a remark about style. To this he added the implied assumption that all art must be representational, and hence that if Modernist colours did not approximate to the 'actual' colours of things, this either meant the artist could not see, or was a liar. The 'unpolished' quality of their works was however claimed to be their greatest single failing. On the other side, National Socialist art was perceived by the Modernists to be at once sentimental and cheap, but also cold, inhuman and remote.

Both, in a sense, were right — how could they fail to be? It is only when one asks what other qualities were signified by these marks of style that the nature of the antagonism between Fascism and Modernism begins to become clear, or, as I should prefer, more complex.

It is too simple to say that one style was progressive while the other was not. In fact, both styles attempted to modernise visual and aesthetic experience in their own very different and largely incompatible ways. Hitler knew that although emotional capital could be made out of an appeal to *völkisch* national sentiment, no culture could succeed which was based entirely on the forms of the past. He was also aware that National Socialist culture had in some sense to be new, not merely a replay of old German forms and images. Industrial modernisation, too, was essential for high employment and national recovery, as well as for eventual military expansion. The design of everyday artefacts could not rest on the practices of the traditional craft industries, since these, however *völkisch*, were inefficient in manufacturing terms and were ergonomically unsuitable for workers in a dynamic modern state. In industry, much National Socialist design was entirely in keeping with *Bauhaus*-inspired ideals of ergonomic suitability and technological effectiveness, shorn of unnecessary decoration.[14] Labour-efficiency was highly desirable in a nation preparing for war, and the forms of everyday objects such as chairs, light-shades and buildings would necessarily have to take this into account.

How then did this basically modernising impulse express itself in the visual art on the Third Reich? An important aspect of National Socialist modernisation lay in a certain kind of return to Classical (and specifically Greek) forms. 'Never was humanity closer to antiquity than today', Hitler had written in *Mein Kampf*, 'It is the marvellous fusion of the most splendid physical beauty with the most brilliant intellect and the noblest soul that makes the Greek ideal of beauty eternal . . . As a rule the spirit dwells, if healthy, only in the healthy body with any degree of permanence'.[15] Classicism, in this context, meant at least two things: the cult of the body, and a tendency towards discipline and militarisation.

In its most negative form, Classicism was made to function as the vehicle of an expansionist, military demeanour, both heavily centralised and highly disciplined — at least on the surface. For, over and above the correspondence of Nazi classicism to the Classicism of Imperial Rome, it must be clear that the very forms and angles of National Socialist architecture were imbued with the values of the harsh, the aggressive and the coercive (*Fig 4*). This was of course not a specifically Nazi idea, but one revived by them from the example and the writings of Julius Langbehn, who had already pointed out the relationships between German Classicism and the forms of the parade ground. The very term 'soldier of the line', Langbehn had written, 'derives from the august and symmetrical lines of troops in formation; the work of art becomes classical when it develops its individual character, both in form and in spirit, along such august and symmetrical lines'.[16] The equation between the concepts *art* (normally classical) and *war* had already been implied in Langbehn's further formulation of 'war fused with art', as 'a Greek, a German, an Aryan battle cry'.[17] The great warrior as artist came to be seen under National Socialism as equivalent to the great artist as warrior. The terms became virtually interchangeable. Wasn't Athena of Greece goddess of both war and art? The analogy extended easily to music. Here, Germany could boast some solemn victories. 'The Stormtroopers are marching for Goethe, for Schiller, for Kant, for Bach, for Cologne Cathedral and for the Knights of Bamberg . . .' (Wilfried Bade is describing Horst Wessel) 'Now we must toil for Goethe with beer-mugs and black-jacks. But once the battle is won, then we will extend our arms and embrace our spiritual heritage'. Werner Sombart had been more specific. 'Militarism is the realisation of the heroic intellect in the material spirit. It is Potsdam and Weimar in the most exalted union. It is Faust and Zarathustra, a Beethoven score in the trenches. Are not the Eroica and the Egmont Overture also the finest expression of militarism?'[18] Presumably Sombart could not have made his point with the Pathetique sonata, or even with the *Grosse Fuge*; then how much less could he have done so with Schoenberg's chamber music, or with Hindemith's?

And yet National Socialist classicism contained other values as well — much nearer to the spirit of a substantial amount of Modernist (and modernising)

136

4. W. Mach, Arcade at the Olympic Stadium, Berlin

culture. The cult of the body, particularly, already had well-established roots within an older German culture and became, within National Socialism, the focal point for a host of moral and sexual predispositions. The concept of a healthy soul inside a healthy body, which had characterised the gymnastic movement of the early nineteenth century, had turned towards the concept of the physical body by the time of Hans Blüher and Stefan George and their esoteric lodges in the closing years of the nineteenth century and the early years of the twentieth. Here, sheer adulation of the physical body was deemed sufficient to guarantee moral and spiritual strength. Whiteness of skin was considered symptomatic of inner purity. Correct proportions effortlessly substituted for intelligence or culture. Artists like

137

Franz von Stück (1863–1928) and Franz von Lenbach (1863–1904) perfected marble surfaces and perfect proportions in their nudes precisely as an expression of inner wholeness and completeness of being—and these were artists at whose feet Kandinsky, Marc, Beckmann and others were students. Sensual euphoria or the craving for physical beauty at the expense of truthfulness was at the centre of the generation of *fin-de-siècle* classicists whose literary and artistic examples were perhaps more important to National Socialism than the merely fabricated examples of Goethe and Schiller (*Fig 5*).

Indeed there was plenty in the recent German past to validate the twin concepts of *smoothness* and *proportion* as being essentially German characteristics, and ones that were far from archaic. A predilection for smoothness was far from absent even in the period we call 'Expressionist', let alone the World War I period and the epoch of the Weimar Republic. It goes almost without saying that Wilhelm II himself was an apologist for the smoothness and finish of Classical art. 'At the sight of the marvellous remnants of antiquity', he said, 'one is overcome by the same feeling; here also dwells an eternal and unchanging law: the law of beauty and harmony, of aestheticism . . . I would like to caution you [artists] that up to this moment the art of sculpture has remained relatively uncontaminated by the so-called modern schools and currents . . . [but] art that disregards the laws I cited is no longer art, it is factory work, handicraft, and that is something art should never become . . . To us, the German people, the great ideals have become enduring values, whereas other people have more or less lost sight of them . . .'[19] Paintings specifically commissioned by the Wilheminian court were consequently conservative in both content and style, they portrayed healthy, contented citizens, depicted within the safe limits of naturalism of technique and Classicism of form or manner. In its notorious discussion of modern art in April 1913, the Prussian Chamber of Deputies was unanimous in condemning the depraved (i.e. distorted and sketchy) development of the fine arts in the hands of younger artists under the thrall of International Modernism.

5. R. Klein, *The Repose*, exhibited in the Grosse Deutsche Kunstaustellung, Munich, 1939

One is tempted at several points in twentieth century history to postulate a relationship between the authoritarian personality structure and a taste for smoothness of form; and a further link between liberal and romantic sentiment and a predilection for sketchiness, informality or looseness of form. (These equations would be convenient if they could be universally sustained; however the descent of 'looseness' into a mere sign for bourgeois freedom on the one hand, and the tendency of authoritarian art to embrace 'tradition' and 'simplicity' rather than smoothness *per se*, show just how difficult the association is.) Whether from personality or aesthetic conviction, Hitler, at any rate, favoured the classicising pole. From the earliest days of Weimar he had been quick to see that sketchiness was to be identified with the political Left, while a tendency to Classicism could be easily enough associated with a politically radical Right. He had personally already taken an interest in triumphal architecture in his days as a would-be student. Perhaps more importantly, he had been struck by the smoothness and opulence of the *Goldschnitt* style in painting and literature from his early days in Munich, in 1918. This emphasised delicate and decorative elements in art through the selection and use of precious materials, and had already provided an important part of the plush interior design style of nineteenth century Munich. Under National Socialism, this became the decorative style of the *Braune Haus,* the official National Socialist building in Munich; of the Obersalzberg buildings (including Hitler's own *Berghof*); of the Munich *Führerhaus* (*Fig 6*) and of the Berlin *Reichskanzlei,* all of which were characterised by superficial opulence and the smooth surface, aided by the example of the saloon car interior and the decor of the German beer-house.

The sketchiness and incompleteness associated with Modernism were associated with other meanings. The first breakage of the surface in modern art had occurred in Impressionism, and Impressionism, perhaps — and despite Göring's personal taste for these works — was an oppositional tendency premised on the destabilization of the art establishment and the incursion of alien perceptions into the value-system of the bourgeoisie: that is, it challenged the imperatives of predictability, ease of movement, comfort of transition from one experience to another, consistency of view, and the uninterrupted 'illusion' of a situation or a character. After Impressionism, the *surface* of art had become the most vigorously contested site of meanings of every kind. The coherence or fragmentation of the means of painting were the very programmes out of which Fauvism, Cubism and Expressionism had been built; they may be said to have suggested moral and political orders that were inconsistent with the Classical conception of life. One senses — from Hitler's 1933 outburst against 'unfinished' art — that he understood these matters (instinctively, perhaps, yet with conviction) moderately well (*Fig 7*).

And yet Hitler either did not realise, or chose to obscure, the fact that Modernism, too, had resorted to Classicism as a means of expressing a utopian, idealising goal. One might even say that it was no less classicising than National Socialism — although its devices took ostensibly very different forms. It contained, for example, the anti-individualising platform of the machine aesthetic, of artists such as Mondrian, van der Leck and the International Style architects of the 1920's and 1930's including those associated with the *Bauhaus*. There is the classical impulse too in Gris, and in crystal Cubism, in Picasso's monumental style of the 1920's, in Wyndham Lewis, in much of Matisse, and in much, much more. The timeless and impersonal appealed to these artists as a valid reaction to the predominance of 'the personal' within earlier Modernism, not as something lying beyond or outside it. And then there are the difficult cases of de Chirico, Severini,

6. The Führerhaus in Munich, designed by Prof. L. Gall and Prof. P. Troost

7. Hitler visiting *Entarte Kunst*, 1937

140

Derain, and others, who turned against subjective Modernism as early as 1918 or 1920 but who did not, in the process, become any less 'modern' than before. De Chirico's 'conversion' in the Uffizi Gallery in 1919 — he heard the sound of trumpets and thought that the sky was about to fall — caused him to react violently against the Modernism of his earlier 'metaphysical' work, and even to paint some overtly classicising paintings in the 1930's, many of them consisting of little else than white horses, Classical pillars and ancient heroes, which at one stage captured the attention of Mussolini.[20] Such facts cannot by themselves be used to fuse together a directly reactionary, even fascistic art with one that knowingly rejects an earlier phase of Modernism in favour of a more developed, Post-Modern sensibility. And yet the two categories stand close together. Art and architecture throughout the Western nations turned backwards to Classical prototypes between 1925 and 1935; and did so without losing their utopian zeal or their urbanist and secular motivations. Thus Modernism in its fullest sense is certainly compatible with Classicism and, like National Socialist art and architecture, may even be said to have relied heavily upon it. At least it cannot be said uncontroversially that the two are necessarily opposed.

Fascism as Post-Modernism

The certainty of an absolute distinction between National Socialist and Modernist art is again contradicted by the fact that both forms — for the moment we must persist in this usage — relied upon exaggerated Romantic yearnings as well as Classical prototypes. Herein lay the redemptive, irrational side of both cultural programmes. For example the 'new politics' of the Nazi period had its roots in a variety of communities and associations which were developed during the nineteenth century in reaction to the loss of traditional religion under the rapid growth of industrialisation. Quasi-religious and mystical groupings such as the German Youth Movement of the late nineteenth century, or the earlier gymnastic association of Father Friedrich Jahn (1778 – 1852), with its slogan of *mens sana in copore sano* (from Juvenal), which sprung up after the Napoleonic conquest of Germany, all sought to satisfy a common yearning for a sense of personal belonging and purpose, explicitly linked to a heroic role for the German nation, in a time of rapid social and ethical change. The *Alldeutscher Verband*, founded in 1891, existed solely to revitalise national consciousness through the support of German interests at home and abroad. At the turn of the century a partially similar impulse was apparent in Expressionism, with or without the aid of Nietzsche. The 1906 *Brücke* Statement, put out by Kirchner and his allies, calls explicitly for a revival of culture; for enthusiasm, for youth, for nation: 'As youth', they wrote, 'we carry the future; and we want to create for ourselves freedom of life and movement against the long entrenched forces of seniority. Everyone who reveals his creative drives with authenticity and directness belongs to us'.[21]

In 1906 and in the years before 1914 the *Brücke* artists were certainly persuaded that modern society had lost touch with the basic needs of the human spirit, and that somehow the ills of civilisation were to be laid at the door of the big city and the habits it had helped to form. The theme of nature worship is a major theme in *Brücke* Expressionism, as well as in National Socialism. Here, in an allegedly untarnished state of grace — the natural world perceived pantheistically and still untouched by the march of technology — members of the Modernist community could find confirmation of the de-individualising monotony of industrial culture.

The theme of the alienating effect of the big city is found again in Nolde, as it was only a few years later in Goebbels and Eberlin. The *Blaue Reiter* formation around Kandinsky and Marc, though particularly the latter, gave expression to a simplified, mystical concept of 'nature' and of 'harmony' in which animals and plants were suddenly more 'genuine' than human beings. Klee became fascinated by the concept of the *Ur-grund*, the descent into the mystical heart of nature, on the grounds it signified the chaos that lay at the heart of all creation and all human will.

Yet these Modernist affirmations are precisely of a piece with the nature-zeal of the National Socialist youth movements. As Glaser puts it in his account of the hiking movement, the ideal of being 'blended into nature' meant a life away from the avenues of civilisation. Campfire discussions would centre on the beauty of Germany and the romance of war, helped by the bonding of a sacred pledge and a commitment to be 'ready for action'. An entire generation was caught up in a variety of semi-cultivated mob Romanticism that found its climax at the Hohe Meissner in 1913. 'Here', says Glaser, 'two thousand members of the youth movement met to celebrate the first Free German Youth Festival and to proclaim guidelines for a life based on self-determination, individual responsibility and inward honesty . . . the view from the mountain-top became a panorama of the nation: it was not the beauty of nature at one's feet, but the beauty of *German* nature'.[22] German Fascism depended upon its romantic slogans, including many of those embraced by Modernism, even if ultimately it developed them to the level of a propaganda aesthetics for consumption on a mass scale. From this point of view its subsequent public altercation with Modernism might easily be read as a marriage tiff between compatible partners, a squabble over detail within an otherwise substantial framework of agreement as to ends.

The more radical argument that National Socialist art was just another form of Modernism — however distinguishable it may have been in style — is not difficult to construct. Its repeated proclamations of contemporaneity, which had appealed to generations of artists of the European avant-garde, were broadly similar to those of the Modernists. Likewise, the utopian zeal with which National Socialist art policy was applied was reminiscent of the Modernist urge to redeem and improve, to create the blueprint for a future society through artistic forms that could be uttered today. The rootedness of National Socialist art in the emotions of the masses — simplified and banalised though these emotions may have been — can likewise be compared to the universalising tendency that is implicit in Modernist aesthetics to the effect that flattened, streamlined or even child-like forms of art can have potentially all-embracing appeal. The masculine bias of National Socialist culture is certainly comparable with that of the Modernism we think we know and understand. Finally, the appeal in National Socialism to some 'radical negation that will free us of the nightmare of the past' can surely be set alongside the negation of traditional and academic genres that was a motif of European Modernism from Impressionism onwards. All that seems to have been lacking in National Socialist aesthetic modernisation was the sometimes intense individualism of Expressionism, Fauvism, and the like.

These parallels as well as discontinuities between Fascist and Modernist thought raise potentially difficult questions about the relationship of 'our' culture — that of Modernism and its variations — to its supposed antithesis in Germany of the 1930's. Are we to neutralise the difficulty by pointing to the possibility that Fascism used modernising means to achieve anti-Modernist or traditional ends?[23] Or that industrial modernisation can be most effectively forwarded by a culture of constraint, which thus takes on a duplicitous, yet anti-liberal character? Or are we to concede that the butt of both Modernist (in its conventional sense) culture and that of National Socialism was the traditional, hypnotised, philistine culture of Sunday artists with its left-over meanings and its fear of even modest change? Certainly the political differences between the democratic-liberal formations and those of National Socialism — differences which are real enough — can seem effectively to vanish in a comparison, say, between the confiscations in Germany between 1933 and 1937 and the de-Nazification sequestrations of thousands of paintings and sculptures by the US Army at the end of World War II. These latter impoundings, and the atmosphere of secrecy that has followed, have resulted in a distortion of twentieth century art history to the effect that National Socialist art did not exist. The works have never been studied, written about or displayed by the academic and museological fraternities in either Europe or the United States. Instead, they have been fastidiously avoided.[24]

It is with the realisation finally that neither Fascism nor liberal democracy has any claim to being the 'natural' state of civil society, that both regimes partake reciprocally in the measures and devices of the other, that the true identity of the National Socialist 'interregnum' begins to present itself. For now each social order begins to look, not like the inverse of the other, nor even like its shadow, but like its mute accomplice. Elements of Modernist nature-Romanticism, of utopianism, of casting aside the past in a zealous race into the future, of messianic redemptiveness, of social cleansing and the desire to begin again culturally — all these have been noticed within the pattern of National Socialist architecture and art. By a similar token, the legacy of National Socialist cultural thinking, though ostensibly now a historical remnant, still proves to be present within liberal democracy in the guise of highly regulated behavioural standards in work and leisure, a blind subservience to the rhythm of the consumption cycle, and in numerous petty coercions and enforcements in the conduct of everyday life. To this list one could add the high level of popular support within both systems for massive levels of military spending and for uncritical investment in reactionary social programmes dependent upon technology.

To say this is to suggest once more that Fascist Post-Modernism — the impulse to destroy a carefully selected 'Modernist' past — is, like its present-day incarnations, most probably part of a wider Modernist dynamic in which all forms are to be renovated and life as a whole is to be transformed and improved. For it seems likely that at a number of points within our Modernist and modernising century, the very apocalyptical nature of the race into the future has meant both a search for tradition as well as an obsession with the speed of time.[25] This is the sense in which Fascism was an early form of Post-Modernism — albeit an authoritarian one — and hence part of that wider network of Modernisms with which we are still trying to get adequately acquainted. Of course, the physical destructions of the *Entarte Kunst* period were infinitely severe in comparison to the ideological adjustments that contemporary Post-Modernists are committed to. But the motives and the inspirations can be directly compared.

Chapter Eight

BRIDGES: PAUL BONATZ'S SEARCH FOR A CONTEMPORARY MONUMENTAL STYLE

Hartmut Frank

'The bridge is a thing and only a thing. As this thing it assembles the Foursome (Geviert).'
'The bridge is a site. It locates a space in which the earth and the heavens, the divine ones and the mortals gain a joint presence.'
Martin Heidegger[1]

In February 1935 Paul Bonatz (1877–1956) gave a remarkable lecture in Stuttgart on 'representative buildings of the people'.[2] He stated that after 'a last, genuine surge of representative architecture' around the year 1800 it had hit a crisis which made 'the act of representing an end in itself'. Few works in the history of modern German architecture escaped his venomous verdict: among them were Wallot's Reichstag building in Berlin, Tessenow's 'house of festivities' (*Festhaus*) in the Hellerau garden city near Dresden, and his own masterpiece, the Central Railway Station in Stuttgart, dating back to the years of World War I (*Fig 1*). According to Bonatz it was in only these few examples that one recognised 'the will to form a representative structure out of a sense of responsibility and the renunciation of everything that was merely fashionable'. He drew the following conclusion: 'Content and form must coincide. Representation for its own sake is nonsense.' Amongst the 'prominent buildings of present-day Germany' there was not one that stood out as 'a work of pure architecture' and which he could regard as representative. All that existed were a few presentable 'technical and semi-technical designs'. It is worth noting that Bonatz made these remarks in the Germany of 1935, expressly including in his judgement highly important examples of state architecture, such as the Reich-Chancellery[3] in Berlin by the *Führer's* architect Paul Troost, and Albert Speer, who was only just coming onto the scene. 'In its mix-up of the severe and the picturesque, tradition and playful Modernism, it is patently inadequate.' Bonatz refrained from again mentioning Troost's plans for the transformation of the Königsplatz in Munich into a place of commemoration for the dead heroes of the Nazi movement. He had pronounced against it as early as June 1934 in a counter-report which he had sent to the *Führer's* deputy, Rudolf Hess. Here he had called Troost's plans 'indecisive' and 'unsuited to the layout of the square'.[4]

1. Paul Bonatz/Friedrich Eugen Scholer: Stuttgart, Central Railway Station (1914–28), Side view

With his criticism of the early works of an emphatically representative new state architecture in Berlin and Munich, as well as of the first, unsuccessful, competitions for important commissions by the new regime[5] Bonatz in no way intended to oppose the Third Reich. On the contrary, his criticism was the sincere expression of his unconditional support for the new state, in which he placed all his hopes. He was intent on finding better possibilities for the architectural self-expression of this state and to this end he offered his experience and his skill. He wanted to participate in the shaping of the new state and recommended a different

145

kind of architecture for it. His report on the Königsplatz in Munich ended with the sentence: 'Only the greatest simplicity and clarity, limpid proportions and noble materials are conducive to that monumental style which is capable of symbolising the pure will of the *Führer*.'

Bonatz demanded that 'the will to representative architecture' come to terms with the products of technology, for 'it is undoubtedly possible to achieve the same authenticity in monumental as in practical design'. Modern technological constructions revealed 'a new will ... ruthlessly clear, sometimes harsh ... They are not born out of the mere calculations of an engineer, but inaugurated by a creative will that demands rhythm, provides tension and gives impetus. What is pleasing in such buildings is their objectivity and sincerity, hence the absence of false representation.'[6]

At first sight Bonatz's argumentation seems familiar. It is an expression of the same faith that all the architects of the German *Werkbund* placed in the power of modern industry and technology to mould a new style. It relied on the familiar demands of Modernism: opposition to all ornamentation, the rejection of historicism and the imploring repetition of the same moral attributes of the new architecture to which he aspired: objectivity, sincerity, renunciation of the fashionable, a sense of responsibility, ruthlessness, clarity and severity. Much of this is reminiscent of the familiar nostrums of Modernism, only the date and the political context of these statements is surprising.

Yet all this is striking only at first sight, for Paul Bonatz was no supporter of *Neues Bauen* but, on the contrary, he was one of its most significant adversaries. He belonged to the generation which founded the German *Werkbund* and he adhered to its traditionalist wing. He was an outright opponent of that part of the Modern Movement which articulated itself in the Berlin *Ring*,[7] the *Bauhaus* and the CIAM (i.e. *Congrès International d'Architecture Moderne*, founded in Switzerland in 1928). It was unacceptable to him for its avowed internationalism, its rejection of racial and local peculiarity and of architectural traditions worthy of being preserved and protected. This kind of Modernism was modish, formalist, insincere and pseudo-technological, in Bonatz's eyes. He was one of the founders and a prominent teacher of the traditionalist 'Stuttgart School', the only training institution for architects amongst Germany's polytechnics which understood itself as a 'school'.[8] Since 1922, the year in which the Central Railway Station in Stuttgart was completed, his reputation as an innovator of German architecture was unchallenged. Bonatz was recognised as one of the celebrities of German architecture after World War I.

The fact that he and Paul Schmitthenner were not invited to take part in the Stuttgart exhibition of the *Werkbund* and its model residential development Am Weissenhof led to a conflict which was to have some of the longest lasting consequences in the history of modern German architecture. Bonatz left the *Werkbund* and, under the leadership of Paul Schultze-Naumburg, he became a cofounder of the *Block*,[9] together with Paul Schmitthenner, Fritz Schumacher and other architects who had been influenced as much by the *Werkbund* as by the movement for the protection of the country's artistic and natural heritage. As declared preservers of tradition they were opposed to the propaganda and the conspirationnal policy of both the *Ring* and CIAM. However, as a result of the world economic depression the *Block* gained no influence on architectural developments. But a number of its leading members changed the site of the struggle and, even before 1933, began to launch political attacks against *Neues Bauen* from inside the ranks of the Combat League for German Culture. Labelling their opponents 'architectural bolshevists' (*Baubolschewisten*) they fought against unsympathetic colleagues.[10]

Although Bonatz did not engage prominently in these political wrangles before 1933 he too believed there was such a thing as 'architectural bolshevism'. In a letter to the co-founder of the *Werkbund*, Karl Schmidt, who lived in Hellerau, Bonatz wrote as late as 1941: 'New Objectivity (*Neue Sachlichkeit*) was a false creed. The only one who is even less objective and more contemptible in architectural and constructional terms than the *Bauhaus* in Dessau is Le Corbusier, whom they but copied . . . This is truly architectural bolshevism . . . a way of building which denies the third dimension, corporeality.' But as he had done in 1935, he disagreed with the stylistic orientation of official building policy in 1941, although he fairly confessed: 'Chance has allowed me to be one of the players in the game.' He deplored both the absence of scale in the architecture that bore the stamp of Speer and Giesler and the ban on criticising it. 'If criticism were possible, I would say this in regard to certain things: dear friends, we must not start out with such rich, coarse and overburdened forms, for we are only at a beginning. Beginning is the word that needs to be recalled again and again for, if you go on like this, then it will be an end . . . What is required now must not be lush and prodigious, but chaste and discreet, it must be clear, pure, bright and radiant. Strong, but not pompous . . . You will see how much more convincingly this will represent Modernity than the *Bauhaus*, which is already looking un-modern. By "Modernity" I mean a type of architecture which is suited both to today's human kind and the future one which we desire.'[11]

Bonatz attacked the semi-official state architecture with the same mordancy as he had employed against the *Bauhaus*, whether it was Speer's architecture in Berlin and Nuremberg, or that of Giesler in Munich, Weimar and Linz. He knew what he was talking about, for he was a player in the same 'game': from 1939 onwards he worked under Speer on the design of a new building for the high command of the Navy in Berlin and under Giesler he planned a new central station for Munich at the same time. On September 30, 1941, he spoke of Speer and Giesler in a letter to his colleague Friedrich Tamms (a collaborator of Speer's): '. . . but if I think about everything that is supposed to go up in Munich and Berlin, and the way in which it is being handled, then my horror becomes still greater. What arouses this horror is a little different in each case, but in the end it is the same thing . . . who will welcome the realisation of this Babylonian project? My only consolation is the knowledge that the harsh situation of real life will greatly cut down and simplify these phantom creations, much to their own advantage.[12]

Bonatz was fighting on two fronts. He wanted a modern architecture different from that of *Neues Bauen* and a traditionalism different from Speer's neo-Classicism. With his experience in the design of technical construction he intended to find a third way. In the lecture quoted at the beginning of this article he said: 'There is no real gulf between healthy tradition and a clear modern will. It is our task to bridge the apparent gulf and to feed the two creative forces into a single channel.'

Frequently Bonatz's works have been regarded as essentially functionalist and ultimately belonging to *Neues Bauen*, yet such an interpretation fails to take account of his fundamentally different view of the relationship between technical requirements and architectural configuration. It was precisely because of his divergence on this point that Bonatz argued so vehemently against the presumed functionality of the *Neues Bauen* architects.

Although he was more concerned with technical buildings than any other German architecture, he never spoke simply of 'building' (*Bauen*), but invariably of the 'art of building' (*Baukunst*; architecture). This means that for him technology as such would never on its own account, without an act of creative will, be capable of producing high ranking works of architecture. He demanded that architect and engineer collaborate sympathetically on the same project. With regard to this collaboration, he wrote in the Frankfurter Zeitung in 1940: 'But they achieve beauty . . . only if they are led to it by a conscious will.'[13]

The fact that Bonatz was so heavily involved with utility buildings like railway stations, factories, dams and especially bridges did not induce him to transfer the forms he developed in this field to other architectural projects such as representative buildings of the state, monuments or residential developments. He found no contradiction in erecting such a 'modern' construction as the steel bridge spanning the Rhine at Cologne-Rodenkirchen (1936 – 41) and, at the same time, such an 'unmodern' one as the castle for Count von der Schulenburg near Salzwedel. In his eyes it was only logical and consistent with his theories to erect a complex like the one made up by the town hall (*Fig 2*) and, next to it, the water supply tower in Kornwestheim near Stuttgart (1933 – 5). The town hall had a fairly traditional hipped roof while the water supply tower, whose lower levels were used for administrative purposes, displayed its rigidly technical structure made out of reinforced concrete.

2. Paul Bonatz: Town Hall in Kornwestheim near Stuttgart (1933 – 35)

The idea of linking the water supply tower and the town hall was not a new one. But unlike the complex built by Fritz Höger at Rüstringen[14], Bonatz renounced any attempt at formal unity. He opted for a monumental design made up of two heterogeneous elements, even accentuating their diversity. He refused to allow any exchange between the traditionalist form of the one and the technical structure of the other. Their character as monuments was to derive not from the transfer of specific formal elements from one to the other, but from the fact that each element of the complex was treated according to its own character. Yet it is the imposing hulk of the water supply tower that bestows on the complex its monumental character. The fact that it is in a style suited only to utility buildings, a style which Bonatz for the purposes of architectural planning simply called 'work-style' (*Arbeitsstil*), does not hamper this overall impression; on the contrary, it produces it.

Bonatz's *Arbeitsstil* was different from the *Industrieform* (industrial form) or the *Zweckform* (functional form) of the protagonists of *Neues Bauen*. For him this *Arbeitsstil* did not signify any objectivisation of his creative activity, nor any scientific transformation of his design work into engineering construction, but it merely fulfilled a subsidiary function in the formulation of a new style, constraining individual, deeply spontaneous and subjective creativity. He saw it precisely in the same way as Hermann Muthesius when, during the *Werkbund* exhibition in Cologne in 1914, the latter became involved in a famous argument with van de Velde by supporting 'typification in place of individualisation'.[15] 'Nothing is further from my inclination than to eulogise the *Arbeitsstil* as an objective and an end in itself; but it provides a cleansing bath and is the best means of education. From the *Arbeitsstil* we learn that even when planning representative works we must first of all pass through the maximum of simplicity . . . In this way the *Arbeitsstil* will become one of the factors that determine the direction of any further development. It should be no more than this and must above all not be imitated, lest it lead to a new formalism.'[16]

Bonatz wished to place constraints on himself, to fit himself into a new order, not just a formal, stylistic one but, as his political hopes for National Socialism revealed, in a new order in a comprehensive sense, that is, in a new social culture. 'Finally the concentrated energy deriving from the communal will ought to be represented. The conditions have never been so favourable as they are now.'[17] Bonatz was looking for ideological commitment and it was for this reason that he quoted a sentence from an essay of 1906 by his 'teacher and master' Theodor Fischer: 'We believe, because we have to believe to work.'[18]

Bonatz needed ideological embeddedness for his work, be it the embeddedness in regional and national architectural tradition or in the constructive and functional advances of the buildings of modern technology. Perhaps he even needed the submission to the strong client, to the dictatorial pressure of the National Socialist state at whose behest he created remarkable works of architecture which pointed to architectural developments well beyond 1945.

In the 1930s and 1940s Bonatz was mainly occupied with buildings for public utilities. Up to the end of World War II his friends were keen to present these works as examples of the most highly developed, modern and contemporary expression of the new National Socialist architectural culture. Bonatz did not object. But despite this or because he made a belated decision in 1944 in favour of emigration to Turkey he became a shining light for a whole generation of architects after the end of the war. To them Bonatz's work, like that of Heinrich Tessenow, provided compensatory architectural examples for coming to terms with defeat in war and the collective involvement of Germans with National Socialism.[19]

The triumph of his *Arbeitsstil* after 1945 did perhaps not necessarily presuppose the German defeat of 1945, as is exemplified by the parallel development of Scandinavian traditionalism, which became a specific and exemplary form of Modernism for post-war German designers and architects and was greatly admired by Bonatz. As in Scandinavia, traditionalist and radical tendencies of *Neues Bauen* converged into a single style in Germany which one might best term the 'new *Neues Bauen*'. Even in 1933 Bonatz had written: 'The contemporary polemics between tradition and modernity will become pointless, something superior will arise from the two, something that will be accepted as a matter of course.'[20]

The ambitious scheme of the Nazis to provide the whole of Germany in a very short space of time with an extremely modern system of motorways,[21] made of concrete and free of junctions, offered Bonatz the chance to exploit his experience in designing public utility buildings on a grand scale. Hitler had placed the overall management of the project in the hands of the civil engineer and 'veteran Nazi fighter', Fritz Todt, who was appointed 'inspector general of the German road system'.[22]

Todt understood that the motorway project involved a complex intervention in the spatial structure of the entire country, which went far beyond the traditional concerns of civil engineers. Right from the start he therefore undertook to involve architects who were willing to cooperate, side by side with qualified engineers. It was the architects' task to help project the construction of the motorways for the purposes of propaganda as one of the most innovative deeds of National Socialism. It was necessary, for this reason, to use every possible means to present the effect of the technical project on the landscape and its spatial structure as an embellishment over previous conditions. The *Autobahn* could only become effective as a means of propaganda if it had presentable qualities that lent themselves to popularisation.

Hence Todt engaged as his 'landscape consultant' the unconventional Munich architect and planner of green spaces, Alwin Seifert. It was on his recommendation that, in 1935, Bonatz became the 'artistic consultant' of the Inspector General for the design of all motorway bridges.[23]

Bonatz threw himself into this work with maximum commitment. He adjudicated all the projects for major bridges, took over the architectural planning of a considerable number of significant projects and did not think it beneath himself to make detailed contributions to the building of innumerable smaller bridges crossing streams and paths in the countryside.[24] At Todt's behest the major consultants held regular training courses at Plassen castle near Kulmbach for the various kinds of technical staff engaged on different construction sites. Within the context of ideological training by the National Socialist party Bonatz and Seifert were given the opportunity to teach the engineers their own design concepts.

In view of its scale, the design of the motorway system turned out to be a surprisingly homogeneous project and the Third Reich's propaganda machine was accordingly able to exploit it for its own purposes. Todt, who was an enthusiastic amateur photographer, launched a national photographic competition with the beauty of the motorway system as its theme. Painters, film-makers and photographers were commissioned and subsidised to portray the 'great work campaign' for the construction of the motorways.[25] Paintings of the large bridging projects were to be seen at the annual exhibitions at the *Haus der Deutschen Kunst* in

Munich and were even used as advertising for construction firms, car manufacturers and insurance companies. The motorway bridges became the National Socialist symbol of progress par excellence. Pictures of them were promoted everywhere, not just in specialist journals such as Todt's *Die Strasse* (The Road) (*Fig 3*), but also in newsreels, illustrated weeklies and daily papers, even on special stamps issued on behalf of the winter relief organisation (a kind of Nazi charity).

3. Titlepage of *Die Strasse*, 1941:
Rhinebridge Cologne-Rodenkirchen
under Construction

Bonatz was well aware of the propaganda effect that his large bridges had, for as early as 1935 he had stated: 'Among the current building projects being carried out by the state, the one which has the most exemplary stylistic force is perhaps the construction of the motorway system . . . The representational effect of bridges will lie in their absolute technical purity and certainly not, as with the bridges around 1900, in any additional elements. Today new kinds of tasks can lead to new forms of expression. And just as in the Roman Empire, works of engineering can represent the power of the state, as long, of course, as they are born out of a great capacity for creativity.'[26]

Bonatz had already worked out all the principles of his new activity in earlier projects, especially in the ten barrages which he had constructed in the 1920s when the river Neckar was canalised (*Figs 4* and *5*).[27] But his experience in the construction of bridges dated back much further, since it had begun with the building of the Wallstrasse bridge in Ulm in 1907. Among the relatively numerous bridges that he went on to build, the purist Neckar bridge he designed for Heidelberg in 1927 attracted the greatest attention.[28]

In his memoirs Bonatz singled out the construction of the Neckar barrages as a preparation for his work on the motorways. 'The enticing problem here was, to

4. Paul Bonatz (in collaboration with the Directors of the Neckar Construction Company): Neckar Barrage in Ladenburg near Mannheim

5. Paul Bonatz (in collaboration with the Directors of Neckar Construction): Neckar Barrage in Heidelberg, 1926

give clear expression to technical necessity and represent the technically indispensable with complete purity, that is without any appurtenances and at the same time to emphasise function through form, making it comprehensible even to the layman by giving it sensuous expression.'[29]

Despite having basically the same function, the barrages were all shaped in different ways. Bonatz attributed this to their having to fit into different landscapes which, in turn, led to the choice of different construction materials. 'When we came to the area of red sandstone Jurassic cement was added to the monolithic concrete, bestowing it with a pinkish-grey tone. When we were working in the plains, near Ladenburg for example, we were happy to work with ordinary concrete. But when, near Hornberg, we ran into fossiliferous limestone, we used limestone for masonry instead of bricks.'[30]

In contrast to the claims made by the dogmatists of *Neues Bauen*, Bonatz held that modern construction materials did not exist, just a modern architectonic mentality. Hence he regarded the bridge over the Lahn near Limburg, built entirely out of stone (*Fig 6*), just as modern as the steel bridge over the Rhine near Cologne-Rodenkirchen (*Fig 7*). It was the very desire to make his bridges into monuments that explains his passion for building in stone. Concrete buildings which were merely faced with natural stone filled him with horror. If stone was to be used then the building had to be made of stone in its entirety, like the Lahn bridge.

6. Paul Bonatz (in collaboration with the engineer, G. Schaper): Bridge over the Lahn near Limburg under Construction (1938–1940)

7. Paul Bonatz (in collaboration with the engineer, Fritz Leonhardt): Rhinebridge Cologne-Rodenkirchen (1939–41)

Even in his monuments to the fallen of World War I (*Fig 8*) he had sought to obtain monumental effects by semi-circular arches with stones or bricks arranged as 'soldiers' to form the rounded lintel. It therefore suited him that natural stone should be so popular with some politicians of the Third Reich because of its durability and its value as a historical architectural remnant in the future (*Ruinenwert*). This even induced him to design an immense open rotunda, a sort of modern Colosseum, which he imagined should consist of a pure succession of regular vaults of stone (*Fig 9*). In his 1937 monograph on Bonatz, Tamms even went so far as to present this project as a sort of culmination of his work.[31]

Despite stone being in vogue, concrete and steel won out for reasons of cost and because of the considerably shorter construction time they allowed. Bonatz by no means spurned these trends and even with the 'new' materials he once again succeeded, in close collaboration with the engineers, Karl Schaechterle and Fritz Leonhardt, in designing bridges of great suggestive power.[32] His pressed concrete bridge on the Drackenstein slope in the Swabian Alb, designed in collaboration with Wilhelm Tiedje, became famous. Almost equally so were the reinforced concrete bridges over the Danube near Leipheim, over the Murr valley near Backnang and over the Saale near Lehesten. Perhaps even more suggestive at the time were the steel beam bridge spanning the Elbe near Dessau and the steel suspension bridge over the Rhine at Rodenkirchen, for which Bonatz himself had a special liking. The fact that this bridge became so well known shows that the architectural

8. Paul Bonatz: Motorway bridge over the Waschmühl valley near Kaiserslautern (1935 –
37) (Foto: Erna Lendvai-Dierksen)

culture of the Third Reich was not based merely on a revival of building in stone.
Work on this bridge was not broken off at the beginning of the war, as happened
elsewhere more or less as a matter of course, but continued with alacrity, for it was
a project of avowed prestige. It was inaugurated with great pomp in September
1941. Bonatz referred with pride to Todt's enthusiasm for this limpid work, based
purely on technical necessity.

Bonatz's many bridges demonstrate that his call for typification did not signify uniformity. In each case he strove for unmistakable and characteristic design
solutions. 'There are no recipes', he wrote in 1941 in his essay entitled *Die Brücke*
(The Bridge). And a few lines before that: 'Technical and sentimental considerations together will determine the system of bridges, the stone viaduct, the piers set
close together or far apart . . . A horizontally laid bridge will convey passion and
sudden force, a high arched viaduct calm and serenity.'[33]

Bonatz was continually torn between his enthusiasm for a demanding
configuration of technological requirements and his desire to build in conformity
with the scale and characteristics of the project in hand. One notices this above all
in his design of Munich's Central Railway Station (*Fig 10*). Fritz Leonhardt

155

9. Paul Bonatz: Open Rotunda (1937) (Drawing by Kurt Dübbers)

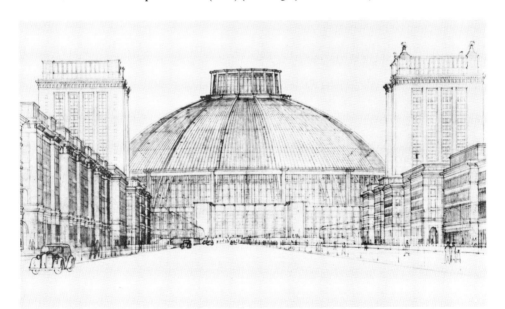

10. Paul Bonatz (in collaboration with the engineer, Fritz Leonhardt): Munich Central Railway Station (1939–1942)

reported: 'Giesler intended this station to be a purely technical construction, and therefore to be built out of steel, not stone or concrete. Surprisingly Hitler agreed to the use of this ephemeral material.'[34] The structure of the dome was put up for competition amongst various specialist contractors. Klönne of Dortmund was awarded the contract. This firm had previously built the Rodenkirchen bridge. The architect responsible for Klönne's design proposal was Paul Bonatz who opened an office in Munich especially for this project. 'I was initially attracted by the engineering and architectural challenge of shaping something purely out of steel, glass and copper. But the pleasure derived from the play with form could in the long run not conceal the knowledge that there was a basic flaw.'[35] He considered the dimensions of the dome, which was to have a diameter of 245 metres, sheer madness, justified only on formal grounds. In his opinion the whole station project was misconceived and instead of the dome he proposed a conventional East-West transit station of decidedly more modest proportions with its entrance hall laid out on one side of the platforms. In his memoirs he described this work as more agonising than the almost contemporaneous project for the Navy High Command in Berlin, with its neoclassicist façades. 'If I had to name a single reason for my emigration, it would have to be the escape from this madness.'[36]

Of all Bonatz's works, the Munich railway station is surely the one that comes closest to the concept of modernity in *Neues Bauen*, both by its choice of building materials and its architecture. The fact that he distanced himself from those concepts so emphatically is due to his fundamentally different conception of the role of architecture in general and of modern architecture in particular. In Bonatz's understanding of Modernism form and content had to be congruent, tradition and technology were to be reconciled. In his architecture Heidegger's 'Foursome' (*Geviert*) was to be united: earth and the heavens, the divine ones and the mortals. Bonatz wanted his architecture to be a bridge.

Chapter Nine

MUSIC AND NATIONAL SOCIALISM: THE POLITICISATION OF CRITICISM, COMPOSITION AND PERFORMANCE

Erik Levi

Throughout history, music has been perceived as an extraordinarily effective medium for transmitting propaganda. This is particularly true of the twentieth century — a period that has witnessed several instances in which music has played a considerable role in consolidating or actually reflecting political change. One of the most conspicuous examples of this process occurred in the Soviet Union, a country in which radical ideology temporarily inspired striking alternatives to bourgeois Western culture. On the other hand in Nazi Germany, cultural and specifically musical developments have been perceived as being primarily nationalist and defiantly conservative. Since conservatism essentially contradicts the conventional interpretation of twentieth century musical history which argues that the language and technique of music has developed along mainly 'progressive' lines, it is hardly surprising that musicologists have on the whole concentrated their attention upon developments in the Soviet Union whereas their assessment of artistic activity in Nazi Germany has been based upon a few ill-informed statements. For example, such an eminently respectable book as William Austin's *Music in the Twentieth Century*[1] barely alludes to the question of music in Nazi Germany, although the nature and quality of Soviet composition is given extended and sympathetic treatment. One explanation for this strange imbalance must be connected with the fact that misapprehensions and rumours of the most superficial nature have tended to dominate any discussion of the relationship between music and National Socialism. Many musicologists, for example, seem to be more interested in speculating as to how far such distinguished musicians as Richard Strauss and Wilhelm Furtwängler collaborated with the regime rather than considering musical life in Nazi Germany in objective terms. Moreover having discussed Strauss and Furtwängler, they then condemn the period as the twentieth century musical equivalent of the dark ages.

Such an assertion is totally misleading since it implies that music did not prosper under the Nazis. Indeed on the contrary, one can argue quite convincingly that the Third Reich positively reverberated to the sounds of music, whether from the massed political rallies with their choral singing, marches and fanfares or from the spectacularly lavish operatic productions presented annually at such places as Bayreuth and Munich. Musicians enjoyed regular employment, composers were courted with generous state prizes and subsidies to opera houses and concert halls increased dramatically as the economic situation improved. In addition, both the radio stations and a greatly expanded recording and film industry offered composers and instrumentalists further opportunities for financial prosperity. The number of books and magazines devoted to music increased substantially during the period 1933 – 1945, whilst music education was encouraged and rewarded through the creation of several newly constituted conservatoires.

Naturally, musical activity on this scale had to be subjected to strict political and racial considerations. Music was but one significant medium in the Nazi party's mounting armoury of propaganda weapons designed to demonstrate to the world the moral, spiritual and cultural superiority of the German nation. Nevertheless music was by no means as malleable an art form as painting. As an essentially abstract medium concerned primarily with the organisation of sound, its emotional message was capable of varying and often contradictory degrees of interpretations. Moreover, Nazi cultural aesthetes found great difficulty in determining the meaning and value of a particular piece of music unless it was allied to an unequivocal political slogan.

In essence, these contradictions, which prevented a clear-cut definition of politically acceptable or unacceptable music, mirror the fluctuating and sometimes equivocal musical tastes of Germany's rulers. There is even some doubt as to whether Adolf Hitler responded positively to music. Certainly the historian Joachim C. Fest suggests that music played a very limited role in the *Führer's* life: 'Although he regarded himself as a lover of music, in actuality, music meant little to him . . . He listened to records only when nothing better offered.'[2]

On the other hand, Ernst (Putzi) Hanfstaengl, a constant companion during the 1920's, presents a completely different view:

> 'I used to play music on the piano to calm him after having to appear as witness in frequent political trials — I played a Bach fugue to which he sat listening in his chair, nodding his head in vague disinterest. Then I started the prelude to [Wagner's] *Die Meistersinger.* This was it . . . He knew the thing absolutely by heart and could whistle every note of it in a curiously penetrating vibrato, but completely in tune . . . He really had an excellent feel for the spirit of the music, certainly as good as any conductor . . . Later I came to see that there was a direct parallel between the construction of the *Meistersinger* Prelude and that of his speeches. The whole interweaving of leitmotifs, of embellishments, of counterpoint and musical contrasts and argument were exactly mirrored in the pattern of his speeches which were symphonic in construction and ended in a great climax, like the blare of Wagner's trombones.'[3]
> (*Fig 1.*)

Whether one accepts Fest's or Hanfstaengl's arguments, there can be no doubt that one musician, Richard Wagner, exerted an enormous influence upon the mind and policies of Adolf Hitler. Much indeed has been written about the *Führer's* links with the Bayreuth master and several scholars have perceived direct parallels between Wagner's essays, published towards the end of his life in his magazine, *Bayreuther Blätter,* and the political ideology of the Nazi party. It is debatable whether Hitler was aware of these writings, but he certainly embraced the chauvinist and racialist prejudices of such Wagnerian disciples as Houston Stewart Chamberlain and Hans von Wolzogen. As a frequent visitor to Wahnfried, the Wagner family home, during the 1920's, Hitler must have engaged in active discussion with some of the more influential members of the Bayreuth circle.

1. The *Führer* lays a wreath at the bust of the composer Anton Bruckner newly installed in the Walhalla in Regensburg in 1937

Whilst documentary evidence suggests that the conversations were dominated by political matters, music was by no means neglected. Indeed, when the Nazis seized power in 1933, Hitler lost little time in attempting to realise some of the musical as well as political objectives held by the Bayreuth circle.

Unquestionably the most important of these was the desire to restore Germany to its former position of pre-eminence in the musical world. During the nineteenth century, the great German tradition extending from Beethoven through Wagner to Richard Strauss had dominated music in a remarkable and almost unique manner. This was the age of Romanticism in which incipient German nationalism was celebrated in such works as Wagner's *Die Meistersinger* and Richard Strauss's *Ein Heldenleben*. However by the time of World War I, musicians had reacted against Romanticism — Paris had replaced Berlin and Vienna as the musical capital of the world. Germany's ignominious defeat at the end of the war had signalled further reactions. The 1920's ushered in a time of intense experimentation, as well as a proliferation of musical activity in countries geographically and spiritually removed from Germany. Despite the fact that cultural ministers, working in the various governments of the Weimar Republic, succeeded in restoring the nation's declining musical fortunes by engaging the services of some of the greatest musicians of the period (for example the composers Ferruccio Busoni and Arnold Schoenberg who held official positions in the Prussian Academy of Arts) and encouraging intense creativity on a scale hitherto rarely experienced in Germany, they were constantly opposed by a section of the musical establishment that was reactionary and provincial in its outlook. The Nazis capitalised upon the fears and prejudices of these musicians by deliberately equating the cultural enlightenment of the Weimar Republic with a dangerous and subversive form of Internationalism — something which could shake the very foundations of German national consciousness.

For the Nazis, the only solution to national recovery lay in crude direct methods of intervention. Music would have to be harnessed for purely nationalist and political purposes, nothing less than total control of all aspects of musical life could suffice. In addition, a programme which supported the complete elimination of alien and undesirable elements had to be undertaken before the dangerous forces of international Modernism could be defeated. These were the clearly stated objectives of Hitler's minister of propaganda, Joseph Goebbels, who pursued a policy that was ruthless in its determination to effect brutal changes in musical life, but somewhat irrational when it came to dealing with individual musicians. It is this dichotomy between musical aims and their execution which forms the central theme of the present essay.

When the Nazis came to power in 1933, they were heartened by the surprisingly large number of influential musicians who passively sympathised with their cultural programme. Although musical activity in the Weimar Republic had been both stimulating and provocative, there were many who became increasingly alienated from the extreme manifestations of avant-garde music-making. In addition, attitudes became more polarised as the economic situation worsened. Thus a remarkable alliance was formed between musicians who had become worried about their future prospects of securing regular employment and conservative composers who had remained embittered by the neglect they were suffering in comparison to their more daring colleagues. Given this state of affairs, it is hardly surprising that many listened with sympathy to the Nazi Party's promises of a regeneration of a genuine and strong national musical style. Even before 1933,

Alfred Rosenberg's *Kampfbund für deutsche Kultur* (Combat League for German Culture) had attracted the attention of musicians of the calibre of the violinist Gustav Havemann and the eminent composer Paul Graener. These men became active participants in this movement, organising concerts, festivals and music seminars and attracting the attention and sympathy of such conservative yet prominent periodicals as the *Zeitschrift für Musik*. This magazine also heralded the formation of the so-called *Nationalsozialistische Reichssinfonieorchester* in 1931 (the personal orchestra of the *Führer*) as one of the most hopeful signs in the continuing struggle to defeat the forces of 'Bolshevik Modernism.'

As more people drifted towards the nationalist cause, the prospects for achieving a totalitarian music policy seemed ever more promising. During the first year of Nazi rule, the *Kampfbund* exercised the most apparent influence through the prominent organisation of musical events such as a special birthday concert for the *Führer* and numerous appearances at summer music festivals. However behind the scenes, a war was being waged for the cultural soul of the Party between two opposing forces — Alfred Rosenberg and Josef Goebbels. When Goebbels gained the upper hand and Rosenberg was consigned to a much less powerful or influential position the *Kampfbund* became largely defunct.[4] Besides, Goebbels, as the master strategist, plundered many of the ideas of the *Kampfbund* but incorporated them within a much grander and more centralised control over all aspects of culture. This newly created body entitled the *Reichskulturkammer* (National Chamber of Culture) in effect gave Goebbels absolute power over all matters of a cultural nature. Within this organisation, the *Reichsmusikkammer* (National Music Chamber) became responsible for the creation of a comprehensive and coherent music policy.

It is worthwhile examining the various functions of the *Reichsmusikkammer* in some detail before commenting on the effectiveness of its policies and the personalities involved. Initially, the number of proposed divisions of the organisation seemed astonishingly wide-ranging, yet cumbersome in appearance. By 1937, however, seven basic areas had evolved. These were: Section 1: the *Fachschaft der deutschen Komponisten* (department of German composers) which encompassed all German composers, soloists, orchestral musicians and those who played in light music orchestras; Section 2: the *Fachschaft Musikerziehung* (department of music teachers), responsible for all music teachers whether at the advanced level of music conservatoire or elementary school; Section 3: *Amt für Chorwesen und Volksmusik* (office for choral affairs and folk music) within which the *Deutscher Sängerbund* (the German Singers Union, an organisation which the Nazis created out of the forced amalgamation of all of Germany's male voice choirs incorporating a membership of over 200,000 people), the *Reichsverband der gemischten Chöre* (the National Association of Mixed Choirs with a membership of nearly half a million), the *Reichsverband für Volksmusik* (National Association for Folk Music) and the *Fachschaft für evangelische Kirchenmusik* (Department for Evangelical Church Music) formed the major components; Section 4 was concerned with the control of concerts, agents and the performing rights of composers, and Section 5 dealt with music publishers, musical instrument manufacturers and dealers. The final two sections were devoted to dealing with aspects of financial organisation and clarification of the laws pertaining to musicians. Beyond these broad divisions, the Nazis appointed various functionaries in the 31 districts of the country to oversee and administer the policies decided by Goebbels and his inner cabinet of influential musicians. This select group formed the public face of the *Reichsmusikkammer*, although their power was severely limited.

Without a doubt, Goebbels scored a massive propaganda coup by persuading Richard Strauss to become the first President of the *Reichsmusikkammer* as well as making Wilhelm Furtwängler his immediate deputy. The presence of two such distinguished musicians, neither of whom was a member of the Nazi party, gave the organisation the kind of national, and indeed international, credibility and respectability that ensured its acceptance even amongst those who were suspicious of Goebbels's real intentions. For a time Strauss, a consistent campaigner for the rights of German musicians, sincerely believed that the *Reichsmusikkammer* could only benefit musical life. Colleagues from abroad seemed astonished at the political naïvety of a man who had witnessed some of the harshest repressions of the Wilhelminian era. In Strauss's defence, it must be said that he believed that his eminence and undoubted influence might protect others from the more extreme manifestations of Nazi policy. Within a few years, however, both he and Furtwängler fell out with the authorities. Strauss suffered a public humiliation when his opera *Die schweigsame Frau* (The Silent Woman) was withdrawn after a few performances because the composer's librettist, Stefan Zweig, was Jewish, while Furtwängler resigned his post at the Berlin Philharmonic Orchestra after defending the cause of Paul Hindemith, the distinguished composer who had been constantly vilified by the Nazi hierarchy. These apparent challenges to Goebbels' authority were in fact turned to the minister's advantage. Strauss was stripped of his post as President of the *Reichsmusikkammer*. Furtwängler withdrew from public life for a time, but found isolation unbearable. Within months, the conductor recanted—his apparent climbdown was hailed in the press as a complete 'rehabilitation' *(Fig 2)*.

In essence, both Strauss's and Furtwängler's resignations from the *Reichsmusikkammer* had only provided momentary embarrassments for the regime. Although public opinion abroad might have been shocked by the shabby treatment meted out to two great musicians, Goebbels skilfully distorted the facts and convincingly accused them of disloyalty. By 1937, Goebbels had reinforced his will over the *Reichsmusikkammer* to such an extent that all potential elements of dissent had been eliminated. Besides, the Nazi government had now established such a hold over the country, that minor scandals no longer threatened the regime's stability. Strauss's successor as President, Dr Peter Raabe, commanded almost universal respect for his considerable achievements as a musicologist and conductor. Moreover Raabe had been a loyal member of the Nazi party for many years and worked with an almost fanatical zeal for the musical reforms espoused by his political superiors. The enthusiasm with which he approached his work can be measured by the fact that he spent much of his time touring the country, making speeches at every important musical occasion and issuing innumerable directives from the *Reichsmusikkammer's* headquarters in Berlin. For a time, Raabe managed to preserve the musical independence of one of Germany's oldest musical organisations the *Allgemeiner Deutscher Musikverein* (General German Music Organisation or *ADMV*), founded by Franz Liszt in 1861, which held annual festivals of new music. However even he could not quell a massively orchestrated campaign, inspired no doubt by Goebbels, which condemned the *ADMV* for its élitism and evident lack of political commitment. In 1937, Raabe was forced to make the most humiliating speech of his career in terminating the activities of the *ADMV*, founded by the very composer whom he most admired.[5]

2. Richard Strauss caricatured as the new Führer of German composers in the magazine *Zeitschrift für Musik* in 1934

Amongst the hierarchy of the *Reichsmusikkammer,* Raabe was by far the most notable musician. Most of his assistants were non-descript party faithfuls who had been rewarded for their loyalty with posts of an often meaningless importance. Therefore despite the fact that opposition from various sectors of the music profession was effectively crushed, the vast bureaucracy set up by Goebbels became incredibly inefficient. Delays in processing vetted applications for concert programmes and approving suitable material for musical publication were legion. Often, contradictory statements were handed out to composers and performers from different officials of the *Reichsmusikkammer.* In truth, the whole edifice which had been master-minded by the ministry of propaganda represented a smokescreen for the realisation of Goebbels' own cherished ideals, which in themselves inclined towards the more 'socialistic' leanings of the Nazi party. Amongst the most notable manifestations of this policy were the schemes to bring music to the ordinary people through the *Kraft durch Freude* (Strength through Joy) movement with, for example, regular orchestral concerts given in factories and sports halls. Goebbels incorporated such events in the annual *Reichsmusiktage* which were held in Düsseldorf from 1935 to 1939. These festivals were designed to demonstrate to the world the extraordinary effectiveness of the policies adopted by the *Reichsmusikkammer*, but the programmes increasingly mirrored the drift away from serious music-making towards concerts that incorporated more overtly political compositions (specially commissioned cantatas, marches and fanfares) and works of a patriotic and popular nature. During the war, Goebbels' hostility towards élitist music became even more extreme. In his posthumously published diaries, we often find him raging against so-called serious composers and admonishing his assistant with responsibility for music in the Ministry of Propaganda for tolerating a situation in which: '. . . popular composers have to give up most of their income to the so-called serious musicians via the STAGMA [the German Performing Rights Society]. This is a downright absurdity. Those who can do their job feed, at least in part, the "serious" ones — that is, often, the failures. I intend to abolish this forthwith . . .' (22 November 1940).[6]

A few days later, he returned to the same theme: 'We should pay more attention to the field of popular music than previously. After all, it represents the major part of our musical activity as a whole . . . Drewes [musical assistant in the Ministry of Propaganda] would like to turn the entire population into Bach enthusiasts. This is, of course, neither possible nor ultimately desirable.' (24 November 1940).[7]

If Goebbels intended to quash the influence of serious music during the war, he was not averse to appearing a year later in front of a specially invited conference of distinguished musicians in Vienna, held to celebrate the 150th anniversary of Mozart's death. Here the minister not only praised the achievements of the Austrian master, but urged his countrymen to learn from the past by writing music of a profound and truly elevating nature. The volatile and overtly opportunistic nature of Goebbels' utterances about music reflect a certain recklessness which infected much of the Nazi party's cultural policy. In truth, Goebbels was out of his depth when dealing directly with composers. On the other hand, with the instruments of mass media, the radio and the press, he was at all times supremely in control.

It could be argued that radio was the most effective and important medium for transmitting musical propaganda. Certainly the statistics bear out the claims made by the Nazis regarding the increased purchase of wireless sets (from 3 million in 1932 to nearly 11 million in 1939) and within the radio stations, the proportion of music broadcasts was raised from 57% in 1932 to nearly 70% six years later. Analysis of the type of music favoured by the authorities points to Goebbels' own prejudices. In the early years of the Nazi period, there was a genuine attempt to maintain a balance between concert and operatic music and lighter fare. But gradually *Unterhaltungsmusik* (light music) gained the upper hand to the extent that by 1938, it accounted for 46% of music broadcasts. Transmissions of symphonies, operas and chamber works barely reached 6% of the total music output. During the War, this proportion was reduced further with most efforts concentrated upon the presentation of the immensely successful *Wunschkonzerte* (Request Concerts) for the Wehrmacht. In this programme, the repertoire could extend from classical symphonies conducted by Herbert von Karajan to the simplest popular melody or march. It was inevitable however that as the War dragged on, this utopian mixture of musical styles could not co-exist. In the end, the Ministry of Propaganda realised that the escapist qualities of popular music were of more immediate benefit to the War effort.

If Goebbels was one of the first politicians to realise the potential of nurturing cultural predilections through the medium of broadcasting, he was equally aware of the power of the written word. While it is difficult to ascertain the extent to which musical criticism was disseminated to the public at large, there is no doubt that musicologists were happier than composers and performers to conform to the Party ideology. Indeed the sheer number of books on music written during this period suggests that musicologists were relishing the challenges of making Nazi prejudices intellectually respectable. No doubt this explains the vast amount of effort expended upon revising standard musical histories such as Emil Naumann's famous *Illustrierte Musikgeschichte* (Illustrated Music History),[8] originally a nineteenth century work, but updated during the Weimar Republic. Moreover this desire to rewrite musical history became entangled with a new and blinkered cultural xenophobia which sought to negate any possible foreign influence upon the great German composers of the past. This insularity of attitude was reinforced in books like Ernst Bücken's *Deutsche Musikkunde*[9] (German Music Knowledge) and Josef Müller-Blattau's *Germanisches Erbe in deutscher Tonkunst*[10] (the Germanic Heritage in German Music) which tried to analyse the very constituents of Germanness in music. The crux of the arguments contained in these books is that the indigenous nature of German folk music is exemplified in clear diatonic themes and strongly defined rhythms which have infiltrated the nation's 'serious' music from the medieval period to the present day. Naturally both Bücken and Müller-Blattau attempt to relate these virtues to the burgeoning influences of Nazi political songs. In essence, their positive melodies and powerful rhythms reflect the nation's spiritual reawakening *(Fig 3)*.

1. Heinrich Himmler, head of the SS and chief of the German police, provides the following motto to Josef Müller-Blattau's book *Germansiches Erbe in deutscher Tonkunst* (1938): 'A nation will live happily in the present and future as long as it remains conscious of its past and the greatness of its forebears.'

Whilst musicologists were prepared to prostitute their ideas about musical nationalism and Germany's heritage of great composers, they were more circumspect about committing themselves with regard to contemporary 'serious' music. Surprisingly few books were published at the time about the new music written during the Third Reich—even the politically committed Müller-Blattau finds space for only three pages of comment on this subject within his 300 page *Geschichte der deutschen Musik* (1938).[11] A possible explanation for this curious state of affairs may lie in the fact that Goebbels had inhibited constructive criticism of contemporary culture in 1936. In addition, instant information, including the necessary panegyrics, could be obtained from reading the numerous music periodicals which from the very outset were controlled by Party activists. Certainly, two of the most influential music magazines which flourished during the Weimar Republic, *Zeitschrift für Musik* and *Die Musik* were afforded very different status under Hitler. The *Zeitschrift*, which had consistently pursued a conservative and nationalist approach during the 1920's (its proprietor, Gustav Bosse of Regensburg, had relaunched the magazine as a broadsheet for the 'spiritual renewal of German music' in 1925), was rewarded with little official interference from 1933–1936. Indeed, the character and format of the magazine hardly changed throughout the period despite the fact that from 1936 onwards all information from the higher echelons of the *Reichsmusikkammer* was officially incorporated within its pages. Moreover, Bosse was allowed to include many articles of a purely musicological and apolitical nature—an important factor in maintaining the *Zeitschrift's* reputation as an internationally respected music journal. On the other hand, *Die Musik* which had gained universal admiration for its independence and perspicacious journalism was subjected to a brutal transformation. Six months after the Nazis came to power, the magazine had become the mouthpiece for the most extreme form of musical tub-thumping. Its June issue, entitled *Das Neue Deutschland*, contained excerpts from political speeches by Hitler and Goebbels together with appeals from approved Nazi musicians to effect a spiritual renewal of all aspects of German culture. Following this, the main articles reiterated the politicians' rallying call—it is unnecessary to comment on the level of intellectual discussion attained in such pieces of journalism as Hans Bullerian's 'Das Deutsche Konzertleben und seine Erneuerung', Hans Joachim Moser's 'Der Deutsche Musikunterricht und seine Neugestaltung', or Willi Hille's 'Nationalisierung der deutschen Musik'. Suffice it to say that subsequent issues of *Die Musik* continued an infinite number of variations on an all-too-familiar theme. In April 1934, Goebbels personally decreed that *Die Musik* should become the official music magazine for the Hitler Youth Movement. Its main task was to brainwash the musical tastes of the younger generation.

Reading through the pages of a periodical like *Die Musik*, one becomes increasingly aware of the fact that musicologists, as well as the Nazi hierarchy, hoped to create a coherent and healthy cultural environment not through positive directives on musical style, but rather by the total elimination of all alien influences. In particular, a policy of anti-semitism was pursued with fanatical consistency and ruthless efficiency. The objectives were perfectly clear—any suspected Jewish element had to be thoroughly purged from German music.

Goebbels postulated four clearly delineated areas in which this could be achieved. Firstly, he decreed that Jews holding positions of influence within German musical life would be expelled from their posts. Wherever possible, he used the newly introduced laws on 'servants of the state' (Laws of the Professional

Civil Service) which sanctioned discrimination on racial and ideological grounds. Within months, conductors of the calibre of Otto Klemperer and Bruno Walter were forced to leave the country. Arnold Schoenberg and Franz Schreker resigned from their teaching positions in Berlin whereas Kurt Weill quietly slipped out of Germany without facing official retribution. This hostility towards conductors and composers was extended to executants of international reputation. In other words, German audiences were deprived of hearing violinists like Jascha Heifetz and Yehudi Menuhin or the pianist Artur Schnabel whether in concert or on commercial recording.

Weeding out prominent Jewish musicians was a relatively easy task. Without exception, most of these people were able to seek refuge in other countries. But the prospects for those who had not attained the fame of a Klemperer or Schoenberg were less clearcut. For a time supposedly independent organisations like the *Berlin Philharmonic Orchestra* refused to countenance the sacking of their Jewish instrumentalists. But when Goebbels threatened the orchestra by suggesting that its future financial position could not be guaranteed, this obduracy was soon removed. As the regime tightened its grip over all aspects of cultural life, a familiar pattern emerged in which Jews were officially forbidden from teaching in music conservatoires or playing in orchestras. To stem the rising tide of international opposition towards this policy, the Ministry of Propaganda proposed the formation of a *Jüdische Kulturbund* which would offer secure employment to Jewish musicians prevented from working in Germany's teaching institutions and concert halls. This form of musical apartheid, which for a time attracted a membership of over 180,000 people, survived the first five years of Nazi rule. But within months of the pogrom known as *Kristallnacht* which took place in November 1938, many of its most prominent musicians had either emigrated or had been deported to concentration camps.

Goebbels' second objective, in his desire to rid the German nation of Jewish influence, took the form of a wholesale ban on the performance of music written by composers of Jewish blood. At first, this was confined to those composers like Schreker, Schoenberg, Toch and Weill who had prospered during the Weimar Republic. But eventually the net was cast wider and popular operetta composers like Offenbach and Kalman were also vetoed. The Mayor of Leipzig ordered the removal of a statue of Felix Mendelssohn which had stood in front of the famous Gewandhaus for many years. Soon his actions would be publicly applauded by the Ministry of Propaganda with the consequent disappearance of Mendelssohn's music from concert halls and publishers' catalogues.

With a concert and operatic repertoire bereft of racially suspect composers, Goebbels turned his attention to music that was guilty, by direct or indirect association, of Jewish connections. I have already referred to Richard Strauss's difficulties with the regime on account of his collaboration with the librettist Stefan Zweig. But Strauss's position was relatively secure and even the Nazi party could not bring itself to ban performances of such operas as *Der Rosenkavalier* just because the work's text had been written by a man who was half-Jewish. However in the case of a relatively unknown composer, the prospects were much less auspicious. A good example of this can be seen when one examines the career of Richard Mohaupt. This composer had been commissioned to write a ballet for the 1936 Olympic Games and was regarded as racially impeccable by the authorities. When his opera *Die Wirtin von Pinsk* (The Landlady of Pinsk) was given its first performance at the *Dresden Opera* in 1938, it was acclaimed by both the critics and the public. Unfortunately, a local Nazi functionary discovered that Mohaupt's wife was Jewish and he instigated a carefully manipulated campaign against the composer and his work. Needless to say, the opera was withdrawn after a few performances and Mohaupt had to flee the country.

Although Party officials maintained a vigilance against the possibility of any music being contaminated by Judaism, they sometimes had to resort to the most ridiculous form of subterfuge in order to protect the public from embarrassing facts. The most notable example of this occurred after Hitler had annexed Austria. During the period in which Jews had been subjected to the most terrible form of persecution, someone examined the genealogical origins of the famous Strauss family in Vienna. When it was discovered that a composer as popular as Johann Strauss had distant relatives who were of Jewish blood, his birth certificate was mysteriously removed from the records office.

It must be emphasised that the campaign against the Jews filled many musicians with a deep revulsion. Nevertheless Goebbels was more interested in shaping the thinking of future generations. To this end, he sustained his war of attrition through skilful and constant use of the propaganda machine. With the help of some influential musicologists, he was able to achieve his third objective of justifying anti-semitism in music on intellectual grounds. Unfortunately there had been a consistent history of racial prejudice in German musical criticism ever since Richard Wagner's controversial essay *Das Judentum in der Musik*[13] had been published in 1851. Despite the fact that Wagner's invective had been largely directed against Meyerbeer and Mendelssohn, he had not formulated any specific forms of racial theory. Neither had he called for the expulsion of the Jews from Germany. But future historians distorted Wagner's opinions to give credibility to their own prejudices. During the Nazi period, musicologists continued to cite Wagner as the sole justification for their anti-semitic programmes. Both Richard Eichenauer in his book *Musik und Rasse*[14] and Karl Blessinger in *Mendelssohn, Meyerbeer und Mahler: Drei Kapitel des Judentums in der Musik*[15] rely heavily on Wagner's extensive writings to support their own particular theories. They also resort to publishing totally misleading information — for example, Blessinger goes to great lengths to try and prove that Mendelssohn borrowed most of his musical ideas from other composers, was openly antagonistic towards the 'Aryan' Schumann, and grossly abused Bach's memory in his 'distorted' revival of Bach's St. Matthew Passion which took place in Berlin around 1830. Not surprisingly, these prejudices were often reiterated in the work of highly respected musicologists with the result that many people accepted them as being totally plausible.

The writings of Eichenauer and Blessinger provided Goebbels with the necessary ammunition for his final objective — a systematic onslaught against the influence of World Jewry upon music. Again, the whole process was nurtured through a supposedly respectable and 'academic' organisation set up by Alfred Rosenberg in Frankfurt with the awesome title of *Institut zur Erforschung der Judenfrage*. Musicologists working at the Institute were officially commissioned to publish a 'Lexicon of Jews in Music' together with a comprehensive work list of Jewish compositions. The editors of this shameful publication based some of their work on information contained within Rosenberg's cultural political archive which included material on over 60,000 persons. They were also influenced to some extent by the apparent success enjoyed by a widely circulated and Nazi inspired encyclopaedia entitled *Judentum in der Musik A-B-C*[16] which first appeared in 1935. There were however considerable differences between the two dictionaries.

LEXIKON DER JUDEN
IN DER MUSIK

Mit einem Titelverzeichnis
jüdischer Werke

Zusammengestellt im Auftrag der Reichsleitung
der NSDAP. auf Grund behördlicher, parteiamtlich
geprüfter Unterlagen

bearbeitet von

Dr. Theo Stengel
Referent in der Reichsmusikkammer

in Verbindung mit

Dr. habil. Herbert Gerigk
Leiter der Hauptstelle Musik beim Beauftragten des Führers
für die Überwachung der gesamten geistigen und weltanschaulichen
Schulung und Erziehung der NSDAP.

BERNHARD HAHNEFELD VERLAG / BERLIN

4. The title page of the standard reference dictionary on Jews in
Music which was first published in 1940

The *Judentum A-B-C* was a largely amateurish affair and perpetrated several inaccuracies including for example the listing of musicians who had no racial connections with the Jews, whereas the *Lexikon der Juden in der Musik*[17] claimed the highest scholarly reliability (*Fig 4*). But musical scholarship did not extend to the entries themselves which were wholly based on innuendo and unsubstantiated prejudice. Despite the fact that Goebbels had ostensibly banned musical criticism from Nazi Germany in 1936, he was quite prepared to allow his team of 'researchers' to resort to the language of the gutter if it was a matter of getting the message across.

The thoroughness with which these Nazi zealots pursued their attempts to

170

tarnish all Jewish music extended beyond the realms of researching composers and their work lists. If World Jewry was to disappear from the face of the earth, any music which had been indelibly linked to Jewish subjects or connections would have to be 'purified'. Thus the Ministry of Propaganda gradually introduced a programme of 'aryanising' great music. Two of the most significant examples of this process can be seen in Nazi approved revisions of famous works by Handel and Mozart. In the case of Handel, most attention was drawn to his oratorios based on events in the Old Testament. Thus the text of *Judas Maccabeus* was subjected to a thorough purification in its various transmogrifications, whether in the version by Hermann Stephani entitled *The Field Marshall: A War Drama,* or as the *Freedom Oratorio Wilhelm of Nassau* as arranged by Johannes Kloecking. Similar treatment was afforded to such stalwarts of the choral repertoire as *Jeptha* and *Israel in Egypt.* With Mozart, the problem rested in the fact that the librettist of such popular operas as *Don Giovanni, The Marriage of Figaro* and *Cosi fan Tutte* was of Jewish birth. However the Nazis ingeniously side-stepped the issue by preventing these operas from being performed in their original language. In addition, after discovering that most opera houses utilised German translations which had been prepared by the eminent Jewish conductor, Hermann Levi, they commissioned totally new versions which they claimed adhered more faithfully to the German spirit of the originals.

In general, the Nazis succeeded in expunging most elements of Jewish influence from their musical life. But anti-semitism was by no means the only area which obsessed the minds of Germany's leaders. Many members of Nazi hierarchy were equally committed to blotting out memories of the artistic achievements of the Weimar Republic. This involved sustained opposition to music written and performed by those sympathetic to left-wing politics. In other words, the few non-Jewish musicians who tried to resist the policies of the Nazi regime were branded socialists and publicly ostracised, if not accused of having Jewish connections. Some of the most important figures in German music, for example the conductors Fritz Busch, Hermann Scherchen and Erich Kleiber voluntarily resigned their posts in protest against what they considered were intolerable working conditions. Critics of the calibre of Heinrich Strobel, Hans Mersmann and Hans Heinz Stuckenschmidt were hounded out of their jobs. At the same time, the socialist composers Heinz Tiessen and Max Butting suffered creative crises when their works could no longer be performed. Other musicians followed a more pragmatic, even opportunistic, line by suppressing their past political affiliations.

The purge of left-wing composers, critics and conductors was accomplished within a remarkably short time. However the regime was less adept at dealing with two of the major manifestations of Weimar culture, namely Jazz and Modernism. Officially the Nazis were totally opposed to Jazz, considering it racially degenerate. But they were unable to stamp it out completely. As we have already seen, *Unterhaltungsmusik* enjoyed Goebbels's approval and became one of the most successful constituents of music broadcasting policy. Goebbels claimed that this form of light music was healthy and invigorating. He also conveniently ignored the fact that it was often highly syncopated and utilised dance rhythms like the tango and the fox-trot. There is no question that double standards were applied when so-called 'serious' composers dared to infect their work with merest hint of either Jazz-inspired instrumentation or rhythmic procedures. Critics were quite eager to accuse men like Rudolf Wagner-Regeny or Boris Blacher of besmirching the holy name of German music with their 'Nigger-infested' compositions.

171

The war against Modernism provided the Nazis with their most intractable problem. On the surface, the regime was implacably opposed to most of the developments in music which took place during the twentieth century and harboured a strong desire to rekindle the flames of national romanticism. Yet their approach to the issues was muddled and often contradictory. The critic, Karl Grunsky, in his pamphlet *Der Kampf um Deutsche Musik*,[18] neatly summed up the objections to most major twentieth century composers accusing them of demonstrating an inability to write clear melodies supported by mellifluous harmonies. Grunsky was in fact one of the first musicologists to use the favoured term 'cultural bolshevism' as a blanket condemnation of music that smacked of stylistic experimentation whether it be primitivism, neo-Classicism or atonality. Nevertheless, such naïvety denied the fact that it was well nigh impossible to roll back the frontiers of musical evolution completely. No doubt Grunsky believed that all composers could write in a style more suited to the nineteenth century. A situation had now been reached where Germany, if it was to regain the musical pre-eminence that it had allegedly lost during the Weimar Republic, would have to turn to a composer of repute and influence for salvation.

Such a man could have been Paul Hindemith, for superficially his credentials, not least the fact that he was completely Aryan, seemed promising. He had initially gained a reputation as a musical iconoclast, but had modified his style considerably in his *Laienmusik* (Lay Music, 1927) even before breaking off his association with artists of the left, most particularly Bertolt Brecht. He had begun to discover the vast riches of German folk music and was therefore implicitly writing in a more 'nationalist' idiom. Indeed, by the time the Nazis had come to power, Hindemith's style could have been described as conservative (while his aesthetic was still 'progressive'), adopting an almost neo-Romantic manner. Yet Hindemith's relationship with the New Germany exemplifies the classic case of an artist who was condemned as Modernist and particularly for the 'sins' of his youth. Ultimately, it was not because of his musical style but because he valued his political independence and thus threatened the very authority of the state.

The background to the conflict between the composer and the Nazis can be attributed almost entirely to the opera *Mathis der Maler* (Mathis the Painter) which Hindemith had begun to write in 1933. Its plot was based on the life of Matthias Grünewald, the 16th century painter who abandons his studio to make cause with the Peasants' Revolt, thus turning against his patron and employer the Cardinal Archbishop of Mainz. The contrast between the ideals for which the peasants are fighting and the reality of their behaviour in war arouses great anxiety and moments of doubt in the painter. These uncertainties are resolved when Grünewald reconciles his relationship with the Cardinal, believing that only by wholehearted devotion to his art can the artist best serve the interests of the people.

It was hardly surprising that an opera based on such a potentially controversial subject would not secure wholehearted approval from the government. In fact *Mathis* was never staged in Nazi Germany despite pressure from some very influential musicians; only the three movement Symphony, which was performed with great success by the Berlin Philharmonic Orchestra in 1934. Within a year, the *Mathis der Maler Symphony* had triumphed all over Germany, and some critics had acclaimed it as a work that could stand comparison with the best of the nation's music. With its sober harmonies and conservative idiom, it could only offend the most die-hard anti-Modernists.

Goebbels on the other hand thought differently. Regarding the subject matter upon which the Symphony was based as potentially subversive he publicly condemned Hindemith and initiated a smear campaign designed to crush the composer's influence once and for all. Invoking evidence that during the 1920's Hindemith had flouted National Socialism by parodying Nazi marches in his *Kammermusik* (Chamber music) and writing an opera (*Neues vom Tage*) in which a soprano was expected to sing an aria stark naked in a bath tub, he branded the composer as culturally degenerate.

Not surprisingly, Hindemith was unable to withstand the pressures of such blatant hostility and he eventually left Germany in 1937. Nevertheless despite the fact that his music was no longer performed in his native country, his influence upon other composers remained considerable. It is surely ironic that other musicians continued to adopt his so-called degenerate and dangerously Modernist idioms yet they were very rarely reproached.[19]

Another illustration of the confusion associated with Modernism can be seen in the attitudes surrounding the use of serial technique in music. Officially proscribed because its main exponent, Arnold Schoenberg, was Jewish, serialism also aroused indignation because its negation of conventional tonality contradicted the Nazi-held view that a strong and healthy German music should be based on the diatonic scale. The ban on Schoenberg's work extended to his 'aryan' pupils Anton Webern and Alban Berg — both of whom found it virtually impossible to get their music performed in Nazi Germany. For example, Webern's *Six Pieces for Orchestra* were scheduled to be heard at the 1933 *Allgemeine Deutsche Musikverein Festival* held in Dortmund. Yet these pieces were withdrawn from the programme without explanation. A year later, the conductor Erich Kleiber introduced fragments from Berg's latest opera, *Lulu*, at an orchestral concert given by the *Berliner Staatskapelle*. The work provoked a near riot. A member of the audience got up and shouted '*Heil Mozart!*' during the performance. Critics were outraged, one declaring that Berg's atonal music was abominable and had been forced upon the public by a clique of Jews. Such prejudice extended to other composers who dared to introduce elements of atonality into their work. Some people however were able to get away with stylistic deviancy if their loyalty to the Nazi party was beyond question. One such person was the composer Paul von Klenau who incorporated serial techniques in his work, but provoked little hostility. Klenau even went so far as to justify his use of serialism as a logical extension of Wagnerian chromaticism. Remarkably, an article written by the composer about his 'discovery' of this technique fails to acknowledge the existence of Arnold Schoenberg.

Whilst Klenau's case is rather unusual, it exemplifies the point that in Nazi Germany, critical attitudes towards a composer's style might be reversed if the personality was deemed politically acceptable. Moreover, a work which had initially aroused feelings of hostility could be rehabilitated without explanation or embarrassment. One of the most amusing examples of this process can be demonstrated in the volatile fortunes of Werner Egk's opera *Peer Gynt*. Its première at the Berlin State Opera in 1938 was certainly controversial. Critics condemned Egk for succumbing to Modernism, citing specific passages in the second act which were dangerously reminiscent of the music of Kurt Weill. In addition, great exception was taken to the scenes in which trolls paraded around the stage in the manner of Nazi storm troopers. After such a reception, both the work's prospects and Egk's promising career seemed doomed. Yet *Peer Gynt* survived simply because Hitler had happened to attend a performance of the opera. After the *Führer* expressed positive approval of the music and personally congratulated the composer, the critics were forced to effect a remarkable volte-face. In the following year, *Peer Gynt* was the featured opera at the officially organised *Reichsmusiktage*!

If critical reversals could take place merely through the whim of a Nazi leader, it is hardly surprising that some composers found themselves both pilloried and approved of at the same time. This situation occurred for example with Igor Stravinsky whose ballet *Jeu de Cartes* was recorded by the Berlin Philharmonic Orchestra whilst simultaneously his music was branded as 'cultural bolshevism' at the special exhibition of *Entartete Musik* held in Düsseldorf during 1938. This exhibition, hastily organised by the *Intendant* of the Weimar Theatre, Hans Severus Ziegler, was perhaps the most forceful and public expression of anti-Modernism in music which had been mounted with the official approval of the Nazi government. Its contents ranged from a reproduction of the painting by Carl Hofer entitled *The Jazzband*, to examples of Modernist theoretical writings on composition and excerpts from magazines devoted to contemporary music. In addition, recordings of music by culturally degenerate composers from Hindemith and Schoenberg to Kurt Weill as well as jazzed-up arrangements of German folk music were made available to the public in specially installed telephone booths (*Fig 5*).

Stravinsky was especially angry that his music had been condemned as degenerate. With a publisher based in Mainz and a pronounced admiration for Mussolini's brand of Fascism, he valued his reputation in Germany. However he

5. Two illustrations from the pamphlet *Entartete Musik: Eine Abrechnung* by Hans Severus Ziegler which accompanied his exhibition of the same name in Düsseldorf in 1938

had fundamentally misunderstood the nature of attitudes prevalent amongst the Nazi hierarchy, namely that Modernism was a manifestation of the dangerous internationalism which had overtaken the Weimar Republic. Since Stravinsky's influence amongst contemporary musicians had been and still was enormous, his music was inevitably regarded with a good deal of circumspection. A policy of cultural isolationism was deliberately encouraged within the Third Reich. Having withdrawn from the International Society of Contemporary Music in 1933 because it was claimed that the organisation was controlled by Communists and Jews, Germany forged musical alliances with composers from countries potentially sympathetic to its political system; for example Italy, Yugoslavia and Hungary. This explains the fact that a composer as radical in style as Bela Bartok was openly tolerated in Nazi Germany despite his outspoken opposition to Fascism.

It is clear from reading through my analysis of Nazi attitudes towards music that the arbiters of cultural indoctrination were more skilful at attacking musicians for transgressions of various kinds rather than suggesting positive alternatives in style, allegiance or subject matter. To arrive at an accurate assessment of the music created during this period, it is necessary therefore to consider those few areas in which the Nazis achieved concrete changes. One particular form of music-making, folksong, certainly experienced a carefully manipulated revival. Convinced of the beneficial effects of singing, the regime believed that folksong would unite people and instill within them a profound awareness of their national roots. Since traditional folk songs were regularly sung in schools and community halls, the Nazis were especially adept at changing the words to suit their own ends. A particularly good example is the Nazi anthem, the *Horst Wessel Lied* whose melody was 'borrowed' from a cabaret number that was popular in Berlin at the turn of the century. Although many of the favoured Nazi songs were based on familiar melodies, some contemporary composers were quite prepared to add to the repertoire and produce completely new material — after 1933 many of the leading music publishers literally flooded the market with collections of political and patriotic songs.[20] The recording industry similarly offered the public a plethora of nationalist music, and by 1939 a gramophone catalogue boasted over 900 different titles devoted exclusively to political folksongs.

Another type of music much favoured by the Nazis was the march, which hitherto had been exclusively associated with the military. Hitler personally took an interest in fostering the cultivation of both marches and fanfares. He was quite insistent that a work like the *Badenweiler Marsch* written during the First World War or the *Nibelungenmarsch* (a cunningly devised potpourri of favourite Wagnerian melodies) should be performed at all official occasions. As the supreme expert in all matters musical, Hitler even decreed that these pieces had to be performed at a metronome speed of crotchet = 80 — a tempo which guaranteed a brisk and confident effect.

It was clearly Hitler's intention that the German nation should become mesmerised by the vast panoply of marches and songs that seemed to be blasted out from every street corner. Nevertheless Nazi ambitions extended to infiltrating other forms of communal music-making. One area which offered tremendous potential was the genre known as *Gemeinschaftsmusik* (community music). Originally evolved during the latter stages of the Weimar Republic by such composers as Paul Hindemith, *Gemeinschaftsmusik* satisfied the socialist wing of the Nazi party in that it encouraged active music making for vast forces of amateur singers and instrumentalists. Although many of its chief protagonists had been committed to left-wing politics (the *Lehrstücke* of Brecht, Weill and Eisler could be regarded as examples of *Gemeinschaftsmusik*), the Nazis successfully hijacked the genre and commissioned several new compositions based on ideologically sound texts.

Since Hitler regarded the indoctrination of the younger generation as being vital to the survival of Nazism, much effort was spent on developing the youth movements. Music played a vital role in this process. Although the various *Hitler-Jugend* songbooks encouraged the regular performance of Nazi songs, Baldur von Schirach, the leader of the organisation, was keen to encourage the creation of compositions of a more ambitious nature. To this end, the *Musikblätter der Hitler Jugend* were published on a regular basis and featured new works of varying technical difficulty specially written by composers such as Heinrich Spitta and Cesar Bresgen. These men were given official posts in the Hitler Youth as music organisers. One of their tasks was to set up annual music festivals in an attempt to improve basic standards of music making. In 1938, for instance, a *Hitler Jugend Festival* devoted to the music of Beethoven was held at Bad Wildbrunn. The highlight of this event was allegedly the performance of the great master's *Eighth Symphony* given by a group of young musicians dressed in official uniforms (*Fig 6*).

Whilst much of the musical activity in the Nazi period seemed orientated towards mass gatherings of singers and instrumentalists with a predominance of political cantatas and occasional works, many composers continued to write for the more conventional genres relating to the opera house and the concert hall. It is in this area that final judgement must be made on the musical legacy of the Nazi period. With over 170 new operas premièred during the Third Reich as well as countless new symphonic works, the only composers to have maintained their place in the repertoire were Richard Strauss and Carl Orff. Since Strauss had developed his musical style in the nineteenth century, his music can hardly be described as typical of the Nazi era despite its conservative and frankly romantic leanings. On the other hand, Orff achieved his first successes under the Nazis. But it would be all too easy to ascribe the simple direct and somewhat primitive style that Orff evolved in such works as *Carmina Burana* to the spectre of Nazism. In fact Orff's music, whatever its shortcomings, owes a great deal to the influence of Stravinsky and was criticised in some quarters for not sounding sufficiently German. Moreover its strong diatonic harmonies are far removed from the world of intense Wagnerian chromaticism.

In conclusion, one is forced to accept the fact that the Nazis were able to effect profound changes upon musical life in Germany. Their policy of musical anti-semitism was carried out with considerable thoroughness and removed at a stroke some of the most stimulating and creative musicians that the country has ever known. On the other hand, their glib attempts at formulating a stylistically acceptable music for the New Germany met with only token response from some musicians. Vindictive campaigns against certain composers who refused to ingratiate themselves with the regime provided controversy, even scandal, but these essentially manufactured affairs were primarily designed to reinforce the authority of the Party over the individual. They were manifestations of a cultural policy that was sometimes dominated by confused prejudice rather than presenting really clear stylistic goals.

Some musicologists suggest that the real problem with music during this period lies in the fact that Germany deliberately isolated herself from musical

6. Hitler Youth with fanfares and legionaries' drums at a Nuremberg party rally

7. Nazi youths from Berlin at a musical event

developments which were taking place in the rest of Europe. Whilst on the surface this policy of cultural isolationism was clearly postulated, the work of some leading contemporary composers such as Bartok, Honegger and Stravinsky was, for a time, freely available to the public. Moreover, for many composers working in Nazi Germany, the process of imposed stylistic simplification demanded by the Ministry of Propaganda parallels developments in other countries where a natural reaction against the radical experimentation of the previous decade was effecting significant and sometimes conservative changes in musical language. Unfortunately, it is difficult for us to recognise, let alone accept, that these similarities exist because the moral repugnance of Nazi philosophy defies objective criticism. Besides, the rights and wrongs of Nazi policy seemed of little importance to the majority of musicians who worked under Hitler. Although one can accept the fact that opportunism was an inevitable consequence of a situation born out of fear, the fact remains that very few members of the music profession were resolute enough to resist the changes imposed upon them by the state.

In this connection it may be worthwhile making a direct comparison between the musical achievements of the Nazi regime and those in the Soviet Union, particularly during the same period. Although both countries actively encouraged music-making on a vast scale, the legacies of Hitler and Stalin seem rather different. In Hitler's Germany, the size of the musical establishment was enormous by any standards. Statistics support this in terms of the number of orchestras and opera houses that flourished and new compositions that were promoted. Moreover, the range of musical styles being cultivated by such composers as Strauss, Hindemith, Orff, Egk, Blacher and Wagner-Regeny can hardly be said to be lacking in variety or originality. Nonetheless, the period as a whole seems bereft of really profound and challenging music. On the other hand, the Soviet musical system was far less sophisticated and conditions of performance were sometimes primitive. But Stalin's repressive policy of Socialist Realism did not suppress the emergence of great and original music. Indeed, one may argue that talented composers in the Soviet Union were more successful in resisting the stultifying hand of the state than in Nazi Germany, where the forced removal of creative freedom ushered in a period of relative sterility and impoverishment that was a tragic monument to the influence of National Socialism.

CHRONOLOGY OF GERMAN MUSIC 1933 – 1945

1933

8th March:
: The Nazis force Fritz Busch to resign from his post as General Music Director of the *Dresden Opera*.

11th March:
: Carl Ebert resigns from the *Berliner Städtische Oper* as he is unwilling to cooperate with the Nazis.

16th March:
: Orchestral concert conducted by Bruno Walter in Leipzig is cancelled after threats from the local Nazi party. A few days later, Walter cancels a concert with the Berlin Philharmonic Orchestra, but Richard Strauss agrees to take his place.

21st March:
: Kurt Weill leaves Germany after his theatre piece *Silbersee* is removed from the repertoire of the Leipzig Opera.

1st April:
: Hitler receives a cable from leading musicians in the United States (Toscanini, Koussevitzky, Reiner etc.) condemning his racial policies.

4th April:
: The director of German Radio responds to this cable by banning all recordings and performances of those people who protested.

7th April:
: Inauguration of new civil service laws which effectively remove non-aryans from employment in opera houses and music conservatoires.

10th April:
: Goebbels rejects an appeal by the conductor Wilhelm Furtwängler not to exclude Jewish musicians, in particular Bruno Walter and Otto Klemperer, from German musical life.

30th May:
: Arnold Schoenberg and Franz Schreker are dismissed from their teaching posts at the Prussian Academy of Arts.

5th June:
: Arturo Toscanini refuses to conduct at the Bayreuth Festival. His replacement is Richard Strauss whose evident cooperation endears him to the Nazi hierarchy.

1st July:
: Richard Strauss's opera *Arabella* is given its first triumphant performance in Dresden. It becomes one of the most frequently heard operas in Nazi Germany.

15th November:
: Goebbels establishes the *Reichsmusikkammer* with Richard Strauss as its president and Paul Graener and Wilhelm Furtwängler as vice-presidents. The *Kraft durch Freude* (Strength through Joy) organisation is inaugurated to bring culture to the people.

30th November:
: First performance of *Feier der neuen Front* by Richard Trunk, a cycle of four choral movements for male voice choir entitled *Hitler, Des Führers Wächter, O Land* and *Horst Wessel* to texts by Baldur von Schirach, leader of the *Hitler Jugend*. Trunk was a highly respected professor of composition at the *Musikhochschule* in Cologne.

1934

12th March:
: First performance in Berlin of Hindemith's Symphony *Mathis der Maler* conducted by Furtwängler.

1st April:
: The magazine *Die Musik* takes over as the official musical forum for the *Reichsjugendführung*.

22nd April:
: The Nazis decree that all German singing societies should be amalgamated into a national *Sängerbund*.

6th June:
: The *Allgemeine Deutsche Musikverein* meets in Wiesbaden to produce a festival of purely German music.

179

11th June:	On his 70th birthday, Richard Strauss receives a framed photograph of the *Führer* with the inscription '*Dem grossen Komponisten Richard Strauss in aufrichtiger Verehung, Adolf Hitler.*' (To the great composer Richard Strauss with deepest veneration, Adolf Hitler.)
29th September:	The *Reichsmusikkammer* issues an order prohibiting performing artists from using foreign sounding names.
1st November:	The *NS Kulturgemeinde* commissions new musical settings for Shakespeare's play *A Midsummer Night's Dream* from Rudolf Wagner-Regeny and Julius Weismann as replacements for Mendelssohn's score. (These works are performed for the first time at the *NSKG Reichstagung* in Düsseldorf in June 1935).
25th November:	Furtwängler's article *Der Fall Hindemith* (The Hindemith Case) appears on the front page of the *Deutsche Allgemeine Zeitung*. He defends Germany's leading composer against a mounting barrage of hostility from the regime, but his incautious use of the words 'political denunciation' bring the whole Nazi hierarchy into unified opposition to the composer.
28th November:	Goebbels' newspaper *Der Angriff* carries a headline 'Why advance musical laurels for musical opportunist Hindemith?'
4th December:	Furtwängler resigns from his position as chief conductor of the Berlin Philharmonic Orchestra and vice-president of the *Reichsmusikkammer*.
6th December:	Goebbels delivers a speech at the Berlin *Sportpalast* in which he denounces atonality as a reflection of moral decay and implicates Hindemith as a pernicious influence. Further attacks upon Hindemith's music appear in the German press during 1935 and he eventually leaves the country in 1937.

1935

25th February:	Furtwängler officially apologises for his defence of Hindemith. Two months later, he is reinstated as principal conductor of the Berlin Philharmonic Orchestra.
20th May:	*Die Zaubergeige*, an opera composed by Werner Egk and based on a Bavarian folk tale about a farmhand who receives a magic violin from the Prince of the Elements and becomes an instant virtuoso, is performed for the first time in Frankfurt. Its success is so considerable that it is heard in virtually every major opera house in Germany during the next few years.
24th June:	*Die Schweigsame Frau*, an opera by Richard Strauss, is given its first performance in Dresden. The Nazi leadership stay away since the opera's libretto was written by Stefan Zweig, a Jew.
13th July:	Strauss is forced to resign from his post as president of the *Reichsmusikkammer* after a letter he wrote to Zweig in which he complains bitterly about Nazi interference in artistic matters is intercepted by the Gestapo. Peter Raabe a conductor, musicologist and Party member, is appointed to succeed Strauss.
30th August:	The *Reichsmusikkammer* issues a decree forbidding Jews and any other non-Aryans from playing in German orchestras.
12th October:	German radio issues a further ban on the broadcast of Jazz calling it '*Jewish Cultural Bolshevism*'.

1936

1st March:	The magazine *Die Musik* issues a special anti-semitic number which includes articles such as 'The Jew as musical manufacturer' and grotesquely distorted photographs of Mendelssohn, Mahler, Weill and Klemperer.

3rd April:	An international music festival in Baden-Baden is organised by the *Reichsmusikkammer* in opposition to the *International Society of Contemporary Music* from which Germany seceded in 1933. It presents contemporary music by composers of purely Aryan blood including Stravinsky, Malipiero, Beck, Larsson and Jean Françaix.
16th August:	The 1936 Olympic Games in Berlin is inaugurated by a performance of Richard Strauss's *Olympische Hymne*. In addition, the Nazis organise a competition to find the most suitable composition to be written in the 'Olympic spirit.' The prizes are awarded to three Germans (Egk, Thomas and Hoeffer) and one Italian (Liviabella).
27th November:	Goebbels decrees that from now on music critics should refrain from expressing personal opinions (either excessive praise or sharp criticism) and simply record accounts of artistic events.

1937

24th May:	International contemporary music festival in Dresden features music by some Modernist but racially pure composers including Bliss, Bartok and Casella.
8th June:	First performance of Orff's *Carmina Burana* at the *ADMV* Festival in Frankfurt.
12th June:	The *ADMV* (*Allgemeine Deutsche Musik Verein*), the last independent musical organisation in Nazi Germany is disbanded by Peter Raabe.
21st December:	The *Reichsmusikkammer* issues a directive banning the distribution of records featuring Jewish or Negro musicians.

1938

10th February:	After a successful first performance at the Dresden Opera, Richard Mohaupt's *Die Wirtin von Pinsk* is banned when the authorities discover that the composer's wife is Jewish.
24th April:	The Fanfare *Grossdeutschland zum 10 April* by Paul Winter, a pupil of Hans Pfitzner, is performed in Vienna as a musical celebration of the *Anschluss*.
1st May:	The *Reichsmusikkammer* prohibits Aryans from teaching music to Jews.
22nd May:	The Exhibition of *Entartete Musik* opens in Düsseldorf. The organiser Hans Severus Ziegler produces an inflammatory booklet in conjunction with the Exhibition which condemns practically every aspect of Modernist music.
24th July:	*Friedenstag* an opera by Richard Strauss is performed for the first time in Munich. Its reception is mixed since the authorities disapprove of its pacifist message.
24th November:	First performance of Werner Egk's opera *Peer Gynt* at the Berlin State Opera. At first, it was subjected to harsh criticism in the Nazi press, but when Hitler heard it for the first time, he was so impressed that he awarded Egk a German government prize of ten thousand Marks.

1939

| 23rd January: | Georg Vollerthun's *Alt Danzig Suite* is performed in Berlin as part of the Nazi propaganda to annex the free city. |
| 21st May: | Goebbels makes a personal address at the *Reichsmusiktage* in Düsseldorf—the last such festival to be staged before the War. |

| **1940** | As Germany and the Soviet Union sign a non-aggression pact, Soviet and Russian music is featured and performed for the first time in Germany. The Soviets reciprocate by staging Wagner's *Die Walküre* at the Bolshoi opera. Similar musical 'treaties' are signed with Italy, Yugoslavia, Finland, Spain, Greece and Bulgaria. |

1941 – 1944   Despite the War, musical life in Germany remains extremely active. In 1941 for example, a grandiose festival of Mozart's music is organised in Vienna in which all the composer's major operas are heard within the space of a fortnight. Contemporary music is also featured with first performances of many new theatrical works including Strauss's *Capriccio*, Orff's *Catulli Carmina* and *Die Kluge* and Egk's ballet *Joan von Zarissa*. In August 1944, however, Goebbels declares 'Total War' and most public musical activities cease to exist.

Chapter Ten

THE POLITICAL POSTER IN THE THIRD REICH

Andreas Fleischer and Frank Kämpfer

The classification of posters as belonging to the world of ephemeral pictures, which often occurs in discussions on tendentious art or on art and kitsch, has not long been free from negative connotations. However, it is our contention that the political posters of the Nazi era are often remarkable both for their mass-psychological effectiveness and for their revelation of the ideological concerns and anxieties of the Nazi regime itself.[1] They must therefore be considered an integral part of the interpretation of Fascism in 20th century Europe.

Not surprisingly, writers in the Third Reich found unambiguous terms with which to characterise the production and purpose of political posters. In a study of 1941, Friedrich Medebach wrote:

> An assessment of the layout of the political poster immediately throws up an important question whose pros and cons have often been discussed. The question is this: is its composition to be seen as art, and must any kitsch therefore be rejected? It should be clearly stated that in principle, the political poster, like any other poster, is not a work of art; the poster is always merely a means to an end. Its value lies purely and simply in its success as an advertisement. Hence no other gauge can apply apart from this one alone: The more the poster succeeds in attracting attention to itself and so to the matter which it is advertising, the more it awakens a political leaning, the more it has fulfilled its purpose, and the more the art of the poster becomes greater for it. The question as to whether it is art or kitsch is an aesthetic one which holds no great meaning for the business of publicity save that the propaganda or agitation should succeed to reach particular sections of society.[2]

The interaction between art and the style of the poster was thoroughly functionalised in Medebach's book. The 'masses', it was perhaps not unreasonably assumed, were accustomed to the 'Realism' of the 19th century and perceived 20th century avant-garde stylistic devices as incomprehensible provocation. So the propagandist had to cope with this accordingly:

> The interaction between the style of art at the time and its influence on the design of the poster will in any case reach its limit in the poster's function. The poster artist will not always be able to turn to the contemporary style of art to compose his poster. He must reckon with the receptiveness of the masses. The eyes of the masses are not to be expected to grasp what an art historian or aesthete can master with no trouble at all.[3]

A large part of Medebach's study was concerned with the 'receptiveness of the masses', and tried to derive laws from the success or failure of the posters of the so-called *Kampfzeit* (years of struggle, 1918–1933) of the NSDAP. If we also include Erwin Schockel's 'psychological assessment' of the political poster[4], which was intended for the NSDAP's internal use and in which Allied posters were also analysed, we can accurately reconstruct the Nazi propagandists' attitude to the medium of the poster. Their phraseology left nothing to the imagination in terms of clarity.

The business of publicity has all the stylistic possibilities for the composition of posters at its command, and can use those which seem the most appropriate for the purpose in hand. Should it engage in stylistic propaganda, that is to say, should it go out of its way to promulgate a particular poster style, then some of the better and more effective formats for its themes will be lost.[5]

The art of propaganda is not an end in itself but serves as an aid in politics. Adolf Hitler says in *Mein Kampf* (p 194), 'Propaganda is a means and must correspondingly be judged in relation to its end.'[6]

Yet it goes without saying that an examination of individual styles can be applied to Nazi posters. Posters by Mjölnir, Matejko or Schiffers are characterised by the personal features of their respective graphic styles. Generalisations about these posters run the risk of straying into a world of false abstraction.[7] The poster artists were as pragmatically eclectic with regard to technique and stylistic execution as was National Socialism itself, both as a policy and as ideology. There is no unified style to be found in the material, and yet it clearly served an ideologically defined purpose. This becomes very transparent in the Nazi writings on posters. If these could be regarded as 'art', then it was only in the sense that propaganda was an art, i.e. a tool of politics and a service to politicians. Covertly referring to the genius of the *Führer* as the supreme propagandist, Schockel defined the poster artists as lowly assistants who had to take their cue from the true men of destiny:

Propaganda must basically be conceived not as a science but as an insight. Its practice is an art. Great propagandists are just as unique as great artists. They are the shining example for the many who faithfully strive to fulfill their duty as helpers of the great men, as the latter pursue their role which fate has allotted to them.[8]

Perhaps we can also say that of the traditional arts, rhetoric is closest to the poster and is sometimes intimately coupled with it. Firstly, the poster drew people to an event at which the demagogue[9] then began his verbal manipulation, and secondly, the slogans, mottos, watchwords, appeals and rhetorical figures of the poster itself were drawn from the rhetoric of the politician. The emphatic intentionality of the poster connected every one of them with an overall strategy which was guided by the latest propagandistic requirements. Starting from the assumption that political language is the vehicle for the achievement or consolidation of political power, we can describe National Socialist poster propaganda as the manipulation of language and images to achieve control over public opinion by a continuous process of mass mobilisation. National Socialist propaganda can accordingly be seen as a particularly purposive rational form of media use.

In the institutes of media research and journalism during the Nazi period intensive efforts were made to put the operation of the media on a scientific basis —

within the bounds of Nazi ideology, of course. Studies of poster propaganda written at the time have remained among the best things written on the subject.

National Socialist poster propaganda did not only disseminate fragmented ideological messages in words and pictures but, together with a corresponding media theory and mass psychology, was embedded in the overall context of Nazi ideology. Nothing would be more natural than to draw the conclusion, based on a vast amount of material, that the poster had a particularly significant meaning (and to draw further conclusions regarding the seductive powers of media activity in general)![10] In 1939 the argument ran like this: 'But in any case we have the political poster to thank for the fact that the liberal and Marxist world views were beaten into the ground, and that National Socialism won over the Reich.'[11]

But when one considers the limited empirical equipment of this field of research in the Nazi era — the studies did not get beyond crude quantitative techniques — one discovers the speculative character of such statements and of so-called 'laws which govern the poster as a journalistic means of leadership.'[12] While today we would only speak of 'particularly significant meanings' with great reservation, the researchers and media practitioners of the Nazi period assured each other of the absolute trustworthiness of ideological generalisations which were paraded as 'laws'. Only with the acceptance of more recent American approaches and the emergence of social psychology did the dominance of mass psychology (Le Bon, Goebbels), propaganda technology (Hitler) and media research (Erwin Doviat, K. de Ester) begin to decline.

Inevitably, the historian will uncover a close integration of posters and their producers with Nazi ideology. This is an incurable effect of the source material: the posters will appear to be a virtually inexhaustible fund of pictures, words and structures of argumentation, to which central importance was once attached by those who commissioned them. At the time, unquestioned faith in the effectiveness of propaganda gave rise to particularly strict control of it — by Goebbels personally. At the beginning, Hitler and Goebbels even composed their own posters.[13] Goebbels never relinquished control over Party and state propaganda, his only limitations being his own capacity for work and the other individuals who were competing with him. Even during World War II he had posters destroyed whose message seemed to him uncertain.[14] In a constant tussle for the greatest effectiveness and clarity of message, discernability of content, conciseness of slogan, image and exhortation, the poster could be made the vehicle of condensed versions of Nazi ideology, which stand out by their extreme compactness and directness, to the point of attacking the viewer by the immediacy of their visual appeal and verbal command. Intensity and extreme concision became the basic characteristics of the semiotics and symbols with which the Nazi organisations surrounded themselves. The aggressiveness of the 'Movement' found its counterpart in pictorial formulae which tried to functionalise existing stereotypes and emotions and which were calculated with a view to providing compositions suitable for the 'masses'.

A representative example of this strategy was the poster entitled *Unsere letzte Hoffnung — Hitler* (Our last hope — Hitler (see *Fig 4*)), which exploited the despair of the unemployed. The anti-semitic posters[15] showed in which direction social hatred was to be channelled. Just how far it is possible to recognise the eventual course of history within the deceptions, tactics and lies which are discernible in these images has not yet been sufficiently ascertained. The material that has been preserved is heterogeneous. There is a great variety of special poster forms such as, for example, the 'motto of the week', extensively illustrated word posters which were hung out in glass cases; 'house posters' which were mounted on wood and which from 1942 were not allowed to be removed from private flats; and 'indoor posters' for offices (above all portraits of Hitler); metal placards, enamel and glass posters and other special poster forms.

1. *Wacht auf! und wählt: den Völkischen Bloch* (Wake up! Vote for the National Block) 1924

In the following section we shall be concerned only with the large coloured bill-posters, that is, posters in the narrower sense of the word, which were used in public places. This analytical restriction must not be allowed to conceal the fact that the 'grand orchestra' (as Goebbels called his propaganda machine) had a whole wealth of other means of visual agitation at its disposal.

Characteristic of the posters of the Nazi movement before the *Machtergreifung* (seizure of power) was a definite predilection for the representation of symbolic scenes of explosive action. Action, activity and 'actionism' was believed to distinguish the NSDAP from the 'bourgeois' parties of the Weimar Republic: it is in this respect that the expression 'Hitler Movement' was fully justified. The use of 'actionism' by the party leaders was a promise to ordinary members, not only to proclaim certain ideological values, but also to realise them in action. This had been practised with great success by Mussolini's version of Fascism, and Hitler perfected the instruments of 'actionism' in the party work of the National Socialists. One of the best-known posters from the early years of the NSDAP was published in 1924, when Adolf Hitler was in prison and the radical Right had consolidated itself within the 'National Block': *Wacht auf! und wählt: den Völkischen Block* (Wake up! Vote for the National Block, *Fig 1*). The fist with the swastika on the sleeve, slamming down and crushing parliament, perfectly visualised the programme of the radical right-wing enemies of the Weimar Republic. The antiparliamentarianism of both the left and right wing extremists is revealed precisely by this pictorial formula, because the 'National Block' had plagiarised this motif from a poster used back in 1920 by the German Communist Party.[16] Another symbolic scene that appeared on posters was derived from the Stormtroopers' continual show of strength on the streets of German cities — the march. The newspaper illustrator Hans Schweitzer (known under the pseudonym of Mjölnir[17]) captured the dynamism of the 'Movement' in his imagery, both retaining the sketchy style of the drawing and yet at the same time answering to the monumental size of the poster: *Nationalsozialismus — der organisierte Wille der Nation* (National Socialism — the organised will of the Nation, *Fig 2*). Mjölnir arranged the sketch in the style of a red chalk drawing with bulky black lettering. This technique clearly reveals that it is a drawing, not a print. The swastika in the white circle behind created an effect and drew attention to the slogan. Just as this encapsulated important concepts of Fascism such as 'organised will' and 'will of the nation', so the image expressed the brutal determination of the NSDAP, through the SA, its paramilitary organisation, to proceed with force against the existing political scenario (the marching direction is towards the left).[18]

Still more laconic and no less violent was the composition of Mjölnir's poster, *Schluss jetzt — wählt Hitler* (That's enough! Vote for Hitler, *Fig 3*), which likewise appeared at a critical phase of the Nazi movement in 1932. In order to understand which particular Hercules — who was depicted in red — was tearing apart the chains and what 'That's enough' referred to we must cite the interpretation of a Nazi contemporary, who was keen to convey the intended audience's way of viewing it:

> 'Every muscle, every sinew, you could say every drop of blood breathes concentrated strength here, together with the unbounded desire for freedom from fetters . . . for the NSDAP as a socialist movement, the well-being of the oppressed and enslaved is paramount. These need only to be freed to break the power of the concept of class struggle and pave the way for a united, powerful Germany which is at the same time free from the foreign yoke.'[19]

2. H. Schweitzer (i.e. Mjölnir),
*Nationalsozialismus — der organisierte
Wille der Nation* (National Socialism —
the organised will of the nation), 1932

The phrase 'freedom from fetters' was intended to refer to the elimination of capitalism as a method of enslavement internally, and, externally, the liquidation of the Allies' demands for reparations ('foreign yoke'), both themes being constant motifs of demagogic National Socialist propaganda. In 1924 Mjölnir had already worked the latter into one of the first anti-semitic picture posters of the NSDAP, in which the slogan 'Down with financial enslavement!' illustrates a corpulent Jewish dwarf riding on a chained giant, suggesting international 'Jewish' capital on the back of the German people.[20] The 'Proletarian Giant' had here, as in other borrowings from the icons of the labour movement, become an expression of the brute force with which the Nazi movement was prepared to assert its claim to power.

The surname of the party chairman, Hitler, the *Führer* (leader), had been stylised for years as the symbol of the 'Movement', even more intensively than was the case in Fascist Italy with Mussolini, known as the *Duce*. Through constant propaganda Hitler's name was made into a relatively fixed symbol of hope for change. The same anticipation of change which the red giant expressed in his 'Vote for Hitler!' was also used to entice the many who were socially downtrodden or

188

3. H. Schweitzer (i.e. Mjölnir), *Schluss jetzt!*
wählt Hitler (that's enough! Vote Hitler), 1932

4. H. Schweitzer (i.e. Mjolner), *Unsere*
Letzte Hoffnung - Hitler (our last hope-
Hitler)

weak. In *'Unsere letzte Hoffnung—Hitler'* (Our last hope—Hitler, *Fig 4*) the picture again represented a symbolic movement, in this case the 'streaming past' of all those who had lost any hope of help from the established parliamentary parties. The graphic style of Mjölnir (evidently influenced by the banned Käthe Kollwitz) was more impressive here than in his painting, which could appear somewhat two-dimensional.

The dynamism of Mjölnir, which was maintained even to his last poster of 1944/5[21], can be regarded as the embodiment of Nazi propaganda art, which nevertheless had further styles and types at its disposal in which the photographic poster, the collage and the photomontage also played a role. Of particular interest is the composition of a Hitler 'icon' which appeared in Munich and which might serve as an example of the sophisticated technique of 'reduction'.[22] The caption consisted only of the word 'HITLER' (*Fig 5*), and the picture showed a frontal view of Hitler's face with a hypnotic look.[23] The only deviation from the principle of reduction (head without neck, surname without first name, black background) was the superfluous dot over the 'i' of the lettering—the impression it conveyed was unforgettable. We quote Schockel again:

> 'The calmness, goodness and strength that radiate from Hitler's face communicate themselves to the observer. The impression it makes on people of unspoilt mind must be powerful. In addition, we had the poster printed white on a black background which at that time served as an eyecatcher in the midst of the otherwise garish colours of the advertising pillars'.[24]

The observer of today, not having this unspoilt relationship with the gaze of Adolf Hitler, might be more inclined to regard this image as an advertisement for a clairvoyant. Yet the Hitler 'icon' showed how well the *Führer*, even in 1932, had succeeded in centering the NSDAP, its organisations and its electorate, on his own personality and in stylising himself as the superego of the nation.[25] At the same time it becomes clear how very certain several poster designers could be that even in this reduced form the *Führer's* charisma would retain its radiating power.

The seizure of power and the enforced ideological conformity (*Gleichschaltung*) that immediately ensued, during which the NSDAP was transformed from an antiparliamentary party of the masses to an organisation supporting the state, required a switch in polarity as far as the propaganda effort was concerned. Since March 1933 Dr. Goebbels had, in his Reich-Ministry for People's Enlightenment and Propaganda, been organising the largest apparatus for the control and direction of mass communication in world history. This propaganda was faced with two principal tasks: firstly, the long-term manipulation of the population in accordance with the aims of the 'National Socialist Movement', that is, manipulation towards acceptance of new values such as *Volksgemeinschaft* (National Community), 'racial purity' and anti-semitism, the '*Führer* myth' and so on; and secondly, the direction of public opinion in accordance with the National Socialist perception of current political problems and priorities.

A characteristic example of the type of poster that served to put the political opponent in the wrong is provided in *Fig 6, Wir starben für Euch! Und Ihr wollt uns verraten?* (We died for you! And you want to betray us?) which was deployed in the 1934/5 struggle to win consent to the reintegration of the demilitarised Saarland into the German Reich.[26] Placed before the public was the poster's pictorial assertion that the dead of 1871/2 and 1914/18 had fallen in the interests of the viewer. The soldiers, who were of different ages, were meant to personify the fathers and

5. *Hitler* poster,
1932

grandfathers of the generation of voters of 1935. They looked down at the viewer from a fluorescently green 'kingdom of the dead'. As loyal forbears in the service of the *Reich* they sternly accused political opponents of betraying the nation, kindling in the living a conflict of conscience which suggested their resolution through suitable electoral behaviour. The poster was launched by the 'German Front', an NSDAP-controlled organisation in the Saarland which was fighting vehemently for reunion with the German Reich. The 'betrayal of the Reich' was the focal point of the campaign to pressurise the population, who eventually voted with 90% in favour of reunification.

Compared with the verbal brutality of political orators and journalists, the language of the poster before the outbreak of the Second World War remained

6. 'German Front' poster: *Wir starben für Euch!
Und Ihr wollt uns verraten?* (We died for you! And
you want to betray us?), 1934/5

relatively restrained. Also, images of the enemy, above all the Jew and the
Bolshevik, on the whole did not enter into monumental propaganda save for a few
well-known exceptions.[27]

Other doctrinal propaganda, with the help of which the National Socialist
system of values was lodged in the minds of the German people, produced conventional works in the field of poster graphics just as it did in the visual arts generally.[28]
The propaganda for the pseudo-corporatist model of social harmony, that is for
the *Volksgemeinschaft*, did not get beyond platitudes in its publicity for the
Workers' Front or for the organisation *Kraft durch Freude* (Strength through Joy).
The poster titled *Damals wie heute: Wir bleiben Kameraden* (Today it must be as it
was then: We remain comrades, *Fig 7*) referred back to World War I in the same
way as *Wir starben für Euch!* but showed the silhouettes of two survivors who, after
the comradeship of war, had moved on to attain the comradeship of the Workers'
Front with the aid of National Socialism. The figures in the foreground were
denoted by their hammer and scientific equipment as 'workers of the fist and the
forehead', a well known stereotype of Nazi propaganda which was designed to
overcome the division of labour by sheer rhetoric. In order to mark the two figures
out as supra-individual personifiations, the artist gave them schematic faces
without eyes, and depicted them in statuesque rigidity, so that they formed a striking contrast to the shadows in the background while nevertheless remaining recognisable as ideal types. The handshake enacted here between the representatives of
polar opposites in the social spectrum (which, as Nazi propaganda endlessly

192

repeated, had until recently been divided by Marxist slogans of class struggle) also sometimes appeared in a tripartite arrangement showing a farmer with a scythe, a worker with a hammer, and a salaried employee with a 'white collar'.[29]

7. Deutsche Arbeits front poster: *Damals wie heute: Wir bleiben Kameraden* (Today it must be as it was then: we remain comrades)

Characteristic of the Nazis' visual propaganda was the constant presence of Party and state emblems, which were reduced to their bare elements despite their variety and the possibility of constantly new combinations. Besides the red flag with its swastika it was above all the eagle, taken from the Imperial German Eagle, which was made into the symbol of the Third Reich with its imperial ideology. In the classicist tradition of the visual arts it could refer back to the Holy Roman Empire, even to ancient Rome, if for instance it was combined with the oak wreath or with emblems of Roman imperalism. Only on few posters is the emblem of the eagle so suggestively elevated to cosmic proportions as in *Tag des deutschen Rechts in Leipzig* (Day of German Law in Leipzig, *Fig 8*), published in 1938. In the lower part of the picture the monumental building of the Supreme Court of the Reich in Leipzig forms the focal point. Above this hovers the emblem of the Nazi Law Guardians' Association in pronounced two-dimensionality — both contained within the monumental eagle whose three-dimensional volume was emphasised by red light cascading from above. This colossal eagle protectively embraces both the building and the emblem of the Nazi Law Guardians' Association, and thus becomes reminiscent of the protective mantle of the medieval Madonna. The monumental eagle was stylised everywhere as one of the most important ideological symbols of the Nazi Reich besides the swastika; it was even used on posters advertising Germany in Italy (which was known to have its own traditional use of the eagle).[30]

8. *Tag des deutschen Rechts in Leipzig* (Day of German Law in Leipzig), 1938

To the ordinary German the use of emblems of power in all areas of public life made one thing above all clear, namely that the state—after the collapse of the politically weak Republic of Weimar—had once again become a power which could deploy political as well as mental strength. The new regime offered the conformist citizen the authority of the *Führer* state with which he could identify and in which he could participate. The same symbols of power had the effect of threatening opposition parties with repression through the ubiquitous control of the Party and state organisations.

During World War II similar strategies of psychological repression were extended in proportion both as the system began to lose support in the population, and as the material basis of life itself became jeopardised. This was certainly the case after the decisive turn brought about by the battle of Stalingrad. The German armies, forced to retreat, left behind 'scorched earth' even when they re-entered Reich territory. Hitler's comment on this problem is well known: 'It is not necessary to consider the fundamental needs of the German people for what would be a worthlessly primitive continuation of their lives. On the contrary, it is better to destroy even the bare essentials for any such life . . .'[31]

To be able to study this last change in Nazi propaganda it is necessary to make a selection from the many war posters which have so far not been systematically analysed. It is only possible here to deal with the *Kohlenklau* (Coal Filcher) poster and two varieties of the *Feind-hört-mit* (The-Enemy-is-Listening) poster in any detail. The appeal for greater thrift in the use of resources during war-time emphasised the extension of the political sphere into everyday life, and the shadow of the unknown traitor came to represent the pervasive mistrust which marked out and held together the *Volksgemeinschaft* in the period before its ultimate fall.

We shall not concern ourselves here with the pictures of fighting, the praise of weapons and military formations, the posters on the theme of 'the Military Front and the Home Front' with their multifarious appeals for participation in the struggle by thrift, work, special donations, and self-sacrifice, and the change from the slogan *Sieg um jeden Preis* (Victory at any Cost) to that of *Endsieg* (Final Victory), and finally to propaganda exhorting the population to hold out against all the odds. All this is neglected in this short sketch in favour of qualitatively superior products of poster propaganda.

Even contemporary observers could not help registering qualitative differences among the posters. In the eyes of Victor Klemperer, the professor of Romance language and literature turned factory worker,[33] the later posters of the Nazis 'began to look uncommonly alike'. The animal violence of the 'brutal and grimly determined' fighters depressed him, in particular.[34] Klemperer believes that the 'wretchedly heroic posters' were monotonous and were therefore perceived as a uniform mass; all that stood out about them, apart from their unimaginativeness, were the flaws in their production: 'On these placards which were produced in dozens of different types, there was no close cohesion or mutual support between the figurative graphics on the one hand and the inscription on the other.'[35] 'All these wretched and heroic posters render only the hack phrases of the monotonous LTI (Lingua Tertii Imperii) into graphics without in any way enriching them.'[36]

But Klemperer also mentions exceptions. Of all the poster images, he believes that only *Kohlenklau* (*Fig 9*) came anywhere near the everyday world of extreme war-time economy measures. A similar degree of suggestiveness, Klemperer maintains, was also attained by the black shadow of the anti-spy posters.

9. A *Kohlenklau* poster, *c* 1940

The illustration of the *Kohlenklau* poster showed the figure from the front, almost as if viewed from below:

'. . . its human shape almost insinuates an animal form. This is exactly how *Kohlenklau* was intended to be imagined; his legs are merely amphibian stumps, an effect which is further enhanced by the flapping tails of his coat. The stooping posture of the thief as he creeps away resembles that of a quadruped. The clever choice of name for the creature contributed to the fairytale effect of the picture: on the one hand it belonged to the realm of popular folklore and the commonplace through the use of the word *Klau* rather than *Dieb* (the former being less emotive a term, on a level with, say, "pilferer" in English, while the latter is an unambiguous term for "thief"); while on the other, the bold formation of the new noun . . . and its alliteration clearly poeticised it and elevated it above the commonplace . . .'[38]

Kohlenklau always wore a cloth cap, formerly the symbol of the working man (as opposed to the top-hat of the capitalist and the felt hat of the 'ordinary citizen').

Everything that could be useful to the war effort could disappear into the sack which he carried around with him, as was also suggested by the accompanying doggerel. The burly figure with the rodent-like teeth and the walrus moustache was a subtle symbol of the weaker side of the German citizen which had to be fended off. No sloppiness and egoism could be tolerated in the new circumstances. Its perpetrators had to be caught and put behind bars. The appeal, *Fasst ihn!* (Catch him!), was expressed in terms of the hunt and pursuit of an enemy, but the viewer was meant to interpret it as an appeal to use scarce resources with extreme circumspection. *Sein Magen knurrt... und gierig schnüffelt er umher...* (His stomach rumbles... and he rumages around greedily...) — this was also true of the average citizen during the war years. Thus it was also a frank appeal by the government for the population to economise further under war-time conditions; but evidently the Nazi propagandists succeeded through *Kohlenklau* in creating an appeal which, thanks partly to its similarity to the world of children's books, was generally accepted.

In a similar way to the 'Squander Bug' of English wartime propaganda, *Kohlenklau* was used as the subject of several cartoon series. The frequent hint that 'there's more about him in the papers!' bore witness to the fact that several different media were acting in concert and, in addition, referred to the learning process of the viewer, for no doubt one had to read several cartoons in order to be able to form a more complete mental picture of *Kohlenklau* and his activities. Moreover, one of the posters[39] testified to the reinforcement of this figure of fantasy in the minds of schoolchildren. It made its appearance in a drawing competition when boys and girls were asked to produce picture stories by the 30th November, 1943. *Kohlenklau* had been launched in the previous winter. Victor Klemperer acknowledged the outstanding success of the figure. He adds that 'subsequently, other attempts were made to achieve a similar effect, but this was never done... *Kohlenklau*, composed of picture and word, would have had every chance of becoming a mythical person, had the Third Reich existed for a longer period.'[40]

The *Feind-hört-mit* posters did not come off quite as well in Klemperer's judgement. He considered the slogan hackneyed at its very inception and criticised the 'Americanism of the omitted (definite) article'[41]. But conceivably he underestimated the project. According to the latest research, this was the most extensive poster campaign of the Nazi era.[42] Here, too, the design challenge was to abbreviate a very complex ideological and military situation to one symbol, while ensuring its general comprehensibility. In this case it was as impossible to fall back on the stylistic devices of caricature as it was to treat the theme in a jokey and jovial manner, since, after all, the deadly serious matter of espionage, treason and secrecy was at stake.

Years of work went into the creation of an unambiguous and easily memorable symbol of espionage. There were no previous prototypes that could be used without thorough modification; the theme posed a considerable challenge for illustrators and copywriters alike. The idea was that when spies were about, then even totally 'upright national comrades' might — however involuntarily — become traitors. Moreover by definition the spy remained 'invisible' and hence without definite contours, and the consequences of any act of betrayal would most probably affect completely different people from those who committed the treachery by their talkativeness in the first place. Hence the illustrators could not assume any unity of place, time or action as a starting point. To accommodate all the functions of an anti-spy poster in a single picture which could be easily compre-

197

hended without risking the plausibility of the representation was an outstanding task in terms of the difficulties which had to be overcome. Attempts to find a solution were correspondingly numerous and varied. It may be helpful to start with an examination of the caption, the shadow as a symbol, and the background, in isolation from each other.

The starting point for considerations of the caption was the slogan issued by the High Command of the *Wehrmacht* during the First World War: *Vorsicht! Der Feind hört mit!* (Beware! The enemy is listening!)[43]. This is perhaps why Klemperer could maintain that the caption was already somewhat second-hand. However, the repetition of something already well-known was important for comprehensibility. *Fig 10* shows one of these posters, featuring two men out walking. The accompanying words are *Dahinten am Waldrand, da liegt . . . Pst! Feind hört mit!* (Over there, at the edge of the woods, there's . . . Sh! The enemy's listening!). The phrase *Feind hört mit!* was taken over from a previous poster. It assumed a 'listening', rather than an observing enemy, and did not mention 'spies' as such. Verbally, at least, this notion was quite absent. The deliberate omission of the definite article signalled a calculated change of meaning, not just an Americanism. Nor was the plural *Feinde* (enemies) used; nor any suggestion of a specific enemy. Only *Feind* was left over — menacing, threatening, evil and omnipresent by the very generality of its concept. The bland assertion *Der Feind hört mit!* was thus transformed into the harrowing warning *Feind hört mit!*, so that only a short appeal or instruction (the *Pst!*) needed adding to ellicit appropriate action on the part of the observer to involve him in a defensive plot.

The majority of the pictures of this campaign showed scenes of everyday communication which, by means of the shadow in the background and a few accompanying words, could be interpreted as situations of betrayal. The *Pst!* made sense in this context and at the same time answered the observer's question as to what it had to do with him. Interestingly, it was not until World War II that this *Pst!* emerged in this function, as did the 'shadow', the visual equivalent of the 'enemy' of the caption.

The evolution of the slogan and of the whole concept of the poster was in fact directly inspired by the competition between several propaganda units. At first it was still *Vorsicht bei Gesprächen!* (Talk with caution!). In 1938 the *Reichspropagandaleitung* (RPL or Reich Propaganda Management) began its campaign with a similarly worded poster by Theo Matejko. In 1940 this slogan was still the property of the *Oberkommando der Wehrmacht* (OKW or Supreme Army Command) — whose poster (to a design by Vogler) was so bad that Goebbels had it withdrawn from circulation on the 6th March 1940. After that, his suggested competition in the propaganda department of the OKW kindled innovation, and the slogan *Schweig!* (Keep Silent!) emerged, which was more effective.

Until Goebbels' own colleagues in the Ministry of Propaganda came up with *Pst!* in 1943 as an unaccompanied caption, various different verbal and pictorial combinations were tried. The small grey *Pst!* (*Fig 10*) was but one of several temporary solutions. These were developed, together with the shadow symbol, in the German Propaganda Studio established by Goebbels' Ministry. There the most highly qualified illustrators and copywriters were employed to work with the best technical equipment on special tasks, without having to concern themselves with the demands of the commercial client or having to worry about an insufficient budget. It was in a special graphics department that the famous posters *Der Feind sieht dein Licht — Verdunkeln!* (The enemy can see your light — Black it out!), with

10. *Pst! Feind hört mit,* after 1943

the skeleton on the bomber; *Harte Zeiten, Harte Pflichten, Harte Herzen* (Hard Times, Hard Duties, Hard Hearts); *Sieg oder Bolschewismus* (Victory or Bolshevism), and *Adolf Hitler ist der Sieg!* (Adolf Hitler is the Victory!) were created. At the same time, Goebbels' *Dreißig Kriegsartikel für das Deutsche Volk* (Thirty Articles of War for the German People) were written there. Article 13 explained the 'enemy-is-listening' slogan: 'Anyone who speculates about the war and its outcome should always choose his words as if the enemy were listening . . .' In February 1944 that slogan appeared as a poster.[44] Within the framework of the measures for 'total war', the other propaganda departments were first reduced and then dissolved. In this way there evolved a unique concentration of skills in the Propaganda Studio. Those who were involved in the enemy-is-listening campaign included, among others, Richard Blank, Erich L. Stahl, Richard C. J. H. Zoozmann and Franz O. Schiffers.

The actual course of the work on the German anti-espionage posters was so complicated that the reader is to be referred to the detailed (unpublished) account by Andreas Fleischer.[45] Apart from the German Propaganda Studio, the RPL, the Reich Propaganda Offices, the OKW and the various propaganda companies all contributed their own designs. Also, propagandistic knowledge of military matters and answers to questions of psychological mobilisation were generated by a whole range of research laboratories, institutes of military science and associations dealing with military politics which cannot be listed here. Of the older established institutions, the universities also contributed to the quality of poster propaganda, for example in the analytical work of Schockel and Medebach already referred to.

199

The 'shadow' image arose, in parallel to the slogan, as a symbol of the enemy. After Stalingrad all propaganda organisations intensified their work to produce oversized pictures of the enemy.[46] The faceless stranger, the shadow of the spy or of the 'enemy within', completed the constellation of pictorial projections which emanated from the Nazi mass propaganda machine. Moreover, at the end of May 1943 there was an official announcement to the effect that 'Greater Germany' was now 'Jew-free', and hence the concept of the Jewish enemy disappeared. However, its 'subversive', 'treacherous', 'furtive' and 'secretive' aspects were preserved in the image of the 'shadow'. The 'shadow' was the last Nazi image of the enemy which was widely disseminated after the other stereotypes had lost their effectiveness. The 'shadow' was the absolute embodiment of the 'enemy within', a potent pictorial extract which, thanks to its very generality, contained everything that Nazi myth could muster, from the 'stab-in-the-back' to the 'world-conspiracy' theory. The 'shadow' became a mere silhouette, a grey form, which offered the observer little more than an outline to stimulate his own interpretations. In the silhouette, the outline of a hat, an arm and a hand was discernible. The inclination of the figure is a particular problem. Indeed, the interaction of the silhouette with other levels of depiction became the main problem of the whole series of posters, for the outlines of the shadow do not enable us to make specific statements about 'his' appearance at all — he wears a hat, he is a civilian, yet beneath the clothes of the respectable citizen he remains faceless and therefore anonymous. The hat, arm and inclination, incidentally, were only developed via a number of intermediary stages before the figure shown in *Figs 10 & 11* was settled on. The hand was such an important instrument that its shape lent the poster a whole new dimension of meaning. It is just possible to make out the rough outlines of a claw, coarseness of which allows the silhouette to be 'read' as lunging, seizing and even strangulating in the immediate future. Since it was accorded the negative attributes of darkness, frightening size and strangeness, the shadow became a symbol of brutality, of the saboteur and of the suspected presence of the dreaded 'Fifth Column'.

In most cases the whole figure loomed from the bottom right to the top left diagonally across the field of vision, and this image was generally cast over the scene of a conservation. As a 'shadow', 'he' could even be looking over the shoulder of the viewer — given the latter's assumed position in relation to the poster. 'He' was evidently listening intently, inclined to the side. The impression of 'listening in' was basically created by this leaning posture — and to translate 'listening in' visually was not an easy task. If this had been the only symbol, the viewer would have known that there were indeed spies about and that he should keep his mouth shut. That was indeed sufficient. This was actually the way in which the later posters of the campaign made their point.

The first ones had more to explain. In them, the symbol of the shadow was linked with a 'realistically' portrayed scene of treacherous and careless conversation. Through the interconnection of the shadow with a picture of men in conversation, darkened through the overlaying technique, there arose problems in the graphics which were hard to solve; thus in the first twenty or so attempts there were definite shortcomings of varying degrees of seriousness. Equally, they testified to a definite intention to hold on to this symbol and exploit its possibilities. The solution suggested by the graphic artist Richard Blank eventually became well known. In a drawing style again clearly inspired by the banned expressionist artist Käthe Kollwitz it showed workers streaming out of the factory with the shadow forming a menacingly greenish-blue backdrop. The examples shown in *Figs 10 & 11* were variations on a different solution. It was the contrasts of light that gave the 'enemy-is-listening' posters a special distinction, rather than the actual colours and stylistic peculiarities (each illustrator maintained his own style and left his signature on the poster). In *Fig 10* the figures on the poster are illuminated like characters in a play, lit up by spotlights on an otherwise darkened stage. Everything else blended into the 'shadow'. The accompanying captions which, apart from the main slogan, were always excerpts of conversations, helped point to the fact that wrongdoers would be exposed to the blazing light of National Socialist publicity. It was only the heads and shoulders of two men which became visible out of the surrounding darkness. Both are dressed in Sunday suits. The older man with the waistcoat, hat, moustache and walking stick was pointing directly at an object outside the picture — and thus became a traitor: 'Over there, at the edge of the wood, there's . . .' The ordinary peace-time concept of the Sunday walk was thus put under suspicion by being juxtaposed with the mysterious shadow of the listening enemy.

The poster in *Fig 11* was by Franz O. Schiffers (1943), who contributed four of the best 'enemy-is-listening' designs. In his imagery he managed to convey situations set in intimate or failing light which at the same time had the 'shadow' falling over them; and all this while retaining a thoroughly detailed, almost photographic realism of scenes from everyday life. His poster told the story of betrayal which literally took place at the last moment: the bus, for which the characters were waiting in the early morning cold, is just about to arrive. The viewer looks into its headlights which beam out from the darkness and can already make out the weak glow of the bus's interior lighting; three faces are lit up in the glare of the headlights; one of the men is just in the process of explaining something with animated gestures. But the shadow lies over him and suggests that he may be about to betray a secret. The picture is clearly reminiscent of a film scene. Its 'naturalistic' specifications are based, incidentally, on considerations in F. Medebach:

> The perceptive faculties of the contemporary masses have had a naturalistic schooling. This requires corresponding pictorial representations which are as true to 'nature' and 'reality' as possible. The mass audience demands that they be 'right' and pose no difficulty to its materialistic perception. Pictorial arrangements which are too far removed from naturalistic reality are for this reason excluded from the political poster . . .[47]

Yet the spray gun technique which Schiffers so effectively employed gave rise to more than just 'naturalism'. The technique of blending subjects into one another and of superimposing several images which comment upon each other and yet which do not disrupt the appeal of the whole replaced older (and generally 'modernist') method of the montage of heterogeneous elements. It made possible new ways of linking incompatible styles (symbolism and naturalism) to new effect. In this way, the technique proved itself a superb instrument for realising the propagandist's dream: to be able to make anything plausible. For, in the pictures of the 'enemy-is-listening' campaign a peaceful world without the terror of bombs is portrayed, which in 1943 had long since ceased to exist. It therefore became a question merely of *recognition*, not of adequate *description* of reality. Despite the civilian atmosphere of these images it is not possible to specify within them a particular point in time, much before the winter of 1941/2: this was one of the tricks they contained.

Through them, however, one thing was made plausible above all: that every

11. Franz Schiffers, *Pst!* 1943

activity in ordinary civilian life might become dangerous for the war effort. In England, the slogan was 'didn't you know, there's a war going on?' The Nazi propagandists went much further than this. Although they were still showing soldiers as inadvertent traitors in the first posters, one can see by taking all the pictures of the campaign together that in the end, every form of communication and every situation was defamed as dangerous, even people innocently chatting while out for a walk. It was a propaganda offensive which plainly criminalised all private communication. The pictures portraying situations which risked becoming acts of betrayal were, it is true — and this must be added in the interests of precision — in many cases indicated specifically by extra captions in the picture, or by notes in the background. In the last posters, however, there was no such delimitation: *Pst!* applied simply to every situation. Life in the Reich had become unsettling as was proved by the 'shadow'. It was now plausible to say: 'The duty to keep secrets applies to all private relationships. Neither kinship nor friendship, neither comradeship nor love remove this first and foremost commitment.'[49] Even the mere suspicion of treachery was sufficient for a death sentence to be pronounced.

Public notices of executions were put up on blood-red bills next to the 'enemy-is-listening' posters. Thus the ubiquity of the enemy had its corollary in the ubiquity of anxiety, both that of the Nazis, who had exiled, persecuted, hanged and gassed so many, and that of the ordinary population, who wondered what would become of them and of Germany after the war. The faceless 'shadow' was, as it were, also the threatening revenge of those who had been banished from their German homesteads. In other words, it would be too simple to explain the 'shadow' merely in terms of the demands of political propaganda. It had other symbolic functions too, even subconscious ones. For the 'shadow' now loomed over that very informality of 'being among friends', over that very same relaxed coziness for the preservation of which so many had been 'sacrificed'. Both the everyday world of people going for a stroll and sitting in coffee houses, and that of business-men and workers newly enveloped by the Nazi regime, became touched by the ghost of those who had been exiled or executed. The mass of the German people was now left behind in desolation, united only by worry and mistrust.

In order to ascertain the specifically National Socialist content of this campaign (in contrast, for example, to the British anti-espionage campaign), we must take its particular context into account. Just as *Kohlenklau's* physiognomy contained an image of the *Untermensch* (the sub-human), so also the symbolism of shadow and light in the 'enemy-is-listening' campaign belonged to the context of the racialist myths. Little could the SS leader Heinrich Himmler know how right he would be when he wrote in 1935: 'Just as night confronts day and light rises against shadow — so the greatest enemy of those who wish to be masters of the earth is man himself.'[50]

Chapter Eleven

FASCINATING FASCISM

(1974)

Susan Sontag

I

First Exhibit. Here is a book of 126 splendid color photographs by Leni Riefenstahl, certanly the most ravishing book of photographs published anywhere in recent years. In the intractable mountains of the southern Sudan live about eight thousand aloof, godlike Nuba, emblems of physical perfection, with large, well-shaped, partly shaven heads, expressive faces, and muscular bodies that are depilated and decorated with scars; smeared with sacred gray-white ash, the men prance, squat, brood, wrestle on the arid slopes. And here is a fascinating layout of twelve black-and-white photographs of Riefenstahl on the back cover of *The Last of the Nuba*, also ravishing, a chronological sequence of expressions (from sultry inwardness to the grin of a Texas matron on safari) vanquishing the intractable march of aging. The first photograph was taken in 1927 when she was twenty-five and already a movie star, the most recent are dated 1969 (she is cuddling a naked African baby) and 1972 (she is holding a camera), and each of them shows some version of an ideal presence, a kind of imperishable beauty, like Elisabeth Schwarzkopf's, that only gets gayer and more metallic and healthier-looking with old age. And here is a biographical sketch of Riefenstahl on the dust jacket, and an introduction (unsigned) entitled 'How Leni Riefenstahl came to study the Mesakin Nuba of Kordofan' — full of disquieting lies.

The introduction, which gives a detailed account of Riefenstahl's pilgrimage to the Sudan (inspired, we are told, by reading Hemingway's *The Green Hills of Africa* 'one sleepless night in the mid-1950s'), laconically identifies the photographer as 'something of a mythical figure as a film-maker before the war, half-forgotten by a nation which chose to wipe from its memory an era of its history.' Who (one hopes) but Riefenstahl herself could have thought up this fable about what is mistily referred to as 'a nation' which for some unnamed reason 'chose' to perform the deplorable act of cowardice of forgetting 'an era' — tactfully left unspecified — 'of its history'? Presumably, at least some readers will be startled by this coy allusion to Germany and the Third Reich.

Compared with the introduction, the jacket of the book is positively expansive on the subject of the photographer's career, parroting misinformation that Riefenstahl has been dispensing for the last twenty years.

> It was during Germany's blighted and momentous 1930s that Leni Riefenstahl sprang to international fame as a film director. She was born in 1902, and her first devotion was to creative dancing. This led to her partici-

pation in silent films, and soon she was herself making — and starring in — her own talkies, such as *The Mountain* (1929).

These tensely romantic productions were widely admired, not least by Adolf Hitler who, having attained power in 1933, commissioned Riefenstahl to make a documentary on the Nuremberg Rally in 1934.

It takes a certain originality to describe the Nazi era as 'Germany's blighted and momentous 1930s', to summarize the events of 1933 as Hitler's 'having attained power', and to assert that Riefenstahl, most of whose work was in its own decade correctly identified as Nazi propaganda, enjoyed 'international fame as a film director', ostensibly like her contemporaries Renoir, Lubitsch, and Flaherty. (Could the publishers have let LR write the jacket copy herself? One hesitates to entertain so unkind a thought, although 'her first devotion was to creative dancing' is a phrase few native speakers of English would be capable of.)

The facts are, of course, inaccurate or invented. Not only did Riefenstahl not make — or star in — a talkie called *TheMountain* (1929). No such film exists. More generally: Riefenstahl did not first simply participate in silent films and then, when sound came in, begin directing and starring in her own films. In all nine films she ever acted in, Riefenstahl was the star; and seven of these she did not direct. These seven films were: *Der heilige Berg* (*The Holy Mountain*, 1926), *Der grosse Sprung* (*The Big Jump*, 1927), *Das Schicksal derer von Habsburg* (*The Fate of the House of Habsburg*, 1929), *Die weisse Hölle von Piz Palü* (*The White Hell of Pitz Palü*, 1929) — all silents — followed by *Stürme über dem Montblanc* (*Avalanche*, 1930), *Der weisse Rausch* (*White Frenzy*, 1931), and *S.O.S. Eisberg* (*S.O.S. Iceberg*, 1932 – 1933). All but one were directed by Arnold Fanck, *auteur* of hugely success- ful Alpine epics since 1919, who made only two more films, both flops, after Riefenstahl left him to strike out on her own as a director in 1932. (The film not directed by Fanck is *The Fate of the House of Habsburg*, a royalist weepie made in Austria in which Riefenstahl played Marie Vetsera, Crown Prince Rudolf's com- panion at Mayerling. No print seems to have survived.)

Fanck's pop-Wagnerian vehicles for Riefenstahl were not just 'tensely romantic.' No doubt thought of as apolitical when they were made, these films now seem in retrospect, as Siegfried Kracauer has pointed out, to be an anthology of proto-Nazi sentiments. Mountain climbing in Fanck's films was a visually irresist- ible metaphor for unlimited aspiration toward the high mystic goal, both beautiful and terrifying, which was later to become concrete in *Führer*-worship. The character that Riefenstahl generally played was that of a wild girl who dares to scale the peak that others, the 'valley pigs', shrink from. In her first role, in the silent *The Holy Mountain* (1926), that of a young dancer named Diotima, she is wooed by an ardent climber who converts her to the healthy ecstasies of Alpinism. This character underwent a steady aggrandizement. In her first sound film, *Avalanche* (1930), Riefenstahl is a mountain-possessed girl in love with a young meteorologist, whom she rescues when a storm strands him in his observatory on Mont Blanc.

Riefenstahl herself directed six films, the first of which, *Das blaue Licht* (*The Blue Light*, 1932), was another mountain film. Starring in it as well, Riefenstahl played a role similar to the ones in Fanck's films for which she had been so 'widely admired, not least by Adolf Hitler', but allegorizing the dark themes of longing, purity, and death that Fanck had treated rather scoutishly. As usual, the mountain is represented as both supremely beautiful and dangerous, that majestic force

205

which invites the ultimate affirmation of and escape from the self—into the brotherhood of courage and into death. The role Riefenstahl devised for herself is that of a primitive creature who has a unique relation to a destructive power: only Junta, the rag-clad outcast girl of the village, is able to reach the mysterious blue light radiating from the peak of Mount Cristallo, while other young villagers, lured by the light, try to climb the mountain and fall to their deaths. What eventually causes the girl's death is not the impossibility of the goal symbolized by the mountain but the materialist, prosaic spirit of envious villagers and the blind rationalism of her lover, a well-meaning visitor from the city.

The next film Riefenstahl directed after *The Blue Light* was not 'a documentary on the Nuremberg Rally in 1934'—Riefenstahl made four non-fiction films, not two, as she has claimed since the 1950s and as most current white-washing accounts of her repeat—but *Sieg des Glaubens* (*Victory of the Faith*, 1933), celebrating the first National Socialist Party Congress held after Hitler seized power. Then came the first of two works which did indeed make her inter-nationally famous, the film on the next National Socialist Party Congress, *Triumph des Willens* (*Triumph of the Will*, 1935)—whose title is never mentioned on the jacket of *The Last of the Nuba*—after which she made a short film (eighteen minutes) for the army, *Tag der Freiheit: Unsere Wehrmacht* (*Day of Freedom: Our Army*, 1935), that depicts the beauty of soldiers and soldiering for the *Führer*. (It is not surprising to find no mention of this film, a print of which was found in 1971; during the 1950s and 1960s, when Riefenstahl and everyone else believed *Day of Freedom* to have been lost, she had it dropped from her filmography and refused to discuss it with interviewers.)

The jacket copy continues:

> Riefenstahl's refusal to submit to Goebbels' attempt to subject her visu-alisation to his strictly propagandistic requirements led to a battle of wills which came to a head when Riefenstahl made her film of the 1936 Olympic Games, *Olympia*. This, Goebbels attempted to destroy; and it was only saved by the personal intervention of Hitler.
>
> With two of the most remarkable documentaries of the 1930s to her credit, Riefenstahl continued making films of her devising, unconnected with the rise of Nazi Germany, until 1941, when war conditions made it impossible to continue.
>
> Her acquaintance with the Nazi leadership led to her arrest at the end of the Second World War: she was tried twice, and acquitted twice. Her reputa-tion was in eclipse, and she was half forgotten—although to a whole generation of Germans her name had been a household word.

Except for the bit about her having once been a household word in Nazi Germany, not one part of the above is true. To cast Riefenstahl in the role of the individualist-artist, defying philistine bureaucrats and censorship by the patron state ('Goebbels' attempt to subject her visualisation to his strictly propagandistic requirements') should seem like nonsense to anyone who has seen *Triumph of the Will*—a film whose very conception negates the possibility of the filmmaker's having an aesthetic conception independent of propaganda. The facts, denied by Riefenstahl since the war, are that she made *Triumph of the Will* with unlimited facilities and unstinting official cooperation (there was never any struggle between the filmmaker and the German minister of propaganda). Indeed, Riefenstahl was, as she relates in the short book about the making of *Triumph of the Will*, in on the planning of the rally—which was from the start conceived as the set of a film spectacle.[1] *Olympia*—a three-and-a-half-hour film in two parts, *Fest der Völker* (*Festival of the People*) and *Fest der Schönheit* (*Festival of Beauty*)—was no less an official production. Riefenstahl has maintained in interviews since the 1950s that *Olympia* was commissioned by the International Olympic Committee, produced by her own company, and made over Goebbels' protests. The truth is that *Olympia* was commissioned and entirely financed by the Nazi government (a dummy company was set up in Riefenstahl's name because it was thought unwise for the government to appear as the producer) and facilitated by Goebbels' ministry at every stage of the shooting[2]; even the plausible-sounding legend of Goebbels objecting to her footage of the triumphs of the black American track star Jesse Owens is untrue. Riefenstahl worked for eighteen months on the editing, finishing in time so that the film could have its world premiere on April 29, 1938, in Berlin, as part of the festivities for Hitler's forty-ninth birthday; later that year *Olympia* was the principal German entry at the Venice Film Festival, where it won the Gold Medal.

More lies: to say that Riefenstahl 'continued making films of her devising, unconnected with the rise of Nazi Germany, until 1941.' In 1939 (after returning from a visit to Hollywood, the guest of Walt Disney), she accompanied the invading *Wehrmacht* into Poland as a uniformed army war correspondent with her own camera team; but there is no record of any of this material surviving the war. After *Olympia* Riefenstahl made exactly one more film, *Tiefland* (*Lowland*) which she began in 1941—and, after an interruption, resumed in 1944 (in the Barrandov Film Studios in Nazi-occupied Prague), and finished in 1954. Like *The Blue Light*, *Tiefland* opposes lowland or valley corruption to mountain purity, and once again the protagonist (played by Riefenstahl) is a beautiful outcast. Riefenstahl prefers to give the impression that there were only two documentaries in a long career as a director of fiction films, but the truth is that four of the six films she directed were documentaries made for and financed by the Nazi government.

It is hardly accurate to describe Riefenstahl's professional relationship to and intimacy with Hitler and Goebbels as 'her acquaintance with the Nazi leadership.' Riefenstahl was a close friend and companion of Hitler's well before 1932; she was a friend of Goebbels, too: no evidence supports Riefenstahl's persistent claim since the 1950s that Goebbels hated her, or even that he had the power to interfere with her work. Because of her unlimited personal access to Hitler, Riefenstahl was precisely the only German filmmaker who was not responsible to the Film Office (*Reichsfilmkammer*) of Goebbels' ministry of propaganda. Last, it is misleading to say that Riefenstahl was 'tried twice, and acquitted twice' after the war. What happened is that she was briefly arrested by the Allies in 1945 and two of her houses (in Berlin and Munich) were seized. Examinations and court appearances started in 1948, continuing intermittently until 1952, when she was finally 'de-Nazified' with the verdict: 'No political activity in support of the Nazi regime which would warrant punishment.' More important: whether or not Riefenstahl deserved a prison sentence, it was not her 'acquaintance' with the Nazi leadership but her activities as a leading propagandist for the Third Reich that were at issue.

The jacket copy of *The Last of the Nuba* summarizes faithfully the main line of the self-vindication which Riefenstahl fabricated in the 1950s and which is most fully spelled out in the interview she gave to *Cahiers du Cinéma* in September 1965. There she denied that any of her work was propaganda—calling it *cinema verité*. 'Not a single scene is staged,' Riefenstahl says of *Triumph of the Will*. 'Everything is genuine. And there is no tendentious commentary for the simple reason that there is no commentary at all. It is *history—pure history.'* We are a long way from that vehement disdain for 'the chronicle-film,' mere 'reportage' or 'filmed facts,' as being unworthy of the event's 'heroic style' which is expressed in her book on the making of the film.[3]

Although *Triumph of the Will* has no narrative voice, it does open with a written text heralding the rally as the redemptive culmination of German history. But this opening statement is the least original of the ways in which the film is tendentious. It has no commentary because it doesn't need one, for *Triumph of the Will* represents an already achieved and radical transformation of reality: history become theater. How the 1934 Party convention was staged was partly determined by the decision to produce *Triumph of the Will*—the historic event serving as the set of a film which was then to assume the character of an authentic documentary. Indeed, when some of the footage of Party leaders at the speakers' rostrum was spoiled, Hitler gave orders for the shots to be refilmed; and Streicher, Rosenberg, Hess, and Frank histrionically repledged their fealty to the *Führer* weeks later, without Hitler and without an audience, on a studio set built by Speer. (It is altogether correct that Speer, who built the gigantic site of the rally on the outskirts of Nuremberg, is listed in the credits of *Triumph of the Will* as architect of the film.) Anyone who defends Riefenstahl's films as documentaries, if documentary is to be distinguished from propaganda, is being ingenuous. In *Triumph of the Will*, the document (the image) not only is the record of reality but is one reason for which the reality has been constructed, and must eventually supersede it.

The rehabilitation of proscribed figures in liberal societies does not happen with the sweeping bureaucratic finality of the *Soviet Encyclopedia*, each new edition of which brings forward some hitherto unmentionable figures and lowers an equal or greater number through the trap door of nonexistence. Our rehabilitations are smoother, more insinuative. It is not that Riefenstahl's Nazi past has suddenly become acceptable. It is simply that, with the turn of the cultural wheel, it no longer matters. Instead of dispensing a freeze-dried version of history from above, a liberal society settles such questions by waiting for cycles of taste to distill out the controversy.

The purification of Leni Riefenstahl's reputation of its Nazi dross has been gathering momentum for some time, but it has reached some kind of climax this year, with Riefenstahl the guest of honor at a new cinéphile-controlled film festival held in the summer in Colorado and the subject of a stream of respectful articles and interviews in newspapers and on TV, and now with the publication of *The Last of the Nuba*. Part of the impetus behind Riefenstahl's recent promotion to the status of a cultural monument surely owes to the fact that she is a woman. The 1973 New York Film Festival poster, made by a well-known artist who is also a feminist, showed a blond doll-woman whose right breast is encircled by three names: Agnès Leni Shirley. (That is, Varda, Riefenstahl, Clarke.) Feminists would feel a pang at having to sacrifice the one woman who made films that everybody acknowledges to be first-rate. But the strongest impetus behind the change in attitude toward Riefenstahl lies in the new, ampler fortunes of the idea of the beautiful.

The line taken by Riefenstahl's defenders, who now include the most influential voices in the avant-garde film establishment, is that she was always concerned with beauty. This, of course, has been Riefenstahl's own contention for some years. Thus the *Cahiers du Cinéma* interviewer set Riefenstahl up by observing fatuously that what *Triumph of the Will* and *Olympia* 'have in common is that they both give form to a certain reality, itself based on a certain idea of form. Do you see anything peculiarly German about this concern for form?' To this, Riefenstahl answered:

> I can simply say that I feel spontaneously attracted by everything that is beautiful. Yes: beauty, harmony. And perhaps this care for composition, this aspiration to form is in effect something very German. But I don't know these things myself, exactly. It comes from the unconscious and not from my knowledge. . . . What do you want me to add? Whatever is purely realistic, slice-of-life, which is average, quotidian, doesn't interest me. . . . I am fascinated by what is beautiful, strong, healthy, what is living. I seek harmony. When harmony is produced I am happy. I believe, with this, that I have answered you.

That is why *The Last of the Nuba* is the last, necessary step in Riefenstahl's rehabilitation. It is the final rewrite of the past; or, for her partisans, the definitive confirmation that she was always a beauty freak rather than a horrid propagandist.[4] Inside the beautifully produced book, photographs of the perfect, noble tribe. And on the jacket, photographs of 'my perfect German woman' (as Hitler called Riefenstahl), vanquishing the slights of history, all smiles.

Admittedly, if the book were not signed by Riefenstahl one would not necessarily suspect that these photographs had been taken by the most interesting, talented, and effective artist of the Nazi era. Most people who leaf through *The Last of the Nuba* will probably see it as one more lament for vanishing primitives — the greatest example remains Lévi-Strauss in *Tristes Tropiques* on the Bororo Indians in Brazil — but if the photographs are examined carefully, in conjunction with the lengthy text written by Riefenstahl, it becomes clear that they are continuous with her Nazi work. Riefenstahl's particular slant is revealed by her choice of this tribe and not another: a people she describes as acutely artistic (everyone owns a lyre) and beautiful (Nuba men, Riefenstahl notes, 'have an athletic build rare in any other African tribe'); endowed as they are with 'a much stronger sense of spiritual and religious relations than of worldly and material matters,' their principal activity, she insists, is ceremonial. *The Last of the Nuba* is about a primitivist ideal: a portrait of a people subsisting in a pure harmony with their environment, untouched by 'civilization.'

All four of Riefenstahl's commissioned Nazi films — whether about Party congresses, the Wehrmacht, or athletes — celebrate the rebirth of the body and of community, mediated through the worship of an irresistible leader. They follow directly from the films of Fanck in which she starred and her own *The Blue Light.* The Alpine fictions are tales of longing for high places, of the challenge and ordeal of the elemental, the primitive; they are about the vertigo before power, symbolized by the majesty and beauty of mountains. The Nazi films are epics of achieved community, in which everyday reality is transcended through ecstatic self-control and submission; they are about the triumph of power. And *The Last of the Nuba*, an elegy for the soon-to-be extinguished beauty and mystic powers of primitives whom Riefenstahl calls 'her adopted people,' is the third in her triptych of fascist visuals.

In the first panel, the mountain films, heavily dressed people strain upward to prove themselves in the purity of the cold; vitality is identified with physical ordeal. For the middle panel, the films made for the Nazi government: *Triumph of the Will* uses overpopulated wide shots of massed figures alternating with close-ups that isolate a single passion, a single perfect submission: in a temperate zone clean-cut people in uniforms group and regroup, as if they were seeking the perfect choreography to express their fealty. In *Olympia*, the richest visually of all her films (it uses both the verticals of the mountain films and the horizontal movements characteristic of *Triumph of the Will*), one straining, scantily clad figure after another seeks the ecstasy of victory, cheered on by ranks of compatriots in the stands, all under the still gaze of the benign Super-Spectator, Hitler, whose presence in the stadium consecrates this effort. (*Olympia*, which could as well have been called *Triumph of the Will*, emphasizes that there are no easy victories.) In the third panel, *The Last of the Nuba*, the almost naked primitives, awaiting the final ordeal of their proud heroic community, their imminent extinction, frolic and pose under the scorching sun.

It is *Götterdämmerung* time. The central events in Nuba society are wrestling matches and funerals: vivid encounters of beautiful male bodies and death. The Nuba, as Riefenstahl interprets them, are a tribe of aesthetes. Like the henna-daubed Masai and the so-called Mudmen of New Guinea, the Nuba paint themselves for all important social and religious occasions, smearing on a white-gray ash which unmistakably suggests death. Riefenstahl claims to have arrived 'just in time,' for in the few years since these photographs were taken the glorious Nuba have been corrupted by money, jobs, clothes. (And, probably, by war—which Riefenstahl never mentions, since what she cares about is myth not history. The civil war that has been tearing up that part of the Sudan for a dozen years must have scattered new technology and a lot of detritus.)

Although the Nuba are black, not Aryan, Riefenstahl's portrait of them evokes some of the larger themes of Nazi ideology: the contrast between the clean and the impure, the incorruptible and the defiled, the physical and the mental, the joyful and the critical. A principal accusation against the Jews within Nazi Germany was that they were urban, intellectual, bearers of a destructive corrupting 'critical spirit.' The book bonfire of May 1933 was launched with Goebbels' cry: 'The age of extreme Jewish intellectualism has now ended, and the success of the German revolution has again given the right of way to the German spirit.' And when Goebbels officially forbade art criticism in November 1936, it was for having 'typically Jewish traits of character': putting the head over the heart, the individual over the community, intellect over feeling. In the transformed thematics of latter-day fascism, the Jews no longer play the role of defiler. It is 'civilization' itself.

What is distinctive about the fascist version of the old idea of the Noble Savage is its contempt for all that is reflective, critical, and pluralistic. In Riefenstahl's casebook of primitive virtue, it is hardly—as in Lévi-Strauss—the intricacy and subtlety of primitive myth, social organization, or thinking that is being extolled. Riefenstahl strongly recalls fascist rhetoric when she celebrates the ways the Nuba are exalted and unified by the physical ordeals of their wrestling matches, in which the 'heaving and straining' Nuba men, 'huge muscles bulging,' throw one another to the ground—fighting not for material prizes but 'for the renewal of the sacred vitality of the tribe.' Wrestling and the rituals that go with it, in Riefenstahl's account, bind the Nuba together. Wrestling

is the expression of all that distinguishes the Nuba way of life. . . . Wrestling generates the most passionate loyalty and emotional participation in the team's supporters, who are, in fact, the entire 'non-playing' population of the village. . . . Its importance as the expression of the total outlook of the Mesakin and Korongo cannot be exaggerated; it is the expression in the visible and social world of the invisible world of the mind and of the spirit.

In celebrating a society where the exhibition of physical skill and courage and the victory of the stronger man over the weaker are, as she sees it, the unifying symbols of the communal culture — where success in fighting is the 'main aspiration of a man's life' — Riefenstahl seems hardly to have modified the ideas of her Nazi films. And her portrait of the Nuba goes further than her films in evoking one aspect of the fascist ideal: a society in which women are merely breeders and helpers, excluded from all ceremonial functions, and represent a threat to the integrity and strength of men. From the 'spiritual' Nuba point of view (by the Nuba Riefenstahl means, of course, males), contact with women is profane; but, ideal society that this is supposed to be, the women know their place.

> The fiancées or wives of the wrestlers are as concerned as the men to avoid any intimate contact . . . their pride at being the bride or wife of a strong wrestler supersedes their amorousness.

Lastly, Riefenstahl is right on target with her choice as a photographic subject of a people who 'look upon death as simply a matter of fate — which they do not resist or struggle against,' of a society whose most enthusiastic and lavish ceremonial is the funeral. *Viva la muerte*.

It may seem ungrateful and rancorous to refuse to cut loose *The Last of the Nuba* from Riefenstahl's past, but there are salutary lessons to be learned from the continuity of her work as well as from that curious and implacable recent event — her rehabilitation. The careers of other artists who became fascists, such as Céline and Benn and Marinetti and Pound (not to mention those, like Pabst and Pirandello and Hamsun, who embraced Fascism in the decline of their powers), are not instructive in a comparable way. For Riefenstahl is the only major artist who was completely identified with the Nazi era and whose work, not only during the Third Reich but thirty years after its fall, has consistently illustrated many themes of fascist aesthetics.

Fascist aesthetics include but go far beyond the rather special celebration of the primitive to be found in *The Last of the Nuba*. More generally, they flow from (and justify) a preoccupation with situations of control, submissive behavior, extravagant effort, and the endurance of pain; they endorse two seemingly opposite states, egomania and servitude. The relations of domination and enslavement take the form of a characteristic pageantry: the massing of groups of people; the turning of people into things; the multiplication or replication of things; and the grouping of people/things around an all-powerful, hypnotic leader-figure or force. The fascist dramaturgy centers on the orgiastic transactions between mighty forces and their puppets, uniformly garbed and shown in ever swelling numbers. Its choreography alternates between ceaseless motion and a congealed, static, 'virile' posing. Fascist art glorifies surrender, it exalts mindlessness, it glamorizes death.

Such art is hardly confined to works labeled as fascist or produced under fascist governments. (To cite films only: Walt Disney's *Fantasia*, Busby Berkeley's *The Gang's All Here*, and Kubrick's *2001* also strikingly exemplify certain formal structures and themes of fascist art.) And, of course, features of fascist art proliferate in the official art of communist countries — which always presents itself under the banner of realism, while fascist art scorns realism in the name of 'idealism.' The tastes for the monumental and for mass obeisance to the hero are common to both fascist and communist art, reflecting the view of all totalitarian regimes that art has the function of 'immortalizing' its leaders and doctrines. The rendering of movement in grandiose and rigid patterns is another element in common, for such choreography rehearses the very unity of the polity. The masses are made to take form, be design. Hence mass athletic demonstrations, a choreographed display of bodies, are a valued activity in all totalitarian countries; and the art of the gymnast, so popular now in Eastern Europe, also evokes recurrent features of fascist aesthetics; the holding in or confining of force; military precision.

In both fascist and communist politics, the will is staged publicly, in the drama of the leader and the chorus. What is interesting about the relation between politics and art under National Socialism is not that art was subordinated to political needs, for this is true of dictatorships both of the right and of the left, but that politics appropriated the rhetoric of art — art in its late romantic phase. (Politics is 'the highest and most comprehensive art there is,' Goebbels said in 1933, 'and we who shape the modern German policy feel ourselves to be artists . . . the task of art and the artist [being] to form, to give shape, to remove the diseased and create freedom for the healthy.') What is interesting about art under National Socialism are those features which make it a special variant of totalitarian art. The official art of countries like the Soviet Union and China aims to expound and reinforce a utopian morality. Fascist art displays a utopian aesthetics — that of physical perfection. Painters and sculptors under the Nazis often depicted the nude, but they were forbidden to show any bodily imperfections. Their nudes look like pictures in physique magazines: pinups which are both santimoniously asexual and (in a technical sense) pornographic, for they have the perfection of a fantasy. Riefenstahl's promotion of the beautiful and the healthy, it must be said, is much more sophisticated than this; and never witless, as it is in other Nazi visual art. She appreciates a range of bodily types — in matters of beauty she is not racist — and in *Olympia* she does show some effort and strain, with its attendant imperfections, as well as stylized, seemingly effortless exertions (such as diving, in the most admired sequence of the film).

In contrast to the asexual chasteness of official communist art, Nazi art is both prurient and idealizing. A utopian aesthetics (physical perfection; identity as a biological given) implies an ideal eroticism: sexuality converted into the magnetism of leaders and the joy of followers. The fascist ideal is to transform sexual energy into a 'spiritual' force, for the benefit of the community. The erotic (that is, women) is always present as a temptation, with the most admirable response being a heroic repression of the sexual impulse. Thus Riefenstahl explains why Nuba marriages, in contrast to their splendid funerals, involve no ceremonies or feasts.

> A Nuba man's greatest desire is not union with a woman but to be a good wrestler, thereby affirming the principle of abstemiousness. The Nuba dance ceremonies are not sensual occasions but rather 'festivals of chastity' — of containment of the life force.

Fascist aesthetics is based on the containment of vital forces; movements are confined, held tight, held in.

Nazi art is reactionary, defiantly outside the century's mainstream of achievement in the arts. But just for this reason it has been gaining a place in contemporary taste. The left-wing organizers of a current exhibition of Nazi painting and sculpture (the first since the war) in Frankfurt have found, to their dismay, the attendance excessively large and hardly as serious-minded as they had hoped. Even when flanked by didactic admonitions from Brecht and by concentration-camp photographs, what Nazi art reminds these crowds of is—other art of the 1930s, notably Art Deco. (Art Nouveau could never be a fascist style; it is, rather, the prototype of that art which Fascism defines as decadent; the fascist style at its best is Art Deco, with its sharp lines and blunt massing of material, its petrified eroticism.) The same aesthetic responsible for the bronze colossi of Arno Breker— Hitler's (and, briefly, Cocteau's) favorite sculptor—and of Josef Thorak also produced the muscle-bound Atlas in front of Manhattan's Rockefeller Center and the faintly lewd monument to the fallen doughboys of World War I in Philadelphia's Thirtieth Street railroad station.

To an unsophisticated public in Germany, the appeal of Nazi art may have been that it was simple, figurative, emotional; not intellectual; a relief from the demanding complexities of modernist art. To a more sophisticated public, the appeal is partly to that avidity which is now bent on retrieving all the styles of the past, especially the most pilloried. But a revival of Nazi art, following the revivals of Art Nouveau, Pre-Raphaelite painting, and Art Deco, is most unlikely. The painting and sculpture are not just sententious; they are astonishingly meager as art. But precisely these qualities invite people to look at Nazi art with knowing and sniggering detachment, as a form of Pop Art.

Riefenstahl's work is free of the amateurism and naïveté one finds in other art produced in the Nazi era, but it still promotes many of the same values. And the same very modern sensibility can appreciate her as well. The ironies of pop sophistication make for a way of looking at Riefenstahl's work in which not only its formal beauty but its political fervor are viewed as a form of aesthetic excess. And alongside this detached appreciation of Riefenstahl is a response, whether conscious or unconscious, to the subject itself, which gives her work its power.

Triumph of the Will and Olympia are undoubtedly superb films (they may be the two greatest documentaries ever made), but they are not really important in the history of cinema as an art form. Nobody making films today alludes to Riefenstahl, while many filmmakers (including myself) regard Dziga Vertov as an inexhaustible provocation and source of ideas about film language. Yet it is arguable that Vertov—the most important figure in documentary films—never made a film as purely effective and thrilling as *Triumph of the Will* or *Olympia*. (Of course, Vertov never had the means at his disposal that Riefenstahl had. The Soviet government's budget for propaganda films in the 1920s and early 1930s was less than lavish.)

In dealing with propagandistic art on the left and on the right, a double standard prevails. Few people would admit that the manipulation of emotion in Vertov's later films and in Riefenstahl's provides similar kinds of exhilaration. When explaining why they are moved, most people are sentimental in the case of Vertov and dishonest in the case of Riefenstahl. Thus Vertov's work evokes a good deal of moral sympathy on the part of his cinéphile audiences all over the world; people consent to be moved. With Riefenstahl's work, the trick is to filter out the noxious political ideology of her films, leaving only their 'aesthetic' merits. Praise of Vertov's films always presupposes the knowledge that he was an attractive person and an intelligent and original artist-thinker, eventually crushed by the dictatorship which he served. And most of the contemporary audience for Vertov (as for Eisenstein and Pudovkin) assumes that the film propagandists in the early years of the Soviet Union were illustrating a noble ideal, however much it was betrayed in practice. But praise of Riefenstahl has no such recourse, since nobody, not even her rehabilitators, has managed to make Riefenstahl seem even likable; and she is no thinker at all.

More important, it is generally thought that National Socialism stands only for brutishness and terror. But this is not true. National Socialism — more broadly, Fascism — also stands for an ideal or rather ideals that are persistent today under the other banners: the ideal of life as art, the cult of beauty, the fetishism of courage, the dissolution of alienation in ecstatic feelings of community; the repudiation of the intellect; the family of man (under the parenthood of leaders). These ideals are vivid and moving to many people, and it is dishonest as wel as tautological to say that one is affected by *Triumph of the Will* and *Olympia* only because they were made by a filmmaker of genius. Riefenstahl's films are still effective because, among other reasons, their longings are still felt, because their content is a romantic ideal to which many continue to be attached and which is expressed in such diverse modes of cultural dissidence and propaganda for new forms of community as the youth/rock culture, primal therapy, anti-psychiatry, Third World camp-following, and belief in the occult. The exaltation of community does not preclude the search for absolute leadership; on the contrary, it may inevitably lead to it. (Not surprisingly, a fair number of the young people now prostrating themselves before gurus and submitting to the most grotesquely autocratic discipline are former anti-authoritarians and anti-elitists of the 1960s.)

Riefenstahl's current de-Nazification and vindication as indomitable priestess of the beautiful — as a filmmaker and, now, as a photographer — do not augur well for the keenness of current abilities to detect the fascist longings in our midst. Riefenstahl is hardly the usual sort of aesthete or anthropological romantic. The force of her work being precisely in the continuity of its political and aesthetic ideas, what is interesting is that this was once seen so much more clearly than it seems to be now, when people claim to be drawn to Riefenstahl's images for their beauty of composition. Without a historical perspective, such connoisseurship prepares the way for a curiously absentminded acceptance of propaganda for all sorts of destructive feelings — feelings whose implications people are refusing to take seriously. Somewhere, of course, everyone knows that more than beauty is at stake in art like Riefenstahl's. And so people hedge their bets — admiring this kind of art, for its undoubted beauty, and patronizing it, for its sanctimonious promotion of the beautiful. Backing up the solemn choosy formalist appreciations lies a larger reserve of appreciation, the sensibility of camp, which is unfettered by the scruples of high seriousness: and the modern sensibility relies on continuing trade-offs between the formalist approach and camp taste.

Art which evokes the themes of fascist aesthetic is popular now, and for most people it is probably no more than a variant of camp. Fascism may be merely fashionable, and perhaps fashion with its irrepressible promiscuity of taste will save us. But the judgements of taste themselves seem less innocent. Art that seemed eminently worth defending ten years ago, as a minority or adversary taste, no longer seems defensible today, because the ethical and cultural issues it raises have become serious, even dangerous, in a way they were not then. The hard truth is that what may be acceptable in elite culture may not be acceptable in mass culture, that tastes which pose only innocuous ethical issues as the property of a minority become corrupting when they become more established. Taste is context, and the context has changed.

II

Second Exhibit. Here is a book to be purchased at airport magazine stands and in 'adult' bookstores, a relatively cheap paperback, not an expensive coffee-table item appealing to art lovers and the *bien-pensant* like *The Last of the Nuba*. Yet both books share a certain community of moral origin, a root preoccupation: the same preoccupation at different stages of evolution — the ideas that animate *The Last of the Nuba* being less out of the moral closet than the cruder, more efficient idea that lies behind *SS Regalia*. Though *SS Regalia* is a respectable British-made compilation (with a three-page historical preface and notes in the back), one knows that its appeal is not scholarly but sexual. The cover already makes that clear. Across the large black swastika of an SS armband is a diagonal yellow stripe which reads 'Over 100 Brilliant Four-Color Photographs Only $2.95,' exactly as a sticker with the price on it used to be affixed — part tease, part deference to censorship — on the cover of pornographic magazines, over the model's genitalia.

There is a general fantasy about uniforms. They suggest community, order, identity (through ranks, badges, medals, things which declare who the wearer is and what he has done: his worth is recognized), competence, legitimate authority, the legitimate exercise of violence. But uniforms are not the same thing as photographs of uniforms — which are erotic materials and photographs of SS uniforms are the units of a particularly powerful and widespread sexual fantasy. Why the SS? Because the SS was the ideal incarnation of Fascism's overt assertion of the righteousness of violence, the right to have total power over others and to treat them as absolutely inferior. It was in the SS that this assertion seemed most complete, because they acted it out in a singularly brutal and efficient manner; and because they dramatized it by linking themselves to certain aesthetic standards. The SS was designed as an elite military community that would be not only supremely violent but also supremely beautiful. (One is not likely to come across a book called 'SA Regalia.' The SA, whome the SS replaced, were not known for being any less brutal than their successors, but they have gone down in history as beefy, squat, beerhall types; mere brownshirts.

SS uniforms were stylish, well-cut, with a touch (but not too much) of eccentricity. Compare the rather boring and not very well cut American army uniform: jacket, shirt, tie, pants, socks, and lace-up shoes — essentially civilian clothes no matter how bedecked with medals and badges. SS uniforms were tight, heavy, stiff and included gloves to confine the hands and boots that made legs and feet feel heavy, encased, obliging their wearer to stand up straight. As the back cover of *SS Regalia* explains:

> The uniform was black, a colour which had important overtones in Germany. On that, the SS wore a vast variety of decorations, symbols, badges to distinguish rank, from the collar runes to the death's-head. The appearance was both dramatic and menacing.

The cover's almost wistful come-on does not quite prepare one for the banality of most of the photographs. Along with those celebrated black uniforms, SS troopers were issued almost American-army-looking khaki uniforms and camouflage ponchos and jackets. And besides the photographs of uniforms, there are pages of collar patches, cuff bands, chevrons, belt buckles, commemorative badges, regimental standards, trumpet banners, field caps, service medals, shoulder flashes, permits, passes — few of which bear either the notorious runes or the death's-head; all meticulously identified by rank, unit, and year and season of issue. Precisely the innocuousness of practically all of the photographs testifies to the power of the image: one is handling the breviary of a sexual fantasy. For fantasy to have depth, it must have detail. What, for example, was the color of the travel permit an SS sergeant would have needed to get from Trier to Lübeck in the spring of 1944? One needs all the documentary evidence.

If the message of Fascism has been neutralized by an aesthetic view of life, its trappings have been sexualized. This eroticization of Fascism can be remarked in such enthralling and devout manifestations as Mishima's *Confessions of a Mask* and *Sun and Steel*, and in films like Kenneth Anger's *Scorpio Rising* and, more recently and far less interestingly, in Visconti's *The Damned* and Cavani's *The Night Porter*. The solemn eroticizing of Fascism must be distinguished from a sophisticated playing with cultural horror, where there is an element of the put-on. The poster Robert Morris made for his recent show at the Castelli Gallery is a photograph of the artist, naked to the waist, wearing dark glasses, what appears to be a Nazi helmet, and a spiked steel collar, attached to which is a stout chain which he holds in his manacled, uplifted hands. Morris is said to have considered this to be the only image that still has any power to shock: a singular virtue to those who take for granted that art is a sequence of ever-fresh gestures of provocation. But the point of the poster is its own negation. Shocking people in the context also means inuring them, as Nazi material enters the vast repertory of popular iconography usable for the ironic commentaries of Pop Art. Still, Nazism fascinates in a way other iconography staked out by the pop sensibility (from Mao Tse-tung to Marilyn Monroe) does not. No doubt, some part of the general rise of interest in Fascism can be set down as a product of curiosity. For those born after the early 1940s, bludgeoned by a lifetime's palaver, pro and con, about communism, it is Fascism — the great conversation piece of their parents' generation — which represents the exotic, the unknown. Then there is a general fascination among the young with horror, with the irrational. Courses dealing with the history of Fascism are, along with those on the occult (including vampirism), among the best attended these days on college campuses. And beyond this the definitely sexual lure of Fascism, which *SS Regalia* testifies to with unabashed plainness, seems impervious to deflation by irony or over-familiarity.

In pornographic literature, films, and gadgetry throughout the world, especially in the United States, England, France, Japan, Scandinavia, Holland, and Germany, the SS has become a referent of sexual adventurism. Much of the imagery of far-out sex has been placed under the sign of Nazism. Boots, leather, chains, Iron Crosses on gleaming torsos, swastikas, along with meat hooks and heavy motorcycles, have become the secret and most lucrative paraphernalia of eroticism. In the sex shops, the baths, the leather bars, the brothels, people are dragging out their gear. But why? Why has Nazi Germany, which was a sexually repressive society, become erotic? How could a regime which persecuted homosexuals become a gay turn-on?

A clue lies in the predilections of the fascist leaders themselves for sexual metaphors. Like Nietzsche and Wagner, Hitler regarded leadership as sexual mastery of the 'feminine' masses, as rape. (The expression of the crowds in

Triumph of the Will is one of ecstasy; the leader makes the crowd come.) Left-wing movements have tended to be unisex, and asexual in their imagery. Right-wing movements, however puritanical and repressive the realities they usher in, have an erotic surface. Certainly Nazism is 'sexier' than communism (which is not to the Nazis' credit, but rather shows something of the nature and limits of the sexual imagination).

Of course, most people who are turned on by SS uniforms are not signifying approval of what the Nazis did, if indeed they have more than the sketchiest idea of what that might be. Nevertheless, there are powerful and growing currents of sexual feeling, those that generally go by the name of sadomasochism, which make playing at Nazism seem erotic. These sadomasochistic fantasies and practices are to be found among heterosexuals as well as homosexuals, although it is among male homosexuals that the eroticizing of Nazism is most visible. S-m, not swinging, is the big sexual secret of the last few years.

Between sadomasochism and Fascism there is a natural link. 'Fascism is theater,' as Genet said.[5] As is sadomasochistic sexuality: to be involved in sadomasochism is to take part in a sexual theater, a staging of sexuality. Regulars of sadomasochistic sex are expert costumers and choreographers as well as performers, in a drama that is all the more exciting because it is forbidden to ordinary people. Sadomasochism is to sex what war is to civil life: the magnificent experience. (Riefenstahl put it: 'What is purely realistic, slice of life, what is average, quotidian, doesn't interest me.' As the social contract seems tame in comparison with war, so fucking and sucking come to seem merely nice, and therefore unexciting. The end to which all sexual experience tends, as Bataille insisted in a lifetime of writing, is defilement, blasphemy. To be 'nice,' as to be civilized, means being alienated from this savage experience — which is entirely staged.

Sadomasochism, of course, does not just mean people hurting their sexual partners, which has always occurred — and generally means men beating up women. The perennial drunken Russian peasant thrashing his wife is just doing something he feels like doing (because he is unhappy, oppressed, stupefied; and because women are handy victims). But the perennial Englishman in a brothel being whipped is re-creating an experience. He is paying a whore to act out a piece of theater with him, to reenact or reevoke the past — experiences of his schooldays or nursery which now hold for him a huge reserve of sexual energy. Today it may be the Nazi past that people invoke, in the theatricalization of sexuality, because it is those images (rather than memories) from which they hope a reserve of sexual energy can be tapped. What the French call 'the English vice' could, however, be said to be something of an artful affirmation of individuality; the playlet referred, after all, to the subject's own case history. The fad for Nazi regalia indicates something quite different: a response to an oppressive freedom of choice in sex (and in other matters), to an unbearable degree of individuality; the rehearsal of enslavement rather than its reenactment.

The rituals of domination and enslavement being more and more practiced, the art that is more and more devoted to rendering their themes, are perhaps only a logical extension of an affluent society's tendency to turn every part of people's lives into a taste, a choice; to invite them to regard their very lives as a (life) style. In all societies up to now, sex has mostly been an activity (something to do, without thinking about it). But once sex becomes a taste, it is perhaps already on its way to becoming a self-conscious form of theater, which is what sadomasochism is about: a form of gratification that is both violent and indirect, very mental.

Sadomasochism has always been the furthest reach of the sexual experience: when sex becomes most purely sexual, that is, severed from personhood, from relationships, from love. It should not be surprising that it has become attached to Nazi symbolism in recent years. Never before was the relation of masters and slaves so consciously aestheticized. Sade had to make up his theater of punishment and delight from scratch, improvising the decor and costumes and blasphemous rites. Now there is a master scenario available to everyone. The color is black, the material is leather, the seduction is beauty, the justification is honesty, the aim is ecstasy, the fantasy is death.

Chapter Twelve

THE RECONCEPTUALISATION OF WOMEN'S ROLES IN WAR-TIME NATIONAL SOCIALISM. AN ANALYSIS OF *DIE FRAU MEINER TRÄUME*

Eva-Maria Warth

In contrast to the wide interest in National Socialist film productions which are subsumed under the heading of 'propaganda films', the seemingly non-propagandistic group of so-called 'entertainment films' have hardly attracted the attention of film scholars and historians of the Nazi era. In this paper, I use Georg Jacoby's *Die Frau meiner Träume* (The Woman of my Dreams, 1944) to investigate some of the ways in which the specific representational strategies developed in the 'entertainment' genre contribute to the naturalisation of National Socialist ideology, particularly in terms of the changing concept of women's roles during World War II.[1]

In order to establish a broader background for my analysis of this particular film, the first part of this paper will present a short overview of National Socialist film politics and the reorganization of film production during the first four years of National Socialist rule. This is followed by a brief account on the typologies generally employed in the classification of Nazi films, which not only serves to situate *Die Frau meiner Träume* in the context of the general film production of the era, but also to motivate the critique of the propaganda/entertainment dichotomy which follows.

NATIONAL-SOCIALIST FILM POLITICS

In a 1932 interview, Hitler declared: 'I detest that politics should be performed under the pretext of art. It has to be either politics or art'.[2] Yet shortly after Hitler's inauguration on 1 February 1933, this clear-cut distinction was rapidly abandoned when Goebbels, the newly-assigned Minister of Propaganda, declared: 'The national revolution will not be limited to politics, it will also encompass economics, culture in general, domestic and foreign politics, and also films.'[3] On an organisational level this concept implied (1) tight censorship at all levels, e.g., direct control of film production, distribution and administration; (2) the nationalisation of the German film industry; and (3) the virtual extinction of art criticism, including film criticism.

In terms of the reorganisation of film production, the first decisive step was the establishment of the *Reichsfilmkammer* (film board) in June 1933. Shortly afterwards, the *Filmkammer* was subsumed under the *Reichskulturkammer* (National Chamber of Culture), with Goebbels as Minister of Propaganda at its head. The *Reichsfilmkammer* was divided into ten departments covering all aspects of film production — artistic, technical, financial and administrative.

The enactment of the Film Law of 1934 resulted in the official registration of all employees of the film industry and the regulation of their work; that of writers, producers, directors, actors, sound engineers, distributors and owners of movie theatres. Only Aryan citizens qualified for this registration, a restriction that resulted in the dismissal of at least 3,000 people formerly employed in the German film industry. Another fundamental feature of National Socialist film politics was direct censorship: before actual shooting could begin, each film script had to be submitted to and passed by the *Reichsfilmdramaturgie*, a subdivision of the *Reichsfilmkammer*. After completion, any film had to be reviewed by the board once more before public release. The casting of important films as well as the assignment of a director were other points where directive measures could be brought to bear to rule out opposition in film production.

Another form of control involved the financial sector. The film credit bank, founded in June 1933, enjoyed a close affiliation with the *Reichsfilmkammer* and provided up to 70% of film budgets. A rating system perfected during the Nazi era served as an additional means of bringing the film industry into line with party politics. The previously existing system of three points on the ratings scale was expanded to eight, including labels such as 'of political or artistic merit' or 'of special merit' (*politisch oder künstlerisch wertvoll*, or *besonders wertvoll*), of folk-loric merit (*volkstümlich wertvoll*) or of value for national education. These ratings formed the basis of a system of financial subsidies, with the result that most films were designed to earn a variety of labels.

The *Reichsfilmkammer* was closely connected to the film department of the NSDAP by personal ties. Thus Goebbels, who as Minister of Propaganda had direct or indirect influence on film production, was also director of party propaganda. These two institutions divided control of the film world between them: the Ministry was responsible for film politics in general, while the *Reichsfilmkammer* supervised and controlled actual production.

The second vital feature of National Socialist film politics was the nationalisation of the film industry, which paralleled the take-over of the press. At the beginning of the 1930s, German film production faced a severe crisis due to sinking export rates and increased production costs. This situation facilitated Nazi nationalisation efforts, a process which was achieved not by decree or special legislation but by a series of steps involving the acquisition of shares of leading film companies such as Terra, Tobis, Bavaria and finally UFA, the largest German film-maker of the 1920s, 1930s and early 1940s. This process was completed by the end of 1937 and by 1938 the German film industry was firmly under the control, administration and ownership of the state. Although most movie theatres, with the exception of a few owned by UFA, remained in private ownership, control was exercised by the registration with the *Reichsfilmkammer* of all cinema proprietors and operators.

The last of the three organisational aspects mentioned earlier refers to film criticism. According to a decree issued in October 1933, all journalists were placed under the control of the Ministry of Propaganda, transforming them into civil servants. The critic's task was considered to be a public one, imposed by the National Socialist state and its ideology. Film criticism was restricted to description alone; judgment was the exclusive province of state and party officials.

Although both Hitler and Goebbels agreed about the importance of film as an instrument to influence the masses, they differed on the appropriate means and strategies to be used. Whereas Hitler and Alfred Rosenberg stressed the explicit political content of film, Goebbels favoured more subtle and indirect means of propaganda, tending even to a certain liberalism towards art forms prevalent during the Weimar Republic (such as Expressionism). But after Hitler's 1935 speech on art and politics in which he strongly denounced Modernist and so-called primitive tendencies, Goebbels also took a firmer stand against these artistic traditions.

In his first meeting with representatives of the film industry in March 1933, Goebbels not only stressed the importance of incorporating Nazi concepts into film, but also cited Eisenstein's *Battleship Potemkin* as a model of the cinema's propaganda possibilities: it proved 'that a work which is politically biased (*tendenziös*) could also be a work of art.'[4] A film like *Hitlerjunge Quex* (The Hitler Youth called Quex, 1933) clearly shows how National Socialist films incorporated the formal elements developed in films of the political left during the Weimar Republic. The film depicts a young boy divided in his allegiance between the communists (his family) and the Hitler-Youth, with the latter finally becoming a family substitute and providing him with a new perspective on life. The film employs formal devices reminiscent of works like *Mutter Krauses Fahrt ins Glück* (Mother Kraus's Journey into Happiness), *Die Dreigroschenoper* (The Threepenny Opera) and Lang's *M*. Throughout, the film contrasts the chaos, anarchy and decadence of the communists with the discipline, subordination and cheerful decency of Hitler-Youth.

In his seminal study *Deutschland erwache!: Propaganda im Film des Dritten Reiches* ('Wake up Germany!' Propaganda in the Films of The Third Reich, 1968), Erwin Leiser offers a typology of Nazi propaganda films in which this film is subsumed under the heading 'brown or red?'. Other categories established by Leiser include a groups of films glorifying the German nation in order to strengthen national consciousness (... *reitet für Deutschland*, — ... riding for Germany, 1941), films on German history in which a rewriting of political and historical events serves as a foil for current issues (*Kohlberg*, 1945), anti-semitic films (*Jud Süss*, Jew Süss, 1940) war films and documentaries (such as the famous film by Leni Riefenstahl on the 1936 Olympics), or newsreels. A typical example of the way in which propagandistic elements were incorporated into the other genres mentioned by Leiser, is *Der Herrscher* (The Governor, 1937), a significantly altered adaptation of Gerhart Hauptmann's *Vor Sonnenuntergang* (Before Dusk), which presented the concept of the lonely leader, deserted by friends and family, left only with his task and his responsibility to the *Volksgemeinschaft*.

Like most typologies of National Socialist films, Leiser's classification is based on a clear dichotomy between overt propaganda and entertainment. This differentiation is also employed in other, more detailed analyses which subdivide total film production into about 14% propaganda and 47% entertainment films. The remaining 39% are subcategorised into 'problem films' (27%) or 'adventure films' (11.2%). That films like *Ich klage an* (I accuse), which makes a case for euthanasia, are often subsumed under the heading of 'problem film' and not classified as propagandistic, clearly indicates the difficulties inherent in these categories.

The rather limited notion of propaganda which still tends to inform most accounts of National Socialist film has been expanded in recent studies on the film musical. However, attempts to raise questions of ideology in the context of 'entertainment' films have so far failed to offer a sophisticated account of the rhetorical and pictorial strategies employed in this type of film. Before examining *Die Frau meiner Träume*, it seems appropriate, therefore, to begin with a critical review of some of the recent assumptions concerning the fascist entertainment film, especially the film musical.

According to a typical characterization of this genre, it 'consciously avoids any realistic portrayal of reality and instead escapes into the illusory world of artists and variety performers, presented in a highly stereotypical manner'.[5] Theories of the genre thus tend to focus on the concept of an alternative world as a major element in this type of film. The ideological content of the genre, it is argued, lies precisely in its exclusion of 'the real world'. Theories of the film musical which attempt to characterize the 'entertainment' film in terms of a distinction between films with a realistic and those with an 'escapist' relationship to reality seem, however, to depend upon a rather simplistic notion of mimesis. Although the sets and decor of film musicals seem to invite interpretations in terms of an alternative world, the following analysis of *Die Frau meiner Träume* attempts to show that the energy and the effects of the film are derived not so much from its distance from the lived world, but precisely from the way in which the film draws on and reworks the viewers' actual experiences of everyday life in the real world of wartime Germany.[6]

On the other hand, recent theories of the genre which avoid the opposition between utopia and reality produce interpretations which 'read' film musicals as dramatisations of female oppression under Fascism, with its typical concentration on 'kids and kitchen'. In this context, the German film musical, with its postulation of marriage as a happy ending, as a space in which all conflicts are transcended, is contrasted with the American musical and its fantasies of social climbing. Viewed from this angle, Julia, the female protagonist of *Die Frau meiner Träume* could be identified as a 'woman without a heart' — the title of her first stage number — and interpreted as cold and superficial, the victim of a process of subordination and taming, who at the end appears purified, in touch with her true feelings and thus ready for marriage.[7]

Although I would basically agree with this attempt to read the film in relation to its specific social reality, my criticism of these approaches concerns the way in which they apply a one-dimensional image of women formed during the early and middle 1930s to the analysis of a film produced in the mid-40s. In view of the major changes which occurred at the beginning of the 1940s, such analytical approaches seem ahistorical.

In contrast, I would argue that certain elements of the plot in *Die Frau meiner Träume* can only be understood by acknowledging the film's specific attempt to address the issue of a significantly changed social reality of the 1940s and the changing role of women. If we ignore this context, the fact, for example, that Julia at one point in the film finds herself barely dressed with no money or baggage in the middle of nowhere, can only be read as a sign of weakness, moodiness or flippancy. If we overlook such allusions to the hasty evacuation experienced by many refugees, or to the experience of destitution and the necessity for improvisation, the events would have to be attributed to the irrationality of the female protagonist, and the film would thus become an example of misogynist Nazi ideology.

The narrative plot of the Georg Jacoby's film is rather straightforward: The singing and dancing revue star, Julia Köster (Marika Rökk), plans to take a break from her stressful job at a large metropolitan theater. She travels to the mountains where she meets Peter and Erwin, two engineers who are supervising construction work in this area. Julia falls in love with the shy Peter who, after a number of turbulent escapades and masquerades, learns to accept the independence and urban lifestyle of Julia. The happy ending of the film differs from earlier National Socialist film narratives in that it does not feature the transformation of Julia into a submissive country housewife. Instead, the lovers are happily united only after Julia's return to the stage where the oppositional concepts represented by the protagonists (urban/rural; old/new concept of women's roles, etc) are taken up once more on a symbolic level during Julia's stage performance.

In the following analysis of the film, I will concentrate first on the examination of the film-rhetorical devices which offer themselves most readily to an exploration of the workings of ideology. This is most clearly the case in the film's references to everyday experience in the 1940s, i.e. in those forms of representation which involve different kinds of transformations: idealisation, comedy and aestheticisation.

Comedy is employed as a crucial means to play down numerous wartime experiences characterized by scarcity and rationing. Thus scenes reminiscent of bomb explosions are not presented threateningly but rather as part of construction works and the technical appropriation of nature. Transformed in this way, they provide the backdrop for such slapstick scenes as when Julia, surprised by a detonation, crashes her motorcycle into a tree. Reference to everyday reality takes place mostly as dramatisations of material scarcity, for example, a food shortage. Thus the dinner prepared for the two engineers at the canteen has to suffice for three, and the meal prepared by Julia exhausts the ration portions so that Erwin has to go without supper. Even members of the upper ranks are confronted with the experience of shortage: the theatre director waiting for Julia at the train station has to make do with cheese, since nothing else is available. The theatre director and Julia's maid having to spend the night without food or bed may be regarded as a reference to and transformation of experiences in war-time bomb shelters.

Whereas food shortages and dangerous situations are mainly taken as material for comic passages, lack of proper clothing is transformed through sexualisation and aestheticisation into an object of voyeuristic pleasure. An impressive example of the idealisation of everyday situations is Julia's provokative combination of slip and fur coat, the erotic associations of which are emphasized by their unselfconscious presentation in a public situation, the train station, as well as in the more private setting of Peter's bedroom after Julia is saved by the engineers (*Fig 1*). This principle of idealisation by eroticisation becomes even more evident in a stage costume Julia wears at the end of the film which, as a theatre prop, is already marked by a distance from everyday reality. At one level the Spanish costume represents a direct fashion quote of the 1940s (*Fig 2*). Even on this level of contemporary fashion we find a tendency to aestheticise scarcity. The combination of different pieces of fabric obtained from used clothes was proclaimed fashionable; the so-called *Aus Zwei mach Eins* (From Two Make One) fashion, in which usually the middle part of a dress — the part which showed greatest signs of use — was replaced by a piece of fabric from another dress (*Fig 3*). This reference to

1. *Die Frau meiner Träume*

2. *Die Frau meiner Träume*

3. *Aus Zwei mach Eins* fashion picture

contemporary fashion, which itself relied on an aestheticisation of want, is one step removed from its counterpart in reality through the erotic aura provided by the choice of revealing lace for the middle part, which thus transforms the condition of scarcity into voyeuristic pleasure. This kind of sexualisation was unthinkable in the entertainment films of pre-war National Socialism. *Die Frau meiner Träume* mobilizes all kinds of energies capable of serving as a basis for creating distance and idealisation, and therefore demonstrates how the politics of the war years — the mobilisation of all resources — is carried out at all levels, including the patterns of entertainment.

It should be evident by now that *Die Frau meiner Träume*, rather than offering simple escapism, reflects the changing conceptions of women's roles which were substantially prompted by the realities of life necessitated by the war situation. I now want to elaborate on how the film raises issues about these changing roles in a more complex fashion.

Whereas the beginning of National Socialist rule was marked by an effort to remove women from the labour force in order to reduce unemployment, after 1937 women were encouraged to resume work (although only in less qualified positions). The expansion of the female labour force encompassed the entire economy and not just the armaments industries. Despite propaganda launched against the female role model associated with this status, the number of female employees increased rapidly. At the same time a tendency towards smaller families with fewer children became noticeable. In her 1981 study *Die Frau im wesensgemässen Einsatz* (Woman at work appropriate to her nature), Annemarie Tröger demonstrates how the inclusion of women in the labour force was not only a means of providing additional labour during the war years, but was to a greater extent a structural feature of Fascism which revealed itself by the end of the 1930s.[8] This led to an increase in the number of women entering the labour force during the 1940s. As a result of this process a new female role-model emerged at the end of the 1930s: education, marriage and motherhood along with (re-)entry into the labour force were now considered to be the various stages of a single biography. The concept that married women should keep their jobs in order to serve as a kind of reserve army which would come into full effect during the war, demanded an integration of various spheres of female life which were formerly considered to be incompatible. Women entered the labour force primarily in new areas of production. There was no longer a strict hierarchy within the sphere of production, and the previously clear distinction between the spheres of production and reproduction was abandoned. Due to this change, a new definition of hierarchical structures and a new demarcation of positions was carried out on a symbolic level.

In order to analyse how these positions and their transformations are articulated in *Die Frau meiner Träume*, it is necessary to examine the language of clothing as an area of symbolisation which also achieved special importance in the fascist system itself: never before was clothing taken so seriously, either as a political instrument (viz. the foundation of the German Institute of Fashion as early as 1933) or as an economic factor (the development of the ready-made clothing industry), as during the National Socialist era. Clothes served both as an indicator and an instrument of the fascist tendency to subsume and reorganize areas of life under the tutelage of the state which had formerly belonged to the private sphere, such as the family, education, housework or leisure.

One way in which *Die Frau meiner Träume* approaches the topic of clothing is the manner in which Julia deals with everyday dress. Her attitude towards clothes serves as a means of presenting character traits and virtues which reflect actual requirements of the time. Julia's talent for organising and improvising manifests itself in the way she succeeds in dealing with situations of scarcity, such as masking it through borrowing, appropriation or alteration. The amount of work required in this process is never actually shown, and remains hidden in the final product.

In addition, the strength of the protagonist is derived from her capacity to constantly transform her own image by means of her clothes. Her refusal to become a passive object offering itself to undisturbed contemplation represents both a trait of emancipation and its reversal. Thus her continuous transformation results in the image of a woman who adapts and transforms herself according to the role required of her in each specific situation. The way in which the readiness to adopt future role requirements is expressed in the improvisation of her dress is especially striking. Thus all the arrangements of everyday clothing which Julia presents seem discordant. With one exception — her professional dress, a black skirt and jacket which appear complete and correct — all her self-dramatisations involving clothes reveal want and incompleteness. Thus clothes are either assembled incorrectly (dirndl and high-heeled shoes) or they don't fit (they are not made for her or are too big) (*Fig 4*). Her openness regarding new roles as further proof of her flexibility is located precisely in this incongruence and incompleteness.

A close examination of these 'incorrect' combinations shows that they represent an attempt to combine and synthesize the props of an out-dated female role image inspired by the modes of the 1930s with those elements of clothing which represent self-sufficiency, independence and a professional career. These attempts, which appear disharmonious because they represent an incomplete synthesis (fur coat and overall, dirndl and high heels, men's clothes which seem too large) serve as visualisations of a conflict which — once resolved — becomes the basis of a new image which is in accordance with the demands of the time.

This conscious use of clothes which *Die Frau meiner Träume* employs in order to represent the conflict of female role patterns in late National Socialist Germany also finds expression through a new concept of masquerade.[9] In the early films, characterisation was always based on the congruence between a person's visual image — including clothes — and her character. In her analysis of *Gilda* (USA 1946),[10] Mary Ann Doane shows how this traditional unity of image and essence begins to dissolve. Especially in the American 'film noir' of the 1940s, whose structure is based mainly on the ambivalence of masquerading and hiding, we find female protagonists who are presented as dangerous to men precisely because of a discrepancy between their projected image and their 'true being'. It is significant that in the context of these American films the conscious manipulation of image is presented as an aspect of 'the bad girl'. In *Die Frau meiner Träume*, however, the protagonist's ability to slip into a variety of roles is not condemned by attributing it to a scheming and threatening woman (as, for example, with the female protagonist of *Double Indemnity*, USA 1944). Also — in contrast to a film like *The Dark Mirror* (USA 1946) — narrative closure is not achieved by reducing the multiplicity of the protagonist's roles to a single aspect and thereby creating the unambiguous and fixed identity which is the mark of the 'good girl' in American 'film noir'. Quite contrary to these US productions, the discrepancy between character and image in *Die Frau meiner Träume* is not represented as a threatening disruption, but as a necessary disposition which allows a greater flexibility in the presentation of social role requirements for women.

This postulation of a new role-pattern, which is most strikingly expressed in

4. *Die Frau meiner Träume*

the iconography of clothes, is also articulated in relation to men. The opposition of 'old' and 'new' woman, which correlates with the dichotomy of country and city, is here expanded by the dichotomy of subordination and dominance. On the narrative level Julia presents the image of the dominating woman in relation to the director of the theatre, the male audience and her Spanish lover on stage. Subordination is a character trait of the 'old' woman is presented in the dirndl maid, Julia's maid servant and in the doll-like Asian dancer on stage (*Fig 5*). The changes in female role patterns also require an alteration in the attitude of men who, like Peter, associate the old and new role model with labels like 'angel' and 'devil'. During the first two parts of the film Peter interprets female masquerade as the impossibility of defining or pinning down women. Only in the third part, after a happy end featuring Julia forever confined to a dirndl is rejected, does he adopt a different reading of her masquerade, which is now no longer interpreted as an opposition to but rather as a completion of the traditional image of women.

Only after men have learned that a certain self-sufficiency, cunning and masculinity do not exclude simplicity, partnership and emotion is the new woman legitimized. If these latter qualities are lacking, however, female self-sufficiency is rejected as superficial. In this context, it is significant that at the end of the film it is Peter who adjusts himself to Julia's world and follows her into the city. The final synthesis between the oppositional worlds and concepts represented by the protagonists is staged in the world of the theater, a place where transformation and flexibility are a part of everyday life. The harmonisation of apparent opposites is performed on two levels, ideally on the stage, and behind the scenes in reality. The synthesis of the two female role-models on the stage (incorporated in the roles of a submissive Asian and a proud and independent Spanish dancer, both performed by Julia), which is expressed in the language of dance as an integration of pair

5. *Die Frau meiner Träume*

6. *Die Frau meiner Träume*

7. *Die Frau meiner Träume*

8. *Die Frau meiner Träume*

dancing and solo numbers, is presented as a happy partnership, which on stage is transformed into a wedding scene. The cut of the wedding gown reiterates the synthesis already presented in the dance numbers, as it conjures up both the dress of the flower girl or prostitute (one of Julia's stage roles at the beginning of the film) and the dirndl in its bodice-like top (*Figs 6, 7 and 8*). The transference of this ideal into reality is staged via the same three steps. Julia leaves the stage in her wedding gown, which at this point, however, no longer bears its explicit signs, the veil and the bouquet. A kiss seems to establish them as a classical couple. The applause of the audience in the street and the black umbrella which is lowered over the final scene duplicates the stage situation. Julia makes her bow and smiles: this, too, is a part, a role, but not necessarily the role of women. I would therefore suggest that the image of wedding and marriage should not be read simply as the closed image of a happy end. I think that because of the twinkle in Julia's eye and the applause of the audience the scene contains a moment of self-distance and irony which seems to relativize the meaning of the wedding. Thus marriage seems no longer to stand for an ultimate and final goal, but rather as a phase, one role among others.

Chapter Thirteen

THE DE-NAZIFICATION OF NAZI ART: ARNO BREKER AND ALBERT SPEER TODAY

Walter Grasskamp

Debates about history and classicism

Four debates during recent years have ensured that the origins and activities of German National Socialism have again become the subject of public controversy. Firstly, the art collector and industrialist Peter Ludwig set off a discussion on whether, and if so how, works by National Socialist artists should be presented in Federal German art museums. Since the Federal Republic has recently been given a collection of National Socialist works of art which had been confiscated by the Allies at the end of the war, such a debate was no doubt unavoidable. But Ludwig gave it a polemical flavour right from the start. After he and his wife had had their portraits made by Arno Breker (*Fig 1*) — at one time Hitler's favourite sculptor — he surprised the public with the statement that the Federal Republic owed a re-habilitation to this and other wrongly judged artists of the recent past.[1]

Shortly before, another Nazi artist had received just such a rehabilitation — Albert Speer, who had once been Hitler's favourite architect. In 1985, the contemporary architect and theoretician Leon Krier dedicated an opulent book to the work of Speer and declared in the introduction that Speer had preserved and given new life to an honourable architectural tradition which was in danger — and according to Krier still is in danger — of being suppressed and eliminated by 'modern' architecture. In Krier's perspective the combination of Speer's classicistic architecture with National Socialist barbarism was a tragic misunderstanding between the participants, while the modern, International Style has in the meantime shown itself to be the true expression of an inhuman industrial society. Krier's book was published in English and French; in 1987 the leading West German architectural magazine *Bauwelt* published a translation of Krier's introduction together with statements by several critics of his thesis.[2]

A third discussion centred upon the Congress Hall in Nuremburg, planned by Ludwig and Franz Ruff, which had been built from 1935 but never completed. This colossal fragment of a building had been used after the Second World War as a storage depot, and now a plan came up to redevelop the skeleton and to construct flats, shops and restaurants as well as a discotheque, a cinema and other leisure centres inside it. Since the ruined building, which would cost 20 million Deutschmarks (7 million pounds) to clear away, is also expensive to maintain, even pro-

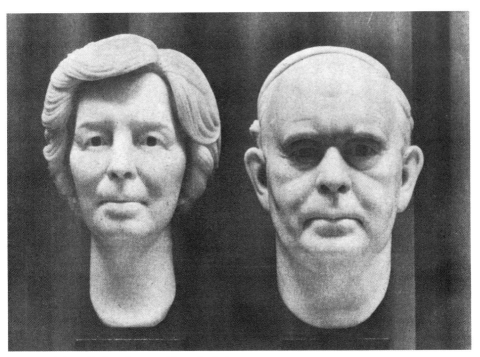

1. Arno Breker, *Irene and Peter Ludwig*

visionally, the proposal to rebuild it for town and private living uses had a certain economic logic. However the plan showed a remarkable lack of historic sensitivity. The granite with which the Congress building is faced was, as a matter of fact, hewn by the inmates of the nearby concentration camp at Flossenbürg. We may already have got used to the idea that the building of high-rise houses and industrial complexes normally costs the lives of two or three of the workers involved, but the idea of an accommodation and leisure complex made out of stones of that kind of origin provoked the resistance of numerous citizens, whose intervention brought the case to an end.[3]

However these debates were not purely theoretical events, for they have their practical application in the question of how to deal with the artistic inheritance of the so-called Third Reich. Decisions have to be made. That is why the discussions attracted public interest; but they were overshadowed by a fourth debate, the so-called *historians' argument* which was not concerned with the continuity of National Socialist classicism but with the question of whether the holocaust of the Nazis can be compared to the 'terror' of the Bolsheviks, and whether its origin was perhaps even a reaction to those Soviet events.[4] The historians' argument concentrated the public's attention upon these and other questions, so that simultaneous controversies on the evaluation of National Socialist art remained rather like episodes in an isolated side-show. These controversies, like the historians' argument, will not provide quick solutions to satisfy all participants, and here too even the form of the discussion is often unsatisfactory. But, taken together, these debates on classicism suggest the conclusion that forty-five years after the defeat of National Socialist Germany the public still finds it difficult to deal with the recent past, which from a moral point of view has always been regarded as settled, but in the historical and aesthetic spheres obviously remains still very problematic.

Modern Art as a Dogma: The Fifties

With the recent debates around Breker and Speer, a new phase in the cultural history of the Federal Republic has been started which one could describe as a late and controversial phase of the de-Nazification of Nazi art. In order to recognise the significance of this process it is necessary to look back to earlier phases of confrontation with the National Socialist inheritance. The first of these phases in the period immediately after the Second World War can be characterized as that of a *cultural policy of the guilty conscience.* The principles of this policy can now be regarded as dogmas, although they were seldom codified as such by the theory of culture but, rather, found expression in the daily work of politicians who worked in culturally-related jobs in urban and regional areas.[5] The first dogma was the view that the art and architecture promoted by National Socialism found itself in conjunction not by chance but by necessity. Works by artists who in those days had preferential treatment at exhibitions and in getting commissions were considered in the post-war years to be the *expression* of National Socialist ideology, as a direct *translation* of its racial and megalomaniacal ideas into the realm of art. This impression was further strengthened when the Allied Powers confiscated all movable art objects from German soil, as if National Socialist art was like a tempting poison which the Germans had to be prevented from tasting. Thus the guilty conscience which the Germans developed regarding their past was also extended to the art which they were formerly meant to admire.

A second dogma supported this view. Because classicistic examples, however much altered and watered down, were still frequently preferred, within the Soviet Union and her allies and in the Communist parts of Germany, the idea developed that totalitarian systems favoured classicism *of necessity*, no matter whether they were Fascist or Communist in doctrine. Because Stalin himself is said to have courted Arno Breker, this idea was even provided with empirical proof; and the discussion about the function of art and architecture in the Third Reich gradually orientated itself around the ideological clichés of the Cold War.

As a new, democratic and practical maxim of post-war cultural policy, demonstrative protectionism towards that modernism which had been reviled as 'degenerate' by the National Socialists gained ground. When post-war Germans realized how far the campaign against 'Degenerate Art' had separated them from the other nations of the West, especially France and the United States, this protectionist attitude became the popular stage for demonstrations of a new liberalism and trendiness among West Germans. The *Documenta* 1955 exhibition supplied proof to the art public of the world that West Germany would be able to catch up on this backlog in just as short a time as it had taken to recover from the damages of war. Public resistance to modernist art was regarded as a left-over from National Socialist propaganda, one which would eventually be eradicated by education and the force of habit.

Indeed the *enthronement of the modern* became the third dogma of this post-war policy. The cultural establishments of the Allies, together with lectures, art clubs and magazines worked jointly to exert the greatest influence on young artists who were amongst the visitors to libraries and exhibitions.

In architecture in these years, the sober and functional *International Style* was imported back into the country of its origin and adapted itself in all its forms, particularly the least demanding ones, to the new concept of re-building the destroyed cities which were now being re-planned along modernist lines. Within a few years the Federal Republic had become a modern country not only in her economy and industry but also in her art and architecture. Whoever wanted to orientate himself to classicistic examples was looked upon as an outsider, or suspected of sympathising with National Socialism.

Thus the actual conflict between the modern and the anti-modern which had governed National Socialism only a short time before was now suppressed altogether by brushing aside classicistic and realist art as a left-over from an unloved and uproductive nineteenth century. This was made easier by the fact that National Socialism had borrowed so much from the art of the 19th century that it — the art of the 19th century — could now be looked upon as fore-runner of Nazi art. In those years a young art historian would not have been able to build an academic career by working on the art of National Socialism, any more than he could with that of the 19th century. The hasty 'enthronement of the modern' made the Federal Republic lose its chance of attaining a balanced and moderate confrontation with modernism which other countries, Great Britain for one, had achieved. Modern art and architecture were prescribed in Germany like bitter but life-saving pills; however, even today one gets the impression that many politicians, industrial executives and observers swallow them with a certain dislike.

Protest in a Vacuum: The Sixties

The period of the guilty conscience apparently ended towards the end of the Sixties, when the student movement claimed the leading role in interpretations of the German past. But the protest movement superseded the phase of the guilty conscience only by taking onto itself the role of a new moral conscience, as the philosopher Odo Marquard remarked in a brilliant autobiographical essay.[6] From the perspective of modern art this movement had two important characteristics. First of all, its anti-modern attitude towards contemporary art was surprising. It rekindled the conservative argument according to which contemporary art represented nothing more than the result of clever manipulation by the dealers, and it treated art accordingly as goods designed specifically for the markets of capitalism. Even if this abbreviated account seems to be a bit unfair, its closeness to the arguments used by the National Socialists was more than embarrassing. Whilst the National Socialist argument had been an openly anti-semitic one, the students of the Sixties were hardly able to recognise the origin and tradition of this argument because the famous Jewish dealers of modern art had long since been driven from the German art market, which in the Sixties, at least in regard to contemporary art, was in a reconstructive phase.

Although modern art had changed drastically in the meantime, the structure of the argument remained the same. The re-installation of modern art in the post-war period turned out not to be very successful. Since the student movement was the first generation which had grown up within post-war democracy, the re-emergence of this argument in the Sixties was more serious than its continued existence among the older generation. Obviously the practice and experience of modern art had not been a collective experience, but had remained confined to 'glamorous' exhibitions, coffee-table books and private collections. But it was also significant that the student movement not only did not develop its own art, but also refused to accept any tradition to which they might have been able to relate, least of all that of classicism, which after all could be regarded as the major anti-modernism of the 20th century, and which had also found a radical democratic expression in the French Revolution. There were two reasons which made such links impossible. First of all, artistic and craftsmanship skills would have been a pre-condition of such a revival and both their use and their teaching had almost completely disappeared from art colleges after the latter had been staffed with artists who had orientated themselves to the example of abstract art.

Apart from that, classicistic examples had been promoted by political systems in the twentieth century with whom anarchistic and radical students could not identify, by Italian as well as German Fascists, and by Stalinism.

If however any links with modern art were established in the student movement then it was only with individual artists whose political work seemed exemplary, like George Grosz or John Heartfield. Such connections could not shake the anti-modernism of the student movement because it was regarded as a purely political appropriation and not an artistic one. The controversial artistic life-style of a George Grosz which was perhaps typical for modern art had completely faded out. Contemporary artists like Joseph Beuys and Wolf Vostell with their happenings and actions might have served as examples for the partly pathetic, partly carnivalesque culture of the demonstration, the procession and the sit-in; but their entanglement in the art market continued to signify an unbridgable gulf between the two worlds.

The almost simultaneous Fluxus movement might easily have served as the art of the student movement. But behind the radically public and actionistic aesthetics of this movement there was hidden a great aesthetic and cultural vacuum, which was collectively and privately being filled with just those fashionable offers of a 'cultural industry' against which, at least in theory, war had long since been declared. A panorama of recklessly consumable culture goods stretching from Walt Disney to Robert Crumb, from *Yellow Submarine* to the Italian Brutalo-Westerns by Leone and Corbucci, from Art Nouveau posters to concert posters for pop-stars and rock groups, presented a not particularly utopian collection. The most convincing, seen against the background of their teachings, seemed to be the gurus and ascetics, who were noticeable in highly influential positions. The utopian element which classicism in its hey-day had embodied, as a unity which could provide both enlightenment and a sense of history, was not called to mind, and certainly not imitated.

From Taboo to Stigma

On the other hand—and this was without any doubt due to the protest movement—the dark side of classicism, its anti-progressive and anti-human aspects, now became a main focus for art-historical research which took a new line in its orientation to National Socialism. Before, in the phase of the guilty conscience, this relationship was dominated by an awareness of the burning of books and the iconoclasm of the National Socialist leaders. Books such as Adolf Behne's *Entartete Kunst* (Degenerate Art, 1947); Paul Ortwin Rave's *Kunst und Diktatur im Dritten Reich* (Art and Dictatorship in the Third Reich, 1949), R. Drews and A. Kantorowicz's *Verboten und verbrannt* (Forbidden and Burnt, (1947), Walter Mehring's *Verrufene Malerei* (Infamous Painting, 1958) and Franz Roh's *'Entartete' Kunst: Kunstbarbarei im Dritten Reich* (Degenerate Art, Art and

Barbarism in the Third Reich, 1962) had been aimed mainly at the rehabilitation of modern art. In 1962 the artist Jürgen Claus organized an exhibition which was reminiscent of the exhibition *Entartete Kunst* which had taken place 25 years before—but without the vilifying captions. These books, as well as the exhibition, suggested that the Federal Republic wanted to dissociate itself from National Socialist iconoclasm, and in demonstratively cultivating modern art offered final proof of its break with the traditions of National Socialism.

The re-orientation in the research on the National Socialist period was prepared by three books which appeared in the sixties: Joseph Wulf's *Die Bildenden Künste im Dritten Reich* (Fine Art in the Third Reich), of 1963, Hildegard Brenner's *Die Kunstpolitik des Nationalsozialismus* (The Artpolicy of National Socialism), also of 1963; and Anna Teut's *Architektur im Dritten Reich 1933–1945* (Architecture in the Third Reich, 1933–1945), Frankfurt/Main 1967. These books not only drew attention to the art which had been persecuted in the Third Reich, but also opened discussion on the kind of art which had been promoted. A new generation of art historians profited from this revision which, in the wake of the protest movement, placed the official art of National Socialism at the centre of methodological research. This re-orientation coincided with the beginning of an important research project by the Fritz-Thyssen Foundation into the art of the nineteenth century. Thus while the Fritz-Thyssen project was encouraging a new evaluation of the nineteenth century, research into National Socialist art policy intended right from the start to make judgements of quality. In most cases the sentence was already a foregone conclusion; *guilty of collaboration*; since for most protagonists of this research, ethics and aesthetics were one ideological unit and the political judgement was merely extended into the aesthetic field.

In any case the issue was not solely the *aesthetic* quality of Nazi art, which was denied right from the start. The question to be answered was rather: what was the contribution of art to the stabilising of the National Socialist regime?

The art of the Third Reich, for some 20 years a taboo, now found itself in a paradoxical position. In illustrations and exhibitions it was presented as in a clinical examination, in which the presence of the patient is necessary in order to study the case, while at the same time the danger of infection makes a certain distance advisable. The fear of contact was grotesquely exaggerated at one large exhibition dedicated to the presentation of National Socialist art, called *Skulptur und Macht: Figurative Plastik im Deutschland der 30er und 40er Jahre* (Sculpture and Power: Figurative sculpture in the Germany of the 30s and 40s), which took place in West Berlin and Dusseldorf in 1983. The exhibition worked on the principle of confrontation, whereby works by sculptors who had not been favoured by the National Socialists were displayed against those who had in those days been official artists. But this confrontation presented works by Arno Breker not in originals but only in large photos. In the introduction to the catalogue the sculptor Rolf Szymanski gave the reason for this by explaining that they wanted to avoid giving the impression of taking the 'non-artist' Breker seriously.

In my opinion this decision was wrong. There can surely be no doubt that Arno Breker is and was an artist, just as there can be no doubt that Adolf Hitler was a politician. In fact the decision not to contribute Breker's works to the exhibition in the original had a symbolic meaning which points to the generally underestimated role of *magical acts* in politics. These magical acts show themselves to be just as central for a democratic as for a tyrannical society, and the most popular act is surely that of *stigmatising* a person or object. To call an artist a non-artist falls into the category of stigmatising acts. But this detail nevertheless illustrates the change of mentality in a nutshell. Whenever the young generation of art historians dealt with the art of National Socialism it was certainly not in order to lift the stigma, but rather to establish it as a learned dogma.

However this development already carried the elements of a transformation within it. Firstly, each one of these exhibitions — ever since the first, which Georg Bussman had been brave enough to organize in 1974 in the Frankfurt *Kunstverein*—had to come to terms with the fact that National Socialist art was still as popular as ever.[8] Thus the clinical detachment with which it was dissected in public collided with the admiration of visitors who were unconcerned about the dangers of aesthetic infection. But since it was implausible to see in this pheno- menon the survival of a fascist mentality, the 'fascination-effect' exerted by these works of art had to be acknowledged and researched far more thoroughly than ever before. Although an appropriate reception-aesthetics had already been developed within the art world, it was not critics and historians, but artists who took up the challenge first: the painter Anselm Kiefer and the film directors Hans Jürgen Syberberg and Rainer Werner Fassbinder.[9]

The intellectual and moral risk which these artists took upon themselves had thus far been confronted within aesthetics only very gingerly — that is, by asking where the fascination of those seduction-effects lay, to which so many observers had fallen (and still fell) victim. This reticence on the part of the art community has since changed. An exhibition which took place in 1987 in West Berlin under the title *Inszenierung der Macht: Ästhetische Faszination im Faschismus* (Stage Managing Power: The Aesthetic Fascination of Fascism) shows just how far.[10]

The Rehabilitation of Arno Breker

This short summary at least makes the background clear against which Peter Ludwig opened the debate around Arno Breker. It is a background of research which is now twenty years old into the official art of the Third Reich, both in books and exhibitions, but which Herr Ludwig has quite obviously taken no notice of. How else can one interpret Ludwig's opinion that the condemnation of Breker 'erases twelve years of German history'?[11] In fact, an unavoidable and unintended result of those publications and exhibitions is the fact that Arno Breker is now amongst the best known of all artists, whose works are reproduced, quoted, assessed and discussed most frequently. A bibliography of the books and essays devoted to research into the art in the Third Reich would easily amount to more than two hundred (mostly German) titles: a recently published selected biblio- graphy by Berthold Hinz lists eighty examples alone.[12]

Ludwig's plea for Breker is not significant therefore because of his desire to acknowledge the artist at long last, but because of his wish to give Breker a place of honour within the art museum. This demand contains, too, a specific notion of *the function of the art museum*. Ludwig apparently pleads for Breker's acceptance from two points of view: firstly, for the sake of *historical completeness*; secondly, for the sake of *aesthetic fairness*. In so pleading, he could have referred to the progres- sive tendency of the bourgeois art museum. After all, it was a decisive innovation of the French museums of the Revolutionary period to incorporate works of art of defeated opponents, instead of destroying them (as had been the case in almost all previous revolutions) or selling them abroad. This integration was historically carried out — and this will prove to be important — within the framework of an education programme which sought to develop historical awareness as well as taste.[13] More recently, the evolution of the art museum suggests that its historical scope as well as its aesthetic criteria have changed several times, and radically.

By itself however this does not allow us to deduce that these institutions either can or must do without any criteria. On the contrary, Ludwig's plea for Breker presupposes precisely that canon-forming aspect of the museum by means of which our criteria for representations of the past are usually formed, regardless of their historical relativity. Ludwig's plea for Breker can therefore be properly understood only if one realizes that it is not the recognition of an artist which is at stake, but the role of the art museum itself in a democratic and pluralistic society. In assuming responsibility for forming the canon, the art museum becomes a moral institution in so far as its criteria are both aesthetic and ethical, without these necessarily being always the same. So even though the modern art museum has contracted not to make the selection of works dependent on the moral integrity of the producer (otherwise it would have to remain almost empty), nevertheless in the exercise of its aesthetic criteria it has managed to retain an important element of moral legislation right up to the present day. Indeed it is precisely in this that the art museum differs from a historical or folklore museum, for whom the completeness of the collections irrespective of aesthetic quality is frequently the main consideration. From the fact that post-Revolutionary French museums integrated works of art of the defeated feudal classes it does not follow that henceforth every defeated political opponent can or must claim aesthetic recognition. Rather, it must be made quite clear that, as always, a work of art possesses an aesthetic quality which will make it more interesting for an art museum than for an army museum, or the archive of a firm.

Regarding the question of Breker's suitability for a museum on the criterion of quality, a solution is in my opinion not all that difficult, although one could make it more complicated than Peter Ludwig has made it. After all, one of the first gallery owners who exhibited the young Breker was Alfred Flechtheim, a cultured and successful Jewish dealer of modern art who had had to flee from Germany whilst his former protegé ascended rapidly in his career.[14] I would be surprised if Flechtheim had been mistaken in his assessment of the abilities of the young Breker; he must have seen a talent well worth noticing, strong enough to mature into an important, even great, artist. Concerning his importance Flechtheim was right, but about the quality of his work he was surely wrong. Looked at from today's point of view, it is no longer relevant what might have become of Breker, but only what *has* become of him. Without doubt he showed a lot of talent during his career in the Third Reich and in the post-war period, but this is one and the same talent of which he has, according to circumstances, made different uses; in particular his remarkable gift for flattering his clients. As long as there was a demand for pithy sculptures of the Nordic superman he supplied them. When after the defeat of National Socialism his new clients were more inclined towards sober and respectable portrait-sculptures he again dealt with the orders extremely obligingly, this time however with a trivializing of the classic form-language, into which he now introduced a host of merely cosmetic considerations.

A comparison between his models and their portraits shows Breker's talent for a profession which unfortunately he never took up, in which he would have achieved much greater fame after the war, that of cosmetic surgeon. His portrait sculptures are compliments chiselled in '*Schmalz*' which ought to be embarrassing for their subjects the moment they discover how cleverly the artist has speculated on their vanity. And I don't think that an artist nowadays deserves art-historical attention only because he managed to banish from his portrait-sculptures any traces of their life histories—which after all shows itself in the faces we carry around with us, whether we like it or not. Since artistic lack of independence is typical of Breker's National Socialist works as well as his flattering portrait-sculptures, I believe that modern aesthetics in its entirety would have to be invalidated before one could open the art museum to Breker's works.

Just observe the creamy hair creations with which Breker has equipped his female portraits for the last fifty years (*Fig 2*), and let us remind ourselves that the shaping of hairstyles was always the Achilles' heel of National Socialist classicism, which in this respect could not refer back to ancient examples but had to make concessions to the taste of the time. Breker's cloying female nudes of the post-war period overstep the boundaries even further; they are merely optical confections, erotic knick-knacks that serve as an old man's clubjokes, male fantasies for which no classical pose is too good to be made a travesty of. Even Rodin's provokative version of *Iris Messenger of the Gods*, (around 1891/92) transforms in Breker's hands into a gynaecologist's perspective, and Aphrodite, born from foam, rises out of the fabric-softener (*Fig 3*). Even more drastic is the case where Breker tries to bring his military form-language up to date with an ornithological gaffe like *Young Europe* (1980) (*Fig 4*)—which showed regrettable timing in making it coincide with the opening of the European Economic Community.

2. Arno Breker, *Portrait of Iris Logothetopulos, c* 1942

3. Arno Breker, *Young Venus*, 1979

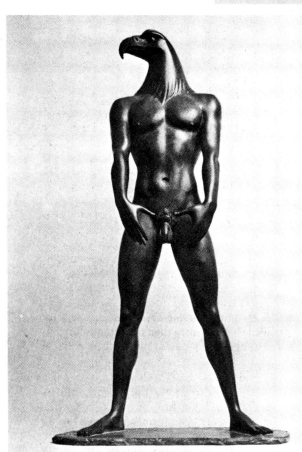

4. Arno Breker, *Young Europe*, 1980

240

Now Breker has—and this must of course flatter his present customers—repeatedly been compared with Michelangelo. The late Max Imdahl looked at this notorious comparison more closely.[15] In different circumstances it might seem absurd that proof of the groundlessness of this comparison had to be produced by a respected art historian who certainly had better things to do; but under the circumstances we must be grateful to Imdahl for having taking the trouble and for having dissociated the two artists so convincingly; we shall be interested to know what Breker's advocates have to say in answer, if they answer at all. Imdahl's criticism is also of interest because it is made from within the tradition of the same ideas of the museum as have been outlined above; in which aesthetic judgement has been regarded as the final guarantor of the sovereignty of the art museum against the demands of the market, the collectors, state art policy and the public.

But our deliberations have so far taken into account only one aspect of the civic museum's policy, namely its aesthetic jurisdiction. The second aspect is the programme of establishing the museum as an agency for historical education. If the chronological hanging of works of art, which has been customary in civic museums only since the nineteenth century, was based on the idea that art can show not only its own history but that of society, then it is difficult to find a reason for excluding Breker or Thorak. But it is not impossible. First of all, we do not in fact exclude the art of National Socialism if the period 1933–1945 is represented by artists who had spent that time in exile. It is a topographically narrow-minded view of German history to believe that only art which was produced within German borders is genuine or *necessary* German art. Breker, in fact, was only representative of the taste of leading members of a régime which completely gambled away its aesthetic credit.

The racist polarisation between superior, useful peoples and worthless, useless races which could be used as slaves or eliminated, formed the core of National Socialist ideology. This was known then as it is today. While it was the function of cartoonists to circulate a negative picture of the 'inferior' races, the art of Breker and Thorak provided, perfected and emphasised a positive image of a Nordic super-race within a scheme of classicising representation. *Stürmer*-caricature and Breker sculpture cannot be separated from one another. They were both equally and simultaneously promoted because they endorsed and illustrated racist policy.

On this basis one could conceivably defend the exhibition of Breker's works in art museums together with the caricatures of the *Stürmer*, providing explanatory notices were used to prevent any misunderstanding; thus at the same time doing justice to Breker's craftsmanship. I believe that such a conception might be defensible for a history museum, but not for an art museum: not because it is superior to the history museum but precisely because it is *inferior* to the history museum. In my book about the social history of the art museum I put forward the thesis that since the French Revolution the art museum has purchased its political tolerance at the price of de-politicising the artistic sphere.[17] Since then the art museum has integrated various epochs and artists at the cost of neutralizing their political colouring.

But this ability to integrate is not limitless. So long as the historically manifest political content of a work of art is still painfully evident to the survivors or descendants of the victims, the art museum has surely reached the limit of its neutralizing possibilities. Beyond this point, the works displayed stand in need of extended commentary and dissociation, for which the art museum is not responsible and never was. In the arguments of David Schoenbaum, Martin

Broszat or Hans-Dieter Schäfer a similar conclusion emerges.[18] Exhibited next to modern art whose themes and forms originate mainly in the brittleness of modern life, works by Breker in an art museum could give the erroneous impression that there was an art which might give meaning and a unified shape to the chaos of the modern, which after all could only be pretended with the greatest difficulty.

Breker's artistic life is a tragedy even though it appears absolutely harmless and privileged compared with all those tragedies which the National Socialist regime, which he glorified and profited by, brought about for millions of people. It is tragic in so far as he has sacrificed his artistic identity to the dream that art and state might one day function together, having existed in a condition of tension, contradiction, resistance and reservation, for about two hundred years. The fact that not only the state, who produced this dream, came to grief, but also the artists who devoted themselves to it, must surely be the lesson which we learn from Arno Breker's work. It is merely a pity that he never learnt it himself. This is surely evident from the astonishing sculpture that Wolfgang Schäche photographed recently in Breker's garden (*Fig 5*). Entitled *Readiness*, it was in fact intended for a monument which Hitler planned to dedicate to Benito Mussolini, but which was never completed (*Figs 6 and 7*). But transforming the figure into a torso, he robs it of all its historical references and associations. He also misuses a model which ordinarily signifies the pathos of the transitoriness and imperfection of art, for the purposes of de-Nazification. If the torso were now acquired for a museum, it might function effectively as an emblem of the now fashionable amputation of historical awareness.

5. Arno Breker, *Readiness* as a torso, photographed by Wolfgang Schäche in 1975

242

6. Arno Breker, *Readiness*, 3m high version of the 11 metre high sculpture for the planned Mussolini monument, 1939

7. Project for a monument dedicated to Benito Mussolini, with Breker's sculpture *Readiness* in the centre, maguette *c* 1940

243

Untimely Utopia: Leon Krier and Albert Speer

The debate on Albert Speer, begun recently by Leon Krier, differs substantially from that on Breker. Today, Speer enjoys a far higher reputation among architects than Breker does among sculptors. Speer has reflected in three books about his part in the Third Reich and has admitted his responsibility, although with some details glossed over.[19] Post-Modernism in architecture has provided Speer as well as other architects with considerable topicality, because the classicising tradition in which Speer situated himself has recently been re-introduced on behalf of a new, anti-modern canon. Speer's apologist Leon Krier is one of the polemicists of anti-modern dogma in the rich field of Post-Modern architectural idiom. Krier looks for and finds in Speer's works from 1933 to 1942 an ally in the fight for classicism against the International Style, and gets himself so involved in sheer adoration for Speer's work that he is even ready to defend the early monumental Speer against the late, self-critical period. One understands Krier's argument as follows: National Socialism was a purely political phenomenon, the realization of whose anti-human targets could only be finally stopped by a purely political measure — war; although much too late. On the other hand industrialization as the core of the modern has still not been attacked in its inhuman tendencies because it is an economic and cultural phenomenon which structures modern society in all departments of life, and does not have a political opponent either in communism or within civil democracy. Its aesthetic expression is the International Style.

Leon Krier entered the contest with Modernism and the International Style early in his career, and to begin with held his own with pure style, like David against Goliath. The stone which he aimed and flung hit his beloved home town of Luxembourg. There, a new building for the European parliament, a hyper-modern complex, was planned in sharp contrast to the Old Town, a confrontation which Krier used to illustrate the mistakes of modern town planning. Krier believed that the Old Town demonstrated the hidden wisdom of traditional, pre-modern building and planning. From that project a publication developed entitled *The Reconstruction of Luxembourg*, which contained such inspired drawings and suggestive pictorial oppositions that Krier quite justifiably became famous over-night; indeed so much so that some University professors had to watch with displeasure at the way their students fell for the personal charisma and utopian zeal of this travelling preacher, and migrated to Krier's methods.[20]

I gladly admit that I myself, although no longer a student, was one of those many admirers. When Krier found out that the private addresses of some of the most enthusiastic followers of modern architecture were charming old houses, and took photographs of them and used them in ridicule, the applause was for him once more. Finally the architect became regarded with something approaching rever-ence when he let it be known that he would refuse to build anything unless *crafts-manship*, which he claimed had given traditional towns and buildings their charm-ing character, was put back in that central position from which it had been driven. The argument that industrial production of pre-fabricated parts dictates that aes-thetic value is the same as economic expediency seemed invincible. Indeed this was the concept on which Krier later based his reconstruction of Albert Speer's works.

However the introduction to Krier's book on Speer has the disadvantage that it mixes new polemic with outdated theses, new intellectual short-circuits with long-established misjudgements, and wished-for projections with diagnosis so completely that it seems almost simpler to reconstruct Luxembourg than it does Krier's own argument.

244

Accepting that architectural anti-industrialism had been exploited by the National Socialists, but could equally well be regarded as a politically neutral reaction to the devastating side-effects and consequences of industrialization, it is difficult to see why Krier wanted to put the National Socialist version of the argument at the centre of his deliberations. He appears to have seen in National Socialist ideology the last hopeful and indeed heroic declaration of war on the evil forces of industrialization. A significant part of early National Socialist propaganda was artisan and small-town romantic; but those who developed this view — as Krier well knows — were castrated politically soon after Hitler came to power and after they had presumably enticed a great number of middle class farmers and romantic intellectuals into the Party.[21] Krier now sees in the surrender of this anti-industrial front Speer's cardinal sin. He believes that Speer betrayed the ideals of his teacher Tessenow; and he believes that National Socialism committed a cardinal sin in not fulfilling its historical promise. Speer's present admission that even National Socialism as a totalitarian regime could not reverse industrialisation means for Krier only a further capitulation in a battle which he intends to go on fighting.

He seems to find comfort in the supposition that National Socialism could easily have realized its anti-industrial utopianism if it had not embraced the industrialisation process necessary for war planning. And yet Krier's insistence on this utopian possibility for National Socialism, for which the young Speer is his main witness, is completely absurd and can only be explained by assuming that a number of historical examinations and interpretations of National Socialism have escaped his notice, namely those which point in particular to the paradoxical industrialisation and modernisation of Germany at the time of the Third Reich.[22] Like every utopian, Krier seems to prefer ideological fiction to historical accounting. We must ask ourselves why he is projecting his utopia back on to a phase of German history which it does not even partially fit.

Krier cannot be suspected of being a National Socialist or fascist sympathiser on account of his ignorance; for Krier and his criticisms stand in a tradition which is older than National Socialism and has many honourable representatives. The fact is however that because National Socialism laid claim to a number of nineteenth and twentieth century anti-industrial critics without being able to realize their conservative utopia, anti-industrial and anti-modern criticism has consequently fallen into thorough disrepute. Critical diagnoses of the modern which were sold and read at the beginning of the 20th century by the thousand either did not emerge from their shadows in the post-war period, or were dismissed as antiquated daydreaming. And it did not matter whether the protagonists of this older criticism had been close to National Socialism, or had been wrongly reinterpreted as forerunners; whether they had gone on spouting Romantic clichés or shown themselves to be knowledgeable in their field. Such diverse authors as Walther Rathenau and Julius Langbehn, Karl Ernst Osthaus and Oswald Spengler did not attain to a fraction of the prominence after the Second World War that they had had in the 'tens, 'twenties and 'thirties.

In that sense National Socialism perpetrated an interruption of an important intellectual tradition. Whilst the student movement managed to re-discover and re-publish writings by socialist authors suppressed during the time of National Socialism, the conservative tradition of industrialisation criticism never did recover, for the social class which once identified with it, the bourgeoisie, had in the meantime come fully to terms with the modern. It is exactly this forgotten tradition of anti-Modernism to which Leon Krier relates (*Fig 8*). But he quotes from it only at second and third hand, in its National Socialist distortion. In so doing he renders perhaps the ultimate disservice to the discussion which he wants to stimulate, the necessity of which is indisputable. Krier articulates his position neither on the level of tradition, nor on the level of the complexity of his self-chosen themes, and appears thus like a figure from that book he could have been a reader of: Fritz Stern's brilliant investigation *The Politics of Cultural Despair* (1961).[23] Thus Krier supplies the proof of a paradox, which is that he who does not study history might even become its victim.

Indeed it can appear extremely puzzling to the reader of the Krier polemic why it should be Albert Speer who is the main witness for his anti-industrialism

8. Leon Krier, *Belvedere*, Seaside, Florida, 1988

246

9. A. Speer, *Model of the North-South axis in Berlin*, from the south, showing the Arch of Triumph (centre) and the Great Hall (top)

campaign, just as it may appear puzzling what Speer's modern classicism has got to do with Krier's anti-industrial nostalgia.

It is perhaps not the historical content of Speer's architecture that Krier has been attracted by, but its shape, from which seemed to shine the splendour of a classicism not capable of being discredited by any political servitude, in his words an 'architecture of longing'. Krier has been so blinded by this 'splendour' that he lets his hero get away with town-planning decisions which he himself would have mercilessly condemned in a modern town plan. Speer's design of the North-South axis in Belin (*Fig 9*) fulfills the facts of a functional monoculture so exactly that one can easily see in it a concession to the shape of the industrial city, that is, to its radical division of functions, which Krier, like many others, regards as the fundamental evil of the modern city.

The Nazi version of this division sought to move the civic emblems of power, like the prisons, out of the town and into the country, thus out of sight of the town, precisely in order to shift the positive representations of power more significantly into the centre. The North-South axis as a representation of power was an important adjunct, which occurred in the expanded prison of the concentration camp and which was now exceeded in the point of its origin, the city, to take in the surrounding countryside as well. Is it not the case that Krier's constant critique of the functional separation of the modern state became less a harmless traffic game for adults than a polarisation between magnificence and squalor? How could Krier have been so blind to the origins of his arguments? It is a longing for a timeless classicism as inquisitor of the modern which enabled Krier to be blinded by the example of Speer. It has also resulted in the political categorising of Speer. While the point of the argument has for a long time been whether Speer's architecture was a *mask* or *expression* of National Socialist rule, Krier chose the popular idea of a *mask*, but without mentioning the other possibilities. By talking of Speer's architecture as having given an aesthetic and ethical *facade* to a nation of lies, he saves Speer's classicism from suspicion of having become a lie in itself.

NOTES

Chapter 1: Aesthetics and National Socialism

1. In the 'Afterword' of his famous essay *Das Kunstwerk im Zeitalter seiner technischen Reproduzierbarkeit* (1936) (The Work of Art in the Age of Mechanical Reproduction) Walter Benjamin said: 'Fascism is out to organise the newly arisen proletarianised masses without touching the property relations at whose abolition the masses are aiming. It is sold on allowing the masses to have ornamental representation, but not justice. . . . Consequently, Fascism amounts to an aestheticisation of political life.' (edition suhrkamp, vol. 28, Frankfurt, 1963, p 48, our transl.) See also Wolfgang Emmerich, "Massenfaschismus' und die Rolle des Ästhetischen. Faschismustheorie bei Ernst Bloch, Walter Benjamin, Bertolt Brecht', in Lutz Winkler (ed), *Antifaschistische Literatur*, vol. 1, Kronberg, 1977; Rainer Stollmann, *Ästhetisierung der Politik. Literaturstudien zum subjektiven Faschismus*, Stuttgart, 1978.

2. Josef Goebbels, Letter to Wilhelm Furtwängler, 1933, quoted in J. Noakes and G. Pridham (eds.), *Nazism 1919–1945, A Documentary Reader*, vol. 2 (*State, Economy and Society 1933–1939*), Exeter, 1984, p 408.

3. Adolf Hitler, *Mein Kampf*, With an Introduction by D.C. Watt, London, 1969, pp 451–2.

4. Cf. the lack of information in such standard German works as *Knaurs Lexikon der modernen Malerei. Von den Impressionisten bis heute*, Munich/Zurich, 1982; Werner Haftmann, *Malerei im 20. Jahrhundert* (2 vols.), Munich, 1965/1983; Karl Ruhrberg, *Die Malerei unseres Jahrhunderts*, Düsseldorf/Wien/New York, 1987; a counter-example is Wolfgang Hütt, *Deutsche Malerei und Graphik im 20. Jahrhundert*, Berlin, 1969 — this book appeared in an East German publishing house.

5. Cf. *'Historikerstreit'. Die Dokumentation der Kontroverse um die Einzigartigkeit der nationalsozialistischen Judenvernichtung*, Piper Verlag, Munich, 1987.

6. E.I. Zamyátin, quoted in *Russian Literature under Lenin and Stalin 1917–1953* by Gleb Struve, London, 1972, p 228.

7. Cf. the analyses by the Communist International and by Georg Dimitroff in *Arbeiterklasse gegen Faschismus* [A Report on the 7th World Congress of the Communist International, 2nd August, 1935], reprint of the Arbeiter-Basis-Gruppen, Munich, 1970s; also Albert Norden, *Lehren deutscher Geschichte. Zur politischen Rolle des Finanzkapitals und der Junker*, Berlin (East), 1947.

8. Sic in Eberhard Czichon, *Wer verhalf Hitler zur Macht? Zum Anteil der deutschen Industrie an der Zerstörung der Weimarer Republik*, Cologne, 1967; against this thesis: Henry Ashby Turner, Jr., *Faschismus und Kapitalismus in Deutschland. Studien zum Verhältnis zwischen Nationalsozialismus und Wirtschaft*, Göttingen, 1972.

9. E. Czichon, op. cit. p 24 ff.

10. Cf. the detailed study by Reinhard Neebe, *Grossindustrie, Staat und NSDAP 1930–1933. Paul Silverberg und der Reichsverband der Deutschen Industrie in der Krise der Weimarer Republik*, Göttingen, 1981.

11. Cf. Alfred Sohn-Rethel, *Economy and Class Structure of German Fascism*, London, 1978.

12. Reinhard Kühnl, *Der deutsche Faschismus in Quellen und Dokumenten*, Cologne, 1975, 4th edition 1979, pp 203–207.

13. J. Noakes and G. Pridham, op. cit., pp 277–95.

14. Cf. ibid. Hitler's memorandum on the Four-Year Plan, August 1936, p 282.

15. Adolf Hitler, op. cit., p 595 and p 598.

16. Cf. Hitler's memorandum on the Four-Year Plan in J. Noakes and G. Pridham, op. cit., p 281.
17. The Marxist, Ernst Bloch, had spoken of the Fascist enemy's 'weapons of deception and the luring dazzle of the devil', in *Erbschaft dieser Zeit* (1935), Frankfurt, 1973, p 19; Bertolt Brecht, 'Über die Theatralik des Faschismus' (from *Der Messingkauf*), in *Gesammelte Werke* 16, Frankfurt, 1967, pp 558–68.
18. Cf. Reinhard Kühnl, op. cit., pp 94–104.
19. Karlheinz Schmeer, *Die Regie des öffentlichen Lebens im Dritten Reich*, Munich, 1956.
20. Hans Jochen Gamm, *Der braune Kult. Das Dritte Reich und seine Ersatzreligion*, Hamburg, 1962.
21. George L. Mosse, *The Nationalization of the Masses. Political Symbolism and Mass Movements in Germany from the Napoleonic Wars through the Third Reich*, New York/Scarborough, 1977, p 207 ff.
22. Klaus Vondung, *Magie und Manipulation. Ideologischer Kult und politische Religion des Nationalsozialismus*, Göttingen, 1971.
23. Hanns Johst, *Schlageter*, Munich, 1933, p 26.
24. Richard Grunberger, *A Social History of the Third Reich*, London, 1971, p 429.

Chapter 2: The Body and the Body Politic as Symptom and Metaphor in the Transition of German Culture to National Socialism

1. Cf. I. Kershaw, *The Nazi Dictatorship. Problems and Perspectives of Interpretation*, London, 1985.
2. The striking similarities between some of Hitler's ideas and those of Jörg Lanz von Liebenfels and Guido von List have been impressively researched by Wilfried Daim, *Der Mann, der Hitler die Ideen gab. Die sektiererischen Grundlagen des Nationalsozialismus*, Vienna, Cologne, Graz, 1985 (2nd edn) and Nicholas Goodrick-Clarke, *The Occult Roots of Nazism. The Ariosophists of Austria and Germany 1890–1935*, Wellingborough, 1985.
3. Cf. M. Weber, 'Science as a Vocation', in P. Lassman and I. Velody, *Max Weber's 'Science as a Vocation'*, London, 1989.
4. M. Scheler, 'Sociology and the Study and Formulation of *Weltanschauung*', ibid., p 91.
5. J. Goebbels, 'Der Führer als Staatsmann', in Cigaretten/Bilderdienst (ed), *Adolf Hitler, Bilder aus dem Leben des Führers*, Hamburg-Bahrenfeld, 1936, p 45.
6. Cf. G. D. Stark, *Entrepreneurs of Ideology. Neoconservative Publishers in Germany, 1890–1933*, Chapel Hill (North Carolina), 1981.
7. Oswald Mosley, quoted in R. Osborn: *The Psychology of Reaction*, London, 1938, p 60.
8. Cf. Lanz von Liebenfels, *Ostara*, Nr. 66: 'Nackt- und Rassenkultur im Kampf gegen Mucker- und Tschandalenkultur', Rodaun, 1913. *Ostara* appeared irregularly between 1905 and 1930. Hitler appears to have been an avid reader.
9. A. Hitler, *Mein Kampf*, tr R. Manheim, London, 1976 (1st edn 1969), p 351.
10. ibid., p 270.
11. H. Spencer, *The Man versus the State*, Baltimore, 1969 (orig. publ. 1881), p 147.
12. A. Hitler, in H. v. Kotze, H. Krausnick and F. A. Krummacher (eds), *'Es spricht der Führer'. 7 exemplarische Hitler-Reden*, Gütersloh, 1966, p 339.
13. Quoted in C. Zentner, *Adolf Hitlers 'Mein Kampf'*, Munich, 1974, pp 108–9.
14. A. Ferguson, *Essay on Civil Society* (1792), quoted in the excellent article by Roy Pascal 'Bildung and the Division of Labour' in *German Studies*, Presented to W. H. Bruford by Pupils, Colleagues and Friends, London (etc), 1962, p 15.
15. F. Schiller, *On the Aesthetic Education of Man in a Series of Letters*, edited and translated by E. Wilkinson and L. A. Willoughby, Oxford, 1967 (German original 1795), p 35.
16. Reproduced in E. Lewis, *Medieval Political Ideas*, vol. 1, London, 1954, p 225.
17. Cf. G. Duby, 'Ternarity' in *The Three Orders, Feudal Society Imagined*, tr. A. Goldhammer, Chicago and London, 1980 (French original 1978), p 81ff.
18. Wallafried Stabo in the year 841, cf. ibid. p 70, p 78, p 247.

19. Reproduced in *Coriolanus,* The Arden Edition of the Works of William Shakespeare, ed P. Brockbank, London, 1976, pp 369–70.
20. F. Hölderlin, *Hyperion oder der Eremit in Griechenland* (1797–9), Stuttgart (Reclam), 1953, p 169.
21. Novalis, *Blütenstaub* (1798), in C. Seelig (ed), *Novalis, Gesammelte Werke,* vol. 2, Zurich, 1945, p 19, cf. also p 20: 'A complete human being is like a small nation.'
22. ibid., pp 23–4.
23. Cf. F. Tönnies, *Community and Society,* tr C. P. Looms, New York, 1963 (German original 1887), expanded 2nd edn Berlin, 1912).
24. Cf. K. Bullivant, 'The Conservative Revolution', in A. Phelan (ed), *The Weimar Dilemma,* Manchester, 1985, pp 47–70.
25. O. Weber, 'Nacktheit und Sozialismus', in *Körperbildung–Nacktkultur, Blätter freier Menschen,* eds A. Koch & H. Graaz, Leipzig, *Sonderheft 7: Nackt,* 1929, p 20.
26. R. Ungewitter, *Nacktheit und Aufstieg, Ziele zur Erneuerung des deutschen Volkes,* Stuttgart, 1920, p 111.
27. O. Weber, op. cit., p 22.
28. Cf. W. van der Will & R. Burns, *Arbeiterkulturbewegung in der Weimarer Republik. Historisch-theoretische Analyse der kulturellen Bestrebungen der sozialdemokratisch organisierten Arbeiterschaft,* Berlin (etc.), 1982.
29. This figure is taken from reports to the police now kept in the Bundesarchiv in Koblenz under the archival mark R 58/630.
30. H. Wilke, *Dein 'Ja' zum Leibe! Sinn und Gestaltung deutscher Leibeszucht,* Berlin, 1939, p 108.
31. H. Surén, *Der Mensch und die Sonne,* Stuttgart, 1924, Preface.
32. In *Fridericus* (Deutschnationale Wochenzeitung), 15.8.1932, quoted in *Körperbildung—Nacktkultur, Sonderheft 14: Körper und Kunst,* Leipzig, 1932, p 40.
33. Cf. *Köperbildung—Nacktkultur,* 'Anklagen und Bekenntnisse', Leipzig, 1925.
34. Cf. *Die Deutsche Freikörperkultur,* No. 2, Feb. 1934, p 20.
35. *Das Schwarze Korps,* 25 Nov. 1937, p 6.
36. E.g.: H. S. Ziegler, *Praktische Kulturarbeit im Dritten Reich,* Munich, 1932; C. Lange & E. A. Dreyer, *Deutscher Geist 1935,* Leipzig, 1935; W. Sluyterman von Langeweyde, *Kultur ist Dienst am Leben,* Berlin, 1937; W. Schultz, *Grundgedanken national-sozialistischer Kulturpolitik,* Munich, 1939 and 1943.
37. For rich and authoritative pictorial documentation see C. Jencks, *Post-Modernism. The New Classicism in Art and Architecture,* London, 1987.

Chapter 3: The Nazification of Women in Art

1. I. Kershaw, *The Nazi Dictatorship. Problems and Perspectives of Interpretation,* London, 1985, Chapter 1, 'Historians and the Problems of Explaining Nazism', pp 1–17.
2. For example in the women's magazine *Frauen-Kultur im Deutschen Frauenwerk* (10, October 1935, p 1) Thorak is constructed as a suntanned 'farmer, hunter or forester' and his own explanation of his female nude sculptures is that while images of men produce thought, women produce experience and the deepest inspiration. 'Mit Männern denkt man, mit Frauen erlebt man, und deshalb geben uns Frauen—wenn sie innerlich sind—die tiefsten Inspirationen'. (ibid., p 1)
3. This functioning-for-Fascism approach is exemplified by, among others: B. Hinz, *Art in the Third Reich,* (1974), New York, 1979, and K. Wolbert, *Die Nackten und die Toten des 'Dritten Reiches', Folgen einer politischen Geschichte des Körpers in der Plastik des deutschen Faschismus,* Giessen, 1982.
4. W. Rittich, *Deutsche Kunst der Gegenwart,* Breslau, 1943.
5. Ibid., p 5.
6. C. Koonz, *Mothers in the Fatherland; Women, the Family and Nazi Politics,* London, 1987, p 69.
7. Cited in Koonz, p 56.

8. Ibid., p 59.
9. L. J. Rupp, 'Mother of the *Volk*: The Image of Women in Nazi Ideology', in: *Mobilizing Women for War. German and American Propaganda, 1939–1945*, Princeton, New Jersey, 1978.
10. Ibid., p 46.
11. Koonz, op. cit., p 71.
12. J. Hermand, 'Alle "Macht" den Frauen. Faschistische Matriarchatskonzepte', *Das Argument*, 26, 1984, pp 539–554.
13. Koonz, op. cit., p 68.
14. Ibid., p 66.
15. J. Stephenson, *The Nazi Organisation of Women*, New York and London, 1981, p 181.
16. *Deutsches Frauenschaffen*, Jahrbuch der Reichsfrauenführung, 1936, p 12.
17. Lydia Gottschewski, deputed by Robert Ley, head of the Labour Front, to integrate Germany's 230 civic and religious women's organisations, called for and was thought to embody a female 'fighting front', Koonz, p 143. Paula Siber, her older rival, in charge of a Co-ordinating Committee for Women's Affairs, cultivated a religious motherly self-image and evolved the strategy of attracting women to practical tasks, Koonz, p 152. To some of the women this seemed rather lacklustre. They demanded a more extreme image of self-sacrifice: '. . . the woman who, uncomplaining as the earth itself, joyfully sacrifices and fulfils her fate.' Koonz, p 157.
18. Koonz, p 185.
19. J. Stephenson, *Woman in Nazi Society*, New York and London, 1975, pp 57–71.
20. Koonz, p 399.
21. Ironically, if *Ripeness* did make viewers think of the reality of women's labour service in farm-work, they might also have been reminded of anti-Soviet propaganda which employed a stereotype of women's forced agricultural labour. In one article sad Russian mothers are described breastfeeding their babies brought by the cart-load during lunch-break in the fields. *Deutsches Frauenschaffen*, 1937.
22. For example the tasks of the Frauenwerk were listed as: 1. People's economy (*Volkswirtschaft*) and housework; 2. Supervision of training courses in motherhood; 3. Ideology. The Education of women as 'the guardianess of spiritual values and cultivator (*Pflegerin*) of a racially pure culture'. *NS-Frauenwarte*, vol. 5, no. 1, 1936.
23. *Deutsches Frauenschaffen*, 1936, p 26.
24. M. Maschmann, *Account Rendered. A Dossier on my Former Self*, London, New York and Toronto, 1964, pp 12–13.
25. Ibid., p 25.
26. Ibid., p 47.
27. Ibid., p 49.
28. Ibid., p 11.
29. M. Klaus, *Mädchen im Dritten Reich. Der Bund Deutscher Mädel*, Cologne, 1983, pp 26–27.
30. A summary and excellent critique of prevailing views may be found in W. F. Haug, 'Ästhetick der Normalität — Vor-Stellung und Vorbild', in: Neue Gesellschaft für Bildende Kunst (NGBK), *Inszenierung der Macht. Ästhetische Faszination im Faschismus*, Berlin, 1987, pp 79–102.
31. Wolbert, op. cit., p 109.
32. W. Rittich, *Deutschlands Werden Seit 1933. Die Kunst*. Reichsbahnzentral für den deutschen Reiseverkehr, n.d. estimated at 1940 by the Bayerische Stadtsbibliothek.
33. For example: M.-A. von Lüttichau, 'Deutsche Kunst und Entartete Kunst: Die Münchener Ausstellungen 1937', in: P.-K. Schuster (ed.), *Nationalsozialismus und 'Entartete Kunst'*, Munich, 1987, pp 83–118.
34. *Die Kunst im Dritten Reich*, April 1937, p 128.
35. This and subsequent references are taken from Hitler's speech as reproduced in P.-K. Schuster, op. cit., pp 242-252.

36. I do not intend to suggest that sculpture demonstrated a consistent trend to minimize gender differences in the sense of creating masculinised female bodies. The repertory of poses given to male and female nudes remains different; for example female nudes are never given clenched fists even when they are given the 'heroic' striding pose. However Klimsch, Thorak, Kolbe and Scheibe all employ similar body-types for their male and female nudes.

37. P. Schultze-Naumburg, *Nordische Schönheit. Ihr Wunschbild im Leben und in der Kunst,* Munich and Berlin, 1937.

38. Ibid., p 80.

39. Ibid., p 100.

40. Ibid., p 100.

41. Ibid., p 102.

42. K. Theweleit, *Male Fantasies,* (1977), Cambridge and Oxford, 1987, documents and analyses examples of the psychological need of the Freikorps soldiers to envisage their own bodies and those of their remote but ideal 'white' women in terms which are compatible with this architectural body-aesthetic: steely, hard-edged. The soldiers fear the dissolution of their own bodies which they associate with an image of the 'red' woman, a mythical communist whore with castrating powers.

43. A very straightforward reproduction of Schultze-Naumburg's Nordic body-aesthetic can be found in an article in a women's magazine on the Danish painter Wilhelm Petersen, an ex-Freikorps soldier. The author praises the female bodies for having narrow hips, long legs, etc. Although they are clear-eyed and cool to the point of being off-putting, she argues 'We women feel our kinship to Petersen's female figures for they are models (*Vorbilder*), mistresses of their duty, who never serve any other people; they always serve — in addition to their husbands — the higher trinity: honour, kindred, *Volk*'. E. Boger-Eichler, 'Frauengestalten des Malers Wilhelm Petersen'. *Frauen-Kultur,* March, 1937, pp 2–7.

44. Preussische Akademie der Künste, Berlin, *Berliner Bildhauer von Schlüter bis zur Gegenwart,* November/December, 1936, p 7.

45. W. Willrich, *Säuberung des Kunsttempels,* Munich and Berlin, 1937.

46. Werner Rittich, 'Architekturgebundene oder freie Plastik?', *Die Kunst im Dritten Reich,* August 1938, pp 251–257.

47. Ibid., p 256.

48. Ibid., p 257.

49. Though I cannot discuss the issue in detail I can summarise the debate in the literature on the possible male psychological need for a desexualised image of woman alongside a more sexual one. One analysis argues that desexualised nudes such as Thorak's *Victory Goddess (Fig 7),* like earlier female allegories, were aiming to displace sexual response into a readiness to die. This they did by representing an imaginary communality beyond the present. Women, in order to represent communality, had to have their threatening erotic power removed. With this removed, woman is to some extent a mother figure who then reinvokes for the male viewer the prohibition on mother love in the Oedipal crisis, and its accompanying fear of death. S. Wenk, 'Aufgerichtete weibliche Körper' in: NGBK, op. cit., pp 119–128. Theweleit's study of the Freikorp male's fantasies demonstrates the interdependence of the hard-edged ideal woman who evokes a desire to die, and the fearful formless red woman who produces in the male sensations of flooding and engulfment followed by phallic hardness of the whole body and trance-like states of dissociation in which the soldier-male wreaks violent revenge on the woman. (Theweleit, op. cit.) George Mosse's study of nationalism and sexuality proposes that as the dynamic *Männerbund* ideals of Nazism prior to office were overtaken by the need to demonstrate respectability to the bourgeoisie, the ideal of heterosexuality was emphatically proclaimed, requiring ruthless suppression of homosexuality. This analysis would account for the outnumbering of the architectural by the erotic female nude. G. Mosse, *Nationalism and Sexuality,* New York, 1985.

50. For example the first *Grosse deutsche Kunstausstellung* catalogue juxtaposed a sculpted female nude *The Call* (Die Berufung), in a pose of eroticised saintliness, swooning back with arms raised and hands with palms upwards, and a painting *The Roll-call* (in the military sense, *Appell*) showing two iron-jawed soldiers, one fingering his belt, the other his hat strap (*Fig 10*). Consciously or unconsciously the catalogue editors again paired male and female equivalents. The men are 'called' to the concrete tasks of war; the woman is 'called' by something unspecific which is to be read from her swooning as an aspect of her female sexuality.

51. R. Scholz, 'Das Problem der Aktmalerei', *Die Kunst im Dritten Reich*, 1940, cited in: D. Klinksiek, *Die Frau im NS-Staat*, Stuttgart, 1982, p 129.

52. Klaus, op. cit., p 44.

53. 'Lively as they [girls] are, they will completely reject the idea of being harnessed into a way of life that will not be relevant to them for another 5 or 10 years'. L. Gottschewski, 1934, cited in Klaus, op. cit., p 43.

54. Ibid., p 43.

55. Ibid., p 44.

56. J. Rüdiger, 1939, cited in Klaus, op. cit., p 45.

57. Ibid., p 46.

58. Ibid., p 44.

59. Ibid., p 41.

60. *Deutsches Frauenschaffen*, 1937, p 66.

61. I. Köhn, *Mischling Second Degree. My Childhood in Nazi Germany*, Foreword by H. E. Salisbury, New York, 1977, p 49. Maschmann likewise is able to distance herself from the 'Nordic Ninnies' in the SS by noting that one bride, dressing herself up in white robes and imagining herself to be a Brunhilda, is in fact fat, dark and nervous. Maschmann, op. cit., p 49.

62. Klaus, op. cit. p 29.

63. A. Rosenberg, cited in *Deutsches Frauenschaffen*, 1937, p 35.

64. *Deutsches Frauenschaffen*, 1936, p 3.

65. W. Rittich, 'Das Werk Georg Kolbes', *Die Kunst im Dritten Reich*, February, 1942, pp 32–39.

66. Martin Klaus, in his analysis of the accounts given of their experiences by former members of the *Bund deutscher Mädel*, maintains that the predominant experience engendered by the rituals, especially singing, was the feeling of community well-being, of togetherness and belonging. Such feelings made the 'individual ego fade into the background'. Individual identity was to depend on Germany's gaining the world's respect. The ideological tenets of Nazism were not successfully indoctrinated in the sense of being positively and consciously embraced. But the girls' loyalty was unconditional. 'The end of individual loyalty was one's own death'. However, whatever the girls were engaged in transcended individual death and was 'more than one's own death.' Klaus, op. cit., pp 26–27.

67. A photograph of Myron's ancient Greek statue of Athena in *Frauen-Kultur* illustrates the story of how the virginal Athena punished the 'Asian' Marsyas for his forbidden look. *Frauen-Kultur*, April, 1940.

68. L. Bauer-Hundsdörfer, 'Und keine Zeit und keine Macht zerstückelt geprägte Form,' *Frauen-Kultur*, November, 1936, pp 2–3.

69. *Frauen-Kultur*, October, 1940, p 5.

70. *Frauen-Kultur*, June, 1935, p 13.

71. See note 2.

72. NSDAP calendar, *Deutsches Landvolk*, 1939, Wiener Library Archives. 'Die Erde, die brach liegt, ist nicht froh, ebensowenig die schön gewachsene Frau, die lange kinderlos bleibt'.

73. NSDAP calendar, *Neues Volk*, 1939, Wiener Library Archives.

74. *Deutsches Frauenschaffen*, 1938, p 4.

75. Kraft durch Freude, *Unter dem Sonnenrad*, Berlin, 1938.

76. L. Gottschewski, 'Von der Formkraft der Bilder', *Frauen-Kultur*, June 1935, pp 9–10.

Chapter 4: The National Chamber of Culture (Reichskulturkammer)

1. K.F. Schreiber, *Deutsches Kulturrecht*, Hamburg, 1936, p 18.
2. Ibid., p 18.
3. Karl Künkler, *Hochschule und Ausland*, March 1935.
4. *News in Brief*, Vol. 3, No. 23/24.
5. *News in Brief*, Vol. 2, No. 17.
6. Karl Künkler, *Hochschule und Ausland*, p 15.
7. *News in Brief*, Vol. 2 , No. 5.
8. *News in Brief*, Vol. 2 No. 17.
9. *Völkischer Beobachter*, 28/11/35.
10. *Völkischer Beobachter*, 22/1/36.

Chapter 5: Artists and Art Institutions in Germany 1933–1945

1. Bruno Paul, report of 13.7.32, HdK-Archive.
2. Bruno Paul, speech 30.6.32, HdK-Archive.
3. Quoted by Abram Enns, *Kunst und Burgertum*, Lübeck, 1978, p 57.
4. Oskar Schlemmer, manuscript of a lecture for the Breslau College of Art, 26.10.30.
5. Oskar Schlemmer, letter to the Minister of Science, Art and National Education, 12.9.31, Berlin, HdK-Archive.
6. Oskar Schlemmer, letter to W.B., beginning of February 1933, in *Briefe und Tage-bucher*, Munich, 1958, p 306.
7. Erwin Graumann, 'An Example to Many' in *Mittelungsblatt des Wirtschaftsverband Bildender Künstler Nordheim-Westfalen*, No. 8, September 1969, p 117.
8. Max Kutschmann, letter to O. Schlemmer, 10.10.33, HdK-Archive.
9. Oskar Schlemmer, letter to Max Kutschmann, 23.10.33, Oskar Schlemmer Archive, Stuttgart.
10. RKS, Writings, 3.9.37.
11. Exhibition catalogue, *Neue Sachlichkeit*, Mannheim, 1925, n.p.
12. G. Richard Bie, 'Der Sachliche Kreis. Georg Schrimpf', in *Deutsche Malerei der Gegen-wart*, Weimar, 1930, p 10.
13. Zimbal, letters, 29.5.37, HdK-Archive.
14. NS Student leader Schuster, letter to Minister of Science, Art and National Education, 3.11.37, HdK-Archive.
15. Report of the Gauleiter office of the NDSAP, 24.11.37, Berlin Document Centre.
16. Willy Maillard, letter to the Minister of Science, Art and National Education, 14.6.33, HdK-Archive.
17. Otto Andreas Schreiber, speech, 29.6.33, reprinted in *Deutsche Allgemeine Zeitung*, Berlin, 10.7.33, HdK-Archive.
18. Bertolt Brecht, *Gesammette Werke*, vol. 12, Frankfurt, 1967, p 553.
19. Kurt Schumacher, letter of 22.12.42, cited in Biernat & Krausse, *Die Schulze-Boyssen/ Harnack Organisation im Antifaschistischen Kampf*, Berlin (DDR), 1970, p 158.
20. Karl Hofer letter to the students' parliament 28.4.49, HdK-Archive.

Chapter 6: Modernism and Archaism in Design in the Third Reich

1. Hans Scheerer, 'Gestaltung im Dritten Reich', in *Form*, Vol. 69, Nos. 1, 2 and 3, 1975.
2. Erika Gysling-Billeter, 'Die angewandte Kunst: Sachlichkeit trotz Diktatur', in: *Die Dreissiger Jahre: Schauplatz Deutschland*, Munich, 1977, p 171.
3. Ibid, p 171.
4. Ibid, p 171.
5. For further discussion of these terms, see Tim W. Mason, 'Zur Entstehung des Gesetzes zur Ordnung der nationalen Arbeit vom 20. Januar 1934: Ein Versuch über das Verhält-

nis 'archaischer' und 'moderner' Momente in der neuesten deutschen Geschichte', in: Mommsen, Petzina and Weisbrod (eds.) *Industrielles System und politische Entwicklung in der Weimarer Republik*, Düsseldorf, 1974.

6. National Industry Conference Board (eds.), *Rationalization of German Industry*, New York, 1931, p VII.

7. 'Zweckmässige Beleuchtung und rationelle Wirtschaft' in: *RKW-Nachrichten*, 4th Year, Nr. 6, 1933, p 171.

8. Ibid, p 171.

9. 'RKW und RAL nehmen Stellung zur Frage der Gütesicherung' in: *RKW-Nachrichten*, 7th Year, Nr. 1, 1933, p 3.

10. 'Siemens & Halske aud der Funkausstellung 1932' in *Siemens Zeitschrift*, August 1932, p 288.

11. Bundesarchiv Koblenz, Bestand R32/1. Quoted in a letter to Dr. E. Römer, 13.2.1933.

12. Bundesarchiv Koblenz, Bestand R32/443. Letter from Dr. E. Redslob to Dr. P. Bruckmann, President of the German Werkbund, p 5.

13. Statistic from 'Wirtschaftsbeobachter' in: *Der Vierjahresplan*, Vol. 3, 1939, p 1028.

14. Paul Walter, *Handwerk auf neun Wegen*, Berlin, 1937, p 12.

15. Ibid, p 34.

16. *Grossdeutscher Handwerktag*, Berlin, 1939, 'Rede des Reichshandwerkmeisters'. Typescript in Staatsbibliothek, Berlin, p 15.

17. Ibid, p 27.

18. Reichsamt Schönheit der Arbeit (eds.), *Das Möbelbuch: Schönheit der Arbeit*, Berlin, 1937.

19. *Moderne Gebrauchsmöbel*, Berlin, 1937.

20. Fritz Spannagel, *Unsere Wohnmöbel*, Ravensburg, 1937, p 6.

21. Ibid, pp 59–60.

22. Ibid, p 5.

23. Kunst-Dienst (eds.) *Deutsche Warenkunde*, Berlin, 1939–40.

24. *Eine deutsche Warenkunde* in: *RKW-Nachrichten*, 13th Year, Vol. 6, Sept. 1939, p 12.

25. Henryk Katz, 'Arbeiter, Mittelklasse und die NSDAP: Randbemerkungen zu zwei amerikanischen Studien' in: *Internationale wissentschaftliche Korrespondenz zur Geschichte der deutschen Arbeiterbewegung (IWK)*, Vol. 3, 1974, p 307.

Chapter 7: Post-Modernism in the Third Reich

1. Charles Jenks, *What Is Post-Modernism?* London, 1986.

2. From a speech by Adolf Hitler, Munich, 27 April 1923, published in Werner Siebarth, *Hitlers Wollen*, Munich, 1936, p 136; and in G. Mosse, *Nazi Culture: Intellectual, Cultural & Social Life in the Third Reich*, London, 1966, pp 10–11.

3. A. Hitler, *Mein Kampf*, 1926; in G. Mosse, op. cit. p 6.

4. See the account offered by B. Schrader and J. Schebera, *The Golden Twenties: Art and Literature in the Weimer Republik*, Yale, 1988, and this author's review in *New Statesman and Society*, 22 April 1988, pp 30–31.

5. E. Nolde, *Achtung, Befreiung, 1919–1946*, Köln, 1967, p 115.

6. A. Rosenberg, Völkische Kunst', *Völkischer Beobachter*, 10th May 1922, cited in R.A. Pois, 'German Expressionism in the Plastic Arts and Nazism', *German Life and Letters*, Vol. XXI, No. 3, April 1968, p 206.

7. A. Rosenberg, *Der Mythus des 20. Yahrhunderts*, Munich, 1938, pp 303–4.

8. H. Brenner, *Die Kunstpolitik des Nationalsozialismus*, Hamburg, 1963, p 67.

9. B.E. Werner, *Deutsche Allgemeine Zeitung*, Berlin, 12 May 1933; quoted in Georg Bussman, ' "Degenerate Art" A Look at a Useful Myth', in *German Art of the Twentieth Century*, Royal Academy, London, 1985, p 117.

10. Cited by C. Fischer-Defoy, 'Artists and Art-Institutions in Germany 1933–1945', *Oxford Art Journal*, 9:2, 1986, p 23; in this volume, p 101.

11. P.O. Rave, *Kunstdiktatur im Dritten Reich*, Hamburg, 1949, p 52.

12. Rave, 1949, p 54; Hinz, p 8.
13. A. Hitler, words quoted in *Guide to the Exhibition of Degenerate Art*, from F. Roh, *'Entartete Kunst' — Kunstbarberei im Dritten Reich*, Hanover, 1962, p 26 ff.
14. See J. Heskett, 'Modernism and Archaism in Design in the Third Reich', *Block* (3) 1980, pp 13–24; in this volume, pp 110–127.
15. A. Hitler, *Mein Kampf*.
16. Quoted in H. Glaser, *The Cultural Roots of National Socialism*, London, 1978, p 42.
17. Loc. cit.
18. Glaser, p 42.
19. Kaiser Willhelm II; quoted in H. Glaser, p 51.
20. For de Chirico's 'conversion' see *Memoirs*, p 73 ff.
21. *Brücke* Statement, 1906.
22. Glaser, pp 209–10.
23. This is argued for example by H.A. Turner, Jr, 'Fascism and Modernization', *World Politics*, XXIV, July 1972, pp 547–64 (see the reply by A.J. Gregor, same journal, Vol. XXVI, April 1974, pp 370–384.
24. The notorious exclusion of German art of the period 1933–45 from the Royal Academy's *German Art of the Twentieth Century*, 1985 is but the latest example in a historic series of exclusions.
25. I owe this formulation to G.L. Mosse, 'Fascism and the Avant-Garde' (1980), in Mosse, *Masses and Man: Nationalist and Fascist Perceptions of Reality*, Detroit, 1987, p 229.

Chapter 8: *Bridges: Paul Bonatz's Search for a Contemporary Monumental Style*

A first version of this essay appeared under the title: 'Monuments in *Arbeitsstil*, Paul Bonatz's public works' in both Italian and English in *Lotus International*, Nr. 47, 1985, Milano. It has since been substantially revised. My research would not have been possible without the kind support of Herr Peter Dübbers who facilitated access to the archives of the Bonatz family in Stuttgart and to whom I owe special thanks.
1. Martin Heidegger, 'Bauen Wohnen Denken', in Otto Barning (ed.), *Darmstädter Gespräche 1951, Mensch und Raum*, Darmstadt, 1952.
2. Paul Bonatz, 'Repräsentative Bauten des Volkes', Stuttgart, 13.2.1935, lecture manuscript, Paul Bonatz Archive, Stuttgart.
3. This is not a reference to the so called *Neue Reichskanzlei* by Speer, which was only completed in 1939, but to a mixed bag of reconstruction work on the Reich-Chancellery by Jobst Siedler in 1930 and, from October 1933 onwards, by Paul Troost and his collaborator in Berlin, Albert Speer. Cf. Angela Schönberger, *Die Berliner Reichskanzlei von Albert Speer*, Berlin, 1981.
4. Paul Bonatz, 'Zur Baufrage: Führer- und Verwaltungsbau der NSDAP in München', an explanatory report, 6.6.1934, Paul Bonatz Archive, Stuttgart.
5. Cf. Winfried Nerdinger, 'Versuche und Dilemma der Avantgarden im Spiegel der Architekturwettbewerbe 1933–35', in: Hartmut Frank (ed.), *Faschistische Architekturen, Planen und Bauen in Europa 1930–1945*, Hamburg, 1985.
6. Bonatz, op. cit. (note 2 above).
7. Der Ring: the group of Berlin architects known as 'der Ring' arose in 1924 as a union of nine architects from the Berlin 'Novembergruppe'. (Otto Bartning, Peter Behrens, Hugo Häring, Erich Mendelsohn, Ludwig Mies van der Rohe, Hans Poelzig, Walter Schildbach, Bruno Taut, Max Taut). Joined by Martin Wagner, the group was known as 'der Zehnerring' (cartel of ten) until in 1926 it was enlarged to 21 members (Richard Döcker, Walter Gropius, Ludwig Hilbersermer, Arthur Korn, Hans and Wassili Luckhardt, Ernst May, Hannes Meyer, Adolf Roding, Hans Scharoun and Heinrich Tessenow — see *Die Form*, 1926, p 225). Later, Otto Haesler, Bernhard Pankok, Hans

Soeder and Karl Schnerder joined. The efforts of Hugo Häring and Richard Döcker to revive 'der Ring' after 1945 failed.

8. Cf. Wolfgang Voigt, 'Die Stuttgarter Schule und die Alltagsarchitektur des Dritten Reiches', in: Hartmut Frank (ed.), *Faschistische Architekturen, Planen und Bauen in Europa 1930–1945*, Hamburg, 1985.

9. Der Block. The society of architects known as 'Der Block' was founded in 1928 at Paul Schultze-Naumburg's house in Saaleck, and included an office in Berlin. The founding manifesto was signed by German Bestelmeyer, Erich Blunck, Paul Bonatz, Anton Gessner, Paul Schmitthenner, Paul Schultze-Naumburg, Franz Seeck, Hernz Stoffregen (published in *Die Baukunst*, Munich, 1928, IV, no 5, p 128).

10. The term *Baubolschewismus* was first used by the Swiss architect, Alexander von Senger, in a polemic against Le Corbusier. In the early 1930s von Senger appeared at a number of meetings of the National Socialist *Kampfbund für deutsche Kultur*. Cf. Hartmut Frank, 'Schiffbrüche der Arche, notes on the re-edition of Paul Schmitthenner's Baugestaltung' in: Paul Schmitthenner, *Das deutsche Wohnhaus, Baugestaltung 1. Folge, 4*, Auflage, Stuttgart, 1984.

11. Letter to Schmidt-Hellerau, Baden-Baden, Sanatorium Quisisana, 10.4.1941. Copy in the Bonatz Archive.

12. Letter to Tamms, Stuttgart, 21.9.1941. Carbon copy in the Bonatz Archive.

13. Paul Bonatz, 'Die Brücke als gemeinsames Werk von Ingenieur und Architekt', in: *Frankfurter Zeitung*, 1941, quoted in: Fritz Schumacher, *Lesebuch für Baumeister*, reprint of the second edition of 1947, Berlin, 1977.

14. Cf. Carl D. H. Westphal, *Fritz Höger, der niederdeutsche Backsteinbaumeister*, Wolfshagen/Scharbeutz, 1938.

15. Cf. Julius Posener, *Anfänge des Funktionalismus, von Arts and Crafts zum Deutschen Werkbund*, Berlin, Frankfurt, Vienna, 1964, p 199ff; also Joan Campbell, *The German Werkbund. The Politics of Reform in the Applied Arts*, Princeton, 1978, p 57ff.

16. Bonatz, op. cit. (note 2 above).

17. ibid.

18. On the life and works of Theodor Fischer cf. Ulrich Kerkhoff, *Theodor Fischer, Eine Abkehr vom Historismus oder Ein Weg zur Moderne*, Stuttgart, 1987.

19. Cf. Hartmut Frank, 'Trümmer. Traditionelle und moderne Architekturen im Nachkriegsdeutschland', in: B. Schulz (ed.), *Grauzonen—Farbwelten, Kunst und Zeitbilder 1945–1955*, Berlin, 1983.

20. Paul Bonatz, 'Welchen Weg geht die deutsche Baukunst?' in: *Die Baugilde*, 1933, Nr. 17/18, p 835.

21. The Nazi motorway scheme was based on plans drawn up prior to 1933, at which time they were violently resisted by the NSDAP. Cf. Kurt Kaftan, *Der Kampf um die Autobahnen*, Berlin, 1955.

22. Eduard Schönleben, *Fritz Todt, der Mensch, der Ingenieur, der Nationalsozialist*, Oldenburg, 1943.

23. Cf. Alwin Seifert, *Ein Leben für die Landschaft*, Düsseldorf/Köln, 1962; also Alwin Seifert, *Im Zeitalter des Lebendigen, Natur-Heimat-Technik*, Planegg near Munich, 1941.

24. Paul Bonatz, 'Die Unterführung der Autobahn', in: *Die Straße*, ed. by the Generalinspektor für das deutsche Straßenwesen, Berlin, Vol. 2, 1935, p 547f.

25. Cf. amongst others Erna Lendvai-Dircksen, *Reichsautobahn, Mensch und Werk, mit einem Geleitwort des Generalinspektors für das deutsche Straßenwesen, Reichsminister Dr.ing. Fritz Todt*, Bayreuth, 1937.

26. Bonatz, op. cit. (note 2 above).

27. The history of the canalisation of the Neckar is closely connected with that of the Württemberg section of the German *Werkbund*. The association for the canalisation shared offices with the *Werkbund* in Stuttgart as well as most of the members of the governing boards. Cf. Karin Kirsch, *Die Weißenhofsiedlung*, Werkbund-Ausstellung: Die Wohnung—Stuttgart, 1927, Stuttgart, 1985, p 10ff.

28. Cf. Peter Dübbers, 'Werkverzeichnis Paul Bonatz', in: *Stuttgarter Beiträge 13, Paul Bonatz 1877–1956*, Stuttgart 1977.
29. Paul Bonatz, *Leben und Bauen*, Stuttgart, 1950, p 129.
30. ibid. p 130.
31. Friedrich Tamms, *Paul Bonatz, Arbeiten aus den Jahren 1907–1937*, Stuttgart, 1937.
32. Bonatz's most important bridges can be found in one of the volumes of the popular series *Die Blauen Bücher*: Paul Bonatz and Fritz Leonhardt: *Brücken*, Königstein im Taunus, 1942 (there were many later editions also in the post-war era).
33. Bonatz, op. cit. (note 11), p 179.
34. Fritz Leonhardt, *Baumeister in der unwälzenden Zeit*, Stuttgart, 1984, p 89.
35. Bonatz, op. cit. (note 27 above), p 179.
36. ibid. p 180.

Chapter 9: Music and National Socialism: the Politicisation of Criticism, Composition and Performance

1. William W. Austin, *Music in the Twentieth Century from Debussy through Stravinsky*, New York 1966.
2. Joachim C. Fest, *Hitler*, London 1973 p 520.
3. Ernst Hanfstaengl, *Hitler, The Missing Years*, London 1957 pp 49/50.
4. The *Kampfbund* was absorbed in 1934 into a new organisation the *Nationalsozialistische Kulturgemeinde* (National Socialist Cultural Community) which was still controlled by Rosenberg. Although Rosenberg's influence upon cultural matters had been considerably diminished, he continued to agitate on behalf of a more radical ideological programme bringing him sometimes into open conflict with Goebbels.
5. Peter Raabe wrote the standard critical biography of Franz Liszt in the German language published in 1931.
6. Fred Taylor, *The Goebbels Diaries 1939–1941*, London 1982 p 181.
7. Op. Cit. p 184.
8. Emil Naumann, *Illustrierte Musikgeschichte* edited by Eugen Schmitz, Stuttgart, 1934.
9. Ernst Bücken, *Deutsche Musikkunde*, Potsdam 1935.
10. Josef Müller-Blattau, *Germanisches Erbe in deutscher Tonkunst*, Berlin 1938.
11. Josef Müller-Blattau, *Geschichte der deutschen Musik*, Berlin 1938.
12. *Die Musik* Vol. 25, June 1933.
13. Richard Wagner, *Das Judentum in der Musik*, Leipzig 1851 revised 1869.
14. Richard Eichenauer, *Musik und Rasse*, Munich 1932.
15. Karl Blessinger, *Mendelssohn, Meyerbeer und Mahler: Drei Kapitel Judentum in der Musik als Schlüssel zur Musikgeschichte des 19. Jahrhunderts*, Berlin 1939.
16. Hans Brückner and Christa Maria Rock, *Judentum in Musik A-B-C*, Munich, 1935.
17. Theo Stengel and Herbert Gerigk, *Lexikon der Juden in der Musik*, Berlin 1940.
18. Karl Grunsky, *Der Kampf um deutsche Musik*, Stuttgart 1933.
19. For example, the music of such composers as Harald Genzmer, Karl Marx and Paul Höffer demonstrates a strong influence of Paul Hindemith.
20. Good examples of collections of new political folksongs were published by Schott of Mainz *Das Neue Deutschland* (1934) and Bärenreiter of Kassel, *Aufrecht, Fähnlein* (1933) and *Lieder der NS Kraft durch Freude* (1936).

Chapter 10: The Political Poster in the Third Reich

1. An overview of the research is given in Frank Kämpfer, *'Der Rote Keil.' Das politische Plakat, Theorie und Geschichte*, Berlin, 1985, pp 29 ff, 48 ff; bibliography pp 314–324. Important for the German political poster is Heidrun Abromeit, *Das Politische in der Werbung. Wahlwerbung und Wirtschaftswerbung*, Opladen, 1972; Gerd Müller, *Das Wahlplakat, Pragmatische Untersuchungen zur Sprache der Politik am Beispiel von Wahlplakaten*, Tübingen, 1978.

2. Friedrich Medebach, *Das Kampfplakat, Aufgabe, Wesen und Gesetzmäßigkeit des politischen Plakats, nachgewiesen an den Plakaten der Kampfjahre von 1918–1933*, Frankfurt 1941, p 116. Cf. also S. Friedländer, *Kitsch und Tod: Der Widerschein des Nazismus*, New York, 1983. 'Gentlemen, in a hundred years a nice colour film will be screened about the terrible days in which we are living. Wouldn't you like to play a part in this film? Hold out now, so that the viewers in a hundred years do not howl and whistle when you appear on the screen.' (Goebbels in April 1945 talking about the film *Kolberg*; Friedländer, op. cit., p 1).
3. Medebach, op. cit., p 117.
4. Erwin Schockel, *Das politische Plakat. Eine psychologische Betrachtung*, Munich (2nd ed.), 1939.
5. Medebach, op. cit., p 131.
6. Schockel, op. cit., p 12 f.
7. Cf. Müller, op. cit., p 250, 'All statements to the effect that the military metaphor is typical of the language of Communism . . . or of National Socialism are therefore highly questionable. This is just as true for all other areas of pictorial representation . . .'
8. Schockel, op. cit., p 12.
9. 'Demagogue' is entirely in the sense used by Rudolf Bartels, *Lehrbuch der Demagogik*, Berlin, 1905. 'Demagogy understood as related to pedagogy. It is a question of political education.' Cf. Kämpfer, op. cit., p 76, 'The statement contained in the political poster is dominated or determined by the written text, which captures the message in words.'
10. Herzstein believes in a near-perfect propaganda machine; see R. E. Herzstein, *The war that Hitler Won. The Most Infamous Propaganda Campaign in History*, London, 1978. Cf. the commentary by I. Kershaw, *How Effective was Nazi Propaganda?*, in D. Welch (ed.), *Nazi Propaganda. Its Power and Limitations*, Totowa, New Jersey, 1983.
11. Schockel, op. cit., p 5.
12. There is also occasional scepticism in Medebach, op. cit., p 151, cf. also p 33, 'There can therefore be no complete and conclusive evaluation of the political poster with regard to this important question (concerning the connexion between writing and colour).'
13. Anthony Rhodes, *Propaganda. The Art of Persuasion, World War II*, London, 1976.
14. Reference in the minutes of the Conference of Ministers in W. Boelke (ed.), *Kriegspropaganda 1939–1941. Geheime Ministerkonferenzen im Reichspropagandaministerium*, Stuttgart 1966, pp 295, 411, 478.
15. Rhodes, op. cit., p 48 ff.
16. Cf. Kämpfer, op. cit., fig 41.
17. Cf. Herzstein, op. cit., p 47.
18. Cf. Kämpfer, op. cit., p 124 f.
19. Schockel, op. cit., p 199.
20. For illustration cf. Schockel, op. cit., p 209.
21. Zeman Zbynek, *Selling the War. Art and Propaganda in World War II*, London, 1982, figs 45 & 46.
22. On 'reduction' cf. Kämpfer, op. cit., p 109 ff.
23. The same head, yet in combination with that of Hindenburg's, is used on the election campaign poster of 1933 ('Never will the Reich be destroyed provided you stay united and true. Vote 1, National Socialists'). Hitler's hypnotic gaze is used on a photo-poster of 1934, being reduplicated there sixteen times! Cf. Kämpfer, 1985, fig 39 Ibid. many examples for the eye contact between the image on the poster and the viewer.
24. Schockel, 1934, p 203; also Kämpfer, 1985, p 87.
25. cf. Hans-Ulrich Thamer, *Verführung und Gewalt. Deutschland 1933–1945*, Berlin, 1986, pp 342 ff.
26. G. Paul. and R. Schock, *Saargeschichte im Plakat 1918–1957*, Saarbrücken, 1987, fig 55; cf. also photos on pp 62–3 and p 86; for more detailed information on the historical background, see G. Paul, *'Deutsche Mutter — heim zu Dir!' Warum es mißlang, Hitler an der Saar zu schlagen. Der Saarkampf 1933–1935*, Cologne, 1984.

27. Cf. Rhodes op. cit., figures on pp 48 ff, 55 ff.
28. A large number of poster designs were popularised in small formats by propaganda post-cards, e.g. the posters for the National Party Congress with designs by Prof. Richard Klein, Munich; cf. Robert Lebeck and Manfred Schuette, *Propagandapostkarten II. 80 Bildpostkarten aus den Jahren 1933–1943*, Dortmund, 1980, fig 14 ff.
29. Kämpfer op. cit., fig 57.
30. Rhodes op. cit., p 99 (Operai italiani arruolatevi!).
31. Cf. H. Guderian, *Erinnerungen eines Soldaten* Heidelberg, 1951 (4th ed.) p 384 f.
32. Cf. Rhodes op. cit.
33. Victor Klemperer, *LTI. Die unbewältigte Sprache; aus dem Notizbuch eines Philologen*, Munich, 1969.
34. Klemperer, op. cit., p 96.
35. Klemperer, op. cit., p 97.
36. Klemperer, op. cit., p 97.
37. Klemperer, op. cit., p 98.
38. Klemperer, op. cit., p 97.
39. Paul Spang, *Von der Zauberflöte zum Standgericht. Naziplakate in Luxemburg 1940–1944*, Luxembourg, 1982, Nr. L-119.
40. Klemperer, op. cit., pp 97 & 99.
41. Klemperer, op. cit., p 98.
42. Andreas Fleischer, *Die Plakatkampagnen 'Ne Boltai!', 'Feind hört mit!', 'Talk Kills!' während des Zweiten Weltkrieges*, unpublished MA, Münster, 1988. So far, 24 posters have been found which combine the shadow of the spy with different backgrounds; another 36 documents exist (posters, bills, leaflets) which deal with the same theme.
43. Fleischer, op. cit., p 85 ff.
44. Fig 294 in Hans Bohrmann (ed.), *Politische Plakate*, Dortmund 1984.
45. See A. Fleischer, footnote 42.
46. Peter Longerich, *Propagandisten im Krieg*, Munich, 1987.
47. Medebach, op. cit., p 117.
48. For a list and analysis, see Fleischer, op. cit., p 96 ff.
49. *Spione, Spitzel, Saboteure. Eine Aufklärungsschrift für das Deutsche Volk*, ed. Reichsamt Deutsches Volksbildungswerk, Berlin, 1938, p 40.
50. Der Reichsführer SS, SS-Hauptamt (ed.), *Der Untermensch*, Berlin, 1935.

Chapter 11: Fascinating Fascism

1. Leni Riefenstahl, *Hinter den Kulissen des Reichsparteitag-Films* (Munich, 1935). A photograph on page 31 shows Hitler and Riefenstahl bending over some plans, with the caption: 'The preparations for the Party Congress were made hand in hand with the preparations for the camera work.' The rally was held on September 4–10; Riefenstahl relates that she began work in May, planning the film sequence by sequence, and super-vising the construction of elaborate bridges, towers, and tracks for the cameras. In late August, Hitler came to Nuremberg with Viktor Lutze, head of the SA, 'for an inspection and to give final instructions.' Her thirty-two cameramen were dressed in SA uniforms throughout the shooting, 'a suggestion of the Chief of Staff [Lutze], so that no one will disturb the solemnity of the image with his civilian clothing.' The SS supplied a team of guards.
2. See Hans Barkhausen, 'Footnote to the History of Riefenstahl's "Olympia,"' *Film Quarterly*, Fall 1974 — a rare act of informed dissent amid the large number of tributes to Riefenstahl that have appeared in American and Western European film magazines during the last few years.
3. If another source is wanted — since Riefenstahl now claims (in an interview in the German magazine *Filmkritik*, August 1972) that she didn't write a single word of *Hinter den Kulissen des Reichparteitag-Films*, or even read it at the time — there is an interview in the *Völkischer Beobachter*, August 26, 1933, about her filming of the 1933 Nuremberg

rally, where she makes similar declarations. Riefenstahl and her apologists always talk about *Triumph of the Will* as if it were an independent 'documentary,' often citing technical problems encountered while filming to prove she had enemies among the party leadership (Goebbels' hatred), as if such difficulties were not a normal part of filmmaking. One of the more dutiful reruns of the myth of Riefenstahl as mere documentarist—and political innocent—is the *Filmguide to 'Triumph of the Will'* published in the Indiana University Press Filmguide Series, whose author, Richard Meram Barsam, concludes his preface by expressing his 'gratitude to Leni Riefenstahl herself, who cooperated in many hours of interviews, opened her archive to my research, and took a genuine interest in this book.' Well might she take an interest in a book whose opening chapter is 'Leni Riefenstahl and the Burden of Independence,' and whose theme is 'Riefenstahl's belief that the artist must, at all costs, remain independent of the material world. In her own life, she has achieved artistic freedom, but at a great cost.' Etc. As an antidote, let me quote an unimpeachable source (at least he's not here to say he didn't write it)—Adolf Hitler. In his brief preface to *Hinter den Kulissen,* Hitler describes *Triumph of the Will* as 'a totally unique and incomparable glorification of the power and beauty of our Movement.' And it is.

4. This is how Jonas Mekas (*The Village Voice,* October 31, 1974) salutes the publication of *The Last of the Nuba*: 'Riefenstahl continues her celebration — or is it a search? — of the classical beauty of the human body, the search which she began in her films. She is interested in the ideal, in the monumental.' Mekas in the same paper on November 7, 1974: 'And here is my own final statement on Riefenstahl's films: If you are an idealist, you'll see idealism in her films; if you are a classicist, you'll see in her films an ode to classicism; if you are a Nazi, you'll see in her films Nazism.'

5. It was Genet, in his novel *Funeral Rites,* who provided one of the first texts that showed the erotic allure Fascism exercised someone who was not a fascist. Another description is by Sartre, an unlikely candidate for these feelings himself, who may have heard about them from Genet. In *La Mort dans l'âme* (1949), the third novel in his four-part *Les Chemins de la liberté'* Sartre describes one of his protagonists experiencing the entry of the German army into Paris in 1940: '[Daniel] was not afraid, he yielded trustingly to those thousands of eyes, he thought "Our conquerors!" and he was supremely happy. He looked them in the eye, he feasted on their fair hair, their sunburned faces with eyes which looked like lakes of ice, their slim bodies, their incredibly long and muscular hips. He murmured: "How handsome they are!" . . . Something had fallen from the sky: it was the ancient law. The society of judges had collapsed, the sentence had been obliterated; those ghostly little khaki soldiers, the defenders of the rights of man, had been routed. . . . An unbearable, delicious sensation spread through his body; he could hardly see properly; he repeated, gasping, "As if it were butter — they're entering Paris as if it were butter." . . . He would like to have been a woman to throw them flowers.'

Chapter 12: The Reconceptualisation of Women's Roles in War-Time National Socialism. An Analysis of 'Die Frau meiner Träume'

Production: UFA-Filmkunst GmbH; Distribution: Deutsche Filmvertriebs GmbH; Director: Georg Jacoby; Script: Johann Vaszary, Georg Jacoby; Camera: Konstantin Irmen-Tschet; Set Design: Erich Kettelhut; Score: Franz Grohe; Choreography: Sabine Ress, Terry Krause; Costume design: Gertrud Steckler; Sound: Heinz Martin, Werner Pohl; Editing: Erich Kobler.

1. A more detailed version of this analysis which I wrote together with Karen Ellwanger was published as 'Die Frau meiner Träume. Weiblichkeit und Maskerade: eine Untersuchung zu Form und Funktion von Kleidung als Zeichensystem im Film', *Frauen und Film,* Vol 38, 1985, pp 58–71.

2. Jerzy Toeplitz, *Geschichte des Films 1934-1945,* Munich, 1987, p 1186 (my translation).

3. Rudolf Oertel, *Filmspiegel. Ein Brevier aus der Welt des Films,* Wien, 1941, p 195, quoted in Toeplitz, *Geschichte des Films,* p 1186.

4. Erwin Leiser, *'Deutschland, erwache!' Propaganda im Film des Dritten Reiches*, 2nd ed., Reinbek bei Hamburg, 1978, p 16 (my translation).

5. Carla Rhode. 'Leuchtende Sterne?' in *Wir tanzen um die Welt. Deutsche Revuefilme 1933-1945*, ed. Helga Belach, München, 1979, p 119.

6. It is significant that this link is most obvious in those apparently fantastic and irrational components which cannot be accounted for by a model of interpretation based on the concept of an alternative world and which therefore have to be categorized as 'narrative surplus' in such a context.

7. Ulea Stöckl, 'Appelle an Wünsche und Traumbilder,' in *Wir tanzen um die Welt*, ed. Belach, pp 94 – 119; and Karsten Witte, 'Gehemmte Schaulust,' ibid., p 20.

8. Annemarie Tröger, 'Die Frau im wesensgemäßen Einsatz,' in *Mutterkreuz und Arbeitsbuch*, ed. Frauengruppe Faschismusforschung, Frankfurt/M, 1981, pp 246 – 73.

9. For a detailed account of this change in terms of costume history see Ellwanger and Warth, 'Die Frau meiner Träume'.

10. Mary Ann Doane, 'Gilda: Epistemology as Striptease', *Camera Obscura*, Vol. 11, p 15.

Chapter 13: The De-Nazification of Nazi Art: Arno Breker and Albert Speer Today

1. All important quotations from Ludwig are documented in Klaus Staeck (ed.): *Nazi-Kunst ins Museum?* Göttingen 1988.

2. Leon Krier (ed.): *Albert Speer. Architecture 1933-1942*, Brussels, 1985; Themenheft 'Die grosse Speer-Feier des Leon Krier oder KLASSIK zum Völkermord', Nr. 28/29 of the journal *Bauwelt*, Berlin (West) 1987 with contributions from Ulrich Conrads, Christoph Hackelsberger, Peter Neitzke, Wolfgang Schäche and Robert Frank.

3. Ulricke Zeuch: 'Die Schande restaurieren? Die Nürnberger Kongresshalle — eine nationalsozialistische Hinterlassenschaft'. In: *Frankfurter Allgemeine Zeitung*, 31 July 1987; Mathias Schreiber: 'Brutale Bauten? Die Nürnberger NS-Last und die Angst vor dem Grossen', in: *Frankfurter Allgemeine Zeitung*, 15 July 1988.

4. Most contributions to this debate are documented in *'Historikerstreit', Die Dokumentation der Kontroverse um die Einzigartigkeit der nationalsozialistischen Judenvernichtung*. Munich, 1987; also Hans-Ulrich Wehler: *Entsorgung der deutschen Vergangenheit? Ein polemischer Essay zum 'Historikerstreit'*, Munich, 1988.

5. Jutta Held: *Kunst und Kunstpolitik 1945-1949. Kulturaufbau in Deutschland nach dem 2. Weltkrieg*, Berlin, 1981; Hermann Glaser: *Kulturgeschichte der Bundersrepublik Deutschland*, Munich, vol. 1 1985, vol. 2 1986, further volumes in preparation; Jost Hermand: *Kultur im Wiederaufbau. Die Bundesrepublik Deutschland 1945-1965*, Munich, 1986; Hans Mommsen: 'Das Dritte Reich in der Erinnerung der Deutschen'. In: Staeck, *Nazi-Kunst*, op. cit., pp 49 – 59.

6. Odo Marquard: 'Abschied vom Prinzipiellen. Auch eine autobiographische Einleitung'. In: Marquard, *Abschied vom Prinzipiellen. Philosophische Studien*, Stuttgart, 1981, pp 4 – 22.

7. *Skulptur und Macht. Figurative Plastik im Deutschland der 30er und 40er Jahre*, Katalog der Adademie der Künste, Berlin (West), 1983; the contributions to a colloquium at this exhibition were edited by Magdalena Bushart, and others: *Entmachtung der Kunst. Architektur, Bildhauerei und ihre Institutionalisierung 1920-1960*, Berlin (West) 1985.

8. The catalogue to the exhibition appeared under the title: *Kunst im Dritten Reich-Dokumente der Unterwerfung*. It was printed several times and distributed by Zweitausendeins-Versand (Frankfurt am Main).

9. Hans Robert Jauss: *Literaturgeschichte als Provokation*. Frankfurt am Main, 1970; Hans Jürgen Syberberg: *Hitler—ein Film aus Deutschland*. Reinbek 1978; on Anselm Kiefer see my essay 'Der Dachboden' in Grasskamp: *Der vergessliche Engel. Künstlerportraits für Fortgeschrittene*. Munich, 1986, pp 7 – 22.

10. *Inszenierung der Macht. Ästhetische Faszination im Faschismus*. Catalogue of the Neue Gessellschaft für Bildende Kunst, Berlin (West), 1987.

11. Interview in *Der Spiegel*, 36/1986, p 187.
12. Berthold Hinz: '1933/45. Ein Kapitel kunstgeschichtlicher Forschung seit 1945'. In *Kritische Berichte* 4/1986, pp 18–33.
13. Walter Grasskamp: *Museumsgründer und Museumsstürmer. Zur Sozialgeschichte des Kunstmuseums*, Munich, 1981, pp 17–35.
14. *Alfred Flechtheim. Sammler. Kunsthändler. Verleger.* Katalog des Kunstmuseums, Düsseldorf, 1987.
15. Max Imdahl: 'Pose und Indoktrination—Zu Werken der Plastik und Malerei im Dritten Reich'; in: Staeck, *Nazi-Kunst*, op. cit., pp 87–99.
16. D. Lucknow, 'Museum und Moderne', in *Museum der Gegenwart, Kunst in öffentlichen Sammlungen bis 1937*. Katalog der Kunstsammlung Nordrhein-Westfalen, Düsseldorf, 1987, pp 33–45.
17. C.F. note 13.
18. David Schoenbaum: *Hitler's Social Revolution. Class and Status in Nazi-Germany 1933-1939.* 1966; Hans Dieter Schäfer: *Das gespaltene Bewusstsein. Deutsche Kultur und Lebenswirklichkeit 1933-1945*, Munich/Vienna, 1981; Martin Broszat: *Nach Hitler. Der schwierige Umgang mit unserer Geschichte*, Munich, 1988.
19. Martin Broszat: 'Zwiespältige Distanzierung zur Vergangenheit: Albert Speers "Sklavenstaat"', in: Broszat, *Nach Hitler*, op. cit., pp 189-193.
20. Leon Krier: 'Projet pour la reconstruction de Luxembourg'. In: Archives d'Architecture Moderne, Nr. 15/1978, pp 42–76.
21. Heinz-Gerhard Haupt: *Die radikale Mitte. Lebensweise und Politik von Handwerkern und Kleinhandlern in Deutschland seit 1848*, Munchen 1985; Berthold Franke: *Die Kleinbürger. Begriff. Ideologie, Politik*, Frankfurt/New York 1988; Bernhard Schubert; *Der Künstler als Handwerker. Zur Literaturgeschichte einer romantischen utopie*, Konigstein 1986.
22. These are the findings of Schoenbaum and Schafer (cf. note 28). In Schafer's view the Third Reich appears as the early model of an industrialised welfare state for racially privileged people.
23. Fritz Stern: *Kulturpessimismus als politische Gefahr. Eine Analyse nationaler Ideologie in Deutschland*, Munchen 1986.

BIBLIOGRAPHY

A. WORKS ON THE SOCIAL, POLITICAL AND ECONOMIC HISTORY OF THE NATIONAL SOCIALIST PERIOD, INCLUDING WORKS ON THE PSYCHOLOGY OF FASCISM

Arbeiterklasse gegen Faschismus (report on the 7th World Congress of the Communist Party, 2 August 1935).

H. Ashby Jr, *Faschismus und Kapitalismus in Deutschland. Studien zum Verhältnis zwischen Nationalsozialismus und Wirtschaft*, Göttingen, 1972.

G. Bataille, *Literature and Evil*, London, 1973.

G. Bataille, *Die psychologische Struktur des Faschismus*, Munich, 1978.

R. Bessel and E. Feuchwanger (eds), *Social Change and Political Development in Weimar Germany*, London, 1981.

R. Bessel, *Political Violence and the Rise of Nazism*, New Haven and London, 1984.

E. Bloch, *Erbschaft dieser Zeit* (1935), Frankfurt, 1973.

W. Boelke (ed), *Kriegspropaganda, 1939–1941. Geheime Ministerkonferenzen im Reichspropagandaministerium*, Stuttgart, 1966.

K. D. Bracher, *The German Dictatorship: The Origins, Structure and Effects of National Socialism*, London, 1973.

R. Brady, *The Spirit and Structure of German Fascism*, (intr H Laski), London, 1937.

R. Bridenthale et al (eds), *When Biology became Destiny: Women in Weimar and Nazi Germany*, New York, 1984.

B. Broszat, *The Hitler State: the Foundations and Development of the Internal Structure of the Third Reich*, London, 1981.

M. Broszat, *Nach Hitler. Der schwierige Umgang mit unserer Geschichte*, Munich, 1988.

W. Carr, *Hitler, A Study in Personality and Politics*, London, 1978.

E. Czichon, *Wer verhalf Hitler zur Macht? Zum Anteil der deutschen Industrie an der Zerstörung der Weimarer Republik*, Cologne, 1967.

W. Daim, *Der Maun, der Hitler die Ide gaben. Die sektiererischen Grundlagen des Nationalsozialismus*, Vienna, Cologne, Graz, 1985 (2nd edn).

W. Emmerich, *Zur Kritik der Volkstumsideologie*, Frankfurt, 1971.

J. C. Fest, *Hitler*, London, 1973.

B. Franke, *Die Kleinbürger. Begriff, Ideologie, Politik*, Frankfurt and New York, 1988.

H. Glaser, *The Cultural Roots of National Socialism*, London, 1978.

H. Gamm, *Der Braune Kult. Das Dritte Reich und seine Ersatzreligion*, Hamburg, 1962.

N. Goodrick-Clarke, *The Occult Roots of Nazism. The Ariosophists of Austria and Germany 1890–1935*, Wellingborough, 1985.

L. Gottschewsky, *Männerbund und Frauenfrage: Die Frau im Neuen Staat*, Munich, 1978.

A. J. Gregor, 'Response to H. A. Turner', *World Politics*, Vol XXVI, no 3, 1974.

R. Grunberger, *A Social History of the Third Reich*, London, 1974.

265

H. Guderian, *Erinnerung eines Soldaten*, Heidelberg, 1951 (4th edn).

G. Hanfstaengl, *Hitler, the Missing Years*, London, 1957.

W. F. Haug, *Der Hilflose Antifaschismus*, Frankfurt, 1970.

H-G Haupt, *Die Radikale Mitte. Lebensweise und Politik von Handwerkern und Kleinhändlern in Deutschland seit 1848*, Munich, 1985.

J. Hermand, 'Alle "Macht" den Frauen. Faschistische Matriarchatskonzepte', *Das Argument*, 26, 1984, pp 539–554.

R. E. Herstein, *The War that Hitler Won. The Most Infamous Propaganda Campaign in History*, London, 1978.

A Hitler, *Mein Kampf*, with an introduction by D. C. Watt, London, 1969.

M. Kafer, *The Nazi Party. A Social Profile of Members and Leaders, 1919–1945*, Oxford, 1983.

I. Kershaw, *The Nazi Dictatorship; Problems and Perspectives of Interpretation*, London, 1988.

I. Kershaw, 'How Effective was Nazi Propaganda?', in D. Welch, *Nazi Propaganda. Its Power and Limitations*, New Jersey, 1983.

M. Klaus, *Mädchen im Dritten Reich. Der Bund Deutscher Mädel*, Cologne, 1983.

V. Klemperer, *LTI. Die umbewältigte Sprache: aus dem Notizbuch eines Philologen*, Munich, 1969.

D. Klinksiek, *Die Frau im NS-Staat*, Stuttgart, 1982.

C. Koonz, *Mothers in the Fatherland: Women, the Family and Nazi Politics*, London, 1987.

H. Krausnick, et al, *Anatomy of the SS State*, London, 1968.

R. Kühnl (ed), *Der deutsche Faschismus in Quellen und Dokumenten*, Cologne, 1975.

W. Laqueur, *Fascism, A Reader's Guide*, London, 1979.

O. Marquand, *Abschied vom Prinzipiellen. Philosophische Studien*, Stuttgart, 1981.

T. Mason, 'Italy and Modernisation', *History Workshop* Journal, no 25, Spring 1988, pp 127–47.

B. Moore, Jr, *The Social Origin of Democracy and Dictatorship*, London, 1966.

G. L. Mosse, *The Nationalisation of the Masses. Political Symbolism and Mass Movements in Germany from the Napoleonic Wars through the Third Reich*, New York/Scarborough, 1977.

G. L. Mosse, *The Crisis of German Ideology*, New York, 1964.

G. L. Mosse, *Nationalism and Sexuality: Respectability and Abnormal Sexuality in Modern Europe*, New York 1983.

R. Neebe, *Grossindustrie, Staat und NSDAP 1930–1933, Paul Silverberg und der Reichsverband der Deutschen Industrie in der Krise der Weimarer Republik*, Göttingen, 1981.

F. Neumann, *Behemoth: The Structure and Practice of National Socialism*, London, 1943.

J. Noakes (ed), *Government, Party and People in Nazi Germany*, Exter, 1980.

J. Noakes and G. Pridham (eds) *Nazism, 1919–1945, A Documentary Reader*, Exeter, 1984.

A. Norden, *Lehren deutscher Geschichte. Zur politischen Rolle des Finanzkapitals und der Junker*, Berlin (East), 1947.

G. Paul, '*Deutsche Mutter — heim zu Dir!' Warum es misslang, Hitler an der Saar zu schlagen, Der Saarkampf 1933–1935*, Cologne, 1981.

W. Reich, *Massenpsychologie des Faschismus*, Copenhagen, 1934.

A. Rhodes, *Propaganda. The Art of Persuasion, World War II*, London, 1976.

R. Sarti, 'Fascist Modernisation in Italy: Traditional or Revolutionary?' *American Historical Review*, Vol LXXV, no 4, 1970.

D. Schoenbaum, *Hitler's Social Revolution. Class and Status in Nazi Germany 1937-1939*, London, 1967.

K. Schmeer, *Die Regie des öffentlichen Lebens in Dritten Reich*, Munich, 1956.

A. Schweitzer, *Big Business in the Third Reich*, Indiana, 1964.

W. A. Sheridan, *The Nazi Seizure of Power: The Experience of a Single German Town*, London, 1984.

A. Sohn-Rethel, *Economy and Class Structure of German Fascism*, London, 1978.

A. Speer, *Inside the Third Reich*, London, 1970.

Spione, Spitzel, Saboteure. Eine Aufklärungsschrift für das Deutsche Volk; (ed) Reichsamt Deutsches Volksbildungswerk, Berlin, 1938.

G. D. Stark, *Entrepreneurs of Ideology. Neoconservative Publishers in Germany, 1890-1933*, Chapel Hill, 1981.

P. Strachura (ed), *The Shaping of the Nazi State*, London, 1978.

J. Stephenson, 'The Nazi Organisation of Women, 1937 – 39', in P. Strachura (ed), 1978.

J. Stephenson, *Women in Nazi Germany*, London, 1975.

J. Stephenson, *The Nazi Organisation of Women*, New York and London, 1981.

F. Stern. *The Politics of Cultural Despair. A Study in the Rise of the Germanic Ideology*, Berkeley, 1961.

F. Taylor, *The Goebbels Diaries 1939-41*, London, 1982.

H.-U. Thamer, *Verführung und Gewalt. Deutschland 1933-1945*, Berlin, 1986.

H. A. Turner, 'Fascism and Modernisation', *World Politics*, Vol XXIV, no 4, 1972.

H. Turner, *German Big Business and the Rise of Hitler*, New York and Oxford, 1985.

Unter dem Sonnenrad, Kraft Durch Freude, Berlin, 1938.

K. Vondung, *Magie und Manipulation. Ideologischer Kult und politische Religion des Nationalsozialismus*, Göttingen, 1971.

D. Welch, *Nazi Propaganda. Its Power and Limitations.* New Jersey, 1983.

S. J. Woolf (ed), *The Nature of Fascism*, London, 1966.

B. BOOKS ON ART, ARCHITECTURE, DESIGN, MUSIC AND FILM IN THE THIRD REICH

A Hundred Years of German Painting 1850-1950, Tate Gallery, London, 1956.

H. Abromeit, *Das Politische in der Werbung, Wahlwerbung und Wirtschaftswerbung*, Opladen, 1972.

W. M. Austin, *Music in the Twentieth Century from Debussy through Stravinsky*, New York, 1966.

H. Belach (ed), *Wir Tanzen um die Welt. Deutsche Revuefilme 1933-1945*, Munich, 1979.

Berliner Bildhauer von Schlüter bis zur Gegenwart, Preussische Akademie der Künste, Berlin, 1936.

H. Bohrmann (ed), *Politische Plakate*, Dortmund, 1984.

A. Breker, *Im Strahlungsfeld der Ereignisse, Leben und Wirken eines Künsters; Porträts, Begegnungen, Schicksal.* Preussich-Oldendorf, 1972.

H. Brenner, *Die Kunstpolitik des Nationalsozialismus*, Hamburg, 1963.

H. Bruckner and C. Rock, *Judentum in Musik A-B-C*, Munich, 1936.

E. Bucken, *Deutsche Musikkunde*, Potsdam, 1935.

M. Busshart (ed), *Entmachtung der Kunst. Architektur, Bilhauerei und ihre Institutionalisierung 1920–1960*, Berlin (West), 1983.

F. Courtake and P. Cadars, *Geschichte des Films im Dritten* Reich, Munich, 1975.

M. Damus, *Sozialistischer Realismus und Kunst im Nationalsozialismus*, Frankfurt, 1981.

Deutsche Künstler und die SS (catalogue) Berlin, 1943.

C. Despiau, *Arno Breker*, Paris, 1942.

A. Dressler (ed), *Deutsche Kunst und entarte 'Kunst': Kunstwerk und Zerrbild der Weltanschauung*, Munich, 1938.

K. Eberlin, *Was ist Deutsch in der Deutschen Kunst?*, Leipzig, 1933.

A. Enns, *Kunst und Bürgertum*, Lübeck, 1978.

R. Eichenauer, *Musik und Rasse*, Munich, 1932.

C. Einstein, *Die Kunst des 20. Jahrhunderts*, Berlin, 1931.

S. von Falkenhausen, *Der zweite Futurismus und die Kunstpolitik des Faschismus in Italien von 1922–1943*, Frankfurt, 1979.

Alfred Flechtheim. Sammler. Kunsthändler. Verleger, Kunstmuseum, Düsseldorf, 1987.

A. Fleischer, *Die Plakatkampagnen 'Ne Boltai', 'Feind hört mit', 'Talk Kills' während des Zweiten Weltkrieges*, unpublished MA thesis, University of Münster, 1988.

H. Frank (ed), *Faschistische Architekturen, Planen und Bauen in Europa, 1930–1945*, Hamburg, 1985.

Frauengrupe Faschismusforschung (ed), *Mutterkreuz und Arbeitsbuch*, Frankfurt, 1981.

S. Friedländer, *Kitsch und Tod. Der Widerschein des Nazismus*, New York, 1983.

H. Glaser, *The Cultural Roots of National Socialism*, London, 1978.

H. Glaser, *Kulturgeschichte der Bundesrepublik Deutschland*, Munich, Vol 1 1985, Vol 2 1986.

W. Grasskamp, *Der vergessliche Engel. Künstlerportraits für Fortgeschrittene*, Munich, 1986.

W. Grasskamp, *Museumsgründer und Museumsstürmer. Zur Sozialgeschichte des Kunstmuseums*, Munich, 1981.

W. Haftmann, *Malerei im 20 Jahrhundert*, 2 Vols, Munich, 1965/1983.

W. F. Haug, *Kritik der Warenästhetik*, Frankfurt, 1971.

J. Heartfield, *Krieg im Frieden. Fotomontagen 1930–1938*, 1982.

J. Held, *Kunst und Kunstpolitik 1945–1949, Kulturaufbau in Deutschland nach dem 2. Weltkrieg*, Berlin, 1981.

J. Hermand, *Kultur im Wiederaufbau. Die Bundesrepublik Deutschland 1945–1965*, Munich, 1986.

H. Hinkel, *Zur Funktion des Bildes im deutschen Faschismus*, Giessen, 1975.

B. Hinz, *Art in the Third Reich*, Oxford, 1979.

B. Hinz, *Die Malerei im deutschen Faschismus—Kunst und Konterrevolution*, Munich, 1974.

B. Hinz, *Die Dekoration der Gewalt. Kunst und Medien im Faschismus*, Giessen, 1979.

Historikerstreit. Die Dokumentation der Kontroverse um die Einzigartigkeit der nationalsozialistischen Judenvernichtung, Munich and Zurich, 1987.

W. Hütt, *Deutsche Malerei und Graphik im 20. Jahrhundert*, Berlin, 1969.

H. R. Jauss, *Literaturgeschichte als Provokation*, Frankfurt, 1970.

C. M. Joachimedes, N. Rosenthal, W. Schmied (eds), *German Art in the Twentieth Century: Painting and Sculpture 1905-1985*, Royal Academy London, 1985.

K. Kaftan, *Der Kampf um die Autobahnen*, Berlin, 1955.

F. Kämpfer, *'Der Rote Keil'. Das politische Plakat, Theorie und Geschichte*, Berlin, 1985.

F. A. Kauffmann, *Die Neue Deutsche Malerei*, Berlin, 1941.

Knaurs Lexikon der modernen Malerie. Von den Impressionisten bis heute, Munich and Zurich, 1982.

L. Krier (ed), *Albert Speer. Architektur 1933-1942*, Brussels, 1985.

Kunst im Dritten Reich: Dokumente der Unterwerfung (catalogue), Frankfurter Kunstverein, 1974.

Kunst-Dienst (eds), *Deutsche Warenkunde*, Berlin, 1939-40.

W. Laqueur, *Weimar, a cultural history, 1918-1933*, London, 1974.

J. Langbehn, *Rembrandt als Erzieher, von einem Deutschen*, 47th ed, Leipzig 1909.

R. Lebeck and M. Schüte, *Propagandapostkarten II. 80 Bildpostkarten aus den Jahren 1937-1943*, Dortmund, 1980.

E. Leiser, *Deutschland Erwache! Propaganda im Film des Dritten Reiches*, Reinbeck bei Hamburg, 1978.

Lieder der NS Kraft durch Freude (Bärenreiter), Kassel, 1936.

F. Medebach, *Das Kampfplakat. Aufgabe, Wesen und Gesetzmässigkeit des politischen Plakats, nachgewiesen an den Plakaten der Kampfjahre von 1918-1933*, Frankfurt, 1941.

B. Miller Lane, *Architecture and Politics in Germany 1918-1945*, Cambridge, Mass, 1968.

Moderne Gebrauchsmöbel, Berin, 1937.

Mommsen, Petzina and Weisbrod (eds), *Industrielles System und Politische Entwicklung in der Weimarer Republik*, Düsseldorf, 1974.

G. L. Mosse, *Nazi Culture: Intellectual, Cultural and Social Life in the Third Reich*, London, 1966.

G. Müller, *Das Wahlplakat, Pragmatische Untersuchungen zur Sprache der Politik am Beispiel von Wahlplakaten*, Tübingen, 1978.

J. Müller-Blattau, *Germanisches Erbe in deutscher Tonkunst*, Berlin, 1938.

J. Müller-Blattau, *Geschichte der deutschen Musik*, Berlin, 1938.

Museum der Gegenwart. *Kunst in öffentlichen Sammlungen bis 1937. Kunstsammlung Nordrhein Westfalen*, Düsseldorf, 1987.

National Industry Conference Board (eds), *Rationalisation of German Industry*, New York, 1931.

E. Naumann, *Illustrierte Musikgeschichte*, Stuttgart, 1934.

Neue Gesellschaft für Bildende Kunst, *Inszenierung der Macht. Aesthetische Faszination im Faschismus*, Berlin, 1987.

E. Nolde, *Achtung, Befreiung, 1919-1946*, Cologne, 1967.

R. Oerfel, *Filmspiegel. Ein Brevier aus der Welt des Films*, Vienna, 1941.

G. Paul and R. Schoch, *Saargeschichte im Plakat, 1918-1957*, Berlin, 1987.

J. Petsch, *Kunst im Dritten Reich. Arkitektur, Plastik, Malerei*, Cologne, 1983.

W. Pinder, *Georg Kolbe: Werke der letzten Jahre*, Berlin, 1937.

V. G. Probst, *Arno Breker. 60 ans de sculpture*, Paris, 1981.

P. O. Rave, *Kunstdiktatur im Dritten Reich*, Hamburg, 1949.

L. Richard, *Le Nazisme et la Culture*, Paris, 1978.

L. Richard, *Deutscher Faschismus und Kultur. Aus der Sicht eines Franzosen*, Munich, 1982.

L. Riefenstahl, *Hinter den Kulissen des Reichsparteitog-Films*, Munich 1935.

W. Rittich, *New German Architecture*, Berlin, 1941.

W. Rittich, *Deutsche Kunst der Gegenwart*, Breslau, 1943.

W. Rittich, *Deutschlands Werden seit 1933*. Die Kunst. n.d.

R. Roh, '*Entartete Kunst*': *Kunstbarbarei im Dritten Reich*, Hanover, 1962.

A. Rosenberg, *Der Mythus des 20. Jahrhunderts*, Munich, 1930.

A. Rosenberg, *Revolution in der bildenden Kunst?*, Munich, 1934.

K. Ruhrberg, *Die Malerei unseres Jahrhunderts*, Düsseldorf, Vienna, New York, 1987.

E. Schokel, *Das politische Plakat. Eine psychologische Betrachtung*, Munich, 1939.

Neue Sachlichkeit (catalogue), Mannheim 1925.

O. Schlemmer, *Briefe und Tagebücher*, Munich, 1958.

H. D. Schöfer, *Das gespaltene Bewusstsein. Deutsche Kultur und Lebenswirklichkeit 1937–1945*, Munich and Vienna, 1981.

A. Schönberger, *Die neue Reichskanzlei von Albert Speer*, Zum Zusammenhang von nationalsozialistischer Ideologie und Architektur, Berlin, 1981.

E. Schönleben, *Fritz Todt, der Mensch, der Ingenieur, der Nationalsozialist*, Oldenburg, 1943.

K. F. Schreiber, *Das Recht der Reichskulturkammer*, Berlin, 1937.

B. Schubert, *Der Künstler als Hankwerker. Zur Literaturgeschichte einer romantischen Utopie*, Königstein 1968.

B. Schulz (ed), *Grauzonen-Farbwelten, Kunst und Zeitbilder 1945–1955*, Berlin, 1983.

P. Schultze-Naumburg, *Kunst als Blut und Boden*, Leipzig, 1934.

P. Schultze-Naumburg, *Kunst und Rasse*, Munich, 1928.

P. Schultze-Naumburg, *Kampf um die Kunst*, Munich, 1932.

P. Schultze-Naumburg, *Nordische Schönheit. Ihr Wunschbild im Leben und in der Kunst*, Munich and Berlin, 1937.

P-K Schuster (ed), *Die Kunststadt München 1937: Nationalsozialismus und Entartete Kunst*, Munich, 1987.

A. Seifert, *Im Zeitalter des Lebendigen, Natur-Heimat-Technik*, Munich, 1941.

V. Silva, *Ideologia e arte del fascismo*, Milan, 1973.

Skulptur und Macht. Figurative Plastik im Deutschland der 30er und 40er Jahre, Akademie der Künste, Berlin (West), 1983.

P. Spang, *Von der Zauberflöte zum Standgericht. Naziplakate in Luxemburg 1940–1944*, Luxemburg, 1982.

S. Spender, *The Temple*, London 1929.

K. Staek (ed), *Nazi-Kunst ins Museum?* Göttingen, 1988.

T. Stengel and H. Gerigk, *Lexikon der Juden in der Musik*, Berlin, 1936.

F. Stern, *Kulturpessimismus als politische Gefahr. Eine Analyse nationaler Ideologie in Deutschland*, Munich, 1986.

R. Stollmann, *Äesthetisierung der Politik: Literaturstudien zum subjektiven Faschismus*, Stuttgart, 1978.

D. Strothman, *Nationalsozialistische Literaturpolitik: Ein Beitrag zur Publizistik im Dritten Reich*, Bonn, 1960.

H-J Syberberg, *Hitler—ein Film aus Deutschland*, Reinbeck, 1978.

F. Tamms, *Paul Bonatz, Arbeiten aus den Jahren 1907–1937*, Stuttgart, 1937.

K. L. Tank, *Deutsche Plastik unserer Zeit*, Munich, 1942.

R. R. Taylor, *The World in Stone: The Role of Architecture in the National Socialist Ideology*, Berkeley and Lost Angeles, 1975.

A. Teut, *Arkitektur im Dritten Reich 1933–1945*, Berlin and Frankfurt, 1967.

K. Theweleit, *Male Fantasies*, Cambridge and Oxford, 1987.

J. Toeplitz, *Geschichte des Films 1934–1945*, Munich, 1987.

R. Wagner, *Das Judentum in der Musik*, Leipzig, 1851 (revised 1869).

P. Walter, *Handwerk auf neuen Wegen*, Berlin, 1937.

H-U Wehler, *Entsorgung der deutschen Vergangenheit? Ein polemischer Essay zum 'Historikerstreit'*, Munich, 1988.

D. Welch (ed), *Nazi Propaganda: Its Power and Limitations*, London, 1983.

D. H. Westfahl, *Fritz Höger, der niederdeutsche Backsteinbaumeister*, Wolfshagen 1938.

W. Willrich, *Säuberung des Kunsttempels*, Munich and Berlin, 1937.

L. Winkler (ed), *Antifaschistische Literatur*, Kronberg, 1977.

K. Wolbert, *Die Nackten und die Toten des 'Dritten Reiches': Folgen einer politischen Geschichte des Körpers in der Plastik des deutschen Faschismus*, Giessen, 1982.

J. Wulf, *Die Bildenden Künste im Dritten Reich: Eine Dokumentation*, Reinbeck 1966.

Z. Zbyrek, *Selling the War. Art and Propaganda in World War II*, London, 1982.

C. ARTICLES ON ART, ARCHITECTURE, DESIGN, MUSIC AND FILM IN THE THIRD REICH

H. Barkhausen, 'Footnote to the History of Riefenstahl's "Olympia" ', *Film Quarterly*, Fall 1974.

L. Bauer-Hundsdörfer, 'Und keine Zeit und keine Macht zerstückelt geprägte Form', *Frauen-Kultur*, November 1936, pp 2–3.

R. Bie 'Der Sachliche Kreis: Georg Schrimpf', in *Deutsche Malerie der Gegenwart*, Weimar, 1930.

E. Boger-Eichler, 'Frauengestalten des Malers Wilhelm Peterson', *Frauen-Kultur*, March 1937, pp 2–7.

R. Bohn, H. Schimmel, E. Serdl, 'Faschismus-Kunst-Homosexualität', in *Sammlung 5*, Frankfurt, 1982.

B. Brecht, 'Über die Theatralik des Faschismus', in *Gesammelte Werke, 16*, Frankfurt, 1967.

G. Bussmann, 'Plastik', in *Kunst im Dritten Reich: Dokumente der Unterwerfung* (catalogue), Frankfurter Kunstverein, 1974.

G. Bussmann, ' "Degenerate Art": A Look at a Useful Myth', in C. Joachimedes, N. Rosenthal, W. Schmied (eds), *German Art in the Twentieth Century, Painting and Sculpture 1905–1985*, London, 1985.

C. Coultass, 'The German Film 1933–45', *Screen*, Summer 1971, Vol 12, no 2, pp 38–42.

I. Dunlop, 'Entarte Kunst', in *The Shock of the New: Seven Historic Exhibitions of Modern Art*, New York, 1972, pp 224–259.

C. Fischer-Defoy, 'Artists and Art Institutions in Germany 1933–45', *Oxford Art Journal*, 9, 2, 1986.

A. Fleischmann, 'Das Bild der Frau in der Plastik des Nationalsozialismus', in *Das Bild der Frau in der Plastik des 20. Jahrhunderts*, Wilhelm-Lehmbruch-Museum, Duisburg 1986 pp 40–48.

L. Gottschewski, 'Von der Formkraft der Bilder', *Frauen-Kultur*, June 1935.

J. Heskett, 'Modernism and Archaism in Design in the Third Reich', *Block* 3, 1980, pp 17–20.

J. Heskett, 'Art and Design in Nazi Germany', *History Workshop Journal*, 6 Autumn 1978, pp 139–53.

B. Hinz, 'Malerei des deutschen Faschismus', *Kunst im Dritten Reich, Dokumente der Unterwerfung*, Frankfurter Kunstverein 1974.

B. Hinz, '1933/45. Ein Kapitel kunstgeschichtlicher Forschung seit 1945', *Kritische Berichte*, 4/1986, pp 18–33.

M. Köhler, 'Lebensform durch Körperkultur', in M. Köhler and G. Berche (eds), *Das Aktfoto*, Munich and Lucerne, 1986 (IInd edn), pp 341–55.

L. Krier, 'Projet pour la reconstruction de Luxembourg', *Archives d'Architecture Moderne*, no 15, 1978, pp 42–76.

M-A van Lüttichau, 'Deutsche Kunst und Entartete Kunst: Die Münchener Ausstellungen 1937', in P-K Schuster (ed), *Nationalsozialismus und 'Entartete Kunst'*, Munich, 1987.

I. Metzger, 'Art in Germany under National Socialism', *Studio International*, March/April 1970, pp 110–2.

K. Pinthus, 'Culture inside Nazi Germany', *American Scholar*, Autumn 1948.

R. A. Pois, 'German Expressionism in the Plastic Arts and Nazism: A Confrontation of Ideologies', *German Life and Letters*, XXI, no 3, April 1968.

A. Rabinbach, 'Beauty of Labour — The Aesthetics of Production in the Third Reich', *Journal of Contemporary History*, London December 1976.

W. Rittich, 'Architekturgebundene oder freie Plastik?' *Die Kunst im Dritten Reich*, August 1938.

W. Rittich, 'Das Werk Georg Kolbes', *Die Kunst im Dritten Reich*, February 1942, pp 32–39.

L. J. Rupp, 'Mother of the Volk: The Image of Women in Nazi Ideology', in *Mobilizing Women for War: German and American Propaganda*, Princeton, New Jersey, 1978.

C. Rhode, 'Leuchtende Sterne?' in H. Belach (ed) *Wir Tanzen um die Welt: Deutsche Revuefilme 1933–45*, Munich, 1979.

T. Smith, 'A State of Seeing, Unsighted: Notes on the Visual in Nazi War Culture', *Block*, 12, 1986/7, pp 50–70.

S. Sontag, 'Fascinating Fascism', in *Under the Sign of Saturn*, London 1983, pp 73–105.

A. Tröger, 'Die Frau im wesensgemässen Einsatz' in Frauengruppe Faschismusforschung (ed), *Mutterkreuz und Arbeitsbuch)*, Frakfurt, 1981.

(unattributed) 'Nazi Art Returns to Germany', *Art News*, New York, November 1984, p 143.

J. A. Walker, 'Total Kultur: Nazi Art and Media', *AND, Journal of Art and Art Education*, no 9, 1986, pp 3–11.

E. Warth and K. Ellwanger, 'Die Frau meiner Träume: Weiblichkeit und Maskerade: eine Untersuchung zu Form und Funktion von Kleidung als Zeichensystem im Film', *Frauen und Film*, Vol 38, 1985, pp 58–71.

NOTES ON CONTRIBUTORS

CHRISTINE FISCHER-DEFOY graduated from the Gesamthochschule Kassel in 1975 and wrote a thesis on workers' resistance to Fascism which was published as *Arbeiterwiderstand in der Provinz* in 1982. A subsequent five year project at the Berlin Kunsthochschule was published as *Kunst Macht Politik — Die Nazifizierung der Kunst- und Musikhochschulen in Berlin* in 1988. She is also a film-maker.

ANDREAS FLEISCHER is a post-graduate student at the University of Münster. His M.A. thesis deals with aspects of National Socialist posters.

HARMUT FRANK is Professor for Analysis of the Built Environment at the *Hochschule für Bildende Künste* in Hamburg. He has published numerous articles in such journals as *Archithèse, Bauwelt, Casabella, Lotus,* and others; he has edited *Lesebuch zur Wohnungsfrage* (1983); *Faschistische Architekturen* (1985); *Stadtgestalt und Heimatgefühl* (1988).

WALTER GRASSKAMP is Professor of History of Art at the University of Aachen. He has published the following books: *Museumsgründer und Museumsstürmer. Zur Sozialgeschichte des Kunstmuseums* (1981); *Der vergessliche Engel. Künstlerportraits für Fortgeschrittene* (1986); *Die unbewältigte Moderne. Kunst und Öffentlichkeit* (1986).

JOHN HESKETT is Associate Professor of Design in the Institute of Design, Illinois Institute of Technology, and author of *Industrial Design* (1979), *Design in Germany 1870–1918* (1986) and *Philips: A Study in the Corporate Management of Design* (1989).

FRANK KÄMPFER is Professor of History and Director of the Centre for East-European History at the University of Münster. Of his numerous publications two are related to his contribution on Nazi posters in this book: *Das russische Herrscherbild von den Anfängen bis zu Peter dem Großen. Studien zur Entwicklung politischer Ikonographie im byzantinischen Kulturkreis* (1978) and *'Der rote Keil'. Das politische Plakat. Theorie und Geschichte* (1985).

ERIK LEVI is lecturer in Music at Royal Holloway and Bedford New College, University of London. He is currently working on a book on music in Nazi Germany. He is also a professional accompanist who has made several commercial recordings, and he broadcasts regularly with the BBC.

ANNIE RICHARDSON is Senior Lecturer in History of Art at Winchester School of Art. Her M.A. thesis (University of Sussex) is on women in Expressionist art.

SUSAN SONTAG is an American writer and critic whose publications include *Against Interpretation, Styles of Radical Will, On Photography* and *Under the Sign of Saturn.* She has written and directed four feature-length films, two of which, *Brother Carl* and *Duet for Cannibals,* have been published as screenplays. She is also the author of *Illness as Metaphor* and *Aids and its Metaphors.*

BRANDON TAYLOR is Reader in History of Art at Winchester School of Art. He is the author of numerous articles on contemporary and modern art, several exhibition catalogues, and *Modernism, Post-Modernism, Realism* (1987) and *Art and Literature under the Bolsheviks* (1990).

WILFRIED VAN DER WILL is Reader in Modern German Studies at the University of Birmingham. His publications include *Pikaro heute* (1967), *The German Novel and the Affluent Society* (1968 — with R. H. Thomas), *Arbeiterkulturbewegung in der Weimarer Republik* (1982 — with R. Burns) and *Protest and Democracy in West Germany. Extra-Parliamentary Opposition and the Democratic Agenda* (1988 — with R. Burns).

EVA-MARIA WARTH is Assistant Professor of American Studies at the University of Tübingen. Apart from articles in journals such as *Frauen und Film* and *English-Amerikanische Studien* her publications include *Edgar Alan Poe and the American Horror Film (1909–1961)* (1988); she has co-edited *Remote Control: Television, Audiences and Cultural Power* (1989) and *Never-Ending Stories: Soap Operas and the Cultural Production of Meaning* (1989).

INDEX